KHRUSHCHEV

A POLITICAL LIFE

KHRUSHCHEV

A POLITICAL LIFE

William J. Tompson

MACMILLAN

DK
275
K5T65
1997

First published 1995 by Macmillan Press Ltd

Paperback edition first published 1997 by
MACMILLAN PRESS LTD
Houndmills, Basingstoke, Hampshire RG21 6XS
and London
Companies and representatives
throughout the world

ISBN 0-333-59927-6 hardcover
ISBN 0-333-69633-6 paperback

A catalogue record for this book is available
from the British Library.

10 9 8 7 6 5 4 3 2 1
06 05 04 03 02 01 00 99 98 97

Printed in the United States of America by
Haddon Craftsmen
Bloomsburg, PA

Ad maiorem Dei gloriam

Contents

Acknowledgements

The relief that I feel in seeing this book approaching completion is matched only by the awareness of my debts to many others who helped along the way. I am indebted to the staffs of the Institute for Scientific Information on the Social Sciences of the Russian Academy of Sciences, the All-Russian Centre for the Preservation and Study of Documents of Recent History (the former Central Party Archive) and the Central State Archive of Social Movements of the City of Moscow (the former Moscow Party Archive). Anton Nesterov of the Institute of General History and Irina Kovaleva of Moscow State University arranged my visa for the autumn of 1992 and my housing in Moscow for the 1992–3 academic year; Anton was also an excellent source of advice about libraries, archives and so on. Valerii Egorov of the All-Russian Political Science Association was gracious enough to assist me in obtaining access to libraries and archives and in arranging my visa for the spring of 1993. I am also especially grateful to Anton, Irina and Valerii for their friendship and encouragement.

Special thanks are due to Professor Archie Brown and Dr Alex Pravda of St Antony's College, Oxford, who supervised my research into the Khrushchev period as a graduate student at Oxford and subsequently encouraged me to tackle Khrushchev's biography. The assistance of Carole Menzies of the Bodleian Library's Slavonics section has been invaluable and has made the whole process quicker and easier. I am grateful to my mother, Elizabeth Tompson, who proof-read the manuscript of this book, a task which required her to suppress instincts developed over a lifetime of teaching English in American schools and to learn British punctuation and usage. Terry Mayer of the Department of Politics and Sociology at Birkbeck College, London, also gave generously of her time in reading through the text in search of typos. Finally, I thank *Europe-Asia Studies* (formerly *Soviet Studies*) for permission to quote from my article 'The Fall of Nikita Khrushchev' (vol. 43, no.

6 [1991], pp. 1101–21), much of which has been reproduced in chapter 10. To all of the above and to many others I say thanks. The credit for any merit this book may possess is in part theirs; responsibility for the errors of fact and judgement which no doubt remain is entirely my own.

William J. Tompson

1 The Donbass Bolshevik

Southern Russia and Ukraine, 1894–1929

Do you want to know just who I am? I started to work as soon as I began to walk. Until I was 15, I tended young calves, I tended sheep and then I tended a land-lord's cattle. Then I worked at a factory, the owners of which were Germans, and after that I worked in mines belonging to Frenchmen; I worked in chemical factories belonging to Belgians, and now I am the Prime Minister of the great Soviet state.

N. S. Khrushchev, Hollywood, 1959[1]

The career of Nikita Khrushchev took him far from the peasant village of his childhood and the industrial town of his youth, but the memories of his peasant-proletarian background remained important to him all his life, informing his views and reinforcing his basic faith in communist ideals and in the Soviet system. Sixty years later, as the leader of a socialist superpower, Khrushchev peppered his speeches with reminiscences, stories from his youth and peasant proverbs. Nikita Khrushchev was a self-made man, and like most self-made men he believed deeply in the system which had fostered his rise. His perceptions of his own career undergirded his belief in that system's essential justice and his buoyant – at times even utopian – optimism regarding its potential. When in 1961 Khrushchev promised that 'the present generation of Soviet people will live under communism',[2] his words reflected personal experience rather than Marxist theory. Born in a pre-industrial village whose inhabitants had only a generation before been little more than the chattel of local landowners, Khrushchev had lived through the industrialisation of Russia's iron age and led her into the space age. He needed no further proof that the

1

workers' paradise could be completed in Russia in another twenty years.

Nikita Sergeevich Khrushchev was born to a peasant family in the village of Kalinovka, Kursk Province, in April 1894. During his lifetime official Soviet sources gave the date as 17 April (5 April according to Russia's old-style, pre-revolutionary calendar), as does Khrushchev in his memoirs.[3] However, the birth certificate for Nikita Khrushchev of Kalinovka, Dmitrevskii District, Kursk Province, gives the date as 3 April, which would be 15 April according to the modern calendar.[4] His mother, Aksiniia Ivanovna, was a peasant girl from a village called Tishkino, where her father had settled after twenty-five years of military service.[5] Sergei Nikanorovich Khrushchev, the son of an old army friend of Aksiniia's father, married her and took her back to Kalinovka, his native village. Their married life began in extreme poverty, as Sergei's father refused to allow the couple to remain in his house or to provide them with wedding gifts. Sergei and Aksiniia had two children, a son, Nikita, and a daughter, Irina.[6]

In an effort to better his lot, Sergei Khrushchev travelled annually to the Donets Basin (Donbass) some 275 miles away, where he worked as a seasonal industrial labourer. Aksiniia and their children stayed behind in Kalinovka. Sergei worked first on the railways, then in a brick factory and finally in the mines.[7] This was a common pattern of life for the peasants of the region: Kursk Province, on the border of Great Russia and Ukraine, was agriculturally rich but cursed with rural overpopulation. Many peasants were driven by rising land prices to become seasonal workers. The most ambitious hoped to save enough money to purchase sufficient land, livestock and draft animals to prosper in the countryside. The incentive to undertake such work was considerable: the average factory wage in Russia was seventeen roubles per month, much more than a poor peasant could earn as a farmhand, and wages in the Donbass were considerably higher than the national average. A skilled coal-cutter in the mines could earn more than thirty-five roubles a month.[8]

Sergei left his family in Kalinovka, where they, like most peasants in the area, led a life of poverty, disease and toil, in which the success or failure of the current crop was a matter of life and death, and all human existence was shaped by the rhythm of the agricultural calendar. Diet was poor, and diseases like typhus and diphtheria were common. Necessity required that Nikita start work at an early age to help support the family. He tended village livestock before going to work as a herdsboy for a local woman named Shaufusova, who owned 500 hectares of land.

Nevertheless, Nikita began to attend the three-year village parochial school at about the age of six. The teacher was a deacon who taught by rote and made free use of the ruler when correcting his young charges.[9] The curriculum at this time would have included, in addition to reading, writing and basic arithmetic, lessons in church history and Old Slavonic, the liturgical tongue of the Russian Orthodox Church. Attendance at church services was mandatory.[10] When Nikita was six or seven, the family moved with Sergei to the Donbass town of Iuzovka for a year or so before returning to Kalinovka to live with Sergei's father, who welcomed them now that his son had saved enough money to ensure that the family would not be a financial burden. When Sergei's money ran out, Nikanor Khrushchev again evicted them.[11]

The family remained in Kalinovka until Khrushchev was fourteen, and it was during these years that he came under the influence of Lidiia Mikhailovna Shevchenko, one of the teachers in the village. Shevchenko was a woman of radical views who upset the local peasants by her failure to attend church. Khrushchev later recalled that it was at her house that he first saw books forbidden by tsarist censorship laws and that her brother, on a visit from the city, gave him some illegal political pamphlets. She was, moreover, an atheist, perhaps the first non-believer the boy had ever met; he later recalled that she 'began to counteract the effects of my strict religious upbringing'.[12] The young Khrushchev's quick mind was obvious to the schoolteacher, and when he left school, having completed four years in all, she encouraged him to go to the city in search of further education. The family could not afford this, however, and Nikita went to work as a shepherd to help support his family, earning five kopecks a day.[13]

Khrushchev witnessed his first revolution while still in Kalinovka. Russia's humiliating defeat in the 1904–5 war with Japan was followed by a rising against the autocracy across the country. In Kalinovka as elsewhere, peasants, driven by poverty and land-hunger, rose up against the regime. The autocracy survived by employing a policy of concession combined with repression. The principal concession to the peasantry was the end of redemption payments on land acquired by peasants after the abolition of serfdom in 1861; this change brought no benefits for landless peasants like Sergei Khrushchev.

Persistent rumours have held that Khrushchev's humble origins were a fabrication and that he was in fact born into a noble family; this view has recently resurfaced in conjunction with attempts based on German and *émigré* Russian genealogical documents to prove conclusively Khrushchev's aristocratic lineage.[14] He would not have been the only major Bolshevik to conceal his high birth: his colleague and rival Georgii Malenkov was the son of a minor nobleman.[15] There was indeed an aristocratic Khrushchev family registered in the genealogies of Kursk and five other provinces.[16] Some have sought to identify Khrushchev's father as Sergei Nikolaevich Khrushchev, a tsarist official and Kalinovka landowner.[17] Such hypotheses are impossible to reconcile with Khrushchev's obvious lack of formal education, with his public behaviour, which scarcely suggested a refined upbringing, and with the fact that his parents lived with him in Moscow in the 1930s.[18] Khrushchev's family were peasants who had in all likelihood simply adopted the surname of local landowners.

In 1908 Sergei Khrushchev again moved to Iuzovka, this time for good, and returned to the mines; Nikita followed soon after.[19] Like his earlier seasonal migrations, Sergei's move was not at all unusual. Most peasant workers came to the Donbass as seasonal labourers with no desire to stay; as time passed and their hopes of becoming prosperous peasants disappeared, however, many reconciled themselves to life in the mines and settled permanently.[20] For the next two decades, Nikita Khrushchev's life and career were to be shaped by social, economic and political conditions in this industrial region of southern Ukraine.

The contrast with Kalinovka, to which he returned only for a brief period in 1918, could not have been greater. The Donbass was one of the most industrially developed regions of Imperial Russia. At its heart was Iuzovka, the company town of the New Russia Coal, Iron and Rail Producing Company, founded in 1870 by the Welsh entrepreneur John Hughes; the town's name was derived from Hughes's surname: Hughes-ovka. By 1908 Iuzovka had an ethnically mixed population of well over 50 000. As in other Donbass settlements, socio-economic cleavages in Iuzovka reflected ethnic ones. Foreigners – mainly British – held the commanding technical and managerial positions but occupied few low-level supervisory or production posts; these were taken for the most part by Russians, who also formed the great majority of rank-and-file workers. Russian entrepreneurs were numerically significant, but operated only on a small scale. Merchants and artisans tended to be Jewish, a fact which contributed to the anti-Semitism of the workers and peasants, and the rural Ukrainian population, which viewed the other groups with some suspicion, avoided entering the mines and steel mills as long as possible. The Ukrainians, whose village ties remained strong and close at hand, were also more likely than Russian peasants to return to the countryside at the first available opportunity.[21]

The rise of the Donbass as a region of company towns gave its social and political life a special character and implanted in Khrushchev's mind an image of industrial capitalism which remained with him all his life. Because of employer opposition, Iuzovka achieved municipal status – and a measure of grassroots political participation – only in 1917; until that time, employers there and elsewhere in the Donbass controlled education, health care, housing and retail trade.[22] This last was a particular barrier to worker prosperity since it meant that workers were often compelled to spend their earnings in company stores, where prices were high and the quality of goods low. Some owners, in violation of the law, paid out wages not in money, but in credits with the company store. In later years, this practice was bitterly recalled by Khrushchev.[23]

The 275-mile move from Kalinovka to Iuzovka was a leap between centuries. At the age of fourteen Khrushchev left

the rural, almost medieval life of the Russian village forever
and entered a city in the throes of Russia's industrial
revolution. Here as in Kalinovka his life was one of work
and poverty, but the rhythm of the work and the nature of
the poverty were different. So was the environment; pre-war
Iuzovka could not have presented Khrushchev with a
sharper contrast to his native village. Konstantin Paustovskii
later provided a vivid picture of Iuzovka on the eve of the
First World War:

> In those days [Iuzovka] was a slummy settlement ringed
> by wooden hovels and clay huts. . . . suburbs were known
> by such names as 'Bitch' and 'Croak', which suited them
> perfectly. The Novorossiisk factory, where I worked,
> stood in the same hollow as the settlement, smoke
> pouring from its chimneys. Smoke also poured from the
> chimneys of the various workshops. It was yellow and
> stank like burned milk. . . . Greasy soot dropped from
> the sky. Nothing in Iuzovka was white. Whatever had
> started out as white was a blotchy, yellowish grey – shirts,
> sheets, curtains, dogs, horses, cats. It rarely rained . . .
> and hot dry winds swept up the streets, stirring up the
> piles of dust, soot and chicken feathers into clouds.[24]

For Khrushchev, the move to Iuzovka, with its foreign-built,
foreign-owned industrial concerns, threw into sharp relief
the backwardness of Russia; for the rest of his life he was
driven by the desire to overcome this backwardness, to
'catch up with and overtake' the most advanced western
countries. Whether working as a local party boss in Ukraine
or Moscow, or as the Soviet premier, Khrushchev's primary
concern throughout his career was economic development.
    After a period as an apprentice to a blacksmith, fifteen-
year-old Nikita was apprenticed to a fitter, a job to which
he was drawn by his love of all things mechanical.[25] All his
life, Khrushchev exhibited a fascination with mechanical
devices, a curiosity about how things worked. According to
his sister-in-law, the young Khrushchev built and maintained
his own motorcycle, using spare parts collected around
Iuzovka.[26] Apprentices in the Donbass tended to be sons

or younger brothers of miners and factory workers and supplemented the family income with their wages. Khrushchev would have earned between 20 and 40 kopecks a day, against a minimum adult wage of 90 kopecks, but the opportunity to learn a trade gave him better long-term prospects than his miner father.[27] Khrushchev later claimed (not without pride) to have earned 20–30 roubles in gold in his best years, triple the pay of most fitters and much more than miners earned; he was able to purchase such luxuries as a bicycle, a camera and a watch.[28] Soon after Nikita started to work, Sergei was able to bring Aksiniia and Irina to join them.[29]

On completing his apprenticeship, Khrushchev went to work as a metal fitter in a generator plant attached to a mine near Iuzovka, a move of great significance for his political development. The miners were politically the most radical element in the Donbass. The better pay and conditions of the steel mills facilitated a much smoother transition to urban life than the mines. Ten per cent of the mill workers were homeowners, and many more could realistically aspire to home ownership; no ordinary miner could hope to own his own home. Mill workers were also more stable in employment and more likely to be married than the miners. The latter tended to be younger, more radical and more violent, caught mid-way in the transition from peasants to urban workers.[30] It is thus no surprise that they were the group from which the Bolsheviks, the most radical and uncompromising of Russia's revolutionary parties, drew their main support in the Donbass.

Though better paid than miners elsewhere in Russia, Donbass miners worked in appalling conditions. A contemporary observer wrote,

It is difficult to say where life is worse for the miner, in the mine or above ground. On the surface he is in a dugout, or in the best case a barrack with dirt, crowding, poor food, drunkenness, an absence of spiritual interests, nowhere to spend his free moments, no one with whom to converse in a civilised manner. Underground there are hard labour, low pay, cave-ins, explosions, flooding, cold, etc., etc.[31]

It was against this background that Khrushchev first encountered the works of Zola and Marx:

> When I read Emile Zola's *Germinal*, I thought that he was writing not about France, but about the mine in which my father and I worked. . . . When, later on, I listened to lectures on political economy . . . it seemed to me as though Karl Marx had been at the mine where my father and I had worked.[32]

Khrushchev's words underscore the extent to which his Marxism was more visceral than intellectual. His political views were born of life experience rather than of any real grasp of Marxist theory. Marxism described to Khrushchev the world in which he lived and offered him a path to a better life.

The Donbass workers' movement was at its nadir when Khrushchev moved to Iuzovka,[33] but as it revived in 1912–14, Nikita became a labour activist. In May 1912 unrest in the Donbass followed the shooting of several hundred striking workers in Siberia. In a report of 26 May the chief of the provincial gendarmerie listed Nikita Khrushchev, an eighteen-year-old metal worker at the German-owned Bosse Engineering Works, as among the men collecting donations for the families of those killed in Siberia. As a result Khrushchev soon lost his Bosse job, but found work at a mine in Rutchenkovo, near Iuzovka. There he first began to take part in organising the circulation and public reading of the Bolshevik newspaper *Pravda*.[34] It was also in 1912 that Khrushchev became acquainted with the *Communist Manifesto*, which he heard read aloud in the hut of a friend and fellow worker named Pantelei Makhinia.[35] Khrushchev played a leading role in a number of strikes during the next few years.[36]

Because coal was a priority industry for Russia's war effort, Khrushchev, as a skilled worker attached to the mines, was exempt from conscription when World War I broke out. He remained in Rutchenkovo, where he began work at a mechanical workshop serving ten local mines in late 1914.[37] Khrushchev and his colleagues went on strike with increasing frequency, demanding better pay and conditions, and agitating against the war.[38] Khrushchev's life was not all politics, however: in 1914, he married Evfrosin'ia Ivanovna Pisareva, the daughter of a fellow machinist in the Rutchenkovo mines.[39] They had a son, Leonid, born in late 1917, just three days after the Bolshevik coup in St Petersburg, and a daughter, Iuliia.[40]

The tsarist autocracy came to an abrupt end in February 1917. The regime had been unpopular even before 1914, and a combination of military defeats, hardship on the home front and its own political ineptitude weakened it still further as the war progressed. When bread riots erupted in the capital, the Petrograd garrison refused to fire on the crowds; instead, many soldiers joined the demonstrators. The government, with no reliable force capable of compelling obedience at its disposal, collapsed. Tsar Nicholas II signed an abdication for both himself and his son, and Russia's monarchy came to an end without anyone having intended to bring this about.

Khrushchev was by this time a Bolshevik sympathiser, though not yet a party member. Although the local councils of workers' deputies which sprang up in the Donbass in 1917 were dominated by the Mensheviks and the Social Revolutionaries (SRs), the Bolsheviks were the dominant force among miners.[41] Khrushchev's critics were later to make much of his 'tardiness' in joining the party,[42] but there is little reason to doubt his sympathies or to attach particular significance to the date of his entry into the Bolshevik party. The distinction between those who formally entered the party before October 1917 and those who did not became a matter of political importance only much later. The Bolsheviks at this time were little more than a faction within the Russian social democratic movement; their bitter quarrels with other factions meant little to most workers and did not hinder the growth of unified grassroots organisations in many areas.[43] Khrushchev himself later recalled that 'in those days joining the party was not the same as it is now. No one campaigned or tried to convince you to join. There were many different movements and groups, and it was difficult to keep them all straight'.[44]

Because his mechanical shop served ten Rutchenkovo mines, all of which he visited at one time or another, Khrushchev was acquainted with, or at least known to, many of the local miners. This probably contributed to his election to the local Council (*soviet*) of Workers' Deputies which was formed after the abdication. The soviet was dominated by Mensheviks and Social Revolutionaries, but Khrushchev reportedly supported the Bolshevik fraction.[45] This did not, however, prevent him from chairing some sessions of the soviet.[46] Differences between the various left parties meant little in many local soviets, as the adherents of the different fractions had to co-operate with one another against common enemies.

The critical months between the end of the autocracy in February 1917 and the Bolshevik coup of October were a time of intense conflict in the Donbass as workers, organised around their soviets, and owners, backed by the provisional government, struggled for control of the region. The owners closed many pits, while the soviets disbanded the police, formed workers' militias and pressed for improvements in pay and working conditions. After an unsuccessful military putsch in August, military-revolutionary committees (*revkomy*) were formed by workers and soldiers across the country. Khrushchev was elected to the Rutchenkovo revkom.[47] By the end of the autumn he was head of the local metalworkers' union.[48]

Around this time he first met his future patron (and later enemy) Lazar M. Kaganovich. The two met when Kaganovich, a Bolshevik organiser, attended two conferences of Donbass miners' representatives at which Khrushchev was a delegate.[49] Kaganovich was only a year older than Khrushchev, but he had been a party member since 1911 and was an energetic organiser. After the Revolution he became one of Stalin's closest aides and supporters and was for a time the *de facto* second-in-command in the Bolshevik leadership. Like Khrushchev, Kaganovich was no intellectual, but he was tough, ruthless and possessed of an enormous capacity for work.

The provisional government in Petrograd floundered

through most of 1917, struggling to establish its authority at home in the face of opposition from both right and left, and refusing to withdraw Russia from the war. It was forced to share power with the soviets of workers' and soldiers' deputies which had sprung up across the country and could hope only to survive long enough to conduct elections to a Constituent Assembly, planned for November. On the night of 24–5 October, however, Lenin's Bolsheviks seized the Winter Palace in Petrograd and arrested the members of the government. The coup itself was an almost comical affair which enraged many of the other parties, but it was allowed to stand, mainly because no one wished to defend the provisional government.

The storming of the Winter Palace was only the beginning of the Bolshevik seizure of power, however:

The Bolsheviks had taken control in Petrograd and, after a week of street fighting, in Moscow. But the soviets that had sprung up in most provincial centres still had to follow the capitals' lead in overthrowing the bourgeoisie (often, at local level, this meant ousting a 'Committee of Public Safety' set up by the solid citizenry of the town); and, if a local soviet was too weak to take power, support was unlikely to be forthcoming from the capitals.[50]

The Donbass was no exception, and fighting soon broke out. Khrushchev joined the Rutchenkovo Red Guard at the head of a battalion of miners. They were involved in their first skirmishes in December 1917 when a number of Donbass towns were subjected to punitive raids by troops under the Cossack General Kaledin.

In early 1918 the Bolsheviks surrendered much of Ukraine to Germany in the Treaty of Brest-Litovsk. German troops moved to occupy the Donbass, and the Red Guards were powerless to halt their advance. Some time around June Khrushchev, fleeing the Germans, returned to his native Kalinovka. He had joined the party during the late spring and, according to his memoirs, he took the post of deputy secretary to the district (*uezd*) party committee in Kalinovka.[51] His claim is not as implausible as it might seem: there were few Bolsheviks in the countryside at this time, and Khrushchev had already been a labour activist and Bolshevik sympathiser for several years. He was, moreover, a man with local roots and considerable natural gifts as an orator and agitator. According to other sources, he also headed the village committee charged with rallying poor peasants to the Bolshevik side and dividing up local landowners' holdings among the peasants of the district.[52] The two positions would not, of course, have been mutually exclusive, and Khrushchev may have held them both. A key role in the land-distribution process would have enabled him to look after his family's interests when the old estates were broken up.

When Khrushchev left Kalinovka and returned to military service in January 1919, the civil war between the Bolsheviks and the various White (anti-Bolshevik) armies had been under way for about six months. He initially served as political commissar of a construction platoon with the Ninth Rifle Division, attached to Semion Budennyi's famous First Cavalry Army, which was then operating in southern Russia and Ukraine. As a commissar, he was charged with indoctrinating Red Army volunteers and conscripts, organising party cells within the army and preventing the chronic desertion which afflicted both sides during the civil war. These political duties did not allow Khrushchev to avoid combat, however, and he was under fire many times. He soon became commissar of a construction battalion, a position which allowed him to take a two-month course for political workers, after which he was promoted to be an instructor in the political department of the Ninth Kuban Army.[53] It was not, by civil war standards, a particularly spectacular rise. Budennyi, a former tsarist cavalry sergeant, ended the war as an army commander and Inspector of the Red Cavalry, and Khrushchev's future rival, Georgii Malenkov, entered the Red Army as an eighteen-year-old private and rose to become political commissar for the Eastern and Turkestan fronts.

After the civil war, Khrushchev was demobilised and sent back to Rutchenkovo as commissar of a labour brigade. Seven years of constant warfare had shattered the nation's economy, and the revival of the Donbass's coal production was crucial to economic recovery. In 1921, Donbass coal output was only 20 per cent of its 1913 level. Miners and other workers with experience of the coal industry were thus among the first to be demobilised; those who refused to return to the mines, which were run with military-style discipline, were treated as deserters. The mine administration in Rutchenkovo consisted of a director and two assistants, one for technical matters and one for political work; Khrushchev became the deputy for political work. The director was Egor Abakumov, a friend of Khrushchev from pre-revolutionary days who would later work with him on the construction of the Moscow Metro.[54] Demobilisation did not, however, mean an easier life. In 1921 there was a drought in the Donbass; a severe famine followed. Brigades of miners were sent into the countryside to take food from the peasantry, and there were instances of cannibalism in some villages. Desertion from the mines rose, and production fell, as miners left in search of food. The situation improved only in late 1922.

By that time, Khrushchev himself had become a widower, losing his wife Evfrosin'ia to typhus at some point during or soon after the civil war. The year of her death is difficult to pinpoint. Evfrosin'ia's sister, Anna Pisareva, recalled that Evfrosin'ia had died in Kalinovka, to which she had fled when the Germans occupied Ukraine, and that Nikita Sergeevich, returning home from the front on leave, arrived just in time to bury his wife.[55] This would suggest that Evfrosin'ia perished in 1919 or 1920, a date compatible with Leonid Khrushchev's claim that his mother had died soon after his second birthday, that is in late 1919 or early 1920.[56] Nikita Sergeevich, however, stated that his first wife perished during the famine in 1921.[57]

As a political worker in the mines, Khrushchev's job was made no easier by Lenin's New Economic Policy (NEP), adopted in March 1921. NEP was a strategic retreat on Lenin's part, involving a relaxation of the harshest policies of War Communism and the reintroduction of a measure of private enterprise. NEP did indeed facilitate both the survival of the regime and the economic recovery of the country, but committed Bolsheviks found it difficult to accept; many regarded it as an outright betrayal of the revolution. A key part of Khrushchev's job was to explain this policy to the miners and to win their support for it. This was no simple task. For rank-and-file workers, the Bolsheviks' strongest supporters, the time was still one of great privation, yet better-off peasants (kulaks) in the countryside and petty entrepreneurs (NEPmen) in the cities took advantage of the conditions created by NEP to enrich themselves. Khrushchev understood the necessity of NEP, but he recognised that it 'was, to some extent, a retreat on the ideological front' and admitted that 'it was . . . difficult and even painful for us to adapt ourselves' to it.[58]

Khrushchev did not remain at the mine for long. In the summer of 1922 he was offered and refused the directorship of the Pastukhov mine, requesting instead to be sent to continue his education in the workers' faculty (*rabfak*) of the new mining institute in Iuzovka. The purpose of the newly created rabfaks was to give capable, politically reliable workers a basic education as rapidly as possible. They were then to go on to more specialised studies in order to provide the country with a new class of politically loyal, technically trained specialists of proletarian origin. There were only eight rabfaks in Ukraine, with a total of about 1500 places; admission was thus a significant achievement and a sign of the party's confidence in a worker. After initial resistance, Khrushchev's request was granted, and he entered the rabfak in August 1922.[59] He also continued to work as deputy director of the Rutchenkovo mine administration.[60]

Khrushchev's desire for further study was great; he was twenty-eight and had had only four years of formal schooling. He was by no means illiterate, however. As a worker in the Donbass, he had, when time permitted, made use of a public library established by a well-known educator and publisher, N. A. Rubakin.[61] Khrushchev developed a love for the nineteenth-century Russian classics and in later life could quote Nekrasov, his favourite poet, for hours on end. He wrote with great difficulty, however, and lacked any sort of specialised or technical qualifications.

Khrushchev's attitude toward education remained ambivalent throughout his career. He valued it highly and consistently sought both to further his own education and to widen access to education for Soviet people.[62] At the same time, he constantly emphasised the importance of practical experience and the limitations of formal or 'theoretical' study in preparing people for 'real life'.[63] This latter emphasis was in part a compensation for his own lack of education, but it also reflected his temperament; he was by nature a man more concerned with experience than with ideas. Knowledge was a tool with which he wished to *do* things, not a good to be pursued for its own sake. In any case, his study at the rabfak was soon subordinated to the demands of 'practical work'. He remained there until 1925, but was principally occupied with politics, not study: shortly after his enrolment Khrushchev became secretary of the party cell in the rabfak, a position he retained until he left the faculty.

Khrushchev's responsibilities extended far beyond managing the cell's internal affairs. As cell secretary, he was deeply involved in the running of the rabfak itself, having a voice in matters connected with personnel, administration and curriculum. His chief concerns were, as might be expected, the political education of students and their employment as agitators among the other workers, but he was also occupied with the construction and equipping of the school. It was up to the students themselves to rebuild the school building, obtain basic equipment and, in some cases, print their own textbooks.

At the rabfak Khrushchev met Nina Petrovna Kukharchuk, a Ukrainian Bolshevik whose career as an agitator had already taken her from underground work in Ukraine and a number of civil war fronts to the Sverdlov Communist University in Moscow, where she had been trained as an instructor in party history and political economy. In the autumn of 1922, she was sent to the Iuzovka regional (*okrug*) party school, which was in the same building as the workers' faculty. Khrushchev was never her student, however, and their relationship developed further only when she was sent to Rutchenkovo as a propagandist for the Petrovo–Mar'inka district party committee (*raikom*) at the end of 1923. Khrushchev was still working in the mines in Rutchenkovo, where he lived with his children, his parents and his sister and her family.[64] In 1924, Nikita and Nina began to live together as husband and wife, although their marriage was not officially registered until 1965.[65]

Khrushchev's rise in the local party apparatus continued. In December 1923 he was a delegate to the Iuzovka regional party conference and was elected to the new regional party committee (*okruzhkom*). This promotion came despite a potentially costly political stumble. The autumn of 1923 had witnessed a struggle over internal party democracy between the supporters of Iosif Stalin and those of his rival Lev Trotsky; Khrushchev was embarrassingly slow to cast his lot with the winning side. At issue was the manipulation of elections, appointments and transfers by Stalin, who used his control of the Central Committee Secretariat to isolate his opponents. Lenin lay dying, and the battle over party democracy was the opening round in the struggle to succeed him. Khrushchev had his doubts about the Stalinist position and wavered for a time in the early stages of the discussion, but he finally came down on the side of Stalin, who was backed by the majority of the Central Committee and whose views therefore constituted the party's 'General Line'.[66] This wavering did Khrushchev no obvious harm, and in January 1924, just a month after his election to the okruzhkom, he was included in the Iuzovka delegation to Lenin's funeral in Moscow, an obvious sign of preferment.[67]

As a result of his promotions, party work took up more and more of Khrushchev's time; he was constantly moving about the region, to mines, factories and educational institutions, representing the regional party leadership. When he left the rabfak in the summer of 1925, he was sent to work as the Petrovo–Mar'inka raikom secretary.[68] Nina Petrovna was still working there as a propagandist. Although formally outranked by her husband, she was better paid than he: propagandists' salaries were paid out of central funds, while Khrushchev, as raikom secretary, drew his pay from the okruzhkom budget.[69]

As secretary of the Petrovo–Mar'inka raikom, Khrushchev found himself in charge of a district encompassing some 400 square miles, including one city, three towns and eleven villages. The district party organisation had 1108 members and candidate members in November 1925, when Khrushchev presided over his first district party conference.

Already at this stage Khrushchev's style of work set him apart from his colleagues in the local party machine. Though he now worked full-time in the party bureaucracy, he was not and would never become a desk-bound functionary. Rather than take advantage of his new position to escape the mud, the frost and the summer heat, Khrushchev moved constantly about his little fiefdom. At the district conference, he described his life as 'itinerant': now in the village of Mar'inka, now in the mines, now in the fields with the local peasants. In the winter he wrapped himself in a sheepskin and roamed about the district in a horse-drawn sleigh, criticising, questioning, encouraging, assisting.[70]

This style of work made Khrushchev unusually accessible for a party official of his rank. One contemporary reported that miners with grievances turned to Khrushchev rather than to the district committee of the miners' union. Another recalled that meetings conducted under his guidance were unusually lively and that he encouraged even rank-and-file communists to take an active part in the proceedings. As his 1925 conference report makes clear, there was no economic or political issue in the district in which he did not take an interest.[71] He became involved even in seemingly petty decisions, because nothing seemed petty to him. Even the provision of glass for the windows of a building in Petrovo was a matter for his attention.[72] His main priorities, to judge from the conference report, were connected with industrialisation, housing, the development of co-operatives and the struggle with 'specialist eaters'.[73]

As a result of civil war, famine and the mass exodus of much of Russia's bourgeoisie, the new Soviet state faced a chronic shortage of trained engineers and other specialists. Those who remained to serve the new regime were members of the old bourgeoisie who had been educated before the revolution. Many Bolsheviks, workers and officials alike, distrusted these old specialists and resented the privileges which they continued to enjoy. Those who were most active in persecuting old technical specialists were known as 'specialist-eaters'; they were more concerned with political reliability than technical expertise. Khrushchev, however, always placed economic work and economic results ahead of other considerations; for him the building of communism was chiefly a matter of 'economic construction', and bourgeois specialists were to be judged on the results they achieved.[74]

Perhaps the most intractable problem Khrushchev faced in Petrovo–Mar'inka was the acute shortage of housing. Many of the miners lived in barracks where poor hygiene, drunkenness and gambling were the norm. This was Khrushchev's first experience of housing problems, but not his last. Housing Soviet people remained one of his major preoccupations for the next forty years: in Moscow in the 1930s, in Ukraine after the war and across the whole of the Soviet Union in the years of his leadership. Khrushchev also faced the problem of managing a largely inexperienced, ill-disciplined industrial workforce made up of men who had been peasants not long before. Strikes were common, and it often fell to Khrushchev to break them.[75] The former labour activist was now part of the management of a workers' state, and his views on labour discipline changed accordingly. By the time he reached Moscow, he was as tough as any of his colleagues in pushing workers to the limit. Khrushchev, of course, saw no contradiction in this, for he believed that he was pushing them to build a better future for themselves.

As a raikom secretary and member of the okruzhkom, Khrushchev was occasionally invited to participate in meetings of the executive organ of the okruzhkom, the bureau, headed by regional party secretary K. V. Moiseenko. Generally speaking, his presence was required when the bureau wished to discuss matters related to Petrovo–Mar'inka district in particular or to district-level party work in general: the state of workers' political education, the work of the Petrovo mine administration, the organisation and conduct of district party conferences and so on.[76] The okruzhkom bureau was the most powerful body in the region, dominating the nominally independent state authorities. In 1926 Khrushchev was present at a closed bureau meeting which planned a purge of the okrug's judges and criminal investigators. Raikom secretaries were instructed to examine ways to 'improve the quality of the staff' of this apparatus in their districts and to report to an okrug commission on the issue. The contents of Khrushchev's report are unknown, but of the seven people's judges in his district, three were removed, one was put on probation, and two were confirmed in their positions; one case was left unresolved.[77] A short while later, Khrushchev participated in another closed session, at which the bureau rejected the state prosecutor's recommendation of long incarceration in a murder case and demanded that the convicted killer be shot.[78]

In November 1926 Khrushchev became a bureau member himself. In December he moved back to Stalino (as Iuzovka had been renamed in 1925) to head the organisational department of the okruzhkom.[79] Khrushchev did not limit himself to party affairs or to organisational questions, however. The division of labour in the okruzhkom was fluid and often did not reflect members' formal titles; though formally chief of the organisational department, Khrushchev dealt with education, housing, workers' pay and productivity, the trade unions and construction,[80] as well as party recruitment, personnel questions and other matters falling within the bailiwick of the organisational department.[81] His growing authority within the Stalino organisation may be inferred from the fact that he headed the okruzhkom bureau and chaired meetings of both the bureau and secretariat, as well as the full okruzhkom, when Moiseenko was absent.[82]

Around the time of Khrushchev's return to Stalino, Nina Petrovna was transferred to Moscow, where she studied political economy in the Krupskaia Communist Academy until the end of 1927. The couple were not reunited until well into 1928, when Nina Petrovna was sent to the Kiev Interregional Party School; by that time Khrushchev himself had also been transferred to Kiev. Even then, Nina Petrovna was able to rejoin her husband only after thwarting an attempt by the personnel department of the Central Committee in Moscow to send her to Tiumen' in central Russia.[83] While his wife was away in the capital, Nikita Sergeevich continued his climb up the party hierarchy, gaining experience of factional struggle and intrigue, both national and local.

The mid-1920s were years of intense political conflict at

the national level, as Lenin's heirs struggled for the right to assume his mantle. Khrushchev was not in a position to influence the course of this struggle, but his status as a party functionary made him both a spectator and a bit player in the unfolding drama. After his wavering during the discussion of intra-party democracy in the autumn of 1923, Khrushchev toed a hard Stalinist line, as did virtually all of the Bolsheviks in the Iuzovka–Stalino organisation. The Ukrainian party was headed from 1925 by Kaganovich, one of Stalin's closest and most dedicated supporters; under his guidance, the Ninth Congress of the Ukrainian party, which Khrushchev attended, took a strong pro-Stalin stand. In December of that year Khrushchev attended the Fourteenth Congress of the All-Union Communist Party as a consulting (non-voting) delegate. This was the congress at which Stalin defeated Grigorii Zinoviev and Lev Kamenev, his former allies in the struggle against Trotsky. Stalin, who as General Secretary of the party controlled appointments to key party posts around the country, was able to pack the Congress with his supporters. The Stalinists heckled and shouted down the oppositionists, effectively silencing all dissent at the Congress; as events were to show, it would not be long before they had silenced dissent within the party altogether. Even Lenin's widow, Nadezhda Krupskaia, was heckled when she spoke. The Ukrainian delegation, and Khrushchev with it, formed part of the Stalinist chorus.[84]

The Fourteenth Congress represented Khrushchev's second opportunity to see both Moscow and the leaders of the country for himself. When Stalin met briefly with the Stalino delegation to have his picture taken with them, the wit and 'democratic spirit' of the General Secretary made a very favourable impression on Khrushchev. At the okruzhkom meeting convened to discuss the congress in January 1926, Khrushchev refuted charges that Stalin's political line had deviated from Lenin's: 'We know that Stalin became General Secretary not after Lenin's death but while Lenin was still alive. It cannot be that Lenin would have had as General Secretary a person with an unclear political line; it is therefore easy for us to deflect the attacks of the opposition.'[85]

Khrushchev was typical of the party members flocking to

Stalin's banner as the struggle to succeed Lenin got under way. The party of the mid-1920s was very different from that which had existed prior to 1917. It had grown enormously before Lenin's death, and it doubled again as a result of the 'Lenin Enrolment', a recruitment campaign initiated in 1924 to commemorate the leader's passing. Thousands of new people moved into the party and into full-time party posts in the 1920s, and they owed their advancement to Stalin. It was to him that they looked for leadership. These new recruits were more likely than the Old Bolsheviks to be workers, and they were distinguished by youth, inexperience and a lack of education. They had no experience of intra-party democracy and little patience for intellectuals and their incessant theoretical debates. Stalin, who managed the party machine, understood these changes better than any of his rivals.

With such a constituency forming within the party, Stalin was able to turn even apparent weaknesses into assets. Unlike Trotsky and some of his other rivals, Stalin was a mediocre orator and a poor theoretician; he made a virtue of this. He spoke to the party's rising new cadres in terms they understood: his arguments were simple and clear, and he made no claim to originality. On the contrary, he insisted that he was merely a disciple and interpreter of Lenin. Stalin's rivals came across to the Khrushchevs of the party as chattering intellectuals, windbag theoreticians from petit-bourgeois backgrounds. And when at the end of the 1920s Stalin abandoned the hated NEP in favour of the five-year plans, these impatient young Bolsheviks saw him as the leader who offered a radical, concrete programme for building socialism, not theoretical justifications of a semi-capitalist status quo. He promised an age of economic heroism to match the military heroism of the civil war, and men like Khrushchev, who had fought that conflict in the hope of building a new world, were ready to follow him.

Khrushchev further demonstrated his Stalinist credentials at the First All-Ukrainian Party Conference in 1926. N. V. Golubenko, an opposition supporter from Odessa, addressed the conference with a statement admitting his involvement in factional politics, renouncing his oppositionist activities and submitting to the will of the party.

That, at least, was what he was supposed to do; the statement was not in fact very apologetic, and Golubenko was given a rough time. He was heckled and interrupted not only by delegates from the floor but also by members of the Ukrainian Politburo.[86] Khrushchev spoke immediately after Golubenko and accused him of 'total irresponsibility and lack of principle', and 'slander against our party organisation'. Khrushchev denied Golubenko's charge that party bodies were being packed with new members so as to facilitate the Stalinists' takeover of leading party posts (in fact, this is exactly what was being done at all levels of the party hierarchy). Khrushchev then accused Golubenko of insincerity. The Fourteenth Congress had agreed that the party would work with oppositionists who renounced their previous views and actions. Yet Golubenko's statement, argued Khrushchev, was insincere, 'only a manoeuvre'; 'acknowledging their mistakes, they are at the same time trying to create for themselves an opportunity to carry on their divisive activity'.[87] Other speakers took a similar line, as did the conference resolutions.[88]

The charge of insincerity was the latest twist in the tactics of the Stalinists. The relatively lenient position of the Fourteenth Congress was to be undermined by 'demands' from the locales that tougher action be taken against oppositionists whose declarations were found to be 'insincere'. The charge was effective because it was generally true: many former oppositionists submitted publicly to the will of the party while continuing to hold oppositionist views. The prohibition on 'factionalism' in the party's ranks was stretched beyond *organisational* factional activity (its original meaning) to cover 'factionalism' at the level of ideas. Lenin had demanded total obedience to the party, but Stalin, who described 'unity of views' as 'the very basis upon which our party is built', soon came to require complete and unquestioning acceptance of its views.[89] In 1926, however, official policy was still more conciliatory than the position of Khrushchev or the Ukrainian conference: *Pravda* had reported in October that 'the Central Committee is able to state with satisfaction that the opposition has in the main accepted the conditions presented to them'.[90]

Though still a staunch supporter of Stalin and of the General Line of the Central Committee, Khrushchev struck a very different note at the Tenth Congress of the Ukrainian party in November 1927:

The comrades who have spoken before me have already talked a great deal about the fact that the line of the Central Committee is correct. Nevertheless, it seems to me that, despite the fact that the struggle with anti-party deviations is now the evil of the day, we must not let the practical questions before us slip from our field of vision.

He went on to devote his speech to organisational questions and to propose changes in the structure and operations of raikoms which, taken together, would have increased the power of raikom officials at the expense of ordinary party activists and reduced the accountability of the former to the party rank and file.[91] Khrushchev's proposals were not acted on, but they give some indication of the direction of his thinking at this time; his remarks anticipated the growth of a more authoritarian party apparatus.

The fact that Khrushchev chose to set himself apart from the mass of speakers at the congress by concentrating on organisational work rather than factional politics is also significant. He was a pragmatist at heart, and his grasp of Marxist-Leninist theory was poor; it is unlikely that he really understood the ideological battles he was witnessing. Khrushchev himself all but admitted as much while describing later struggles in the Moscow party organisation: 'I don't even remember exactly what the differences were between Bukharin and Rykov on the one hand and Syrtsov and Lominadze on the other. Rightists, oppositionists, right-leftists, deviationists – these people were all moving in basically the same political direction, and our group was against them.'[92]

Khrushchev's membership of the credentials commission at the Ukrainian congress indicated that he was on the way up. The following month he was one of eleven voting delegates from the Stalino organisation at the Fifteenth

Congress, where he witnessed the expulsion from the party
of those who had constituted the opposition at the
Fourteenth. At the Fifteenth Congress he saw for the first
time Lenin's last testament, a document in which the dying
leader had been very critical of Stalin and had advocated
removing Stalin from the post of General Secretary. The
testament was distributed to the delegates on 27 December,
but Khrushchev's faith in Stalin remained unshaken.

Back in Stalino Moiseenko ceased to attend meetings of
the bureau and secretariat at the beginning of August 1927;
he had been called to Kiev, where he attended a number
of sessions of the Ukrainian party Politburo, evidently to
discuss his case.[93] On 26 September a plenum of the full
okruzhkom confirmed (in Moiseenko's absence) a decision
of the Central Committee of the Communist Party (bolshevik) of Ukraine (CP(b)U) and the okruzhkom bureau
releasing him from his duties as regional party secretary 'in
accordance with his personal request'.[94] No explanation of
the reasons for his removal was presented at the plenum or
given in answer to delegates' questions at the regional party
conference in November.[95] Two years later, an article in the
party's organisational journal accused Moiseenko of a host
of sins, including bad management, bullying party members, excessive drunkenness, petty corruption and the
'whitewashing' of responsible officials.[96] He was not, however, expelled from the party apparatus altogether; instead
he was transferred to work in the Poltava region.

Khrushchev derived considerable benefit from Moiseenko's demise. While Moiseenko was in Kiev, Khrushchev
served as *de facto* secretary of the Stalino regional committee, one of the largest and most important in the USSR.
He continued in this capacity until Moiseenko's successor,
V. A. Stroganov, arrived in mid-October.[97] Moreover, the
Ukrainian Politburo's consideration of the Moiseenko case
gave Khrushchev a major political opportunity: in early
September he participated in the Ukrainian Politburo
meeting which decided to replace Moiseenko. This enabled
Khrushchev to develop his relationship with Kaganovich
and to make himself known to other members of the
Ukrainian party leadership. Khrushchev then reported on
the Politburo's decision to colleagues in Stalino, first to the

party bureau and then to the plenary session of the okruzhkom.[98] There was, however, one slip in his management of the transition. The protocols of the 26 September plenary session show five items on the agenda; a sixth item has been both inked out and papered over, but is still legible: Khrushchev reported to the plenum that the okruzhkom bureau had earlier that day confirmed the selection of Stroganov to succeed Moiseenko.[99] In reality this is undoubtedly what happened, but formally the bureau could do no more than 'recommend' Stroganov to the committee; only the full okruzhkom could confirm him in office. This was done at a plenary session in November.[100]

Khrushchev later claimed that the move to oust Moiseenko had originated in the Stalino organisation and that the Ukrainian Central Committee had become involved only after an attempt was made to remove him. The CC commission investigating the affair sided with the rebels, and Moiseenko was sacked.[101] Khrushchev's deep involvement in the affair at every turn suggests that if the impetus for a change of leadership really did come from Stalino, then he himself was one of the instigators of this effort.

Khrushchev did not remain in Stalino long after Stroganov's arrival. By his own account, he had to move in order to avoid undermining his new boss: because of Khrushchev's local roots, people with problems were bypassing the newcomer Stroganov and turning to Khrushchev for help. As a result, relations between the two men became strained.[102] This explanation is entirely plausible, particularly in light of Khrushchev's role during the months preceding Stroganov's arrival. Khrushchev may not have been eager to give up the authority which he had enjoyed during the interregnum.

In any case, he was soon on his way; at the beginning of 1928, Kaganovich offered him the post of deputy chief of the organisational department of the Ukrainian Central Committee, a major promotion. The offer was motivated not only by the good personal relationship which Khrushchev and Kaganovich had developed, but also by class considerations: it was felt that not enough of the officials in the apparatus of the Ukrainian Central Committee had working-class backgrounds. After initially resisting the offer,

Khrushchev reconsidered and agreed to move to Khar'kov, then the capital of Ukraine.[103] The job in Khar'kov did not last long. Khrushchev says in his memoirs that he found it most disagreeable: it involved too much paperwork and too little involvement with 'the flesh-and-blood world'. The Khar'kov post was undoubtedly ill-suited to Khrushchev's temperament and may also have been difficult for a man with his lack of education. He requested that Kaganovich transfer him at the first available opportunity.[104] By early May Khrushchev had been transferred to Kiev, where he headed the organisational department of the okruzhkom.[105] He had been in Khar'kov less than four months.

One reason for sending Khrushchev to Kiev may have been to put a reliable Russian into a key position in the local committee. According to Khrushchev, the Kiev organisation was considered to be unstable, riddled with deviationist elements; Ukrainian nationalism was a particular concern.[106] Fear of Ukrainian nationalism had been the principal reason for the selection of Khar'kov rather than Kiev, Ukraine's largest city, as the capital of the Ukrainian Soviet Socialist Republic. Suppression of any hint of nationalism was one of Kaganovich's principal tasks during his three years at the head of the Ukrainian party; as a result, Kaganovich was unpopular with Ukrainian Bolsheviks, a fact which contributed to the development of close relationships with Russian communists from the Donbass like Khrushchev. The Ukrainian party was divided along a Kiev–Khar'kov axis which pitted Donbass Bolsheviks, who were mainly ethnic Russians, against Ukrainians from further west.[107] Khrushchev recalls the Kievans' negative attitudes to the Donbass in his memoirs.[108]

In Kiev as in Stalino Khrushchev soon emerged as *de facto* second-in-command, running the local party machine during okruzhkom Secretary N. N. Demchenko's frequent absences.[109] The protocols of the bureau of the Kiev okruzhkom from 1928 show that a great deal of attention was devoted to the struggle with nationalists, Trotskyites and other anti-soviet elements in the area. Khrushchev himself made several trips to the Central Committee in Khar'kov, at least some of which were made in connection with these issues. Both the protocols and Khrushchev's memoirs also make references to demonstrations, unemployment and problems with labour discipline; the Bolsheviks were less secure in the Ukrainian city of Kiev than in the Russian-dominated Donbass. The bureau was especially concerned for the safety and security of activists and collectives operating in the countryside, where communist influence was at its weakest.[110]

By 1929, the focus in Kiev, as in the rest of the country, had shifted to the so-called 'right deviation'. Stalin was moving to occupy the political positions of his vanquished rivals on the left of the party and to destroy its right wing, which had supported him against Trotsky, Zinoviev and Kamenev. Khrushchev remained firmly in the Stalinist camp but viewed the struggle in practical rather than theoretical terms. At a joint plenum of the Kiev regional and city party committees in April 1929, Khrushchev addressed the issue:

> Comrades, we have conducted many meetings discussing the issue of the rightist deviation and the need to struggle decisively against this deviation and those who have a conciliatory attitude toward it. But comrades, our cells and our members do not always carry on the struggle with the right deviation in their everyday work.[111]

Khrushchev then went on to equate the struggle against the right deviation with the proper conduct of party work in every sphere. He criticised party workers for taking too little interest in economic affairs. Local secretaries, he charged, were conducting meetings of party activists to discuss theoretical issues rather than concrete economic tasks. Party cells in economic enterprises which failed to press actively for higher quality and reduced costs were also failing to translate their opposition to the right into practical action. Khrushchev criticised raikoms for making managers and enterprise party cells into whipping boys rather than taking responsibility for poor economic performance. The notion of party officials' responsibility for economic affairs runs through the entire speech.[112] It remained one of Khrushchev's pet themes for the next thirty-five years.

Khrushchev adopted a similar tone in his address at the Second All-Ukrainian Party Conference in Khar'kov that same month. After a savage attack on rightists and 'conciliators' he turned to practical matters:

> Talking about the need to struggle with the rightists, we sometimes overlook vital problems, the solution of which would help the party to handle its basic difficulties and overcome the hesitations and vacillations which some unsteady party members display. I believe that we should work for a more precise organisation of work, check on whether everyone does his work, ensure the correct conduct of affairs and thus help the party to master all difficulties and to struggle with the right deviations which arise from them.[113]

As his thirty-fifth birthday approached, Khrushchev's thoughts again turned to the need to complete his education. The age limit for Ukrainian higher educational institutions was thirty,[114] so further study there would be impossible. Knowing that it would be too late if he waited much longer, Khrushchev approached Demchenko and the new Ukrainian First Secretary, Stanislav Kosior, with a request that he be allowed to go to Moscow to study in the Industrial Academy established by the Supreme Council of the National Economy. The academy was founded to train future heads of industrial trusts, large enterprises and other economic institutions. Many of its students were men and women already well advanced in their party or managerial careers; the age limit of the academy, if there was one, was therefore somewhat higher than in most other institutions. In March of 1929, he received permission to go to Moscow to the academy; he was released from his duties in Kiev in August.[115]

2 The City Father
Moscow, 1929–37

> *The arbitrary behaviour of one person encouraged and permitted the arbitrariness of others. Mass arrests and the deportation of many thousands of people, execution without trials or normal investigations gave rise to insecurity, fear and bitterness.*
>
> N. S. Khrushchev, The Secret Speech, 1956[1]

Khrushchev travelled to Moscow alone in September 1929; Nina Petrovna remained in Stalino until the following summer, looking after their newborn daughter Rada, and her stepchildren, Leonid and Iuliia.[2] Khrushchev's first task in Moscow was to win admission to the Industrial Academy, which was reluctant to take him on account of his poor educational background. On his first approaches he was told that he was not ready for the course there and would be better off to enrol in the Central Committee's course in Marxism-Leninism. Khrushchev, however, was determined to enter the academy and turned for help to Kaganovich, then a Secretary of the Central Committee. With Kaganovich's assistance, he won admission to the academy and took up residence in a nearby dormitory.[3]

The Industrial Academy's brief was to provide its students with a grounding in general economic management, as well as a technical specialisation; in Khrushchev's case, it did neither. He left the academy sixteen months later without having completed his course, but his work there did more to advance his career than any diploma could have. At the time of Khrushchev's arrival, the Industrial Academy was in a political ferment. The Moscow party organisation had been a bastion of support for the right opposition until a purge in 1928 had replaced the Moscow party leadership with reliable Stalinists. By late 1929, however, the right had again grown active in the capital, reacting to Stalin's First Five-Year Plan and the appalling human and economic costs of the forced collectivisation of agriculture.

The city to which Khrushchev moved was in the midst of an economic crisis brought on by Stalin's First Five-Year Plan. Production increased rapidly, but growth rates were well short of the ambitious tempos set by the plan and were declining; agriculture was in a disastrous state as a result of the drive to force the peasants onto collective farms. For workers in the capital this meant a halving of real wages between 1928 and 1932, a series of draconian new labour laws, and acute shortages of food and housing. Food shortages in turn triggered strikes and aggravated the housing shortage, as peasants fleeing starvation in the countryside poured into the cities, despite some attempts to seal off urban areas.[4]

The Industrial Academy was among the institutions in which opponents of Stalin's new course were active. The academy's political significance, moreover, was far greater than that of most educational institutions: its mission was to prepare leading officials to manage the most important trusts and enterprises in the country, and its student body consisted largely of former city and district party secretaries, men and women of considerable political experience. The health of its party cell was therefore a matter of concern to the party leadership, which followed developments within the academy closely.[5] The rightists and their supporters were disciplined by the leaders of both the cell and the local raikom in October, but this was not enough.[6] On 3 November the Moscow party newspaper attacked the rightist group within the cell, charging that its links reached far beyond the academy's walls.[7] A cell meeting addressed the issue on the following day; the accused implicated other students, and a second closed meeting had to be convened. The cell's leaders were charged with taking too soft a line in their dealings with the right, and a new cell bureau was elected to defuse the crisis.[8] Khrushchev was not elected to the new bureau, but he was among the most outspoken Stalinists at the meeting, demanding the rightists' expulsion from the academy.[9]

Khrushchev's own account of the struggle within the cell suggests that the conflict had a generational dimension: the rightist 'Old Guard', as Khrushchev called them, were older men, former factory directors and trade union leaders who had pre-revolutionary party experience. (Roughly one-third of the academy's students had entered the party before the revolution.[10]) The defenders of the General Line, by contrast, had joined the party after the revolution and came primarily from the industrial party organisations of the south, such as the Donbass and Dnepropetrovsk, which were Stalinist strongholds. Khrushchev claimed that his election to the bureau was successfully blocked by the rightists several times.[11] Another reason for the deviance of the academy cell was that many of the students had left or been removed from other posts during purges of various opposition tendencies and had sought refuge in the academy. Khrushchev himself noted indignantly that 'the enemies of the Central Committee were just about the only people in the country who were able to take advantage of our institutions of higher learning'.[12]

Soon after the November crisis the academy cell, in an effort to demonstrate its support for the General Line, sent a letter to Stalin requesting that the academy be renamed in his honour.[13] In April 1930 a student delegation was sent to the Kremlin to ask him to address the academy's commencement ceremonies. Though still in his first year at the academy, Khrushchev was included in the delegation and was thus once more able to see the General Secretary in person; Stalin again impressed him greatly.[14]

In the spring of 1930, Moscow's Stalinist party chief, K. Ia. Bauman was scapegoated for the excesses of the previous year. Stalin was retreating somewhat from the unbridled radicalism of 1929, and Bauman was sacked for going too far in the collectivisation drive in Moscow province; he was replaced by Kaganovich. Stalin's retreat in general and Bauman's fall in particular encouraged the right to mobilise once again, and on 21 May the Industrial Academy cell elected a number of known rightists as delegates to the upcoming district party conference. Many speakers at the meeting openly attacked the party's General Line.[15] Khrushchev, by then a prominent Stalinist in the academy cell, had been sent on a trip to the countryside and was thus conveniently out of the rightists' way.[16]

Although the cell's errors were acknowledged at another meeting the following day, proposals to withdraw the delegates were rejected.[17]

On 26 May *Pravda* attacked the cell's leadership for its close ties to the rightist former bureau members who had been removed the previous autumn and for its failure to mobilise the cell against the right. The local raikom secretary, A. P. Shirin, ordered the cell to convene another meeting on 26 May.[18] With Khrushchev in the chair, this meeting voted to withdraw the conference delegates and elect a new bureau; the new cell secretary was Nikita Khrushchev.[19] The new bureau was instructed to investigate those members who had exhibited rightist tendencies in the past and to expose those who had concealed their rightist leanings.[20] Similar purges were carried out in the Timiriazev Agricultural Academy and the Trade Academy in the days that followed.[21]

Khrushchev served as cell secretary of the Stalin Industrial Academy until the end of 1930. During much of this time he was preoccupied with purging the cell and turning it into a bulwark of the General Line. Cell members were reprimanded, demoted or expelled, often on flimsy evidence. Members with past connections to known rightists found themselves under fire; others were accused of maintaining relations with anti-soviet relatives. Some members acknowledged their errors – though their self-criticism was frequently judged insufficient – while others tried to defend themselves.[22] Most of those purged were members who had entered the Bolsheviks' ranks before the Revolution.[23] Khrushchev attracted considerable attention with his campaign against the right; the cell's resolutions on this issue were often published in the press as examples for other organisations to follow.

On at least one occasion, however, Khrushchev overreached himself. On 20 November, *Pravda* carried a statement by the former rightist leader Nikolai Bukharin submitting to the will of the party and accepting the decisions of the party's Sixteenth Congress. The cell adopted a resolution criticising Bukharin's statement, which it called 'a new attempt to manoeuvre, to avoid accountability . . . and await a more convenient moment for a new attack on the party'.[24] This was similar to Khrushchev's criticism of Golubenko's submission in 1926. The Central Committee disagreed: on 22 November it pronounced Bukharin's statement satisfactory.[25] The cell bureau met that same day and acknowledged that the cell had committed 'a political mistake of a leftist character'; a full cell meeting was convened to correct the resolution.[26]

Ironically, the misstep on the Bukharin issue came just days after Khrushchev had addressed a cell meeting with a glowing report on the work of the bureau. The praise heaped on the cell's leaders in the discussion of the report was so unrestrained that one member protested: 'Some comrades while speaking have sung eulogistic dithyrambs about the work of the bureau. Is this necessary? I think not.'[27] Necessary or not, such praise was soon to become a regular feature of Khrushchev's career and would land him in political trouble more than once.

Ensuring the political orthodoxy of the cell was by no means the extent of Khrushchev's political responsibilities. The cell secretary of the academy played an important role in its governance. Thus Khrushchev and his bureau gave the administration of the academy instructions for dealing with scheduling and with shortages of textbooks and teachers; the director of the academy reported to the cell on progress in addressing these problems.[28]

Khrushchev's tenure as cell secretary turned out to be as brief as it was busy. In January 1931, mid-way through his second academic year, the Moscow Committee of the party 'recommended' Khrushchev to the Bauman raikom as its new secretary.[29] He was duly elected by the Bauman organisation and shortly thereafter became a member of both the Moscow Committee of the party (MK) and the Moscow City Soviet.[30]

Khrushchev attributed his remarkable rise in the Moscow party machine to his relationship with Stalin's wife, Nadezhda Alliluyeva, a fellow student and party group organiser in the academy. Khrushchev regarded their acquaintance as his 'lucky lottery ticket'. Alliluyeva had frequent dealings with him on party business and, he later claimed, spoke favourably of him to her husband.[31] Western and Soviet scholars have cast doubt on this, pointing to persistent rumours that Alliluyeva was known to sympathise with the right, in which case she would hardly have spoken well of the Stalinist Khrushchev.[32] Nothing can be said about Alliluyeva's political views with confidence, however; it is entirely possible that she mentioned the cell secretary from the Donbass to her husband, and that her favourable impression of him assisted his rise. Nevertheless, Khrushchev was still too lowly a figure to enjoy Stalin's patronage directly; Khrushchev's patron was Kaganovich, and the significance he later attached to his friendship with Stalin's wife probably reflected a desire to avoid acknowledging his debt to a man who later became a bitter enemy.

Some scholars have argued that Kaganovich helped Khrushchev win admission to the academy with a view to having Khrushchev take control of the cell and purge it.[33] Kaganovich may have been aware of the state of affairs in the academy cell in September 1929 and of the advantages of adding a reliable Stalinist like Khrushchev to it, but it is unlikely that his political thinking went further than that. Even this cannot be taken for granted, since Kaganovich was not yet running the Moscow party at the time. If politics had been uppermost in Kaganovich's mind in September 1929, he would surely have arranged Khrushchev's election to the bureau at the first available opportunity – the November 1929 crisis. Instead Khrushchev was elected only after Kaganovich's own election to head MK. This suggests that when the May 1930 crisis in the cell erupted, Kaganovich simply found it convenient to advance 'his' man in the academy. When Khrushchev performed as required, he was rewarded with the promotion to Bauman raikom.

The position of a raikom secretary in Moscow was almost impossibly difficult at this time. The First Five-Year Plan had established incredible targets for industrial development without providing the investment needed to meet these targets. At district level, this meant that the raikom secretary was responsible for the performance of enterprises which could not possibly meet their obligations under the plan. Raikom officials had little help from above in dealing with local problems, but higher authorities were quick to shift the blame for failures down to the districts

and enterprises. The raikom secretary was also responsible
for party affairs. He was expected to know every party cell
in his district (there were several hundred) and all the
heads of important institutions located in his jurisdiction.[34]
There was also a lack of clarity about officials' responsibilities and powers. As one western historian has written,

> Arbitrariness combined with confusion describes the
> atmosphere of party life in 1931 and 1932. . . . There was
> a sense of urgency about the Plan, and about solving
> immediate local problems connected with it, but little in
> the way of solid guidance for local officials. . . . It was
> unclear who was responsible for what, difficult problems
> could be handed on.[35]

For a man of Khrushchev's temperament, the sheer enormity of the task may have been one of the attractions of the
job: the party was re-creating economy and society virtually
overnight, and he was playing a leading role in the transformation. This period and its impact on those who lived
through it cannot be understood unless its heroism, as well
as its brutality, is kept in mind. The absence of clear lines
of authority would have suited a man with Khrushchev's
activist style of management; the 'shapelessness' of this
bureaucratic environment made it easier for Khrushchev to
interfere in anything and everything within his urban fiefdom.[36]

Khrushchev remained in Bauman district only six
months, hardly long enough to make much of a mark. He
carried on with his noisy campaign against the right: the
raikom adopted resolutions condemning 'right-opportunist
theory and practice' in the people's commissariats of
transportation and foreign trade, an all-union oil trust and
other institutions located in Bauman district. Even the party
cell of the State Planning Commission of the Russian
Federation was criticised for 'political shortsightedness and
suppression of self-criticism'. A publishing house was
rebuked for failing to 'react to the publication of ideologically harmful books'.[37] Khrushchev achieved unspectacular

results in industry; plan fulfilment was mediocre. Someone was pleased, however, for Khrushchev soon received
another promotion.

While in Bauman Khrushchev first became acquainted
with Demian Korotchenko, then serving as chairman of the
Bauman District Soviet, having been appointed at the same
time as Khrushchev.[38] Korotchenko worked under Khrushchev in a variety of positions in Moscow and Ukraine over
the next eighteen years. He became Chairman of the
Council of People's Commissars (premier) of Ukraine in the
1940s and entered the top leadership in Moscow as a
Khrushchev client in 1957.

While Khrushchev was still settling into his new situation
in Bauman district, a fabricated scandal across town was
setting the stage for his next promotion. In July 1931 the
secretary of the Red Presnia District, I. I. Kozlov, was under
attack over the state of affairs in 'Kommunar', a large
district co-operative concerned with food supplies. Red
Presnia was the most prestigious district in the capital;
its organisation provided more cadres for the secretariats
of the Moscow city and provincial party committees than
any other, and its raikom secretary enjoyed a certain
precedence over his colleagues in other districts.[39] The
scandal at Kommunar therefore received considerable press
attention.

Pravda criticised Kommunar's management for poor
accounting, long queues, large overhead expenditures and
a lack of self-criticism in the co-operative's party cell; the
co-operative was also running at a loss. In fact, Kommunar's
problems were a direct result of the capital's food
shortages, but *Pravda* attributed them to 'right-opportunist
practice'.[40] Three days later *Pravda* attacked the raikom
leadership for failing to prevent these practices, charging
that it had consistently resisted pressure to take action.[41] On
24 July the raikom bureau granted Kozlov's 'request' to
release him from his duties as secretary.[42] He had been
scapegoated for the food shortages caused by government
policies. Even *Pravda* admitted that the queues at Kommunar had grown longer after the change of management.[43]

Shortly before Kozlov's removal Khrushchev was summoned to a meeting of the bureau of the Moscow City

Committee (MGK) of the party, chaired by Kaganovich. Khrushchev was asked to recount briefly his biography. For some reason he spoke haltingly, mispronouncing many of his words, and he did not make much of an impression on some bureau members. E. G. Goreva, a department head within the committee secretariat, later recalled that Khrushchev came across to his listeners as 'a man with a low level of basic literacy'. In a whisper Goreva asked a colleague how such a man could be put in charge of Moscow's leading raikom. Kaganovich, however, had already made up his mind on the appointment; after the meeting he rebuked Goreva for her question, which he had overheard, and threatened to fire her for such behaviour in future.[44] MGK recommended Khrushchev for the post in Red Presnia and he was duly 'elected' by the district organisation on 24 July.[45]

Khrushchev remained in Red Presnia only until January 1932. His time there was taken up principally by economic issues. Virtually all of the raikom bureau meetings were concerned with the achievement of plan targets, implementation of government decrees and the administration of enterprises in the district.[46] The bureau meeting of 2 October was typical. Eight of the sixteen items on the agenda for the meeting concerned the management of industry and construction, including such issues as the provision of raw materials to enterprises, plan targets for the fourth quarter of the year and the organisation of workers' committees in several large plants. Four agenda points addressed aspects of the food supply situation, which did not improve despite the changes of leadership in Kommunar and the raikom. The rest of the agenda included the construction of workers' dormitories, a credit reform introduced by the government, and a pair of items concerned with the guidance of party cells in the district.[47]

Nevertheless, Khrushchev and his raikom colleagues found time to produce a number of resolutions and statements attacking Trotskyites, rightists and other opponents of the party's general line.[48] Among those caught up in this campaign was a certain historian named Slutskii. In 1931 Stalin wrote to the editors of the party's historical journal, *Proletarskaia revoliutsiia*, attacking Slutskii for having suggested that Lenin did not understand the dangers of German Social Democrats' middle-of-the-road position before 1914; Stalin denounced Slutskii as a Trotskyite.[49] The unfortunate historian lived in Red Presnia, so the raikom was obliged to react. A raikom resolution attacked Slutskii for the 'deliberate use of party literature to propagandise Trotskyism, the spearhead of the counter-revolutionary bourgeoisie'.[50] The raikom was later praised for expelling 'the Trotskyite Slutskii'.[51]

Khrushchev's most significant venture in Red Presnia was the organisation of the Stalin *estafette* in the district. The estafette involved the mobilisation of the entire district for single days or ten-day periods to achieve specific tasks. At the end of October 1931 a ten-day campaign to accelerate the preparation of candidates for full party membership and to speed up fulfilment of fourth-quarter industrial plans was declared. Participation in these campaigns was mandatory, and they were accompanied by increased pressure to subscribe to 'voluntary' state loans, the organisation of 'shock brigades' whose work was based on the 'progressive and premium piecework system' or *progressivka*, and increases in workers' production norms. Workers' collectives demonstrated their enthusiasm by presenting 'counterplans' which were more demanding than the official plans which they had received. According to Pistrak, the estafette was first adopted in Red Presnia and was then emulated elsewhere.[52] *Pravda* reported that it was such a success that 'workers in leading factories appealed to all the proletarians of Moscow to extend the Stalin estafette until 1 January 1932, transforming it into a forty-day Bolshevik campaign for the early fulfilment of the industrial-financial plan'.[53]

Whether or not the estafette was a 'Khrushchev innovation', as Pistrak asserts, there is no doubt that its adoption in Red Presnia first showed Khrushchev to be a true Stalinist. He was not to be outdone in the vigour with which he implemented Stalinist labour policies. During his six months in Red Presnia 12 000 workers were organised into 2250 new shock brigades working on the progressivka. Under the progressivka workers' pay per unit of output was held very low until it reached a certain specified level, beyond which they were paid at a bonus rate; needless to say, the point at which the bonus rate began to apply to additional output was steadily increased. In other words, the progressivka worked like a constantly accelerating treadmill.

All this took place against the backdrop of a general tightening of labour policy nationwide, which would be codified in the infamous labour laws of 1933: in order to reduce labour turnover, workers were deprived of the right to choose or leave their place of work; they were made accountable for the condition of their plant and equipment, including problems which resulted from faulty manufacture or installation; and wages were held down as production norms increased. In 1933 *Pravda* went so far as to attack managers and trade unionists who thought that 'a worker's wife giving birth' or 'moving to new living quarters' constituted a reason for a worker to be absent from his job for a day.[54]

At the time of the Thirteenth District Party Conference in January 1932 Khrushchev had been on the job for less than six months, but the conference was full of praise for 'the Bolshevik restructuring of the raikom under the leadership of Comrade Khrushchev'. Said one speaker, 'The Moscow Committee has corrected us in a paternal manner, and, with the help of new leadership in the person of Comrade Khrushchev, for which our Red Presnia District ought to thank MK, we have corrected our mistakes in a Bolshevik way and come to the Thirteenth Party Conference with colossal victories.'[55] The enthusiasm for Khrushchev was not limited to the district conference; *Rabochaia Moskva* also praised him.[56] By the end of the month Khrushchev had been promoted out of the district, this time to the post of Second Secretary of MGK, of which Kaganovich was the head.[57] It is a measure of the speed of his rise that of the fourteen members of the MGK bureau, only Khrushchev and I. P. Gaidul', the secretary of the Proletarskii raikom, had joined the party after the Revolution.[58]

Khrushchev knew to whom he owed his rapid advancement. His speech at the Moscow Party Conference just days before his promotion was full of praise for his patron

Kaganovich. Khrushchev attributed the transformation of Moscow industry 'from chintz to metal' to Kaganovich's appointment as Moscow party secretary; it was then that 'after those excesses, deviations and distortions [of the previous leaderships] . . . the true line was adopted'. He praised Kaganovich's involvement in 'all questions, right down to petty details'. This was a typically Khrushchevian compliment: Khrushchev never believed much in delegating authority and thought that a good leader understood and decided even the smallest of matters under his authority. Khrushchev's praise for Kaganovich paled by comparison with his adulation of Stalin, whom he repeatedly called the *vozhd'*, or leader, of the party and the working class. Use of the term *vozhd'*, as opposed to other Russian words for leader, implied that Stalin possessed absolute, unquestioned authority.[59]

It was at this conference that Khrushchev first proposed a scheme to improve housing construction which he was to push for several years. Arguing that construction was being hindered by the proliferation of small trusts, housing unions and administrations in the capital, he called for their replacement by a handful of large housing trusts. The presence of fewer and larger organisations, he maintained, would make party guidance of housing construction easier.[60] Khrushchev also called for the construction of small power-stations in the coal basin outside Moscow. This would make it possible to generate electricity on site and transmit it to Moscow, thereby reducing both rail shipments to, and air pollution in, the capital. The overall approach to economic matters expressed in the speech is close to that which Khrushchev espoused throughout his career. He called for ever more intensive party guidance of industry and construction; the party, he argued, ought to give detailed instructions to every worker, shop foreman and supervisor.[61]

Kaganovich at this time held three posts: he was a Central Committee secretary, second only to Stalin himself, and first secretary of both the Moscow provincial and city party committees. He concentrated on his work in the Central Committee Secretariat, so the running of MK and MGK was largely delegated to his deputies. His voice was decisive in matters of real importance, but the day-to-day management of the Moscow party organisation was in the hands of his second secretaries, K. V. Ryndin at MK and Khrushchev at MGK.

Khrushchev's rapid rise continued. In January 1934, Kaganovich, who was devoting increasing time to the country's vexing transport problems, handed over the job of First Secretary of MGK to Khrushchev. At the Seventeenth Congress of the party later that month, Khrushchev was elected to the Central Committee and for the first time addressed an all-union party congress.[62] It was an appropriate moment for the national début of this loyal Stalinist: the Seventeenth Congress was dubbed the 'Congress of the Victors', in recognition of the Stalinists' triumph over their opponents within the party and without. In early 1935, Kaganovich took over the USSR People's Commissariat for Transportation, handing over the leadership of MK to Khrushchev.

The former peasant from Kalinovka, now forty years of age, found himself in charge not only of the capital city, but of the surrounding Moscow Province as well. Taken together, they were roughly equal in size and population to a small European country.[63] Aware of the uncertainties of Soviet high politics, Khrushchev even then kept his old metal-working tools at hand – just in case.[64] Kaganovich continued to take a keen interest in his protégé, offering him frequent criticism and advice.[65] Khrushchev, for his part, continued to praise Kaganovich for his help and guidance in the running of Moscow.[66]

Khrushchev's meteoric rise catapulted him and his family into the world of the Soviet power élite. The family occupied a large flat in the building on Kamennyi Most which housed top party and government leaders – a sharp contrast with Khrushchev's industrial academy days, when the five of them (plus a nanny) had occupied two rooms at opposite ends of a long corridor in a dilapidated dormitory. The additional living space made it possible for Nikita Sergeevich to bring his parents to live with him in Moscow. The Khrushchevs' neighbours now included ministers, Politburo members and Central Committee officials, but their lifestyle remained relatively simple, and the flat was modestly furnished. Nina Petrovna, who worked as a party organiser until 1935, used her own surname and concealed the fact that her husband was the capital's party chief. On one occasion, her astonished boss rang the Secretary of MK only to find his subordinate, Nina Kukharchuk, answering the phone. After the birth of their son Sergei in 1935, Nina Petrovna left her job, although she continued to take on lecturing assignments from the local raikom. A second daughter, Elena, was born in 1937.[67]

Work in the Moscow party organisation presented certain unique opportunities and dangers. As a leading figure in the party organisation of the capital, Khrushchev enjoyed a prestige and a degree of access to the country's highest leaders which his counterparts in the provinces could only envy; by the same token, however, he was subjected to closer scrutiny than they. Khrushchev himself drew attention to this in a speech in early 1934: 'Working in Moscow, we are under the daily guidance of our Central Committee, directly under the guidance of Comrade Stalin. . . . On all those questions on which the city party committee is now working, we have the directives of the Central Committee, we have the direct personal instructions of our beloved vozhd', Comrade Stalin.'[68] The result of this tutelage was a heightened vulnerability to criticism from above and a lack of independence. Many issues which in other places could be resolved more or less independently by local party leaders had to be negotiated with central institutions in Moscow.[69]

Stalin, moreover, was particularly interested in the development of Moscow at this time. The June 1931 plenary meeting of the Central Committee had adopted a resolution calling for the capital to be turned into a model socialist city. This led to a massive programme to rebuild the city, which culminated in the adoption of the General Plan for the Reconstruction of Moscow (the 'Stalin Plan') in 1935. The task was enormous. The Moscow of the 1920s had little in common with a developed twentieth-century capital city; housing, sewage, transport and other facets of its infrastructure were primitive and inadequate. Collectivisation and industrialisation only added to the strain: the population of the capital increased by 1.3 million between January 1929 and January 1934.

Khrushchev's principal concerns in his first years at MGK were thus related to the rebuilding of the city. A number of enormous construction projects were set in motion: the Moscow–Volga Canal, the Kuibyshev Electrical Plant, a number of large industrial enterprises and the Moscow Metropolitan. These grandiose projects could not conceal the continuing hardships of the bulk of the population, however. The famine brought on by collectivisation meant that workers in Moscow were going hungry, and it fell to Khrushchev to oversee the city's rationing programme and to implement various schemes for producing food in the city itself: enterprises were instructed to raise rabbits to supply their kitchens, and there was a plan to raise mushrooms in cellars and ditches around Moscow.[70] The continuing growth of the city's population further aggravated the housing situation, as did the pulling down of old apartment buildings in order to clear space for the construction of factories. While targets for industrial growth were extremely ambitious, the rate of housing construction was slower than during NEP.[71] More housing was demolished than built in Moscow during the First Five-Year Plan.[72]

Nor was it only housing which was pulled down: Moscow lost much of its best pre-revolutionary architecture during these years. A host of old boulevards were razed, and numerous churches, including the famous Cathedral of Christ the Saviour, were destroyed. Khrushchev, who oversaw the implementation of many of these decisions, was unapologetic, arguing that, in rebuilding Moscow, 'we should not be afraid to knock down a tree, a little church or some cathedral or other'.[73] To a Moscow party conference he said,

Some Bolsheviks, it is true, shed tears at the Central Committee plenum: 'What you are pulling down!' I would say that in shedding tears these Bolsheviks, though they may be old, resemble the heroes of *The Cherry Orchard*. . . . One cannot sacrifice the interests of the whole city to please people living on this rubbish.[74]

The final decision in such matters was not, of course, Khrushchev's. When on one occasion he mentioned to Stalin that Muscovites were protesting the demolition of some old buildings, the vozhd' replied, 'Then blow them up at night.'[75] This was the same Stalin who, according to Khrushchev, 'looks after Moscow literally as after a beloved baby'.[76]

Although he did not take the key decisions himself, Khrushchev managed every aspect of the reconstruction in as much detail as time would permit. At various times he was occupied with such matters as the poor operation of public baths and laundries (the laundries took too long, he said, and underwear often came back from the wash having changed colour), the unsatisfactory operation of the city's trams and the shortage of public toilets, a problem brought to his attention by Stalin himself.[77] He criticised builders who had taken 'the path of oversimplification, the construction of "boxes", and had succeeded in ruining certain buildings and neighbourhoods'.[78] He also attacked them for designing flats with little attention to small details which would render them much more comfortable for their inhabitants.[79]

In all of these endeavours Khrushchev adopted and encouraged subordinates to adopt a very tough style of management, to the point of advocating the prosecution of enterprises which failed to fulfil plan obligations. He urged managers and directors to master even the pettiest details connected with the operations of their enterprises and demanded that they take a hard line in dealing with workers. At his most extreme he denounced those who advocated easing workers' output norms as reflecting 'petty bourgeois' tendencies and 'kulak counter-revolutionary elements'. In other words, economic views or demands that contradicted the plan were not merely erroneous or unacceptable, they were counter-revolutionary. Khrushchev also called for wider employment of the progressivka and shock work, while at the same time denying that productivity increases required greater capital investment; all that was needed, he said, was better management.[80]

By far the most grandiose project associated with the reconstruction of Moscow was the building of the first and second lines of the Moscow Metro. The first experimental strip was set aside in December 1931, but construction did not get under way in earnest until early 1934, when the order was given to bring the first line of the Metro into operation by Revolution Day (7 November).[81] The need for an underground railway was questionable, and much could have been achieved at lower cost by improving surface transport.[82] Steps were taken in this direction; Khrushchev was behind the creation of the first electric trolleybus lines in the USSR.[83] The trolleybuses were quieter than regular buses and did not generate air pollution. The motivation for building a subway system in fact had more to do with considerations of national prestige than with Moscow's transport needs. Such considerations also dictated the speed with which it was built: the construction of 'the best metro in the world' was to demonstrate what the Soviet system could do.

Khrushchev, who was brought in on the project on account of his mining experience, admitted, 'When we started building the Moscow Metro, we had only the vaguest idea of what the job would entail.'[84] This lack of preparation, combined with the pressure for speed, led the builders to take extraordinary risks, as one chief engineer acknowledged.[85] By his own account, Khrushchev spent 80 per cent of his time on the Metro, even walking back and forth to work through the tunnels.[86] He and Kaganovich, who was in overall charge of the project, participated in the resolution of all major technical decisions, including the choice of a method of tunnelling, the selection of a wagon design and the use of escalators rather than lifts.[87] Drawing on his mining experience, Khrushchev suggested the use of horizontal tunnels and compressed air for tunnelling, which greatly improved working conditions.[88]

In his determination to meet the 7 November 1934 deadline, Khrushchev pushed his subordinates relentlessly. In late October he ordered that a freezing station, which refrigerated water-soaked silt in order to prevent landslides, be moved in order to make way for the upcoming Revolution Day parade; the machine had taken four months to assemble and had to be moved and reassembled in a few days, but Khrushchev disregarded engineers' warnings that when the refrigeration was turned off, the weight of water might cause the shaft to collapse while people were working in it.[89] When the chief of Metro construction, P. P. Rotert, ordered a halt to tunnelling under some unstable houses until their foundations could be strengthened, Khrushchev told the workers to carry on anyway.[90] Together with Kaganovich he exerted a constant pressure to increase the speed at which tunnelling equipment was employed, to a rate four times that recommended by experts.[91]

Shifts were lengthened and workers were made to serve as many as five consecutive shifts on duty. Workers in the subterranean caissons were given shifts of ten or eleven hours, despite the fact that more than four hours was considered dangerous to human life.[92] Such a punishing work regime was bound to lead to accidents, particularly given the risks being taken. Even accounts written at the time to glorify the building of the Metro could not ignore them; stories of underground catastrophes were recounted in such a way as to strengthen the sense of heroism surrounding the whole endeavour. Underground fires and floods were not uncommon, nor were instances of caisson disease, brought on by rapidly decreasing pressure.[93]

Despite these dangers, workers were poorly paid, since wage rates were often calculated on the assumption of shock work.[94] In some respects, the workers' situation was not much better than slave labour. Chief Engineer Lomov said that in his sector military men were brought in to establish discipline among the 'ill-assorted mob' that worked there.[95] One I. N. Kuznetsov was appointed Assistant Chief of Construction: his previous career included 'the battlefront, the Cheka [the secret police] and nothing else'.[96] A foreign communist who worked on the project estimated that 90 per cent of Metro workers were in some sort of trouble or disgrace.[97]

In the end, the Revolution Day deadline was not met; the first line of the Metro began operations only in May 1935. Even that was a remarkable feat, however, and Khrushchev was duly rewarded with his first Order of Lenin. He was, moreover, allowed a share of the glory which was heaped on Kaganovich in books and press articles published to celebrate the event. It was unusual for anyone other than

Stalin to enjoy the sort of adulation that Kaganovich received in connection with the metro, which was even named for him. The praise given to Khrushchev was more remarkable still.

> The closest assistant to Comrade Kaganovich on the metro is Comrade N. S. Khrushchev. All of the engineers, brigadiers and shock-workers on the project know Nikita Sergeevich. They know him because he is on the construction site every day, because he daily gives directives, checks the work, criticises, encourages and gives advice to this or that shaft foreman, this or that party organiser, concerning all concrete and urgent problems. The office of Comrade Khrushchev has turned into the office of one of the leaders of metro construction, where party organisers, shaft overseers, engineers and brigadiers work out detailed plans for fulfilling the bold, daring tasks given by their experienced leader, L. M. Kaganovich.[98]

The metro was indeed spectacular. The stations of the first and second lines contained more marble than all of Russia's tsarist palaces combined. Granite, bronze, porphyry and other expensive materials were used in great quantities in the stations, which were decorated with sculpture, stained glass, mosaics and murals. And the trains were fast and frequent.[99] The economic cost – quite apart from the human costs discussed above – was staggering: some 350 million roubles were spent on Metro construction in 1934 alone, as against the 300 million roubles per year spent on consumer goods production for the entire country during the First Five-Year Plan.[100]

The demands of administering the capital during those turbulent years left Khrushchev little time for agriculture, and Moscow province was not a particularly important farming region. The oft-repeated goal of making Moscow a net producer rather than consumer of food was utterly unrealistic. Nevertheless, a certain amount of time was devoted to these issues. Khrushchev's first concern was the quality of administrators and specialists attached to the new collective farms. In order to achieve the speediest possible results, he sent 500 party workers and forty-five teams of agricultural specialists into the province's rural districts in 1936; as a longer-term solution Khrushchev worked hard to promote the mass education of the collective farmers themselves. Nearly all the collective farm (*kolkhoz*) chairmen and rural party organisers in the province were brought to Moscow for short courses in the Timiriazev Agricultural Academy; some 50 000 kolkhoz activists also took courses to prepare them for their work. In 1936 province-wide correspondence courses were established for farm chairmen and brigade leaders; the quality of instruction left much to be desired, owing to a lack of qualified teachers, but some basic training was provided.[101]

The other issue which attracted Khrushchev's attention was the size of the new kolkhozes. Many of them were too small to make the introduction of new technology economically sensible. Khrushchev's response to this problem was simply to order, based on his own rough calculations, that the 3800 small farms in the province be amalgamated into 1812 larger farms. The opinions of farm workers and agricultural specialists were ignored. Although the results of this reorganisation were less than impressive, kolkhoz amalgamation was an idea to which Khrushchev would return in later years.[102]

Khrushchev's position as Moscow party chief made him especially vulnerable to criticism. The central authorities had no difficulty in finding out what was happening in the capital, whereas they were often extremely ill-informed about affairs in other provinces.[103] Moreover, the Moscow party chief's high profile made him more likely than his colleagues to be criticised or disciplined as an example to others, as the case of Bauman in 1930 had demonstrated. Khrushchev twice came under fire in connection with his handling of party affairs in Moscow. During 1933-7 the leadership launched a series of operations intended to purge the party of undesirable elements. Several hundred thousand communists were expelled from the party, and tens of thousands were arrested in conjunction with their expulsions. In December 1935 the Moscow organisation was criticised at length for the low rate of expulsion achieved that year.[104] Khrushchev and his organisation took the criticism to heart and increased the number of expulsions sharply in the months that followed,[105] only to be attacked in March 1937 for having expelled too many members. The Muscovites were accused of expelling many 'honest communists' in an effort to raise expulsion rates.[106] Khrushchev defended himself and his organisation at length, but the Moscow party again changed tack; expulsion rates dropped and Khrushchev survived.[107]

Khrushchev was also harshly criticised at the February–March 1937 Central Committee meeting for fostering a local cult of personality. Iakov Iakovlev, a leading member of the party's Central Control Commission, attacked

> that style of party work which has been condemned by the party, where thoroughly assiduous people, no matter what they are talking about . . . repeat after every fact a formula, according to which everything good or rational which happens in Moscow happens only 'on the initiative or according to the instructions of Nikita Sergeevich'.[108]

There was in fact considerable truth to Iakovlev's claim, though Khrushchev was far from alone among provincial bosses in this respect. Khrushchev tried to deflect Iakovlev's criticism by pretending that the issue was not the praise which subordinates heaped upon him but the practice of calling him by first name and patronymic (traditionally the formal style of address in Russian) rather than simply 'Comrade Khrushchev'. There was a slip of the tongue, which Khrushchev used to get a few laughs:

> [Iakovlev] was perfectly right when he spoke of the inappropriate use of first name and patronymic when addressing or referring to party leaders. Such a form of address is uncalled for, no one needs it. . . . It is necessary to struggle with this, and Iakov Arkad'evich's criticism is correct. Excuse me, Comrade Iakovlev, I called you Iakov Arkad'evich. I did it unintentionally. Evidently this is the force of inertia. (Voice: There is no sin in using name and patronymic.) It is no sin, Valerii Ivanovich (laughter). (Voice: Caught him!)[109]

Others interrupted from the floor in an effort to draw
Khrushchev back to the central issue, which was his
mini-cult. He answered with jokes and thus avoided real
discussion of the problem. Khrushchev implicitly acknowledged the justice of Iakovlev's remarks at the Moscow party
conference in May, however, when he attacked the atmosphere of self-congratulation in the Moscow organisation,
saying that 'any excessive praise or noisy ovations must be
cauterised with a hot iron' and admitting his own guilt in
allowing such an atmosphere to develop around him.[110]

By the time Khrushchev entered the Central Committee
in 1934, the victory of the Stalinists over all other factions
in the party was – and had long been – complete. The
Stalinists themselves, however, were divided on many issues
into relatively more moderate and radical tendencies.[111]
Both official policy and the tenor of Stalin's own statements fluctuated between the two poles, leaving many to
wonder which way Stalin himself was really inclined. Stalin
had not yet reached the height of his power, and some
scholars believe that he was sometimes pressured by
moderate colleagues into accepting compromises.[112] Others
see his shifts as purely tactical moves, and still other
observers believe that he had not made up his mind about
many issues and was keeping his options open.[113]

Economic policy was a major point of contention. Stalin's
lieutenants had all supported collectivisation and the First
Five-Year Plan, but they were unable to agree on growth
tempos for the Second Five-Year Plan. The radicals wished
to maintain the rapid tempos of the first plan, but the
moderates prevailed with Stalin's backing, and the January
1933 Central Committee meeting adopted a plan with
relatively modest targets.[114] So deep did this disagreement run that at the Seventeenth Party Congress a year
later Molotov continued to press for higher targets. He
was opposed by Sergo Ordzhonikidze, the Commissar for
Heavy Industry, and the Congress witnessed the extraordinary spectacle of open disagreement between Politburo
members.[115]

Khrushchev was not senior enough to be involved in the
conflict over the Second Five-Year Plan targets, but his
public statements leave no doubt that he shared the rad-

icals' contempt for the moderates' approach. Khrushchev took the view that virtually any tasks set by the party might be achieved regardless of so-called 'objective conditions', provided that the necessary enthusiasm and leadership were provided. In 1933, Khrushchev told construction officials that higher plan targets could be met despite labour shortages and falling capital investment by better organisation of labour.[116] Celebrating Kaganovich's success in improving rail transport, he heaped scorn on the 'lovers of "objective causes"' who believed that the problems of rail transport stemmed from a shortage of rolling-stock; later in the same speech he advocated shock-work as a means of increasing output despite falling capital investment.[117] During construction of the Metro Khrushchev repeatedly cast aside expert opinion and pressed for faster tempos and riskier methods.

Khrushchev was also an enthusiastic supporter of the Stakhanovite movement. Aleksei Stakhanov was a miner who on the night of 30–1 August 1935 hewed 102 tonnes of coal, fourteen times his quota. His feat was based on a rearrangement of the division of labour which freed him from a number of auxiliary tasks and enabled him to exceed his norm many times over. Stakhanov was lauded as a hero and an entire movement arose out of the emulation of his feat in every branch of industry and construction. Stakhanovism was yet another weapon for the radicals in their struggle to regain control of economic policy. They used it to put pressure on conservative managers and specialists, in an effort to win an upward revision of production norms and a renewal of the rapid growth tempos of 1929-32.[118] The movement faced intense opposition. Managers and specialists regarded it as economically counterproductive: the special conditions required for Stakhanovite feats frequently required considerable support and disrupted the work of many other workers. The result was often massive overfulfilment of plans by a few élite workers and underfulfilment by whole enterprises. Ordinary workers resented the Stakhanovites' privileges and rightly feared that Stakhanovite productivity records presaged increases in their own output norms.[119]

In late 1935 Khrushchev praised the Stakhanovites and

warned of efforts to sabotage their work. He called for
vigilance in preventing this and for the severest possible
treatment of those who tried to obstruct the introduction of
Stakhanovite methods.[120] Khrushchev and others thus
identified opposition to Stakhanovism with sabotage, a
move which would have grave consequences in 1936–7,
when thousands of managers and specialists who failed to
evince sufficient enthusiasm for Stakhanovism were arrested and shot as saboteurs. By the end of 1935 the Central
Committee had clearly identified 'executives, engineers and
technicians' as the principal opponents of the movement.[121]
Khrushchev was never much of a 'specialist-eater' as such,
but his views on Stakhanovism placed him on the side of
those who would soon engineer the wholesale slaughter the
country's managers and technical specialists. He called for
the work of party organs in Moscow to be evaluated according to their support for the Stakhanovite movement. MK
and MGK launched a campaign to organise Stakhanovite
work in every branch of industry and to promote the
breaking of productivity records by Stakhanovites.[122] Once
again, Khrushchev had gone too far; in March the Central
Committee condemned the blind pursuit of records and
criticised a resolution by Moscow Stakhanovites calling for
a month-long campaign of Stakhanovite record-breaking.[123]

   The treatment of defeated opposition leaders was
another point of conflict between radicals and moderates
in the leadership during the mid-1930s. Radicals like
Kaganovich pressed for ever harsher sanctions against
defeated oppositionists, while more moderate Stalinists
wished to allow them to return to the fold and serve the
party; Lenin, they pointed out, had more than once
accepted errant colleagues back into the leadership.
Khrushchev, like his mentor, consistently adhered to the
radical line, even when this left him apparently out of step
with Stalin. In Ukraine and at the Industrial Academy
Khrushchev had already taken stands on the treatment of
the opposition which were harsher than the Central Committee line. Such an approach was in keeping with both his
temperament and his interests. A conciliatory policy which
left men like Bukharin, Piatakov and Kamenev in high
positions would block the political rise of less senior

Stalinists like Khrushchev, who could not compete with Lenin's colleagues in terms of education, experience or authority. The struggle to protect and purify the party's ranks was thus closely linked to political ambition.

In early 1934, policy at the national level was relatively conciliatory: defeated oppositionists were allowed to address the Seventeenth Congress and to remain in the Central Committee; many continued to occupy high party and state posts. Stalin himself told the Congress, 'There is, it would seem, nothing to prove and no one left to fight.'[124] On the eve of the Congress, however, Khrushchev warned of the continuing rightist danger in Moscow:

> There are still among us . . . people who in their words have confessed and repented but in fact are still awaiting 'their hour', and hoping to reappear on the political stage. True, they will not see that "hour" . . . but vigilance against them is particularly necessary.[125]

Just days later, he denied that there was any such danger, telling the Seventeenth Congress that 'we have finished with all anti-party endeavours in the Moscow organisation'.[126] Outside the halls of the Congress, however, he continued to call for greater vigilance, notwithstanding Stalin's claim that there was 'no one left to fight'.[127]

The political atmosphere soon changed, however, and Stalin found plenty of enemies to fight. On 1 December 1934 Leningrad party leader Sergei Kirov was assassinated by a disaffected former Bolshevik. Many aspects of the case remain shrouded in mystery, but it is clear that the secret police were involved, and Stalin may well have been behind the killing.[128] Kirov was a relative moderate and according to many accounts was widely seen as an alternative to Stalin as leader.[129] The assassination became the pretext for a series of show trials of former oppositionists over the next few years. Initially only Kamenev and Zinoviev were accused, and their responsibility was described as 'moral': they had inspired the assassin Nikolaev to kill Kirov but had not ordered him to do so. As time went on, however, both the charges and the number of accused multiplied, until virtually all of the former oppositionists and their supporters, as well as many who had no connection with them, stood accused of involvement in a host of far-reaching conspiracies to assassinate party leaders, sabotage industrial development, weaken the state's defences, spy for foreign governments and restore capitalism in the USSR.[130]

Each stage of this process gave rise to calls by the regime for greater vigilance in exposing enemies of the party and the people. Khrushchev demanded heightened vigilance in almost every speech for the next four years.[131] In early 1937 he warned Moscow party workers,

> Sometimes a man sits with enemies crawling around him, almost stepping on his feet, and he does not notice and puffs himself up: 'In my organisation there are no wreckers or alien elements'. This is a result not of the absence of enemies but of his deafness, his political blindness, his carelessness.[132]

The Moscow party chief was too lowly a figure to have much influence on the course of events during this time, but his was among the loudest voices in the chorus of condemnation howling for the defendants' blood during each successive trial. On 30 January 1937 he addressed a meeting of 200 000 people called to applaud the conviction of leading ex-Trotskyites. After accusing them of attempts to wreck the country's economy, enslave the workers, restore capitalism and hand over much of the USSR to foreign imperialists, Khrushchev turned to the defendants' most heinous crime:

> Judas-Trotsky and his band . . . raised their evil-doing hand against Comrade Stalin. Raising their hand against Comrade Stalin, they raised it against all of us, against the working class, against the toilers! Raising their hand against Comrade Stalin, they raised it against the teachings of Marx, Engels and Lenin! Raising their hand against Comrade Stalin, they raised it against all of the best that humanity has, for Comrade Stalin is our hope, he is the beacon of all that is good and progressive in humanity. Stalin is our banner! Stalin is our will! Stalin is our victory![133]

In early June he savaged Ian Gamarnik, the head of the Political Administration of the Red Army, who had committed suicide after being accused of connections to anti-Soviet elements.[134] Just three days before his suicide Gamarnik had been elected to MK at a conference conducted under Khrushchev's leadership.[135]

Khrushchev excelled at praising Stalin no less than he did at denouncing Stalin's enemies. Twenty years later it was Khrushchev who came forward at the Twentieth Party Congress to denounce the cult of personality which had developed around his predecessor, the 'sickening adulation' which was heaped upon him,[136] but in the 1930s Khrushchev's praise of Stalin far surpassed that of most of his colleagues. In the early 1930s he was among the first to call Stalin vozhd';[137] at the Seventeenth Congress, he called Stalin 'the genius-vozhd'', a term that *Pravda* still applied only to Marx and Engels.[138] By early 1937 the General Secretary was 'the great continuer of Lenin's cause, the vozhd' of the peoples of the USSR, the friend of toilers the world over'.[139] No Khrushchev speech until the 1950s was complete without extravagant praise for Stalin.

In 1937 the whole complex of conflicts between radicals and moderates in the leadership came to a head in a blood purge of the party, managerial and military élite which lasted into the following year. The power of the secret police, the NKVD, reached its zenith under the leadership of the notorious People's Commissar for Internal Affairs, Nikolai Ezhov. Under the pretext of a campaign to exterminate 'enemies of the people', Stalin used the secret police to eliminate anyone he chose. None of the major opposition leaders of the 1920s survived. Molotov, the premier, spearheaded a purge of the state economic apparatus, eliminating supporters of his rival Ordzhonikidze, who had been driven to suicide. Managers and specialists who did not support the Stakhanovite movement were arrested and shot. Provincial and republican party bosses were all but wiped out. Officials at every level denounced colleagues, bosses and subordinates in an effort to demonstrate their class vigilance and so protect themselves. The terror spread like an epidemic; anyone with close to connections to an arrested person was in danger of suffering the same fate. Many personal and political scores were settled in this way, and many careers advanced. Every high-level arrest triggered several promotions, so there was an incentive to denounce one's superiors.

There is no consensus among scholars as to the death toll of the Great Purge, largely because it is unclear to what extent the purge touched the populace at large as opposed to the élite; estimates range from 100 000 to several millions.[140] It was undoubtedly less bloody than the collectivisation campaigns of a few years before, but the élite was devastated. Of the 1966 delegates to the 'Congress of the Victors', 1108 were shot; only fifty-nine of the survivors returned as delegates to the Eighteenth Congress four years later. Ninety-three of the 139 Central Committee members and candidates elected at the Seventeenth Congress were arrested and shot; five were driven to suicide. Only twenty-four returned as delegates to the Eighteenth Congress.[141]

Khrushchev was still too junior an official to play a major role in the direction of the purge, but he was far from idle. In the Central Committee he voted for the expulsion and condemnation of many of his colleagues.[142] On factory visits and other public appearances he repeatedly encouraged his listeners to 'seek out the enemies of the people' and 'expose traitors and spies'. Within a few days of such an exhortation to the workers of a machine-building plant in southern Moscow, twenty-one people were arrested.[143] Speaking of party functionaries whose work was unsatisfactory, he told an MGK plenum, 'It is necessary to annihilate these scoundrels. Annihilating one or two or ten, we advance the cause of millions. Therefore it is essential that our hand not falter, it is necessary to step over the corpses of enemies to the good of the people.'[144] In another speech he attacked officials who tried to defend subordinates who had come under suspicion.[145]

Khrushchev's public utterances added to the growing hysteria within the party. Sometimes matters threatened to get out of control. At the opening session of the 1937 Moscow Party Conference, he warned that spies, wreckers and enemies remained unmasked; often, he said, they were among the best workers, hiding their intentions behind their excellent work and waiting for the decisive moment to do their destructive deeds. His listeners took this call for vigilance to heart, and several of the NKVD-approved candidates for election to the new party committee came under unexpected attack from the floor.[146]

Khrushchev's friend and future rival, Georgii Malenkov, then the head of the party's powerful Department for Leading Party Organs, was among them. Recounting his biography, Malenkov stated that his regiment was in Orenburg for a time during the Civil War. 'Were there Whites in Orenburg?' asked a voice from the floor. 'Yes', replied Malenkov, 'there were Whites in Orenburg.' 'That means he was with Whites', came the answer from the floor. Khrushchev intervened at this point: 'Comrades, I think that such questions may lead the conference into confusion. There were Whites on the territory of Orenburg, but Comrade Malenkov was not on their side.'[147] Khrushchev himself felt obliged to acknowledge his own wavering in the 1923 discussion of party democracy; he assured his listeners that this had been a brief episode and that he had fought for the General Line ever since. He also pointed out that this history was known to Stalin and the Politburo and that they continued to have confidence in him.[148] According to his memoirs, Khrushchev twice came in danger of being caught up in the 'meatgrinder'; on each occasion Stalin played a game with him, telling him of the evidence which had been given against him and observing his reactions. In both instances, nothing more came of the allegations.[149]

The Moscow organisation was thoroughly purged. Only three of the thirty-eight secretaries of MK and MGK escaped the terror; all three were transferred to work in other regions of the country. Ten of the 146 district and city party secretaries under the supervision of MK and MGK survived.[150] Among the survivors was Khrushchev's client Korotchenko, who was promoted and sent to work in Smolensk.[151] Similar purges were conducted in the state administration, the trade unions, the Communist Youth League and other institutions.

Khrushchev himself did not, for the most part, choose the victims of the purge; this was in the hands of the NKVD, which also vetted all promotions or transfers within the party. Action against an individual by party bodies generally followed rather than preceded arrest. In the protocols of MK and other bodies the reason most frequently given for removal from a post or expulsion from the party was arrest by the NKVD as an enemy of the people.[152] On occasion, however, party officials sought to protect themselves by taking action against individuals thought likely to be arrested.

Such was the case of Boris Treivas, the Kaluga raikom secretary. Treivas had worked with Khrushchev in the Bauman raikom; Khrushchev thought well of him and the two were friends.[153] Treivas was released from his duties by the bureau of MK on 1 April 1937 for having issued party cards to nineteen people later arrested as Trotskyites. He was also accused of having hindered the NKVD in their struggle against wrecking, a charge which suggests that he sought to protect his associates from the terror. Treivas was arrested within a few days, and on 10 April Khrushchev denounced him as a Trotskyite and an enemy of the party.[154] Khrushchev may well have feared that Treivas's fall might lead to his own demise. The two had worked together since 1931. It was Khrushchev who had nominated Treivas to head the Kaluga raikom. There may also have been a family connection: according to one account, Khrushchev's son Leonid was married to Treivas's niece.[155] Khrushchev is alleged to have broken up the marriage after Treivas was shot. The family connection is at least plausible; Khrushchev's son-in-law and aide, Aleksei Adzhubei, has written that Leonid's first wife was arrested in the terror.[156]

As the purge progressed, Khrushchev became uncomfortably aware of the number of his close associates arrested as enemies. In explaining his apparent lapse of viligance to a joint MK–MGK plenum in 1938, he said that in the struggle to expose enemies he had 'worked and strove with all his strength', but 'many enemies and villains remained'. The fact that so many of his former associates had been unmasked only after he had worked with them for many years was proof that 'one cannot say: if he worked with so-and-so, don't touch him'.[157] In the event, no one touched Khrushchev; when the terror ended, he was not in the prisons of the NKVD but in the Politburo of the Central Committee. Nor was he in Moscow, for in January 1938 he was dispatched to Kiev to take control of the Ukrainian party organisation and complete the purge that had begun there under Stanislav Kosior.

3 The Viceroy
Kiev, 1938–44

We're united and solid and no one will dare
To touch our young land, which is clean as first love.
As fresh and as young with his silver-gray hair
Is Stalin's companion, Nikita Khrushchev.
To the Great Stalin from the Ukrainian People[1]

During the Khrushchev era, the January 1938 Central Committee plenum, which elevated Khrushchev to candidate membership of the Politburo, was regarded as the beginning of the end of the terror.[2] Khrushchev's entry into the party's highest organ and his move to Kiev, which followed the plenum, were thus dissociated from the bloody excesses of the previous year. Such an interpretation was essential to maintaining the myth of Khrushchev's innocence in connection with the terror; it was also a falsification of the historical record. Khrushchev was sent to Ukraine not to liquidate the purge but to extend it. According to NKVD documents, the proportion of those arrested who received the death penalty increased to nearly 100 per cent after his arrival in Kiev.[3] His first months there were the bloodiest of his career.

The resolution of the January plenum sharply criticised the treatment of party members who had been unjustly expelled and demanded their reinstatement and the punishment of those responsible.[4] It was on this basis that Soviet accounts in the 1950s and 1960s sought to present January 1938 as a turning point in the terror. In fact, the resolution concerned not NKVD arrests but the treatment of rank-and-file party members by party officials. Such accusations against party functionaries were nothing new and had been common throughout the terror. The January plenum expressed confidence in the NKVD and its Commissar, Ezhov, and noted that NKVD intervention had saved party members slandered by officials. The result was a new wave of violence aimed at party officials charged with such offenses. It was with such a 'mission' before him that Khrushchev returned to Ukraine in January 1938.

The CP(b)U had already been through more turmoil and bloodshed than most party organisations. The Ukrainian Central Committee meeting at which Khrushchev became Acting First Secretary (his formal election took place at a Ukrainian party congress several months later) was attended by only fifteen members and four candidates, all that remained of the 102 members and candidates elected seven months before.[5] Khrushchev's election was accompanied by the expulsion of fifteen Central Committee members and candidates, including four members of the Ukrainian Politburo.[6]

The purge continued unabated until the Fourteenth Congress of the CP(b)U in June. By the end of April, nine more Central Committee members and two more candidates had been arrested.[7] All but three of the remaining seven were removed in May.[8] Between February and June all twelve provincial first secretaries in Ukraine were replaced, as were most second secretaries.[9] In April Khrushchev himself became the third man to head the Kiev regional and city committees in as many months.[10] The government was replaced *in toto*.[11] In March Khrushchev and the commander of the Kiev Military District, S. K. Timoshenko, reported that 3000 enemies of the people had been exposed among the troops in the district since January; 1000 of them had been arrested. Nearly all corps and division commanders were replaced.[12]

Nor was the turmoil limited to the élite. Expulsion rates in some party organisations reached 18–20 per cent. In Kiev compromising material was submitted on half of all party members; in one district the figure was 63 per cent.[13] Ezhov himself gave added impetus to this process on a visit to Ukraine in February 1938, when he estimated that there were still some 30 000 enemies of the people in Ukraine yet to be arrested and shot.[14] Between June 1937 and June 1938 55.8 per cent of secretaries and party organisers in primary party organisations (PPOs, as cells were now called) were replaced, as were 32 per cent of members of party committees.[15]

All the while, Khrushchev called for more vigilance in unmasking enemies of the people. On 26 May he told a mass meeting in Kiev that 'we have still not exposed all of them, and we all need to know this'.[16] Ten days later he warned a party conference that 'we must not relax, because the enemy will never, under any circumstances, cease to conduct his subversive work against our state'. He went on to blame the poor supply of potatoes and other vegetables on saboteurs.[17] 'We must not', he said, 'lower the political intensity of the struggle with enemies.'[18] At the party congress in June he warned the enemies of Soviet Ukraine that 'for every drop of honest workers' blood we will shed a bucketful of the black blood of the enemy'.[19] At the CP(b)U Congress, Ukrainian NKVD chief A. I. Uspenskii told the delegates that Khrushchev 'guides the organs of our NKVD daily, ceaselessly, surely, paying more attention to them than to any other area of work, and he guides them justly, in a Bolshevik manner'.[20]

It is still impossible to provide a full assessment of the extent of Khrushchev's guilt; in the 1950s archives in Moscow and Kiev were 'cleansed' of materials concerning Khrushchev and the Great Purge. This cleansing operation was carried out under the supervision of his client I. A. Serov, who was then serving as Chairman of the KGB.[21] The documents involved were withdrawn to Khrushchev's personal files, now in the Presidential Archive in the Kremlin; in October 1964 Khrushchev's opponents threatened to use them against him if he did not surrender his party and state posts.[22] For the most part his role was that of an executor and cheerleader, but he was involved to some degree in the decision-making process as well, and he participated in the work of the three-man tribunals, or troikas, which condemned thousands of the victims of the terror.[23]

Khrushchev voted in the Central Committee for the resolutions adopted in 1937–8 expelling other Committee members and handing them over to the NKVD for trial; these included resolutions againt Bukharin and Rykov in February 1937, the military commanders in June and a number of others in the autumn and winter. These votes were always unanimous, save for Stalin who usually left his ballot blank. The closest thing to a dissenting voice was that of Lenin's widow, Nadezhda Krupskaia, who wrote 'agreed' (*soglasna*) on her ballots rather than 'for' (*za*), thereby implying acquiescence in these decisions rather than support for them.[24] Khrushchev seems to have gone along out of fear, conformity and obedience to Stalin rather than any real thirst for blood; as a member of the commission appointed to prepare a resolution on Bukharin and Rykov after the inconclusive December 1936 plenum, Khrushchev was among those who favoured expelling them from the party but opposed shooting them. (Stalin had not yet advocated execution at this stage.)[25]

The question of Khrushchev's role in the purge is also related to the issue of his survival. The very fact that he lived through the purge in such high posts is to some degree an indictment of his role. His unquestioning co-operation in the process provides only a part of the explanation for his good fortune; many of the most active and enthusiastic purgers in due course fell victim to the terror themselves. Khrushchev's survival may to some degree be explained in connection with theories of the terror itself. Some scholars maintain that the principal purpose of the purge was to exterminate the Old Bolsheviks and, with them, any memory within the party of its pre-revolutionary (and pre-Stalin) history. Khrushchev would have been safe from such a purge. Many Old Bolsheviks participated in and survived the terror, however, while thousands of newer party members died.[26] Others have seen the terror chiefly as an attack by economic radicals on moderate managers and officials[27]; on this view also Khrushchev would be expected to survive. But much of the bloodshed during the terror does not reflect this cleavage: some well-known moderates survived, while many radicals perished.[28] Space does not permit the consideration of every other explanation of the terror. In any case, no theory of the purges is complete, and no explanation of Khrushchev's survival which rests on his membership of this or that group is wholly satisfactory.

The alternative is to see how his own personal characteristics kept him in favour with Stalin. Khrushchev's peasant background, crude manner and lack of education led many of his colleagues to view him as something of a buffoon, an image he did little to dispel. On the contrary, Khrushchev appears to have reinforced this impression by his ceaseless chatter, which caused him to be regarded as a bit of a babbler. In fact, although Khrushchev talked constantly, he never did so carelessly, being very much aware of the need to guard his tongue. His untrammelled flow of talk camouflaged more than it revealed; he later remarked that a politician 'is given a tongue in order to hide his true thoughts'.[29] These qualities concealed Khrushchev's considerable intelligence and great skill as a political in-fighter, leading many of his rivals to underestimate him. Stalin never took Khrushchev seriously enough to see him as a potential successor, and this was no doubt to Khrushchev's advantage. Malenkov and others made the same mistake after Stalin's death and paid dearly for it. Like Junius Brutus, Khrushchev outlived a tyrant in part by playing the fool.[30]

Khrushchev survived because he represented 'that rarest of creatures, a devoted tiger'.[31] Total loyalty was not enough for Stalin; he wanted aides whose fidelity was matched by energy and ruthlessness in carrying out his will. Khrushchev shared this combination of traits with Molotov, Zhdanov, Kaganovich and others of Stalin's inner circle who survived.[32] Khrushchev's loyalty and ferocity secured for him a place in their ranks; he would turn on his master only after the dictator was dead.

The situation in Ukraine stabilised after the Fourteenth Congress of the CP(b)U in June 1938. The turnover in party and state bodies, although it remained high through 1940, dropped from its peak, and arrest rates fell sharply. Khrushchev increasingly turned his attention to the task of rebuilding the shattered CP(b)U. This was no simple matter, not least because party organisations remained overcautious in admitting new members, who might later be exposed as enemies. Party officials did not wish to accept responsibility for such a politically sensitive matter, and the Ukrainian leadership spent considerable energy pressuring local party organisations to speed up recruitment.[33] These efforts were not without results: at the Fifteenth Congress of the CP(b)U in 1940, Khrushchev reported that 235 000 new members and candidates had entered the party since the Fourteenth Congress, an 85 per cent increase in the size of the party.[34]

Many of the men promoted in the upheavals of early 1938 were to help Khrushchev govern Ukraine for the next decade and would go on to important careers in all-union politics during the Khrushchev era and beyond. Two of them were men with whom he had worked closely in Moscow: Korotchenko, who was transferred from Smolensk to become Chairman of the Council of People's Commissars,[35] and M. O. Burmistenko, an official in the all-union Central Committee apparatus whom Khrushchev brought from Moscow to serve as Second Secretary of the Ukrainian Central Committee.[36] A number of others were officials already working in Ukraine who received rapid promotion in 1938; these included A. I. Kirichenko, Z. T. Serdiuk, L. P. Korniets, A. P. Kirilenko and L. I. Brezhnev.[37]

One reason for the intensity of the purge in Ukraine was external security. Western Ukraine, which Moscow wished ultimately to absorb into the Ukrainian Soviet Socialist Republic, then formed part of a hostile Poland. Moscow made frequent demands for the 'reunion' of the Ukrainian and Belorussian peoples under Soviet rule and charged that Poland planned to extend its rule into Soviet Ukraine and Belorussia.[38] In Germany high Nazi leaders spoke of the importance of Ukraine to the Third Reich and openly courted anti-Soviet Ukrainian *émigrés*. This threat was reflected in Khrushchev's rhetoric; he frequently railed against 'the Polish-German fascists' and their 'bourgeois nationalist' agents in Ukraine. Enemies of the people were routinely charged with plotting to hand over Soviet Ukraine to 'Polish barons', German fascists or both. The achievements of Soviet Ukraine were contrasted with conditions in the Polish-held Western Ukraine.[39]

Khrushchev's transfer to Kiev and the near-total destruction of the Ukrainian party apparatus were in part a response to these concerns. Moscow's doubts about the reliability and security of Ukraine had been aggravated by the fact that Kosior, Postyshev and other leaders sent to Kiev from elsewhere seemed to have 'gone native' and adopted positions which were too independent for the

centre's liking. Stalin was determined to destroy any
vestiges of independence in Kiev and to bind the second-
largest Soviet republic more closely than ever to Moscow.
The replacement of Kosior, an ethnic Pole, by Khrushchev
and the destruction of the Ukrainian party élite formed
only one aspect of this campaign.

Nationality policy was another. By the time Khrushchev
went to Kiev in 1938, little remained of post-revolutionary
efforts to develop minority languages and cultures or to
make a priority of the advancement of non-Russians to
leading posts in their native republics.[40] Nevertheless, even
lip-service to these goals virtually disappeared after 1937.
Scores of nationalist plots were 'uncovered' by the NKVD;
there were over 100 such cases in the 1930s, the great bulk
of them in the last years of the decade.[41]

The most spectacular case concerned education. V. P.
Zatonskii, the Ukrainian People's Commissar for Education,
was pronounced an enemy of the people in January 1938.[42]
The Commissariat itself was then subjected to a severe
purge in which most of its leading officials were denounced
as Trotskyites, rightists or bourgeois nationalists.[43] Their
crime was to have operated schools for national minorities
in which the language of instruction was Polish, German,
Czech or some other 'foreign' tongue. As both accused and
accusers knew, the Soviet constitution guaranteed minorities the right to be educated in their native tongues.[44]
Nevertheless, the schools were denounced as bulwarks of
anti-Soviet bourgeois nationalist influence and reorganised
into Russian or Ukrainian schools; special sections for
minority language instruction in vocational and higher
educational institutions were liquidated.[45] A short time later
the study of Russian was made mandatory in all schools
where Ukrainian was the language of instruction.[46] This
required the retraining of 20 000 teachers whose command
of Russian was poor.[47] Local leaders were rebuked for slow
fulfilment of these decisions.[48]

At the Fifteenth Congress of the Ukrainian party in June
1938, Khrushchev denounced the wrecking wrought by
anti-party elements in culture and education, charging that
'they did everything to cut off the Ukrainian people from

the fraternal Russian people'. He then turned to the specific question of language policy:

> Comrades, all peoples will now study Russian, because Russian workers . . . raised the banner of revolt in October 1917. Russian workers set an example for the workers and peasants of the whole world as to how to struggle, how to deal with their enemies and how to win freedom. . . . The enemies of the people and bourgeois nationalists knew the strength and influence of the Russian tongue and Russian culture. They knew that this was the influence of Bolshevism, the influence of the teachings of Lenin and Stalin on the minds of the Ukrainian people. . . . Therefore, they threw Russian out of the schools.[49]

In conjunction with the preparation of a new Ukrainian dictionary, a campaign was launched to 'purify' Ukrainian from 'bourgeois-nationalist rubbish', a reference to non-Russian (mainly Polish) linguistic influences. Words with Polish roots were replaced by words with Russian roots.[50] There was considerable leeway to do this, since Ukrainian often contained words with the same meaning drawn from both sources: Polish roots were most common in the western regions, while eastern areas had been under Russian influence for centuries.

Other cultural institutions were also affected. The Ukrainian Politburo under Khrushchev's leadership adopted resolutions concerning the liquidation of ethnic German and other minority districts within the republic.[51] The Moldavian province was left intact but forced to replace the Latin alphabet with the Cyrillic. This was intended to foster the cultural separation of Soviet Moldavians from their brethren across the border in Bessarabia.[52] Ukrainian history was rewritten to emphasise Ukraine's close 'fraternal' ties to Russia.[53] In connection with the approaching 125th anniversary of his birth, Taras Shevchenko, Ukraine's greatest poet, was reinterpreted so as to make him acceptable as a Soviet cultural hero.[54] The events marking the anniversary were overseen by a Ukrainian Politburo commission, headed by Burmistenko and Korotchenko.[55]

The new leadership in Kiev also attempted to put Ukraine's collective farms in order. The collectivisation of agriculture at the beginning of the decade had been resisted more fiercely in Ukraine than anywhere else and had been completed only after much of the republic was subjected to a man-made famine.[56] Yet collective farms in many areas existed only on paper. Kolkhoz statutes were frequently ignored. Peasants' private plots and private livestock holdings were larger than allowed by law, and kolkhoz property and land were often 'leased' to peasants; in some cases they simply took possession of it with impunity, not even bothering with the formality of leasing.[57]

This state of affairs was allowed to persist because local party leaders understood that the easiest way to maintain social peace in the countryside was to ignore such practices. In February 1939, Khrushchev reminded local leaders of the decisions of the USSR government with respect to such matters and warned them that in areas where these decisions were violated 'the responsible chairman of the rural district executive committee and the secretary of the corresponding district party committee will be held accountable as violators of the law'.[58]

Throughout his twelve years in Ukraine Khrushchev devoted considerable time and energy to mastering agricultural issues. He did not shy away from direct interference in such technical issues as methods of sowing, and he encouraged lower party officials to do likewise. Ukraine's farming sector was vital to the Soviet economy, and Khrushchev believed that its rich potential could be realised only by maximising direct party involvement. The management of Ukrainian agriculture also provided him with an outlet for his love of things mechanical. He suggested the development of a number of simple agricultural machines, including a 'comb' to raise stalks beaten down by rain so that they could be harvested and a beet-cleaning machine for combatting beet weevils. Khrushchev consulted with engineers and even drew his own sketches of some of these devices. Several prototypes of the beet-cleaning machine were built, but they failed to perform as had been hoped.[59]

In all of these areas Khrushchev's actions and those of the Ukrainian Politburo as a whole reflected policies established in Moscow. As a candidate member of the all-union Politburo from January 1938 and a full member from March 1939, Khrushchev had a part in formulating these policies, but his was far from the most influential voice in the leadership, not least because he was in Kiev and was thus unable to attend most Politburo meetings.[60] He had, moreover, been sent to Kiev not to set policy but to implement it. Aware of the fate which his immediate predecessors had suffered, Khrushchev gave no hint of any disagreement with Moscow during his early days in Ukraine. He faithfully executed central policies and underscored his loyalty by continued flattery of Stalin.

His flights of rhetoric in this connection reached new heights in Ukraine: Stalin was 'our great genius, our beloved Stalin'; 'the greatest genius of humanity, the teacher and vozhd' who leads us towards communism, our great Stalin'; and 'our great leader of the peoples, our friend and father, the greatest man of our epoch'.[61] The Stalin cult was by this time in full flower across the USSR, but even against this background such phrases marked Khrushchev as a sycophant of exceptional ability; his Politburo colleagues were generally more restrained. In Khrushchev's defence it must be noted that they were in Moscow, daily under the watchful eye of Stalin, while Khrushchev was not. Given Stalin's suspicious nature, Khrushchev's move to Kiev probably required him to go to ever greater lengths to prove his loyalty and subservience.

When Khrushchev had been in Ukraine for a year and a half, he was presented with a new challenge: the absorption into the Ukrainian republic of the formerly Polish regions of Western Ukraine. The secret protocols of the Nazi-Soviet non-agression pact of 1939 (the Molotov–Ribbentrop pact) agreed to a partition of Poland along the line of the rivers Nurew, Vistula and San. Moscow was to be given a free hand in territories east of that line. Khrushchev was informed of the pact only after it was signed, but he welcomed it as a necessary manoeuvre to buy time.[62] Soviet

leaders knew that war with Germany was coming but hoped
to forestall it for a few more years. The pact opened the way
for Hitler to invade Poland, thus triggering a war between
Nazi Germany and the French and British. While Hitler and
the democracies fought, Moscow planned to consolidate its
new position in Eastern Europe and to carry on with its
programme of rapid rearmament.

The pact was concluded in late August, and the German
invasion of Poland followed on 1 September, triggering
declarations of war by France and the United Kingdom on
3 September. On 17 September units of the Red Army
moved into eastern Poland on the pretext of liberating
Ukrainians and Belorussians living there from the 'yoke of
Polish oppression' and protecting them from the advancing Germans.[63] Although Soviet accounts of the welcome
given to the Red Army by local Ukrainian and Belorussian
populations are exaggerated, local people seem to have
accepted the invasion with cautious optimism. There was, at
any rate, little opposition except from the Polish population, which consisted largely of former Polish soldiers and
officers who had been settled in the area in order to secure
Poland's grip on it.[64] The process of sovietisation which
followed the invasion soon turned much of the population
against the new rulers, however.

The absorption of the new provinces of Ukraine had
been prepared well ahead of time. Soviet officials smuggled
into Western Ukraine before the invasion organised temporary local administrations which were alleged to be spontaneous local responses to the collapse of Poland.[65] There
was no native, pro-Soviet organisation on the ground, since
Stalin had ordered the dissolution of the Communist Party
of Western Ukraine in 1938; its leaders had been arrested
and shot. Khrushchev himself entered Western Ukraine on
the day of the invasion; he arrived in L'vov, the largest city
in the region, on 22 September and then travelled from city
to city exhorting the troops and explaining the significance
of the liberation to his new subjects.[66]

Khrushchev also managed to find time in his busy
schedule to look after one item of personal business. He
telephoned Nina Petrovna in Kiev and told her that he had
arranged for her to travel to her native village of Vasilev to

collect her parents and bring them east. Vasilev had fallen into the hands of the Red Army but was located to the west of the Molotov–Ribbentrop line and would have to be handed over to the Germans. Nina Petrovna later recalled that she was almost arrested by the village's newly-formed Soviet administration, which refused to believe that Vasilev was to be ceded to Germany. Khrushchev's first meeting with his in-laws followed soon after.[67]

In October 'elections' to a People's Assembly of Western Ukraine were conducted under the supervision of the Red Army. According to the official results, almost 85 per cent of the local population voted for the 'bloc of communists and non-party Bolsheviks'.[68] On 27 October the assembly proclaimed Soviet rule in Western Ukraine, and on 29 October it asked the USSR Supreme Soviet to incorporate the western provinces of Ukraine into the Ukrainian Soviet Socialist Republic. This was done in November.[69] The next year witnessed two more election campaigns, as deputies were chosen for local, republican and all-union soviets; the official results claimed 95–7 per cent support for Soviet rule.[70]

Local adminstrations, party committees and soviets were comprised almost exclusively of Soviet Ukrainian officials brought to the region from eastern provinces. Even symbolic posts which had no real power were filled with eastern Ukrainians appointed from Kiev.[71] The inadequacy of total reliance on easterners soon became apparent, however. The Ukrainian Politburo in October 1940 rebuked officials in Western Ukraine for their lack of trust toward former members of the Communist Party of Poland, who were henceforth to be drawn more actively into party work.[72] Khrushchev also directed efforts to strengthen the party in the new provinces, especially in rural areas. Little was achieved before Soviet rule was interrupted by the German offensive of 1941, however.

The local Polish population was quickly dispossessed. The NKVD supervised three waves of deportations of Poles from the area to Siberia, Kazakhstan and the Soviet far north in 1939–40; altogether almost 1.2 million Polish military settlers, officials, landowners, gendarmes and their families were subject to deportation or imprisonment without investigation or trial. These deportations deprived many areas of doctors, teachers and other badly needed skilled personnel.[73] The Poles were also the principal victims of the nationalisation of land, industry, trade and the banks in the first weeks of Soviet rule.[74]

The Soviet authorities' handling of the land question soon lost them the support of much of the Ukrainian peasantry as well. Land confiscated from landowners, churches, monasteries and state officials was, in theory at least, to be distributed to peasant households by local peasants' committees. This process moved forward in 1939–40, but more than half the available land was not distributed; it was instead incorporated into new state farms and similar agricultural enterprises. This disappointed expectations aroused by the Soviet occupation and ensured that the peasants remained land-hungry, a condition that may have been intended to make poorer peasants more amenable to collectivisation and more supportive of the authorities in the coming struggle with the kulaks, who remained as yet untouched. The kulaks were left alone for security reasons: the Ukrainian Politburo warned that a campaign against them in border areas 'might be used by elements hostile to Soviet power'.[75] In 1940 the first state and collective farms were organised in the new provinces. Although only 12.8 per cent of households were collect-ivised by the time of the German invasion in 1941, this officially voluntary process was accompanied by mass de-portations of unco-operative peasants and other coercive measures. Many of the kolkhozes so established were 'paper kolkhozes'.[76]

The Ukrainian leadership's suspicion of the local popu-lation and its maintenance of tight police controls also alienated segments of the population which had previously been prepared at least to accept Soviet rule. The Ukrainian Politburo regarded no less than a quarter of the population as 'people who are alien to us and do not plan to change'.[77] These included not only the former bourgeoisie (few of whom remained) but also many citizens with anti-Polish and socialist convictions, whose only sin was to have belonged to a political party other than the Bolsheviks.[78] This under-mined efforts to strengthen the party's local roots.

On 22 June 1941 the rapid sovietisation of Western Ukraine was interrupted by Hitler's Wehrmacht. Khrushchev, in Kiev, was among the first to whom news of Operation Barbarossa was reported. As a member of the Military Council of the Kiev Special Military District (KOVO), he was well aware of the state of Soviet defence preparedness in Ukraine. The KOVO Military Council had reported to Stalin in February that the fortification of border districts was proceeding too slowly; Khrushchev had offered to transfer 100 000 workers to such projects in order to bring construction to a more advanced stage by 1 June. Khrushchev and General M. P. Kirponos, the KOVO commander, had travelled extensively in border areas and expressed serious concern about German preparations for war.[79] In April 1941 they again proposed to Stalin to accelerate the pace of defence construction in border areas.[80]

The evidence available on Khrushchev's war record makes the evaluation of his role extremely difficult. Because he is most frequently on record as having acted as a member of the military council of this or that theatre or front, it is impossible to know the extent to which he actually influenced decisions as opposed to simply signing off on those made by the professional military men on these councils. Moreover, the memoirs of most of his wartime comrades were published either when he was in power, in which case there was great pressure to inflate his role, or during the Brezhnev era, when it was barely possible to mention Khrushchev in print in any context. The memoirs of Marshal Zhukov, for example, were edited in the Brezhnev years in such a way as to exaggerate Khrushchev's responsibility for the Khar'kov disaster of 1942 and minimise his role in the victory at Stalingrad.[81]

Remarkably, the few references to Khrushchev in Soviet military memoirs published during the Brezhnev years are generally favourable. This suggests that his professional military colleagues held him in high regard, though he was certainly not seen as an equal in military matters. Thus Marshal A. M. Vasil'evskii wrote in the 1970s:

It is necessary to say that on those fronts where I was the

representative of the headquarters of the Supreme
Commander-in-Chief, N. S. Khrushchev, as a member of
the military councils of those fronts and of the Politburo,
always maintained the closest links with me and almost
always went with me to visit the front.[82]

During the war Khrushchev, while remaining First
Secretary of the Ukrainian party, served with the rank of
Major General as a political officer and a member of the
military councils of the Southern, Southwestern, Stalingrad,
Voronezh and First Ukrainian fronts and of the Southwestern Theatre.[83] As a political general, Khrushchev was
responsible for such matters as party affairs in the armed
forces, the morale and indoctrination of the troops, and the
supervision of the military commanders with whom he
worked. There was often considerable tension between
professional military men and their 'politicals', but Khrushchev seems to have gotten on well with his generals. As a
Politburo member he could be useful to them; more than
once Khrushchev used his access to the highest political
leaders in Moscow on behalf of his commanders.[84]
Although his job was officially to watch over field commanders on behalf of Stalin, he sometimes represented the
former to the latter.

Khrushchev, in Kiev, was closer to the chaos of the first
weeks of the war than his colleagues in Moscow. The western provinces of Ukraine and Belorussia were overrun with
such speed that one general pronounced the war lost on
the fifth or sixth day and shot himself in Khrushchev's
presence.[85] The Germans advanced more than 125 miles
per week; Kiev was under threat by 11 July, three weeks
after the offensive had begun. On that day Stalin sent word
to Kiev that the Germans must be prevented from crossing
the Dnepr river at all costs and warned Khrushchev and
Kirponos that 'if you take even one step in the direction of
withdrawing troops to the left bank of the Dnepr . . . you
will all suffer severe punishment as cowards and deserters'.
Khrushchev and Kirponos replied with assurances that they
had no intention of yielding the right bank.[86]

In addition to preparing the defence of Kiev, Khrushchev
was responsible for economic questions connected with the

war effort in Ukraine: the organisation of defence production, the evacuation of industrial equipment and other property in the face of the German advance, and the implementation of a scorched-earth policy as the Red Army retreated. Khrushchev was instructed in the opening days of the war to organise production of mines, rifles and other war matériel locally in Ukraine; the centre could not guarantee supplies.[87] Decisions about what to remove to the east and what to destroy before the Germans could seize it had to be cleared with Moscow in some detail. Factories had to be dismantled and moved, livestock shipped east, bridges destroyed and so on. Even the question of where to sow and where to annihilate the crops required consultation with Moscow.[88] Khrushchev's first evacuation proposals were submitted to the headquarters of the Supreme Commander-in-Chief on 7 July; the following day Stalin rebuked him for moving too quickly. Stalin feared that too aggressive a policy of evacuation-cum-scorched earth would demoralise the population and the troops.[89] The result of Stalin's intervention was to slow the pace of evacuation and destruction while the German advance continued at full speed, thus leaving more behind to be captured.

On 3 August the Southern Front command, of which Khrushchev was a member, sent a telegram to Moscow concerning the behaviour of the ethnic German population in Ukraine. They reported that the Germans along the Dnestr were shooting at retreating Red Army troops and welcoming German units with bread and salt, a traditional sign of hospitality. The front command requested that the local authorities be given the power to organise the resettlement of ethnic Germans to the east. Moscow's response was a decree ordering the Ukrainian NKVD to arrest all ethnic Germans believed to be anti-Soviet and to organise all remaining German males aged sixteen to sixty into 'construction battalions' for work in the eastern Soviet Union.[90]

The German advance had been checked some 10–12 miles west of Kiev by mid-July. In late July, however, the German blitzkrieg resumed. On 4 August Stalin repeated his order to hold the right bank of the Dnepr at any price, and Marshal Budennyi ordered Khrushchev and Kirponos

to move on to the offensive no later than the morning of 6
August. The latter, after complaining of shortages of both
troops and supplies, agreed.[91] In the days that followed
Stalin maintained the pressure on Khrushchev and Kirponos to hold Kiev at all costs; help from the centre was
promised but never sent.[92] Stalin pressured Khrushchev and
Kirponos into repeated assurances that they would hold
both the city and the left bank of the Dnepr. Stalin then
used these promises to justify his rejection of a General
Staff recommendation that Soviet troops be pulled back to
the eastern bank of the river.[93] The Germans forced the
Dnepr and continued to drive towards Konotop to the
north of Kiev and Poltava and Khar'kov to the south. The
Ukrainian capital formed the tip of an increasingly narrow
salient with German troops both northeast and southeast of
the city.

By 9 September the salient was more than 40 miles deep;
with no reserves available to halt the German pincer
movement closing around Kiev, Khrushchev and Kirponos
resolved to pull out. On 11 September Stalin emphatically
rejected this option and dispatched Timoshenko to Kiev to
replace the incompetent Budennyi in overall command of
the defence of Ukraine; units from elsewhere on the Southwestern Front were ordered to Konotop to stem the Nazi
advance, but to no avail. By 15 September the corridor
leading out of the Kiev salient was closed. Stalin did not
authorise even a partial withdrawal from Kiev until the
morning of 17 September. By the end of that day the
Military Council in Kiev decided, in contradiction to
Stalin's orders, to abandon the city and attempt a breakout.
But valuable time had been lost, and the Germans had
succeeded in consolidating their encircling position. The
result was catastrophic. The attempt to break out of the
encirclement resulted in hundreds of thousands of Soviet
casualties and prisoners. Khrushchev, Timoshenko and
Budennyi escaped by aeroplane, but Burmistenko and
Kirponos, attempting to fight their way out with the troops,
were killed.

Khrushchev saw the Kiev disaster as a product of Stalin's
failure to grasp what was happening at the front and his
lack of trust in, and support for, commanders in the field.[94]

In strategic terms, however, the defence of Kiev may have been more successful than Khrushchev wished to acknowledge. Stalin's refusal to countenance a withdrawal undoubtedly made the loss of Kiev much more costly than it might have been, but it also slowed the German advance. Many German commanders, including Halder and Guderian, believed that the time lost in the battle for Kiev was critical in thwarting German plans to take Moscow before winter.[95]

With virtually all of Ukraine occupied by late 1941, increasing emphasis was devoted to the development of effective partisan operations behind German lines. On 27 June – two days before the first directives on partisans were issued by the centre – Khrushchev appointed an 'operational group' of party and government officials to organise partisan detachments in all provinces of Ukraine; provincial party committees were ordered to establish such operational groups locally as well.[96] Plans for partisan operations had been prepared prior to Barbarossa but came to nothing on account of the speed of the German advance and the severity of Nazi reactions to partisan activity. In the early days of the war, most partisan units quickly fell apart.[97] The scope for operations by those that survived was limited by topography: 80 per cent of Ukraine is open steppe, ill-suited to guerrilla warfare. Ironically, the wooded areas of Western Ukraine, where anti-Soviet feeling was strongest, were among the regions with excellent conditions for partisan warfare; this was to cause the Red Army considerable trouble after 1943. Partisan activity achieved little in 1941 and early 1942, but this picture changed as a result of the Nazis' brutality towards their Ukrainian subjects.

The aim of partisan operations was not only to hinder the German war effort but also to 'bear witness to the vitality of Soviet power' and thereby to discourage or punish collaboration.[98] This was a vital necessity; in many areas the general population was more inclined to welcome than to resist the invaders. It was thus logical that many of the partisan detachments be formed from NKVD troops. Altogether more than 17 000 NKVD and border troops were organised into partisan units.[99] The Ukrainian Partisan Staff was placed under the command of Timofei Strokach, a career NKVD officer. The staff was formed in September 1941 and formally attached to the command of the Southwestern Theatre, of which Khrushchev was a member.[100] In reality it was controlled by the Central Staff of the Partisan Movement in Moscow.

Party work formed a second facet of Khrushchev's involvement with operations behind German lines. In October 1942 the so-called Illegal Central Committee of the Communist Party (Bolshevik) of Ukraine was formed to provide political leadership for the partisan movement in Ukraine and to 'transform it into an all-people's movement against the German occupiers'. Khrushchev was in Stalingrad at the time and was therefore not a member of the illegal committee, which was headed by three members of the regular Ukrainian Politburo. These, however, reported regularly to Khrushchev, who also participated in the committee's planning of partisan operations for 1942–3.[101]

Early 1942 found Khrushchev with the Military Council of the Southwestern Theatre, headed by Marshal S. K. Timoshenko. With Stalin's support, but against the advice of the General Staff, the Southwestern Theatre Command attempted in May of that year to mount a major offensive with the goal of liberating Khar'kov. The operation was based on the erroneous assumption, shared by the theatre command and the General Staff, that the main Nazi thrust in early 1942 would again be towards Moscow, and that an offensive against German forces in the area would require only limited resources to achieve a major success.[102] In reality German forces in the area were preparing an offensive of their own, a fact of which Soviet intelligence became aware even as Timoshenko was launching his attack; this information did not reach the Southwestern Theatre Command for four days, however.[103]

On 12 May 1942 Soviet armies on the Southern and Southwestern Fronts went onto the offensive. For several days all went well, but on 17 May the Germans launched their own offensive against the 9th and 57th armies of the Southern Front, both of which were short of reserves and overextended. By 10 a.m. that same day German forces had penetrated 12.5 miles beyond the 9th army's front. Moscow promised reinforcements from the Voroshilovgrad Front, but these would not arrive until 20 May at the earliest. At this point the General Staff proposed cessation of the Khar'kov operation to Stalin, but he refused, persuaded by Khrushchev and Timoshenko that the danger to the Southern Front was being exaggerated and that the offensive should continue. The situation continued to deteriorate on 18 May, but Khrushchev and Timoshenko made no mention of ending the offensive in their report to Stalin at 12.30 a.m. on 19 May. A personal report sent by Khrushchev to Stalin an hour and a half later said nothing about halting the Khar'kov offensive or taking action to repel the German attack. Only during the afternoon of 19 May, when the Germans had opened up a 50-mile breach in the Southern Front, was the Khar'kov operation called off.[104] It was too late to halt the German advance, which continued until late June. Soviet losses were enormous.

The Khar'kov operation remains a matter of some controversy. Although his reports of the early morning of 19 May make no mention of ending the offensive, Khrushchev later claimed that the theatre command took the initiative and called it off (evidently on 17 or 18 May) only to have the order countermanded by Moscow. Theatre Chief of Staff I. Kh. Bagramian implored Khrushchev to take up the matter with Stalin personally, but Khrushchev called Vasil'evskii first; only when Vasil'evskii, insisting that Stalin had made up his mind, refused to raise the question with the vozhd' did Khrushchev ring the Supreme Commander's dacha. Malenkov answered, and Khrushchev had to converse with Stalin through him, because Stalin would not come to the phone. According to Khrushchev, Stalin accused him of calling off the offensive without Timoshenko's approval and insisted that the operation continue.[105]

Zhukov denies this account, insisting that Timoshenko and Khrushchev advocated continuing the offensive as late as 18 May.[106] Vasil'evskii recalls that he first suggested ending the offensive on the afternoon of 17 May but that Stalin was persuaded by Timoshenko to let it continue. According to Vasil'evskii, Khrushchev did call him late in the afternoon of 18 May; Khrushchev told him that Stalin had refused the theatre command's request to call a halt to the operation and begged him to take up the issue with Stalin himself. Vasil'evskii told Khrushchev that he had tried more than once to convince Stalin of this, but the latter had rejected his advice, pointing to the more optimistic assessment of the theatre command. He recommended that Khrushchev call Stalin directly. Khrushchev subsequently called Vasil'evskii back and reported on his conversation with Malenkov. Only on 19 May did Timoshenko agree to halt the offensive; Stalin accepted this decision.[107] Bagramian also recalls that it was Timoshenko who held out longest against halting the offensive and that he (Bagramian) turned to Khrushchev in the hopes that Khrushchev would persuade Stalin to override Timoshenko.[108] It is significant that both Vasil'evskii and Bagramian wrote their accounts, which to some degree exonerate Khrushchev, during the Brezhnev years.

It would thus appear that Khrushchev's recollection of events is broadly correct except as to dates; he and Bagramian tried to end the offensive much later than his account suggests. It is curious that in his memoir he blames Stalin rather than Timoshenko, but this may reflect the later development of his attitudes to both men. He and Timoshenko were friends, while Stalin's handling of the war effort was one of the points for which Khrushchev later criticised him most severely. Khrushchev also knew the extent to which Timoshenko's advice to Stalin was shaped by the need to tell the dictator what he wished to hear.[109] Timoshenko's 'stubbornness' may have resulted from his belief in Stalin's determination to carry on.

When the scale of the catastrophe had become clear, Stalin ordered the dissolution of the Southwestern Theatre; Bagramian was demoted to chief of staff of the 28th army, while Timoshenko was placed in command of a single front, subordinate directly to the headquarters of the Supreme Commander. In a telegram to Bagramian, Timoshenko and Khrushchev, Stalin compared the Khar'kov disaster to the worst defeats in Russian military history and warned them, 'If we were to report to the country about the full extent of the catastrophe – with the loss of 18–20 divisions – which your front has been through and is still going through, I fear that they would deal with you extremely severely.'[110] Given Stalin's treatment of some other commanders who failed him, Khrushchev and his colleagues could count themselves lucky indeed.

That Stalin had not completely lost confidence in Khrushchev is indicated by the fact that he was appointed to the Military Council of the Stalingrad Front in July.[111] The defence of Stalingrad in late 1942 is generally recognised as the turning point of the war in Russia, and Khrushchev to the end of his life remained proud of his participation in it. In 1943 V. I. Chuikov, who commanded the defence of the beleaguered city, said that Khrushchev and Malenkov were there 'practically all the time between September 12 and December 20'.[112] Khrushchev's military role cannot have been critical, however, as even the edition of Chuikov's memoirs published while Khrushchev was in power says nothing about it. The one contribution of substance with which Chuikov credits Khrushchev consisted of compelling the Chief of the Soviet Rear, V. I. Vinogradov, to improve the supply of ammunition to the 62nd army.[113] Khrushchev also intervened with Moscow to secure the delivery of 500 tonnes of winter lubricants to Stalingrad in November.[114]

Chuikov most often presents Khrushchev as a conduit for information between commanders at the front and headquarters in Moscow, now relaying the centre's questions or orders to Chuikov, now pressing Moscow for greater air support for Stalingrad.[115] Khrushchev himself presents his activities in a similar light, laying stress on the fact that even the smallest decisions had to be cleared with Moscow. He also claims to have defended the front commander, A. I. Eremenko, against Stalin's wrath on one occasion.[116] Khrushchev's service at Stalingrad apparently did not displease the vozhd', for Khrushchev was decorated and elevated to the rank of lieutenant-general soon after.[117]

From the victory at Stalingrad Khrushchev moved westward with the advancing Soviet force, entering Kiev on the eve of Revolution Day 1943. The Ukraine to which he returned had been utterly devastated by the fighting and by the scorched-earth policy of the retreating Germans. Kiev was practically a ghost town. As the front moved west, therefore, Khrushchev's military duties receded into the background and he became increasingly preoccupied with the reconstruction of Ukraine. In connection with this task, he became premier of the republic in February 1944, while remaining First Secretary of the Ukrainian Central Committee.[118] At the time of his election as premier he was the only man in years to hold both the leading posts in his republic; Ukraine was, moreover, the largest of the non-Russian Soviet republics.

Shortly after Stalingrad the war brought a personal tragedy to Khrushchev. His son Leonid, a fighter pilot, was shot down. What happened next is a mystery. According to Soviet military archives, Leonid Khrushchev perished on 11 March 1943, the day he was shot down over Zhizdra.[119] No other pilots flying with him that day saw him go down, however, and no remains were recovered. Nor did Khrushchev organise a search for his son's remains after the liberation of Zhizdra.[120] It is therefore strange that Leonid was regarded as dead rather than missing in action from 11 March; according to the military archives, a condolence letter was sent to his father that very day, although there was still no proof of his death.[121]

Colonel-General I. A. Kuzovkov, once the Deputy Director of the Main Administration of Cadres of the USSR Ministry of Defence, claimed that Leonid Khrushchev was captured on 11 March but was returned in an exchange of prisoners at Khrushchev's request. While still in an NKVD 'filtration' camp for ex-POWs, Leonid was accused of having co-operated with his German captors. According to Kuzovkov, he was tried by a military tribunal and sentenced to death. Khrushchev pleaded with Stalin to spare his son's life, but the latter refused and the younger Khrushchev was shot. Other versions of the story maintain that Stalin himself ordered the execution.[122] There is no basis for this account in the archives of the Ministry of Defence, but some Soviet military historians have charged that Leonid Khrushchev's files were altered after the war.[123] Molotov, who may have known first-hand what happened, later maintained that Khrushchev hated Stalin because the latter refused to prevent Leonid's execution.[124]

According to Khrushchev's daughter, Rada Adzhubei, Leonid was badly wounded in action and was sent to convalesce in a hospital in Kuibyshev, whither Khrushchev's wife and younger children had already been evacuated. While in hospital, Leonid drank, and, under the influence of alcohol, shot a man. As punishment, he was sent to a forward detachment, where he perished.[125]

If Leonid Nikitich Khrushchev was indeed executed on Stalin's orders, then his fate cannot but have influenced his father's changing perceptions of the genius-vozhd'. The war in any case marked a turning point in Khrushchev's opinion of his leader and patron, quite apart from any role Stalin may have played in the death of his son. Unlike Malenkov, Molotov and other Politburo colleagues, Khrushchev spent most of the war at the front rather than in Moscow. He was not a member of the State Defence Council, which was formed to run the war effort in 1941, and he spent little time at the headquarters of the Supreme Commander-in-Chief, where most of the others were based. At the front Khrushchev daily encountered the centre's often ill-informed interference in the activities of commanders on the scene; in the early days of the war he knew first-hand how out of touch with reality was Moscow's perception of events. In later years Khrushchev never claimed to have defended colleagues during the purges or to have questioned any of Stalin's deeds in the 1930s. This makes his claims to have done so during the war all the more credible, and suggests that the war did indeed transform his view of Stalin.

There is, moreover, other evidence that Khrushchev's views changed markedly during the course of the conflict. His remarks after the liberation of Ukraine suggest gratitude for the loyalty to the regime demonstrated by the Soviet people and a desire to reward this loyalty with higher living standards. Much of the population anticipated that the relatively liberal ideological climate of the war years would continue, and there were even rumours among the peasants that the kolkhozes were to be broken up.[126] Such hopes had been bolstered by the expansion during the war of the private plots which the peasants were allowed to cultivate for profit or personal consumption. Khrushchev himself reinforced expectations of a better life to come:

During the war years our people have had to bear many

trials. The peoples of the Soviet Union have suffered many losses . . . and have endured much privation, devoting all of their labours to winning victory over the enemy. The toiling people of Ukraine suffered much during the black days of the German occupation. Our Bolshevik party and Comrade Stalin personally are devoting exceptional attention to improving the material and cultural life of the Soviet people, the victor-people . . . special attention will be given to the expansion of consumer goods production and the raising of the living standards of working people.[127]

Khrushchev also took a much more relaxed attitude to police controls. At a Ukrainian Central Committee meeting in 1945 he rebuked two provincial party secretaries for the speed with which they employed repression against politically deviant behaviour. Khrushchev told them that, in the first instance, such cases required not police repression but the pastoral guidance of the party. He was particularly severe with a speaker who carelessly applied the kulak label to a peasant woman who had had the temerity to complain about shortages of salt and kerosene. Khrushchev stated that she was right to complain and demanded proof that she was a kulak:

> It is easy to do this. I don't like this speech, so I can say that the orator is a kulak. I know how this happens. You were preparing for the plenum. People began preparing materials for you, giving you three positive facts and three negative ones. You did not verify them and now you are just repeating them. . . . I am sure that an intelligent chekist (secret policeman) would not arrest such a person, because she needs an explanation, not an arrest.[128]

The contrast with the Khrushchev of 1938, with his hysterical demands for greater vigilance and more arrests, could hardly have been greater.

Hopes for rising living standards and greater freedom were soon disappointed, however. Stalin had no intention of taking a more liberal political line at home, and the needs of rapid reconstruction were to be met by returning to the economic approach of the pre-war five-year plans. Heavy industry and agriculture were the priority sectors for reconstruction; hopes for a better deal for the consumer receded into the future. The Soviet people, exhausted by sixteen years of upheaval and war, were to be driven to the limit. Ukraine was no exception. Stalin expected his viceroy in Kiev to govern Ukraine no less ruthlessly after the war than before it.

4 The Counter-heir
Kiev and Moscow, 1944–53

*All of us around Stalin were temporary people. As long
as he trusted us to a certain degree, we were allowed to
go on living and working. But the moment he stopped
trusting you, Stalin would start to scrutinise you until
the cup of his distrust overflowed. Then it would be your
turn to follow those who were no longer among the living.*
N. S. Khrushchev, *Khrushchev Remembers*[1]

The Ukraine to which Khrushchev returned lay in ruins.
Industry was devastated, and agriculture faced shortages of
seed, labour and machinery. There was insufficient housing
for the population that remained, and millions of people
were flooding into the republic – evacuees from the Urals,
demobilised soldiers, former POWs and *gastarbeiten* who
had been taken to Germany as labourers during the occupation. In 1945 Ukrainian industry reached only a quarter
of its pre-war output, and grain procurement was worse
than in the previous year, despite the fact that not all of the
republic had been liberated in time for the 1944 harvest.

The most pressing problem was the revival of farm production. Constant pressure to accelerate the return to pre-war
levels of output led Khrushchev to bully both his officials and
the Ukrainian peasantry. At Ukrainian Central Committee
meetings he subjected officials reporting on agricultural
questions to constant interruptions. In June 1945 he did not
even allow Dnepropetrovsk Secretary Naidenov to complete
his first sentence:

Naidenov: The successful conduct of the spring sowing
for this year (Khrushchev: Was the sowing better in your
province or in Zaporozh'e? Do the Zaporozhites have
better grain?) Naidenov: I haven't been there. (Khrushchev: I will come to you soon. Comrade Matiushin, how

did you come to Kiev, did you fly or drive? Matiushin: I drove.) Naidenov: The successful conduct of the spring sowing for 1945 was preceded by . . . mass political work, which was conducted in the winter and during the spring sowing. (Khrushchev: In the spring Matiushin's province is better than any other. When the harvest begins, things get worse there, and when the procurements campaign arrives, he says that the situation was worse there than in Depropetrovsk.)[2]

Naidenov's 'speech' occupies fourteen pages in the transcript of the plenum. Much of it consists of Khrushchev's conversation with Zaporozh'e party chief Matiushin, with the rest being Khrushchev's detailed interrogation of Naidenov concerning the sowing of melons and grapes.

The situation was much the same at the December 1945 plenum; one secretary after another endured criticism and even verbal abuse from Khrushchev.[3] Faced with the need to meet unrealistic plan targets, Khrushchev's contempt for 'objective' circumstances as a justification for non-fulfilment of plan tasks resurfaced: 'Certain officials have until now tried to hide their shortcomings . . . by pointing to so-called objective reasons – there's a war on, we don't have enough of this or that – but these people themselves make no efforts to overcome difficulties'.[4] Khrushchev told Matiushin that he was 'a very bad boss', accusing him of poor work, poor memory, deception and irresponsibility.[5]

The drive to increase agricultural production led to ever tougher labour discipline on the kolkhozes. Labour collectives on Ukrainian farms were empowered to order the exile from the republic of members who did not work their allotted share of work-days on the farm. Over a two and a half year period some 11 991 people were deported to the east under this decree, many of them old people and invalids whom the kolkhozes did not wish to support. The measure was also used for the settling of personal scores by kolkhoz officials. Khrushchev regarded this as a 'very effective measure' and recommended to Stalin that it be adopted for other republics.[6]

Khrushchev's other great agricultural task was the

collectivisation of agriculture in Western Ukraine, which he promised to complete by the end of 1947.[7] This process proceeded slowly, on account of both armed opposition and a shortage of resources. Under pressure for quick results, Khrushchev relied on inflated statistics on the number of households collectivised. The few machine and tractor stations (MTS) established to maintain and operate agricultural machinery for the kolkhozes before Barabarossa were in total disrepair, since the speed of the German advance had left no time to evacuate them, and collectivisation could not move forward without them. The catastrophic harvest of 1946 and the famine that followed caused further delays. By January 1948 only 7.5 per cent of peasant households in Western Ukraine had been recollectivised; mass collectivisation was not launched until later that year.[8]

Khrushchev's problems in reimposing Soviet rule in Western Ukraine were compounded by the guerrilla struggle waged there by anti-Soviet partisans in the first years after the war. Some of the partisans were Ukrainians who had served the Germans during the occupation, while others had fought against both German and Soviet forces during the war. The largest of these was the Ukrainian Insurgent Army (UPA), a force of 40–50 000 men which enjoyed considerable successes against the Germans in 1943–4 and which ambushed and killed General Nikolai Vatutin, a leading Red Army commander. During 1944–6 Soviet troops conducted three major offensives against the UPA and other groups, suffering thousands of casualties. Garrisons of troops from the security and internal affairs ministries were maintained in virtually every village and town of Western Ukraine.[9]

The guerrilla war was also closely linked to collectivisation; the collectivisation drive alienated the peasantry and increased support for the partisans, but where collective farms were established it was easier for the authorities to cut off food supplies to the resistance. The methods by which collectivisation was imposed, however, made it relatively easy for the partisans to avoid this problem. Teams of 'enforcers' went systematically from village to village organising kolkhozes. The result was that the new farms were formed in close proximity to one another and maintained close links. This made for more stable kolkhozes, but it slowed the spread of collectivisation to new regions. For a long time the partisans had simply to avoid collectivised districts.[10]

For all practical purposes, the Soviet authorities had imposed an occupation regime in Western Ukraine. The security organs (NKVD and NKGB) in the area were staffed by outsiders; only 10 per cent of NKVD/NKGB officials even spoke Ukrainian. Most party workers did, but they too were drawn mainly from the eastern provinces of Ukraine, and many of them wished to return there. Local administrations and party organs were woefully understaffed despite the transfer of 3000 party workers from other regions in April 1944. Hundreds of partisan attacks against them took place in the months following liberation; as a result, party officials in some areas refused to work because of the partisan threat.[11]

Khrushchev oversaw the military struggle against the partisans, but his role was secondary to that of the security organs; his principal concerns were with the rebuilding of the party in both Eastern and Western Ukraine. The first step taken in this direction was a thoroughgoing purge of both officials and rank-and-file party members who had collaborated or otherwise compromised themselves during the war.[12] Turnover among lower level officials remained high for several years after liberation; it was especially high in rural western areas, where frequent purges were a response to the slow pace of recollectivisation. Khrushchev reported in late 1946 that during the preceding eighteen months 38 per cent of raikom secretaries, 64 per cent of chairmen of local soviets and over 60 per cent of MTS directors had been replaced.[13]

Khrushchev was under constant pressure from Moscow to put his shattered republic back into order at speed. As early as November 1944 the all-union Central Committee had characterised party propaganda work in Western Ukraine as unsatisfactory. The resolution called for tougher supervision of the press, better education of the party's oral agitators and closer attention to the work of 'mass organisations'.[14] The low educational level of many professional agitators posed a serious problem. The agitators represented the party to the populace, but many were no better informed than their audiences; one thought that Harry Truman was an Italian fascist, while another identified 'the Italian or English writer Dickens' as the author of *Anna Karenina*.[15]

Propaganda work was made more difficult by cultural policies imposed from Moscow after 1946. In the battle for the hearts and minds of the Ukrainian people after Barbarossa, Khrushchev and his colleagues had made use of appeals to Ukrainian national sentiment. These had formed a key element of Soviet propaganda during the war and continued for some time after liberation.[16] Khrushchev himself employed them, although he was always careful to stress the close ties of the Ukrainian people with the Russian people.[17] In mid-1946, however, the relative liberalism of the war years came to an end. A Central Committee resolution based on a report by Andrei Zhdanov established a new standard for cultural and scientific work. Zhdanov denied that such work could be apolitical. It was therefore not enough that art and literature avoid anti-soviet themes: they must forcefully advance Marxist-Leninist ideals.[18]

The effect of this new line was to rob the Soviet Ukrainian leadership of any opportunity to make use of national themes in a bid for popular support. All scope for the expression of Ukrainian national identity was eliminated: Ukrainian theatre, music, literature and historiography were attacked for their failure to produce works of sufficient ideological merit.[19] Khrushchev himself was quick to get into the act, criticising Ukraine's principal newspapers for their shortcomings soon after the publication of Zhdanov's report.[20] The poet Maksim Ryl'skii was subjected to particularly vicious attacks.[21] A subtle but real softening of official attitudes was evident from late 1947, as Ukrainian colleagues of Khrushchev spoke out against 'cosmopolitan' tendencies, which viewed all manifestations of national cultures as remnants of bourgeois ideology. The writer Korneichuk, a close friend of Khrushchev, stressed the diversity of national forms in which socialist content might be expressed.[22]

Even as Zhdanov's cultural crackdown was getting under way, Khrushchev was headed for a political crisis. The first sign of trouble came in July 1946, when Ukrainian leaders were ordered to report to the all-union Central Committee on measures to strengthen lower party groups. The problem remained especially acute in Western Ukraine, where primary party organisations were few, weak and slow to develop.[23] At first glance there seemed to be nothing for Khrushchev to worry about; he had addressed this problem over the preceding two months and could therefore claim to be taking appropriate action.[24] The Central Committee, however, produced a resolution which was sharply critical of the measures taken by the CP(b)U. The Ukrainians were criticised for paying too little attention to 'the selection and political-ideological education' of party and soviet officials and of underestimating 'the significance of ideological work'. Khrushchev acknowledged the validity of this criticism in mid-August.[25]

Khrushchev's troubles on the political front were compounded by an economic crisis. Ukraine and Russia suffered a drought in 1946 which led to a severe famine the following year. The famine was largely the consequence of official policies. The state forced collective and state farms to give up 52 per cent of the harvest, more even than it had demanded during the war, despite a harvest that was considerably worse than the poor harvest of 1944–5. Even so, the authorities managed to procure only 17.5 million tonnes of grain in 1947, 2.5 million tonnes less than in 1945 and half the procurement of 1940.[26] In any case, there was no need for such extreme measures against the farms; the government reckoned that the grain procured, plus state reserves, would be enough to feed the country.[27] The state, however, wished to conserve the reserves accumulated in 1946 rather than to use them to supplement the harvest.

In addition to conducting a procurement campaign that left the peasants on the edge of starvation, the authorities reduced the demand for state grain supplies by simply removing non-farm workers in rural areas from the rationing system. The exclusion of these workers and their families, in addition to the farm population, relieved the state of some 100 million mouths to feed.[28] By confining the famine to remote rural areas, the authorities were able to conceal it from the outside world. As in the early 1930s, the country's leaders fed the towns and maintained the pace of industrial growth by starving the rural population. In some regions peasants resorted to cannibalism to survive.[29]

Khrushchev insists that he did what he could for Ukraine. He appealed to Stalin and the central government, both on paper and in person, for ration cards and food supplies. Stalin was enraged by his request and flatly refused; evidently he believed that Khrushchev was becoming a spokesman for Ukrainian interest groups rather than his vicar in Kiev. As the severity of the famine became clear, however, Stalin relented and aid was provided.[30] The General Secretary was nevertheless displeased with Khrushchev. He was making poor progress in pacifying Western Ukraine and completing the collectivisation of agriculture there; the famine now left him vulnerable to attack on agricultural questions as well. Moreover, a Khrushchev cult had developed in Ukraine on a scale that could not have escaped Stalin's notice. Stalin himself was always given pride of place, but Khrushchev was not far behind. His portrait was to be seen all over Kiev. The praise heaped upon 'the faithful comrade-in-arms of Stalin and the glorious leader of the Ukrainian people' grew ever more elaborate; he was celebrated in poems about the liberation of Ukraine and credited with the successes of post-war reconstruction.[31]

In February 1947 Stalin called an all-union Central Committee meeting to discuss agriculture. The main report was given by A. A. Andreev, a Central Committee Secretary and a strong proponent of the theories of agronomist Vasilii Villiams, who advocated the sowing of spring wheat in all of the USSR's grain-growing regions. Khrushchev was convinced that winter wheat gave better yields in Ukraine and had resisted pressure to sow spring wheat there. He was sharply criticised for this at the plenum.[32] The spring wheat/winter wheat controversy can only be described as idiotic: none of the leaders involved had mastered the technical issues at stake, nor do they seem to have grasped that differences in local conditions made it unwise to impose a uniform policy across the entire country. After the plenum Stalin suggested to Khrushchev that Kaganovich be sent to 'help' him in Ukraine.[33]

In early March Khrushchev was released from his duties

as First Secretary of the Central Committee of the Communist Party of Ukraine; he was replaced by his erstwhile patron and mentor Lazar Kaganovich, a strong advocate of spring wheat. The official pretext for the change was the need to separate the posts of premier and First Secretary of the republic, but criticisms of agricultural performance appeared in the press as well.[34] Factional politics also played a role; the appointment of Malenkov's client N. S. Patolichev as Second Secretary suggests that Malenkov wished to exploit his rival's weakness. Khrushchev also gave up the secretaryships of the Kiev provincial and city party committees.[35] He retained the post of Ukrainian premier, in which capacity he delivered a self-critical speech to the republican Supreme Soviet later in March; although he acknowledged some shortcomings in his work, he continued to oppose the sowing of spring wheat in Ukraine.[36] Apart from an appearance on May Day, he disappeared from the Ukrainian press until September. Most observers expected further demotions to follow, certain that Khrushchev's brilliant career was coming to an end.[37]

Khrushchev states in his memoirs that he was ill with pneumonia and almost died during this period, a claim which western scholars have viewed with great scepticism; the conventional assumption has been that Khrushchev's only illness was political.[38] Aleksei Adzhubei, however, has written that his father-in-law did indeed become seriously ill at this time, although he does not attribute Khrushchev's demotion to illness or deny that Khrushchev's relations with Stalin were tense.[39] Whether physically ill or not, Khrushchev was politically unwell. After a decade in Kiev he found himself playing second fiddle to Kaganovich, a man whose political career had reached its zenith more than a decade before and was now in decline. By the end of the year, however, Kaganovich was recalled to Moscow and Khrushchev returned to the post of First Secretary, handing the premiership over to his protégé Korotchenko.

When in the late 1950s Kaganovich was expelled from the party leadership, his appointment in Kiev was presented in a light favourable to Khrushchev. Kaganovich's transfer was attributed to Stalin's desire for harsher rule in Ukraine, and Kaganovich was accused of abusing his power and of conducting a witch hunt against alleged Ukrainian nationalists.[40] Kaganovich's tenure in Kiev, like the January 1938 plenum, was thus interpreted in such a way as to dissociate Khrushchev from some of the worst excesses of Stalinism. Adzhubei, however, insists that his father-in-law maintained good relations with Kaganovich in Kiev.[41] Indeed, the two seem to have agreed on a division of labour: Khrushchev concentrated on agriculture, while Kaganovich addressed himself mainly to Ukrainian industry.

There were, moreover, no changes in policy dramatic enough to lend credence to a 'soft Khrushchev–tough Kaganovich' interpretation. The campaign against nationalist deviations did indeed become more intense, but it had begun the year before under Khrushchev; policy in this area was in any case set in Moscow, as Khrushchev himself acknowledged.[42] Khrushchev claims that Kaganovich was planning to convene a Ukrainian Central Committee plenum on the issue at the end of 1947 but was recalled to Moscow before he managed to do so. This possibility cannot be ruled out. The first signs of a softer line came in the late summer of 1947, about the time that Khrushchev's name again began to appear on party and government decrees in Ukraine.[43] The campaign against the poet Ryl'skii, whom Khrushchev claims to have defended against Kaganovich, ended after Kaganovich left Kiev. Kaganovich's unpopularity with Ukrainian officials seems to have had more to do with his arrogance and bullying of subordinates that with substantive issues of policy, however; this is evident even in Khrushchev's account of the period.[44]

Nationality policy is the only specific issue on which Khrushchev claims that he and Kaganovich disagreed in 1947. The struggle with anti-soviet partisans was intensified in 1947, but this followed the assassination of a Polish general in May, not Kaganovich's transfer in March.[45] Khrushchev, in any case, can hardly be said to have taken a softer line than Kaganovich on this issue. Finally, changes were undertaken in the method of recollectivisation, but its pace did not increase markedly until after Kaganovich's departure. There is no evidence of disagreement over any aspect of economic policy, and 1947 turned out to be the best year since the war for both industry and agriculture.

In retrospect it would appear that the decision to send Kaganovich was a blessing in disguise for Khrushchev. The two men had been friends and had worked closely together in the 1920s and 1930s, and there is no evidence that they had fallen out by this time, although Kaganovich may have felt some jealousy at Khrushchev's rise. As a Jew, Kaganovich was effectively excluded from the field of contenders to succeed Stalin; he would therefore not have had the same interest in ruining Khrushchev as did rivals for the succession like Malenkov. Finally, it is unlikely that Khrushchev would have weathered the crisis of 1947 had not Kaganovich reported favourably about him to Stalin. Adzhubei claims that Kaganovich himself asked to be transferred back to Moscow once Khrushchev had made a full recovery from his illness;[46] if true, this suggests that Kaganovich viewed his role as that of a troubleshooter and was ready to go when his job was done.

Having weathered the storms of 1947, Khrushchev served two more years as First Secretary in Kiev. This was the most tranquil period he had known since before the revolution. The country was at peace, Ukrainian industry and agriculture had for the most part recovered from the war, and the last armed resistance to Soviet rule in Western Ukraine was finally being crushed.[47] In Moscow, to be sure, Politburo politics were as treacherous as ever; Stalin was in obvious physical and mental decline, and his increasing inability or unwillingness to attend to affairs of state intensified the conflicts among his would-be successors. Khrushchev was not unaware of these events or untouched by them, but he was able to view them from a distance and to minimise his own involvement in Kremlin intrigues.

Khrushchev lived at this time in a dacha in the village of Mezhigor'e, some 20 miles from Kiev. Although he had lived and worked in industrial cities since boyhood, Khrushchev never completely accepted the conditions of urban life. He was strongly drawn to nature and loved to stroll about the countryside near his home at the end of a day's work. He walked a kilometre or two every morning before leaving for work and spent at least a quarter of an hour walking around the village every evening, no matter how late he returned from Kiev. According to Adzhubei, who became acquainted with his future in-laws at this time, Nina Petrovna ran the Khrushchev household 'strictly and with no "appeals process"'; order rather than warmth predominated. In the presence of their children, Nikita Sergeevich and Nina Petrovna used first name and patronymic when speaking of or to one another. Khrushchev himself was rarely home except on Sundays, and even those he preferred to spend visiting construction sites or kolkhozes before going on to the theatre in the evening.[48]

Agriculture remained Khrushchev's main preoccupation during this period. After the war, he travelled constantly about the provinces of Ukraine, inspecting farms and meeting with both rural officials and ordinary farmworkers. The collectivisation campaign in the western provinces, which finally took off in 1948, met with stiff resistance on the part of the peasantry there. Punitive taxes were imposed on private livestock holdings in an effort to make the kolkhozes more attractive than individual farming; many peasants slaughtered their livestock in response. In an effort to foster a 'class war' between different sectors of the peasantry, poor and 'middle' peasants were freed from taxation, while taxes were increased on those considered to be kulaks. Anti-soviet partisans, though reduced in numbers, were still capable of mounting terrorist attacks, and they directed many of their operations toward disrupting collectivisation. In some regions it was difficult to recruit officials (still mainly easterners) on account of the threat of assassination.[49] Moreover, violations of kolkhoz statutes on the newly collectivised farms were common; the problem of 'paper kolkhozes' was yet to be resolved.

During his last years in Kiev Khrushchev also began peddling the agricultural initiative which, after his return to Moscow, would become the basis for his ill-fated 'agrotown' scheme. His dream was to eliminate the relative poverty and cultural backwardness of rural areas – the 'contradictions between town and country' in Bolshevik parlance. Khrushchev wished to turn the peasants into skilled agricultural labourers, a rural proletariat whose mindset and way of life would differ little from that of urban industrial workers.

Peasants were to be resettled into much larger communities than the villages; these larger settlements would facilitate the provision of electricity and water as well as such cultural amenities as libraries, nurseries, cultural centres, clubs and other modern conveniences. In January 1949 he spoke of 'transforming all our villages in the very near future'. As a demonstration of what could be achieved, he called for turning the Cherkessy district into such an agricultural community; this was to be 'a great step on the path to the elimination of the contradictions between town and country'.[50] The agrarian city so created was presented to Stalin as a seventieth birthday present in December.[51]

At the end of 1949 Politburo politics at last drew Khrushchev back to Moscow. Stalin summoned him to the capital to become both a Secretary of the Central Committee and the head of the Moscow party organisation. Khrushchev believed, probably rightly, that Stalin intended for him to be a counterweight to Malenkov in Moscow.[52] Malenkov remained the ageing dictator's heir-apparent, but Stalin was anxious to keep him in check. This had been increasingly difficult since the death of Zhdanov the year before; Malenkov had formed a close political alliance with Lavrentii Pavlovich Beria, the Politburo member who ran the organs of state security, and was in a position too powerful for Stalin's liking.

Khrushchev himself was not happy about the return to Moscow. In Ukraine he had for twelve years been Stalin's vicar over a republic comparable in size to France and had operated with a degree of independence which men like Malenkov had never known. He had been spared the ordeal of daily encounters with the increasingly paranoid Stalin and the constant scrutiny of his Politburo rivals. In Kiev he had to toe the party line, of course, but the day-to-day management of affairs was in his hands, and there was at least some scope for independent initiative. In Moscow every step he took would have to be cleared with his master. A 'Moscow Case' was being prepared, and Khrushchev feared being caught up in it.[53] Nevertheless, when Stalin gave an order, Khrushchev obeyed. He returned to the capital in December 1949, just in time for the celebrations marking Stalin's seventieth birthday.

Khrushchev's remarks on this occasion demonstrated that he had lost none of his talents as a sycophant while in Kiev:

All the peoples of the Soviet Union and progressive humanity of all the world are marking this dear date, the 70th birthday of our genius-vozhd' and teacher, Iosif Vissarionovich Stalin. . . . The name of Comrade Stalin is the banner of all the victories of the Soviet people, the banner of the struggle of toilers of all the world against capitalist slavery and national oppression, for peace and socialism. . . . all the peoples of our country with exceptional warmth and a feeling of filial love call the great Stalin their own father, their great vozhd' and their genius-teacher.[54]

Among the Politburo members who spoke, only Beria and Marshal Kliment Voroshilov spoke in similar tones; Molotov and Malenkov, by contrast, were remarkable for their restraint. Khrushchev also made frequent references to Ukraine in his speech, evidently in an effort to maintain his influence in that republic, which was now under the leadership of L. G. Mel'nikov, a Russian who was closer to Malenkov than Khrushchev.

The first thing Khrushchev did after arriving in Moscow was to purge its party organisation. Within three months he had replaced all of the secretaries of MK and MGK and the leadership of the Moscow City Soviet.[55] The purge did not, however, lead to a 'Moscow Case'. There is no doubt that such a case was in the works when Khrushchev returned to the capital. His predecessor, Georgii Popov, had made many enemies during his time in Moscow, including Beria. Anonymous letters charged Popov with conspiring against Stalin.[56] Stalin took up the matter with Khrushchev, who assured the dictator that there were no grounds for believing the charges; according to Khrushchev, it took some time to persuade Stalin to leave Popov alone.[57] Popov did survive, however; the resolution dismissing him from his post criticised him for conceit, insufficient attention to political work and suppression of criticism within the Moscow organisation, but it dismissed the charges of conspiracy as 'unconfirmed and slanderous'.[58]

It is unlikely that Khrushchev's opinion was decisive in persuading Stalin to spare Popov, although it is impossible to say what Stalin's reasons were. He may never have intended to prosecute the matter in the first place. In all likelihood the potential Moscow Case was opposed by other members of the Politburo; a blood purge in Moscow so soon after the Leningrad Case raised the spectre of a return to the politics of the 1930s, a prospect that none of Stalin's lieutenants could view with equanimity.

As head of MK once again, Khrushchev's chief concern in connection with the development of Moscow was housing. Housing construction in the capital had returned to pre-war levels only in 1949, but the population of the city had grown by another million people in the course of the decade. The housing construction targets for Moscow in the 1946–50 Five-Year Plan were only 48.7 per cent fulfilled. In response, Khrushchev in 1950 called for a major expansion of Moscow's construction industry and began to press for the mass construction of houses by 'industrial-velocity methods'. In other words, aiming for both speed and low cost, he adopted the methods of 'oversimplification' and 'the construction of boxes' which he had condemned in the 1930s. This emphasis was to continue during his tenure as leader of the Soviet Union, when hundreds of thousands of more or less identical five- and six-storey blocks of flats were built. The flats were small and the buildings ugly; the public nicknamed them *Khrushcheby*, a pun on the Russian word for slums (*trushcheby*). Khrushchev, however, was concerned with speed, not aesthetics; the pace of housing construction in Moscow during 1951–3 was triple the rate of 1946–50.[59] The much-maligned Khrushcheby still house some 60 million citizens of the former Soviet republics today.[60]

Khrushchev's principal concern remained agriculture, however. In addition to being responsible for the farms of Moscow province, he was the Central Committee secretary with responsibility for agriculture, replacing A. A. Andreev, the spring wheat advocate who had criticised him in 1947.

Khrushchev quickly made his mark by launching an attack on the kolkhoz structure which had been in place throughout Andreev's tenure. The first step was to end the so-called link system in collective agriculture. At issue was the size of the labour collective which was to be the basis for organising work on the kolkhozes. Since 1939 this had been the link, a team of six to eight farm workers. In February 1950 *Pravda* attacked the link system on the grounds that it was inappropriate for mechanised farming. *Pravda* advocated greater reliance on a larger labour collective, the brigade, which usually consisted of at least three dozen people.[61] *Pravda* did not mention another drawback of the link: it made political control more difficult, because there were too many links and too many link leaders for party officials to monitor effectively.[62] Within a week of *Pravda*'s broadside, Andreev published an apology and acknowledged the superiority of the brigade.[63]

Khrushchev then masterminded a drive to amalgamate small kolkhozes into larger farms. This was to be his *idée fixe* for several years. Exhibiting an almost limitless faith in the benefits of scale, Khrushchev pressed for the formation of larger and larger farms. The campaign began with a *Pravda* article which appeared under his name on 8 March. In it he argued that the amalgamation of small farms into larger ones would facilitate the employment of advanced technology in agriculture and reduce the number of people employed in administrative and other non-productive tasks on the farms.[64] The kolkhoz amalgamation also had political implications, since it would lead to fewer farms without party organisations and a higher percentage of party members among farm officials. Given that the party was still very poorly represented in many rural areas, this was a significant consideration.[65]

The government decree governing the kolkhoz amalgamation warned that it should not be turned into a crash campaign and that the 'voluntary principle' must be observed.[66] These strictures were routinely enunciated with respect to changes in agricultural policy but rarely observed in practice. The 1950–1 kolkhoz amalgamation was no exception. In Moscow province, where Khrushchev managed the process himself, a crash campaign was conducted, and the wishes of farm officials and workers were ignored.[67] By June the number of kolkhozes in the province had been reduced from 6069 to 1668.[68] The result was the creation of farms too large to be managed efficiently by a single chairman.

Many if not most of these amalgamations led to little change in the way that farms were run, however. This was inevitable given the nature of most collective farms at the time. All but the largest and wealthiest collective farms were based on the old villages which had existed before collectivisation. Amalgamation thus created 'farms' which consisted of several villages located as much as ten miles from one another; the imposition of a single chairman on these farms neither brought these villages together into a coherent unit nor changed the layout of their fields. It was in part the desire to make kolkhoz amalgamation a reality which led to Khrushchev's next and most grandiose scheme.

In June 1950 Khrushchev initiated a pilot scheme in Moscow province along the lines of the agricultural town created in Ukraine in 1949; resources adequate to the task were not provided, however. By the spring of 1951 the farmers were simply to move to the locations of the new settlements, where 'large, comfortable houses' would 'gradually be built later'.[69] The chairman of one of the affected farms complained in early 1951 that the farmers from four villages had simply been moved at their own expense to a fifth, where they had had to construct their own huts.[70] Khrushchev, however, was not to be deterred. On 4 March 1951 he published a plan for constructing a large number of such 'agrotowns'.[71] In Moscow province alone Khrushchev proposed to move 93 000 peasant houses and to build 10 000 new houses, 1000 administrative buildings, 2300 clubs, libraries and cultural centres, 2300 kindergartens and nurseries, and 3350 other buildings.[72] In addition to 'liquidating the contradictions between town and country', the construction of agrotowns was intended to carry further the benefits of the kolkhoz amalgamation in terms of both mechanisation and political control. It would also reduce the role of the peasants' private plots in agriculture, since these were to be smaller and located outside the agrotowns.

Khrushchev disliked the private plots, which peasants were still allowed to work for their own profit. They had been a small concession to the peasantry during collectivisation, but Khrushchev believed that many peasants made good incomes from their plots while shirking their share of collective labour on kolkhoz lands.[73]

Khrushchev had overreached himself. On the following day the newspapers carried a disclaimer explaining that his proposals had been published 'only as a basis for discussion'.[74] No discussion followed, however, and the proposal was quietly dropped. The speed of this reversal is surprising, given that Khrushchev's scheme had been under discussion for two months; it had been foreshadowed by *Moskovskaia pravda* on 6 January and elaborated in a speech by Khrushchev on 18 January. The article on 4 March was thus no surprise to anyone in the leadership; it was cleared in advance only to be disavowed a day later, which suggests that its publication was permitted only in order to let Khrushchev go out on a limb before humiliating him.

A Politburo resolution was adopted on the basis of a report prepared for Malenkov by D. T. Shepilov and I. D. Laptev. It criticised the agrotown scheme for a number of ideological sins. Khrushchev's proposed reorganisation of peasant life, it charged, embodied a 'consumerist approach', ignoring the 'main and defining role' of production in the development of society; its conception of the contradictions between urban and rural sectors was 'unscientific'; and it violated the principle of 'the combination of personal and social interests' by subordinating the general interest to peasants' personal needs.[75] I. A. Benediktov, who was USSR Minister of Agriculture at the time, recalled later that Stalin himself had dismissed the proposal as 'the pure water of hare-brained scheming', a product of Khrushchev's 'mania for endless reorganisations'.[76]

Khrushchev acknowledged his errors to the Politburo, and by the end of March even MK had adopted a resolution criticising the agrotown idea and annulling the December 1950 resolution which had laid the groundwork for it.[77] Khrushchev himself practically vanished from public view for several weeks and was still on the defensive in the summer of 1952, when he told the Moscow party conference that 'in the conduct of work on the amalgamation of collective farms shortcomings and mistakes were permitted; these consisted of an incorrect consumerist approach to questions of collective farm construction and attempts to force the massive resettlement of villagers into large collective farm settlements'.[78] Malenkov criticised the scheme at the Nineteenth Party Congress a few weeks later.[79]

The agrotown episode was not a complete disaster for Khrushchev, however. He had demonstrated a willingness to take the initiative and advance innovative policies without awaiting Stalin's orders. And though the agrotown adventure may have seemed more foolhardy than bold at the time, Khrushchev reacted quickly enough; he admitted his mistakes, dropped the proposal and survived. Moreover, it is significant that although the proposal ignored both economic reality and the psychology of the peasants, it was criticised chiefly on *doctrinal* rather than practical grounds. The fact that it addressed the living conditions of farm workers *at all* was its principal offence; from a Stalinist viewpoint the most serious criticism was the charge of a 'consumerist' rather than 'production-oriented' approach. Soviet economic policy for two decades had been geared to extracting as much as possible from the countryside while giving as little as possible in return. The agrotown scheme was the first indication that Khrushchev wished to improve the lot of the long-suffering peasants.

Khrushchev was relieved of responsibility for agricultural policy in the Central Committee Secretariat after the agrotown episode, but he remained responsible for Moscow province's farming sector. In this capacity he began to interfere increasingly in purely technical matters, of which he often had little understanding. In particular, he pushed specific methods of sowing potatoes, cucumbers, cabbages and tomatoes.[80] In Moscow as in Ukraine he campaigned against the 'squandering' of kolkhoz land and property, which continued to be appropriated by kolkhoz members for private use.[81] He also supported efforts to increase the educational levels of leading workers on the farms and to provide them with more specialists; Khrushchev had devoted considerable attention to this issue during his previous tenure as Moscow party boss. As in the past, however, he

stressed that emphasis on education should not lead one
to underestimate the value of 'practical men trained up by
the party and the collective farm, who, although they
lack specialised education, have great practical experience
and know how to run collective farms and obtain good
results'.[82]

The public bullying of subordinates which had been in
evidence in Ukraine continued in Moscow. When a farm
director addressing an agricultural conference disagreed
with Khrushchev concerning the relevance of certain
problems, Khrushchev kept him at the rostrum for over an
hour, firing question after question at him in an effort to
catch him out. When after more than sixty highly technical
questions, the director admitted that he did not know an
answer, Khrushchev heaped abuse on him. A district
agricultural official who called for more investment in rural
construction was subjected to a similar public interrogation.
Speakers were told that their views were 'nonsense', and
Khrushchev often called publicly for legal indictments,
expulsions from the party and other punishments. One
speaker who tried to defend his position was told, 'You are
lying; I am not mistaken', and dismissed from the rostrum.
When the need to define the rights and duties of agronomists attached to the kolkhozes was raised, Khrushchev
replied, 'It is a nonsensical question. What do rights and
obligations mean? If he is a clever agronomist, everyone
will listen to him.'[83]

Every aspect of Khrushchev's life and work during this
period was overshadowed by the presence of Stalin. In Kiev
he had been the king; now he was merely a member of the
court – not infrequently the jester. Even Stalin's sleeping
habits shaped those of his lieutenants. His nocturnal ways
meant that senior officials had to work long, late and often
irregular hours; a midnight telephone call from the vozhd'
must not find them away from their desks. For those chosen
to be Stalin's dinner companions, the burden was even
greater. Khrushchev tried to nap daily at lunchtime for fear
of appearing sleepy in the master's presence. Stalin would
summon his associates to the Kremlin during the afternoon. There they would watch foreign films – chiefly
American westerns – for hours at a time, discussing busi-

ness between reels. When the last film ended, often at one or two in the morning, Stalin would then 'invite' them to join him for dinner at his dacha; attendance at dinner was mandatory, as was heavy drinking. This was in part Stalin's way of finding out what his colleagues were really thinking, but it also appears that he simply enjoyed getting them drunk.

He undoubtedly enjoyed humiliating them. On one famous occasion he ordered Khrushchev, then approaching sixty, to perform the *gopak*, a Ukrainian folk dance, in front of a group of high party officials. This was both embarrassing and physically uncomfortable for Khrushchev, but he pretended to enjoy it. As he later remarked to Mikoian, 'When Stalin says dance, a wise man dances.' When dining with his colleagues Stalin insisted that someone else be the first to taste each dish served, yet another sign of his growing paranoia. At various times he accused Voroshilov, Mikoian and Molotov of being foreign agents, and he had ceased to trust Beria long before 1953. While business was sometimes discussed at these all-night sessions, Khrushchev believed that their principal aim was to occupy Stalin's time and help him combat his loneliness.[84]

Stalin's deteriorating mental and physical condition made the jockeying among those who would succeed him all the more intense. Much of the history of post-war Soviet politics is the history of various factional struggles waged between rival pretenders to the role of heir-apparent. From 1946 to 1949 the chief axis of conflict was between Andrei Zhdanov and his supporters on the one hand and a faction led by Malenkov on the other. Malenkov sustained some serious defeats, and for a time was expelled from the leadership altogether, but with the help of the secret police chief, Lavrentii Beria, he soon recovered.[85] Zhdanov died in 1948, and the Malenkov–Beria team destroyed his heirs the following year in the infamous Leningrad Case.[86] The years that followed witnessed other local 'cases', including the Mingrelian Case and the Crimean Case. Khrushchev's position in this conflict is unclear; he was not closely associated with either side. It appears that Stalin recalled him to Moscow in 1949 to restore the balance upset by the destruction of the Zhdanovites.

Stalin's principal target in 1951-2 was Beria, who, in addition to overseeing the organs of state security for more than a decade, had also been Stalin's vicar in the Transcaucasian republics. Beria's close associate, V. S. Abakumov, was removed from his post as Minister for State Security and replaced by S. D. Ignat'ev, a man with no connections to Beria. Beria clients were removed from office (and in some cases shot) in an extensive purge of the Georgian leadership; it was against Beria and his supporters that the case of the so-called Mingrelian Nationalist Organisation was fabricated.[87] Khrushchev was uninvolved in these affairs, though he later admitted that he may have signed the death warrants:

> In those days when a case was closed – and if Stalin thought it necessary – he would sign the sentencing order at a Politburo session and then pass it around for the rest of us to sign. We put our signatures on it without even looking at it. That's what was meant by 'collective sentencing'.[88]

In January 1953, less than two months before Stalin's death, *Pravda* announced the arrest of a group of doctors accused of sabotaging the health of leading political and military figures; they were said to have killed Zhdanov and hastened the death of another Politburo member, A. S. Shcherbakov. Acting as agents of foreign powers they had also conspired to undermine the health of a number of leading military officers.[89] The case was a fabrication, as was acknowledged after Stalin's death; it appears to have been the prelude to a new purge in which Stalin intended to destroy many of his Politburo lieutenants, including Beria, Molotov and Mikoian. The first steps in arranging such a purge had already been taken at the Nineteenth Party Congress the previous October, and it is necessary to consider the Congress in some detail before returning to the case of the Kremlin doctors.

The decision to call the Nineteenth Congress came as a surprise to Stalin's colleagues. The party statutes called for a congress to be held every three years, but it had been more than thirteen since the Eighteenth Congress; the

Central Committee had not been convened since February 1947. Stalin chose Malenkov to deliver the General Report of the Central Committee to the Congress, thus confirming Malenkov's status as heir-apparent; the report on the Fifth Five-Year Plan was assigned to M. Z. Saburov, a Malenkov associate who had become Chairman of the USSR State Planning Commission after his predecessor, Nikolai Voznesenskii, was arrested in connection with the Leningrad Case in 1949. Khrushchev was assigned the report on changes in the party statutes.[90] He modelled his report on a similar report given by Zhdanov at the Eighteenth Congress in 1939, padding it with numerous examples to illustrate each of his points. At Beria's insistence the original draft of the report was shortened by eliminating these examples. As a result, the most important speech of Khrushchev's career to that time lasted only about an hour – extremely short by the standards of party congresses.[91]

The ideological climate in the run-up to the Congress recalled the late 1930s and the years of Zhdanov's post-war crackdown. Calls for discipline and vigilance against enemies became increasingly common in the press, and particular stress was laid on the protection of state and kolkhoz property. Khrushchev echoed these themes in his report to the Moscow party conference preceding the Congress, a report which was otherwise remarkable only for its lukewarm praise of Stalin, who was scarcely mentioned.[92] When Khrushchev stated that the Soviet people were 'indebted for all their victories to the wise leadership of the party and its Leninist-Stalinist Central Committee',[93] the omission of Stalin himself was difficult to miss. Khrushchev understood that Stalin, who had been in poor health for some time, would soon die. The time had come to carve out a slightly more independent political identity.

Khrushchev was somewhat freer in his praise of Stalin when delivering his report on changes in the party statutes to the Congress. He was also more aggressive on the vigilance issue:

Many people, carried away by economic successes, forget the instructions of the party on the need to take every measure to increase vigilance. We must always remember capitalist encirclement, remember that the enemies of our socialist state have tried and will continue to try to send their agents into our country to do subversive work. In order to achieve their base aims, they try to . . . take advantage of careless chatterboxes who do not know how to keep party and state secrets.[94]

Nationality policy was also an unusually prominent theme both before and during the congress, as attacks on 'bourgeois nationalism' multiplied. There was no mention, however, of the corresponding sin of the Russians, 'Great Russian Chauvinism'. This was entirely consistent with post-war Soviet nationality policy, which had been uncompromisingly, even stridently pro-Russian. The tone was set by Stalin's victory toast, offered at a Kremlin banquet on 24 May 1945:

I should like to propose a toast to the health of our Soviet people and above all of our Russian people. I drink in particular to the health of the Russian people because it is the most outstanding of all the nations of the Soviet Union. . . . Russia in the war has won the right to be recognised as the leader of the whole Union.

Stalin went on to praise the 'lucidity, strength of character and patience' of the Russians.[95] Since Zhdanov's death, deviations in nationality policy had been at the centre of a number of bloody purge operations, including the Mingrelian and Leningrad cases; its prominence in the autumn of 1952 therefore had sinister implications. Moreover, a number of speakers addressing the issue at the local party conferences preceding the congress made the unusual claim that they were acting on Stalin's personal instructions.[96] At the congress itself, no fewer than twenty-three speakers condemned bourgeois nationalism.[97]

The combination of vigilance, discipline and Russian nationalism in the propaganda preceding the Congress is

exactly what might be expected if Stalin wished to create a
political atmosphere suitable for launching another top-
level purge. Mikoian, Molotov, Voroshilov and Beria were
already under threat, and Stalin's actions suggest that an
even wider purge was planned. Immediately after the
Congress, the new Central Committee met to 'elect' a new
Politburo. Stalin, who had only briefly addressed the
Nineteenth Congress, opened the plenum with a proposal
to replace the Politburo, which had eleven full members
and one candidate member, with a Presidium of twenty-five
members and eleven candidates. He then read off the list
of those to be included in the new body. The size of the
Secretariat was doubled from five to ten. Both the proposal
and the nominations were unanimously accepted without
debate. As Khrushchev observed,

> When Stalin proposed something, there were no ques-
> tions, no comments. A 'proposal' from Stalin was a God-
> given command, and you don't haggle about what God
> tells you to do – you just offer thanks and obey.

Stalin also proposed the creation of a Bureau of the Presidium, which included himself, Malenkov, Beria, Khrushchev, Kaganovich, Saburov, Pervukhin and, surprisingly,
Voroshilov. Molotov and Mikoian were excluded.[98]
The creation of the new Presidium effectively down-
graded all of the members of the old Politburo, who were
now, formally at least, on an equal footing with men who
had previously been their subordinates. The enlargement of
the party's highest body also provided Stalin with a pool
of new men whom he could advance to key posts at the
expense of his older comrades. The composition of the
Presidium underscored the seniority of Khrushchev and
Malenkov among Stalin's associates: they alone among the
members of the Presidium (apart from Stalin) had clearly
identifiable clients included in its ranks. Seven members
and three candidates of the Presidium were close associates,
if not clients, of Malenkov. One member and one candidate were obvious 'Khrushchev men' in 1952; a number of
others were to enjoy his favour in later years and may
already have been close to him.[99] Khrushchev nevertheless

insists that no other members of the old Politburo – with the possible exception of Kaganovich – played a part in either the proposal to create a Presidium or the selection of its members.[100]

The vigilance campaign continued into the new year and reached a climax when the arrest of the Kremlin doctors was announced. The announcement triggered a further intensification of the campaign, which grew increasingly anti-Semitic. A number of major economic ministries came under attack for 'slackness' and indiscipline, and attacks on bourgeois nationalism in the non-Russian republics also continued. Interestingly, the leading roles in this campaign were played by junior members of the leading group, including M. A. Suslov, N. A. Mikhailov and F. R. Kozlov.[101] Kozlov published an article in *Kommunist*, the party's main theoretical journal, hinting that another great purge was in the offing.[102] The members of the old Politburo, including Khrushchev, all but disappeared from the central press.

Khrushchev and his colleagues were now in no doubt that another purge was in the works; the identity of the intended victims, however, was unclear. Beria, Molotov, Mikoian and Voroshilov were undoubtedly under threat, and others may also have been in danger. Unless it is assumed that Stalin intended to exterminate completely the members of the old Politburo, however, there is no reason to count Khrushchev and Malenkov among the intended victims. Both had apparently been in Stalin's good graces at the time of the Congress: each had delivered a key report and their associates had been promoted. Neither ever claimed later to have believed that he was in danger of removal or arrest.[103] Khrushchev, who discusses the danger that others were in at this time, might have been expected to make such claims in his speech to the 1956 Congress, the so-called Secret Speech, or in his memoirs. It is with this in mind that the evidence linking Khrushchev and Malenkov to the Doctors' Plot must be considered.

The case against the doctors was acknowledged to be a fabrication after Stalin died. Significantly, it was denounced as a fraud by the Ministry of Internal Affairs, not the Central Committee or the Council of Ministers; Beria was therefore the only member of the leadership personally associated with the decision.[104] Khrushchev made no attempt to use the Doctors' Plot (as he did the Leningrad Case) against Malenkov during their power struggle in 1954–5.[105] Discussion of the case would have been as awkward for Khrushchev as for Malenkov.[106] The doctors were 'unmasked' by the Ministry for State Security, then under Beria's enemy, S. D. Ignat'ev; Ignat'ev was sacked from the party's leading organs organs after the plot was denounced but became first secretary of Bashkiria after Beria's fall. Andrei Malenkov identifies Ignat'ev as a client of his father,[107] but Ignat'ev did not suffer any political setback at the time of Malenkov's demotions in 1955 and 1957. Khrushchev speaks well of Ignat'ev in his memoirs and defends Ignat'ev's role in the Doctors' Plot, insisting that he was under intense pressure from Stalin to conduct the case.[108] After Beria's fall it was not Ignat'ev but ex-Deputy Minister for State Security M. D. Riumin who was tried and executed for fabricating the plot.[109] Finally, a number of officials who appear to have been marked for advancement in connection with the purge and who suffered reverses when it was aborted were promoted again to important posts by Khrushchev and Malenkov after Beria's fall.[110]

It would be going far beyond what the evidence warrants to suggest that Malenkov or Khrushchev engineered the Doctors' Plot or other moves in the direction of another Great Purge. It is difficult to see either man as being enthusiastic about the Zhdanovite tone of propaganda at the time, and the campaign against slackness and indiscipline was directed to a great extent against the economic ministries, which formed Malenkov's political base. Many of those marked out for advancement in the planned purge had no links to either man. It is much more likely that Malenkov and Khrushchev co-operated with Stalin in preparing the ground for Beria's political and physical demise. Their joint participation ensured that the Doctors' Plot would never become a weapon in the struggle between them in the way that the Leningrad Case eventually did.

The full scale of the planned purge will never be known, for Stalin died before it could be executed. On 28 February he dined with Khrushchev, Malenkov, Bulganin and Beria at his dacha. The dinner lasted until four in the morning; Stalin drank heavily and grew irritated with his companions; there were members of the leadership, he said, who believed that they could get by on their past merits, but they were mistaken. When he finally broke off his monologue and went to bed, the others went to their cars and returned to Moscow. Sometime during the night the old man suffered a stroke. The staff and security detail at the dacha began to worry at noon on 1 March but dared not disturb their boss. At 6.30 p.m. a light went on in the bedroom, and all breathed a sigh of relief. There were no further signs of life from the room, however, and at 11 p.m. two of Stalin's bodyguards and his maid at last entered the room and found him on the floor, partially paralysed and unable to speak. They lifted him onto the divan and telephoned Minister for State Security Ignat'ev.[111]

Ignat'ev told them to phone Beria and Malenkov, but Beria, whose permission was required before any doctors could be summoned, was nowhere to be found, and Malenkov would not act without him. Finally Beria was located, and he and Malenkov went to the dacha; it was by then about 3 a.m. on 2 March. Beria quickly examined the dictator and sharply rebuked the staff, telling them that Stalin was obviously asleep and ought not to be disturbed. He and Malenkov then left. When Stalin's condition did not change, they were called to the dacha again, this time bringing Khrushchev with them; they arrived around 9 a.m. on 3 March. The other members of the Bureau of the Presidium soon followed and doctors were finally called – forty-eight hours or more after Stalin suffered his stroke. Beria threatened them loudly in an effort to demonstrate his loyalty to Stalin; the doctors needed no reminder that if their patient died, it could cost them their lives. At some point Molotov and Mikoian were also summoned.

For the next two days, while Stalin lay dying, the members of the leadership stood watch over him in turns. After Stalin lost consciousness, Beria made little effort to conceal his joy at the imminent demise of the vozhd'. According to Khrushchev,

No sooner had Stalin fallen ill than Beria started going

around spewing hatred against him and mocking him.
. . . as soon as Stalin showed . . . signs of consciousness
and made us think he might recover, Beria threw himself
on his knees, seized Stalin's hand and started kissing it.
When Stalin lost consciousness again . . . Beria stood up
and spat.[112]

Khrushchev's account may well be an exaggeration, but
other witnesses noticed Beria's obvious pleasure at the
dictator's death.[113] Stalin's senior lieutenants also plotted
their next moves as they waited for him to die. Khrushchev
and Bulganin discussed the danger posed by Beria, while
Malenkov appears to have come to some agreement with
the secret police chief. The end came at 9.50 a.m. on 5
March 1953. As soon as it was clear that Stalin was dead,
Beria ran to his car and raced back to Moscow. Khrushchev,
Voroshilov, Kaganovich and others wept openly for a time,
but soon they followed Beria back to the city. The post-
Stalin era had begun.

5 First among Equals
Struggles within the Presidium, 1953–5

We were scared – really scared. We were afraid the thaw might unleash a flood, which we wouldn't be able to control and which could drown us. How could it drown us? It could have overflowed the banks of the Soviet riverbed and formed a tidal wave which would have washed away all the barriers and retaining walls of our society.

Khrushchev Remembers: The Last Testament[1]

Stalin's death was made public on 6 March 1953.[2] That evening the decisions of a joint meeting of the USSR Council of Ministers, the Presidium of the USSR Supreme Soviet and the Central Committee were announced. On the surface everything appeared to bode well for a smooth and speedy succession: Malenkov was named Chairman of the Council of Ministers, while retaining his position in the Secretariat; Beria, Molotov, Bulganin and Kaganovich were all named as first vice-chairmen. Beria's new lease on life was further confirmed by his appointment as Minister of Internal Affairs; he also took charge of the former Ministry of State Security (MGB), which was merged into the Ministry of Internal Affairs (MVD). Khrushchev was released from his duties as First Secretary of the Moscow Committee of the party in order to concentrate on his duties in the Central Committee Secretariat. The selection of Malenkov, Beria and Molotov as the funeral orators created the impression that these three formed a new leading triumvirate; Khrushchev's appointment to head the commission charged with organising the funeral was generally overlooked.[3]

The new party Presidium and Secretariat were also announced. At a stroke Stalin's surviving lieutenants reversed the October 1952 plenum. The Presidium was reduced from twenty-five members and eleven candidates to ten and four respectively; the number of Secretaries fell from ten to eight. The new men elevated by Stalin after the Nineteenth Congress were demoted *en masse*. The full membership of the Presidium consisted of those who had been in the Bureau of the Presidium since October, plus Molotov and Mikoian.[4] The new line-up looked extremely promising for Malenkov; three of the secretaries and four of the Presidium members and candidates had risen to high office with his assistance.[5]

Khrushchev later claimed that Malenkov and Beria had agreed in advance the first steps to be taken following Stalin's death and had simply presented their colleagues with a *fait accompli*.[6] This is entirely plausible. The other members of the leadership feared Beria's power over the security organs and would have been especially anxious to avoid open conflict with him at a time of such uncertainty. After Beria's arrest Khrushchev told the Central Committee that the leadership had needed to 'close ranks' when Stalin died and that an attack on Beria at that point would therefore have been 'ill-timed'.[7] The new leaders' sense of insecurity was underscored in a joint party–government statement on 6 March which demanded 'the greatest unity of leadership and the prevention of any kind of disarray and panic'.[8] The population was in no less a state of shock than the leadership. When the House of Unions was opened for citizens to pay their last respects, the authorities were unprepared for the throngs of people. Hundreds perished as a result of the disorders which occurred. Khrushchev, as chairman of the funeral commission, was among those responsible for the poor planning which led to this tragedy.[9]

The downgrading of the late vozhd' began with his funeral on 9 March. In contrast to Molotov, who remained faithful to his master, Malenkov and Beria were extremely restrained in their praise of Stalin.[10] When the USSR's rubber-stamp legislature, the Supreme Soviet, convened on 15 March, the tribute paid to Stalin was no greater than that given to Czechoslovak communist leader Klement Gottwald, who had drunk himself to death the day before.[11] Stalin's name and portrait began to disappear from the central press. For a few days, a Malenkov cult seemed to be emerging. He was widely quoted in the central press, and his report to the Nineteenth Congress was treated as an authoritative statement of party policy. *Pravda* carried his picture three times in as many days; on 10 March it carried an old photograph of a large group of Soviet and Chinese leaders which had been doctored to show only Stalin, Mao and Malenkov standing side by side.[12]

The faked picture caused Malenkov acute embarrassment in front of his colleagues. At a Presidium meeting on 10 March he condemned it and cited it as an example of the incorrect practices which had developed as a result of the cult of personality. Malenkov's denunciation of the photograph may have been sincere: the conventional assumption has been that he was behind its publication, but the picture may actually have been intended to damage him politically. The Presidium in any case agreed that the cult of the leader must be ended and appointed Central Committee Secretary P. N. Pospelov to oversee the press in this connection. Khrushchev was instructed to monitor publications, films and other materials being prepared to commemorate Stalin.[13]

Khrushchev's attitude toward Stalin was somewhat contradictory at this time. He came down hard on Konstantin Simonov, the editor of *Literaturnaia gazeta*, over an editorial on 19 March which called on writers to 'render the image of Stalin immortal'.[14] At the 10 March Presidium meeting, he told his colleagues, 'I, Khrushchev, you, Klim, you, Lazar, you, Viacheslav Mikhailovich – we should all offer repentance to the people for 1937.'[15] On 16 April, a *Pravda* article by L. Slepov, a man with ties to Khrushchev, proclaimed 'collectivity' the highest principle of party leadership. Slepov's discussion of violations of this principle in party life was an unmistakeable indictment of Stalin's leadership, although Stalin was not mentioned by name. These actions contrast sharply with Khrushchev's proposal to display Stalin's body alongside Lenin's in the mausoleum on Red Square and his later idea of building a Soviet 'pantheon', in which Stalin and other great Bolsheviks could be buried.[16] Khrushchev was also initially in favour of proposals to change the name of the Leninist Communist

Youth League to the Leninist-Stalinist Communist Youth League and to transform Stalin's dacha into a museum.[17]

Malenkov's apparently smooth assumption of Stalin's mantle was disrupted on 14 March. A second Central Committee meeting agreed 'to grant the request of Chairman of the USSR Council of Ministers G. M. Malenkov to be released from the duties of Secretary of the Party Central Committee'.[18] In all likelihood Malenkov was forced by Presidium colleagues to choose between his party and government posts. This was a major victory for Khrushchev, who was henceforth the senior member of the Central Committee Secretariat, although he as yet had no title to distinguish him from the other secretaries. Along with Malenkov he set the agenda for Presidium meetings.[19]

As many in the outside world had surmised, the leadership was now dominated by three men – not by the three funeral orators, however, but by Malenkov, Beria and Khrushchev. Formally Georgii Malenkov was first among this trio of equals; he was head of government, and in this capacity he chaired meetings of the Presidium, now the most powerful political institution in the country. Malenkov was no ideologue; throughout his career he had been concerned less with theory and ideology than with the efficient, practical management of affairs. He had a considerable power base among the managers and administrators of the economic ministries, who shared his commitment to a rational, commonsense approach to management. Some have regarded him as leading a constituency of would-be technocrats.[20]

Lavrentii Beria had made his career in party and secret police organs in Transcaucasia before being brought to Moscow to replace Ezhov as NKVD chief in 1938. Malenkov, then working in the Central Committee's Department for Leading Party Organs, offered his name to Stalin as a suitable candidate for the post.[21] This was the beginning of a long and successful political alliance. In 1946 Beria was able to return Malenkov's favour; Stalin had demoted Malenkov and sent him to work in the east, and Beria played a key role in Malenkov's return to Moscow and the central leadership. From then on, according to Malenkov's long-time aide D. N. Sukhanov, Beria dominated their partnership.[22] The Malenkov–Beria alliance came under strain in 1951–2 when Malenkov's position as heir-apparent was being confirmed, while Stalin (not without Malenkov's co-operation) prepared to destroy Beria. It was renewed after Stalin died but did not last long.[23]

Although he had not actually been Minister of Internal Affairs since 1946, Beria was the Politburo member responsible for the security organs throughout the post-war period. In 1951–2 Stalin had replaced many Beria clients in the MVD and MGB, but these new officials were unable to hold their positions once their patron was dead. Beria conducted a swift purge of central and republican security officials.[24] He likewise replaced the leadership which Stalin had installed in Georgia to weaken Beria's grip on that republic.[25]

Control of the MVD provided Beria with enormous power. He had under his authority several hundred thousand uniformed security troops, including tanks and armoured personnel carriers, the border guards, a small air-force, the Soviet atomic weapons programme, the uniformed police and a substantial economic empire run with the slave labour of the GULAG. He was also in a position to spy on his colleagues and their subordinates, as indeed he did.[26] Yet even this state within a state was insufficient as a basis for seizing power. Beria needed more than brute force to back him up; he needed a policy programme which would attract enough support among the élite that he might take power as something more than an armed bandit or terrorist. Beria was thus the most active of the three in advancing his own policy initiatives.

In his funeral speech, Beria had devoted considerable attention to the constitutional rights of Soviet citizens, an issue neither Molotov nor Malenkov addressed. It was Beria who proposed the amnesty declared at the end of March for certain categories of prisoners.[27] This was calculated to trigger an influx of common criminals into the major cities, giving Beria a pretext to maintain an MVD troop presence in them. It also enabled him to free certain of his associates who had been imprisoned by Stalin. In early April the Doctors' Plot was renounced as a fraud by the MVD itself, rather than by the government or the Central Committee.[28]

This ensured that the decision would be identified with Beria. In the weeks that followed, a number of other articles stressing the inviolability of the rights of Soviet citizens appeared in the press; several singled out the MVD for praise in connection with the amnesty and the repudiation of the Doctors' Plot.[29]

Beria's most potent policy weapon was the nationalities issue. At the Nineteenth Congress he had taken a strong pro-minority stand, diametrically opposed to the Russo-centric line of the other speakers.[30] In his funeral oration Beria again addressed the nationalities issue at length, taking a much more liberal line than Malenkov or Molotov.[31] In the weeks that followed, the nationalities problem received a great deal of attention in the press. In May and June attention shifted from broad statements about nationality policy to the specific question of training and promoting non-Russian officials in the republics, a matter which Beria had raised at the Nineteenth Congress. Beria persuaded the Presidium to adopt a resolution calling for first secretary in every republic to be a member of the titular nationality of the republic.[32] Other decrees called for the conduct of official correspondence in local languages and the replacement of officials who did not know the local tongues of the places where they served.[33]

If strictly applied, these decisions would have led to the removal from office of thousands of Russian officials and their replacement by non-Russians who would have owed their appointments to Beria. In the space of a few months he would have constructed for himself a following among party and state functionaries which would otherwise have taken years to build. The most significant immediate result of this pressure was the removal of Khrushchev's successor in Kiev, L. G. Mel'nikov. Mel'nikov was a Russian and a Malenkov supporter. Among the errors for which he was criticised at the time of his removal were sending too many Russian officials to Western Ukraine and converting its institutions of higher education to Russian-language instruction.[34] A number of other personnel changes in Ukraine followed soon after, and party leaders across the republic were criticised for sins similar to Mel'nikov's.[35] In Latvia and Lithuania Russians in key posts were charged with violations of the party's nationality policy and replaced by native cadres.³⁶ In Belorussia Second Secretary M. V. Zimianin was to replace the Russian N. S. Patolichev as First Secretary. The Belorussian Central Committee backed Patolichev in defiance of Moscow, however, and were supported in their protest by Khrushchev. Beria's arrest settled the issue in Patolichev's favour.³⁷

Beria also pressed for a revision of policy on Germany. It is not clear how far he deviated from Stalin's line on this issue. East German defectors reported that Beria was engineering a change of leadership in East Berlin and that he wished to compel the GDR to adopt more liberal policies at home and abroad. They regarded Beria as responsible for the Soviet delay in responding to an East German request for troops when a rising in East Berlin erupted on 16 June.³⁸ His Soviet colleagues, however, charged that Beria's policies would have led to the eventual liquidation of the GDR.³⁹ This is not as implausible as it sounds; for a time after World War II Moscow had considered the possibility that its security interests would be better served by a united Germany, neutral and disarmed, than by the creation of two German states. Beria may have held this view in 1953. He was also accused of unauthorised attempts to move towards a normalisation of relations with Yugoslavia, which had been anathema to Moscow since 1948.⁴⁰

Khrushchev for much of the spring feigned friendship for Beria in order to protect himself and find out what Beria was planning.⁴¹ Khrushchev backed Beria's purge of the Ukrainian leadership in June; Mel'nikov was replaced as First Secretary by A. I. Kirichenko, a Khrushchev client. At the same time, however, Khrushchev was receiving reports on Beria's activities in Ukraine and elsewhere. In June Lt.-Gen. T. A. Strokach, the former Ukrainian partisan commander and longstanding acquaintance of Khrushchev, was relieved by Beria of his position as the MVD chief for L'vov Province in Ukraine. He was summoned to Moscow, where he expected to be arrested, but before Beria could act, Strokach submitted a detailed report on Beria's use of the MVD apparatus in Ukraine to spy on and undermine local party organs.⁴² Similar information was reaching Khrushchev from other sources. Sometime in the late spring Khrushchev approached Malenkov about the need to block Beria's initiatives; the premier agreed to support him, and Beria suffered a number of defeats at the next few Presidium meetings.[43] This provided Khrushchev with an opportunity to test the degree of support he might expect from other Presidium members.

Finally Khrushchev persuaded Malenkov that the time had come to remove Beria from office altogether. They began to lobby other members of the Presidium. This was no simple matter owing to the fear which Beria inspired in his colleagues and their awareness that his operatives might be bugging their conversations at any given moment. Khrushchev's first visit with Voroshilov came to nothing on account of the latter's fear of 'Beria's ears'. One by one, however, Malenkov and Khrushchev secured the support of the other Presidium members. All that remained was to set and spring the trap before word of what was afoot could reach Beria.[44] The sense of urgency about the plot was reinforced by reports that Beria was secretly concentrating military forces around Moscow and taking other measures to prepare a coup.[45]

The arrest took place at a Presidium meeting on 26 June. Khrushchev and his allies were prepared for a possible civil war. The Commandant of the Kremlin summoned to the capital units under his son's command, and the cadets of a Moscow military academy were mobilised. A division of MVD troops at Lefortovo prison was surrounded by regular army units. When the Presidium meeting opened in the Kremlin, Marshal Zhukov and General K. S. Moskalenko, the acting commander of the Moscow Military District,[46] were waiting in the next room with a group of hand-picked officers. They were to enter the meeting room at a signal from Malenkov and arrest Beria.

Malenkov chaired the meeting and read out a report on Beria's activities. Beria was charged with having been an English agent in the 1920s as well as preparing to seize power in the months since Stalin's death. What happened next is unclear. According to Khrushchev and Molotov, several other Presidium members then spoke in turn; these included Khrushchev, Molotov, Bulganin and Mikoian;

Mikoian advocated allowing Beria to reform himself and remain in the collective leadership.[47] Molotov claimed that Beria himself addressed the meeting and asked not to be expelled from the party; while Beria was speaking, Malenkov pressed the bell summoning the officers.[48] According to Khrushchev, Malenkov, who was supposed to sum up the discussion before summoning Zhukov and his men, lost his nerve and failed to do so. Khrushchev took the floor and proposed that Beria be released from all his posts; while he was speaking, Malenkov, by then in a state of panic, summoned the officers.[49]

In any case, the officers entered the meeting at Malenkov's signal and arrested Beria. He was held in the Kremlin until late at night, when he could be moved in secret to a secure location; in the days that followed he was moved from place to place for reasons of security and secrecy. On 27 June the MVD guards in the Kremlin were replaced by regular army officers and the military took temporary control of the MVD building. Beria's arrest was not announced until 10 July, several days after the Central Committee had discussed the case. He was tried in secret along with five of his closest supporters; all six were executed in December 1953.[50] Although no one knew it at the time, Beria's fall marked the end of an era in Soviet politics: the competition for power was never again a struggle in which the losers died, and police terror was never again used against members of the ruling élite. This was perhaps the most significant change in Soviet politics after Stalin's death, for it meant that Khrushchev and his colleagues were deprived of the most potent instrument Stalin had possessed to ensure the loyalty and subservience of the élite.

The Beria case was discussed at a Central Committee meeting on 2–7 July. Malenkov gave the initial report, charging Beria with abusing his power as Minister of Internal Affairs, spying on his colleagues, conducting an independent foreign policy through MVD channels, misusing his authority over the atomic weapons programme and manipulating the amnesty and rehabilitation processes to increase his own power.[51] Molotov accused Beria of fostering dissension among the peoples of the USSR, while

Khrushchev added that Beria had worked to obstruct the resolution of problems connected with agriculture.[52] The agricultural policies at issue were not specified, which suggests that Khrushchev was simply taking advantage of the opportunity to blame the country's food-supply problems on Beria.

The agricultural connection also enabled him for the first time to draw attention to the sorry state of agriculture and to express his own bread-and-butter view of socialism. He worried about the impact of shortages of meat, milk, potatoes and cabbage on the international standing of the USSR: 'After all, our friends may say to us, "Listen, dear comrades, you are trying to teach us to build socialism, but you don't know how to raise potatoes in your own country, you cannot provide for the people, there is no cabbage in your capital".'[53] This is typical of Khrushchev's approach to foreign relations. His own faith in the Soviet system was born of experience, not theory, and he was convinced that it was Soviet achievements rather than Soviet ideas which would impress other countries and lead them to emulate the USSR.

The discussion of Beria's case at the July plenum did serious damage to Stalin's reputation. The Presidium members who spoke presented him not as a criminal or tyrant but as an ailing and out-of-touch old man who had been easily manipulated by the evil Beria.[54] Khrushchev's comments were typical: 'We all respect Comrade Stalin, but the years take their toll. In his last years Comrade Stalin did not read state papers, he did not receive people, because his health was weak. The scoundrel Beria used this condition adroitly, very adroitly.'[55] Malenkov and Molotov specifically included Stalin among those whose lack of vigilance had allowed Beria to remain so long in high posts. Molotov admitted that 'Beria found certain human weaknesses in I. V. Stalin, but who does not have them? He was able to exploit these adroitly for a number of years.'[56] The effect of this line was twofold: first, it punctured the myth of Stalin's infallibility forever; secondly, it tied the leaders' hands with respect to the Stalin question. It was easy to blame Stalin's mistakes on Beria in July 1953, but it soon became clear that the decision to do so had reduced their freedom of manoeuvre.

These criticisms of Stalin and the cult were publicised in more general terms in the weeks that followed. Stalin was not criticised by name, but the central press carried a number of articles decrying the cult of personality.[57] A party history published shortly after the plenum called for the elimination of 'the incorrect, un-Marxist interpretation of the role of the individual in history, which is expressed in propaganda by the idealist theory of the cult of personality, which is alien to Marxism'.[58]

Anxious to prevent a repetition of the crisis just passed, the Khrushchev–Malenkov leadership rapidly dismantled Beria's MVD empire. The security services were again taken out of the jurisdiction of the Ministry of Internal Affairs and reorganised into the Committee for State Security (KGB). The KGB was subordinated directly to the Central Committee in order to ensure that the secret police remained accountable to the party, and was also deprived of the powers which its predecessors had enjoyed to try, sentence and punish; it could only investigate and arrest. A separate Ministry of Medium Machine Building was established to run the atomic weapons programme.

The elimination of Beria removed one contender for Stalin's mantle, but it did not resolve the succession. The praise for the virtues of collective leadership which appeared in the press thus reflected necessity as well as preference.[59] Khrushchev and Malenkov remained rivals in the leadership, dividing between them authority over party and state. Victory in the struggle between them would depend not only on their skill in factional manoeuvring but also on their ability to address the pressures for change which the regime as a whole faced. There was pressure for change from at least three sources. First, there was the pressure to raise living standards for the population as a whole; secondly there were pressures from within the élite for greater physical security and a greater degree of regularity in the administration of party and state; and finally there was a need to establish a new basis for the legitimacy of the regime, which had for years been tied ever more closely to the person of Stalin.[60] Malenkov and Khrushchev each sought to advance policies which would simultaneously strengthen his political base and win him greater prestige and authority by making progress in solving the problems which faced the regime.

Malenkov's power now rested in the central state apparatus, which he began to strengthen in March with the reorganisation of the forty-five ministries existing at the time of Stalin's death into thirteen new ones.[61] This was intended to strengthen ministerial decision-making and thereby to shift the locus of power from party to government bodies.[62] A decree of 11 April 1953 endowed ministers with a range of new powers to run the affairs of their ministries.[63] The decree was remarkable less for the significance of the powers it transferred to ministers than for what it revealed about their impotence under Stalin. *Pravda* nevertheless hailed it as a major step, and called for further expansion of the powers of ministers and department heads; it decried 'the lack of independence which has characterised the ministries' and demanded the strengthening of 'one-man management' in them.[64] Malenkov was also closely identified with substantial cuts in retail prices which were announced on 1 April and with the reduction in annual state bond sales, which, although technically voluntary, were in practice obligatory. This resulted in savings of 20.2 billion rubles for Soviet taxpayers.[65]

Khrushchev's task was twofold: to strengthen his own position within the party and to strengthen the party apparatus relative to other institutions, especially the central state machinery. He therefore set about the long process of reviving the party and in particular its Central Committee. This body had scarcely met since the war and had not played a significant role in Soviet politics since Stalin's defeat of Bukharin in 1929. The Central Committee's powerlessness stemmed not from the expansion of the Politburo's authority, but from the draining of the Politburo's power by Stalin himself.[66] After Stalin died, his power passed to a collective, the Presidium; conflicts within that body meant that the Central Committee might again come to enjoy a measure of influence. Khrushchev was the first of the Presidium members to grasp the significance of this development. Thus Lazar Slepov's *Pravda* article on collective leadership concentrated on the prerogatives of party committees generally and referred to the Central Committee as the Soviet 'Areopagus'. The CC included the best representatives of all spheres of Soviet life, wrote Slepov, and it was therefore the best forum for the resolution of significant questions in the life of the party and the country.[67]

Khrushchev took up two other issues in the first weeks after Stalin's death: the party's right of oversight (*kontrol'*) of state and social organisations, and the condition of agriculture. This was a theme Khrushchev had taken up, to no avail, in 1952.[68] On 8 May *Pravda* complained that party officials had underestimated the importance of party oversight of local soviets and their bureaucracies; the newspaper stressed that the perfection of the work of state institutions 'depends largely on party organisations' correct guidance of, and help to, soviet agencies'.[69] Kontrol' was also to be exercised more vigorously with respect to economic enterprises. The call for more active party involvement in the running of enterprises and soviet organisations reflected both the approach to party work which Khrushchev had developed in the course of his own career and his political interests in the spring of 1953.

In a series of articles published in May and June *Pravda* also made it increasingly clear that the party was taking up agriculture as an area of primary interest. This too was in keeping with both Khrushchev's convictions and his interests. A number of late Stalinist agricultural policies came under attack. Little was yet presented in the way of an alternative to Stalinist orthodoxy, but *Pravda* did uphold the principle of 'material incentives' in agriculture; in other words, farm workers should be rewarded for better work.[70] Papers and journals associated with Malenkov, by contrast, remained faithful to Stalinist dogmas in agricultural policy.[71]

After co-operating in the struggle with Beria, Malenkov and Khrushchev divided the spoils of victory carefully. S. N. Kruglov, who succeeded Beria as MVD chief, does not appear to have been especially close to either man, while the identity of the KGB chairman appointed in 1953 is still unknown; he was in any case replaced in April 1954 by I. A. Serov, a long-time Khrushchev associate. The Ministry of Medium Machine Building was given to Malenkov's client

Malyshev. No one replaced Beria as a full member of the Presidium, but Ponomarenko, a Malenkov supporter, and Khrushchev's man Kirichenko (who was left in place in Kiev) were elected as candidates.

The next major move was Malenkov's. In early August he told the Supreme Soviet that 'the government and the Central Committee of the party consider it necessary to increase significantly investment in the development of the light, food and fishing industries, and in agriculture, and to improve greatly the production of consumer goods'. He promised a 'sharp increase' in the production of consumer goods, to be financed by a shift in investment away from heavy industry. Malenkov's answer to Soviet agricultural problems was to improve the performance of traditional farming regions, raising yields via greater investment in electrification, mineral fertiliser, irrigation equipment and agricultural machinery, as well as greater reliance on material incentives.[72] The shift in investment priorities which he sought required a revision of party doctrine on the issue of investment priorities, which held that heavy industry was the 'main foundation' of the Soviet economy and the priority sector for investment. Malenkov made no attempt to overturn this doctrine outright, but his programme required that it at least be modified in favour of light industry.[73]

The following month Khrushchev used a Central Committee plenum as the platform for launching his own agricultural initiative. It was calculated to be popular with both the élite and the public and to produce quick, highly visible results. Agriculture was an issue on which Khrushchev could hope to challenge Malenkov successfully, for several reasons. First, it was a much more promising field for party activism. The state ministries were less involved in running agriculture than industry, and local party secretaries already played a key role in running the farms. Secondly, Khrushchev had long been interested in agriculture and could claim some expertise in the field. Finally, Khrushchev was not as closely associated with the agricultural policies of the post-war period as Malenkov, and would therefore not be damaged by an acknowledgement of failures in this area. Discussion of the grain problem was particularly embarrassing to Malenkov, who in 1952 had pronounced the grain problem in the USSR 'finally and irreversibly solved'.[74] In fact, per capita grain production was 25 per cent lower in 1952 than it had been in 1913.

Khrushchev's report on the state of agriculture at the September Central Committee meeting was the frankest public assessment that had been made of the state of Soviet agriculture. The aim of agricultural policy for decades had been to guarantee sufficient food supplies to maintain a growing industrial workforce at a basic level of subsistence as cheaply as possible. This it had done, but the centralised administrative system established to achieve these objectives had impoverished and alienated the peasantry and left agricultural production in an abysmal state. The livestock herd was smaller than it had been before the revolution.[75]

At the September plenum Khrushchev joined Malenkov in calling for an increase in the procurement prices which the state paid farmers for agricultural produce, and for strengthening material incentives, but he stressed that these measures, though important, did not constitute 'the main path for the development of collective agriculture', for further increases in procurement prices could not be funded from the state budget and would necessitate retail price increases. Khrushchev called instead for the expansion of the country's grain-growing regions to include the south-eastern part of European Russia, West Siberia and Kazakhstan, and for an increase in the sowing of maize for animal fodder.

Khrushchev had already been a strong advocate of maize in Ukraine, where its cultivation had indeed been beneficial. His proposals on this score were modest and sensible enough in 1953, but, like so many of his agricultural initiatives, Khrushchev's corn campaign got out of hand. As his enthusiasm for this crop grew, he pressured subordinates to sow it ever more widely, with the result that maize was cultivated in many areas where other grains would have brought better yields. The acreage devoted to rye fell by 25 per cent over the coming decade, and that under oats by almost two-thirds, but the maize cultivated in place of traditional crops failed to produce anything like the yields promised by Khrushchev.

Khrushchev severely criticised Minister of Agriculture A. I. Kozlov, a Malenkov associate, and proposed a re-organisation of agricultural management which would greatly reduce the role of this ministry in managing the farms. The ministry's district-level branches were to be abolished, and supervision of the kolkhozes was to become the task of the Machine and Tractor Stations (MTS), which in turn were to be subordinated to the raikoms. An MTS secretary and a team of party instructors – all accountable to the raikom – were to be appointed for each MTS.[76]

Khrushchev's approach was considerably cheaper than Malenkov's, relying chiefly on better organisation and administration to raise output. As he had done so often in the Stalin years, Khrushchev argued that more active leadership on the part of local party organs would tap the 'hidden reserves' and 'rich local potential' of the farms. He argued that any collective farm could be raised to the level of the best farms in its area without new investment. Khrushchev's proposals would thus require no changes in party doctrine. Khrushchev directly contradicted Malenkov's proposed shift in investment priorities, pointing out that the machine-building industry was critical to the development of agriculture.[77]

In May 1954 the party theoretical journal, *Kommunist*, carried an article evaluating the results of the September reforms. The author complained that party instructors and raikom secretaries had proved no less bureaucratic and dictatorial than the local commissioners from the ministry, whose posts had recently been abolished.[78] What Khrushchev failed to grasp was that the pressures of the planned economy itself created the incentives which led to such behaviour. Replacing local commissioners from the ministry with local party officials achieved nothing, because the environment in which they worked remained essentially unchanged. Khrushchev's hope – indeed, his expectation – was that party officials would heed his call and provide the kind of detailed, on-the-spot, mud-on-the-boots leadership which had characterised his own career as a territorial party secretary. This hope was to be disappointed repeatedly, and Khrushchev's struggle against the 'bureaucratic methods' of local officials was to be one of the toughest and least successful battles of his career.

In the autumn of 1953, however, such struggles still lay in the future. Khrushchev had used the September plenum to good effect in his competition with Malenkov and had received an additional boost when the plenum formally confirmed him as First Secretary of the Central Committee; his pre-eminence in the Secretariat was now official. There was little activity on the agricultural front for the next few months, and Khrushchev turned his attention to party apparatus itself. Between Stalin's death and the end of 1953 party leaders were replaced in Georgia, Armenia, Azerbaijan, Moscow, Leningrad and Ukraine. Khrushchev did not make such personnel decisions unilaterally, but his position as First Secretary placed him in the best possible position to influence these appointments. In every case except Moscow, where a Malenkov client was installed for a short time, he secured the appointment of men who were well-disposed to him; in several cases they were long-time associates.

In early 1954 Khrushchev's client Z. T. Serdiuk was appointed First Secretary in Moldavia, and a Khrushchev protégé replaced the Moscow Secretary appointed in March 1953.[79] Khrushchev also made his mark further down the hierarchy. During the autumn and winter of 1953–4 two-thirds of the provincial party secretaries in the Russian Federation were replaced.[80] The turnover in the party apparatus reached levels not seen since the Great Purge as Khrushchev consolidated his grip on the party machine. Malenkov likewise consolidated his position in the government: Pervukhin, Tevosian, Malyshev and Saburov were named deputy premiers in December 1953.[81]

Not all of the politics of late 1953 were directly linked to the succession struggle, however. There was wide agreement within the leadership on a number of initiatives which were taken in the second half of the year. A decree promulgated in September established regular working hours for state agencies, thereby freeing officials from the bizarre work schedules which had resulted from Stalin's nocturnal ways. This matter may seem trivial, but it represented a significant improvement in the lives of thousands of high-level officials and was an important sign that the new leaders intended to manage party and state affairs in a more regular and rational way.[82]

In the second half of 1953 a trickle of rehabilitated victims of police repression began to return from the labour camps of the GULAG; others were rehabilitated posthumously. Rehabilitation was limited at this point to the most prominent victims of police repression and to those with close connections to people in powerful positions, but a start was made. Roughly 1000–1200 victims of past repression were returned from the camps by the end of 1953. In September the Supreme Court was given the authority to review the verdicts of the notorious secret police tribunals which in Stalin's time had tried political cases and passed sentence without any involvement by the courts or the procuracy. The review was to be conducted in co-operation with the USSR Procurator-General, R. A. Rudenko.[83] (Rudenko, who had been appointed after Beria's fall, had been Procurator-General of Ukraine under Khrushchev.) In early 1954 Khrushchev instructed Rudenko and Minister of Internal Affairs Kruglov to prepare concrete data on past repressions; the memorandum which they presented to him on 1 February stated that 3 777 380 people had been convicted by special police tribunals from 1921 to 1953; 642 980 had been executed, while 2 369 220 had been imprisoned for twenty-five years or less, and 765 180 had been sentenced to internal or foreign exile.[84]

Nineteen fifty-three also witnessed the first departures from Stalin's line in foreign policy. In his funeral speech Malenkov had stressed the 'Leninist-Stalinist thesis of the long-term coexistence and peaceful competition of two different social systems – capitalism and socialism'.[85] This was followed by a number of press articles suggesting that the new leaders intended to take a much softer line in East–West relations.[86] On 30 May Moscow dropped Stalin's claims to a Soviet military presence in the Turkish straits. Ambassadors were exchanged with Greece and Yugoslavia, and a ceasefire agreement in Korea was concluded on 27 July. The new leaders needed a more relaxed international environment, but they feared that any accommodation with Washington would freeze America's military superiority and political hegemony in place.[87] Even Malenkov, whose investment priorities and desire for defence cuts made him the strongest proponent of *détente* in the Presidium, stated that negotiations for the relaxation of tensions could take place only after 'the appropriate prerequisites' had been realised.[88]

There was also agreement on the need to liberalise cultural policy, although there was no agreement about how far to go in this direction. In late April *Literaturnaia gazeta* mentioned several critics who had disappeared from public view during Zhdanov's campaign against 'cosmopolitanism'; a week later it published some love poems for the first time in years.[89] Ol'ga Berggol'ts opened a debate on the freedom of writers to express and defend their own subjective views; she was joined by such eminent writers as Ilia Ehrenburg and Konstantin Paustovskii.[90] The publication in December of Vladimir Pomerantsev's 'On Sincerity in Literature' caused a sensation, although, as Rita Orlova later observed, 'Pomerantsev only asserted that a writer should write what he really thinks.'[91] At the time, however, this was an extremely controversial position. Nor was literature the only field affected. Previously-banned composers returned to prominence,[92] and jazz, which had been condemned as 'alien' and 'harmful pseudo-art', was openly performed.[93]

This easing of cultural policy was limited, however. The principle of party direction of the arts was never questioned; it was accepted by the leadership, the creative intelligentsia and the public alike. The liberal writers' articles were full of professions of fidelity to the principles of socialist realism and party spirit (*partiinost'*) in literature. What was at issue was how much latitude the party would allow artists and writers. It was a time for cautious experimentation and the testing of limits rather than genuine artistic freedom. Ilia Ehrenburg captured the mood of the moment in the title of his novel *The Thaw*. It became a byword for the post-Stalin relaxation in culture and other spheres, albeit one with which the leadership was uncomfortable.[94] Ehrenburg's image evoked more than the coming of spring after a long winter; it suggested 'times of instability, uncertainty, incompleteness and fluctuations in temperature . . . when it is difficult to foresee what turn the weather will take or when'.[95]

There is no evidence that Khrushchev opposed the cultural thaw, but neither is there any reason to believe that he actively supported it at this point. On the contrary, the evidence suggests that the driving force behind it was Malenkov. He had pressed for abandonment of the most conservative theories in drama in early 1952 and had called for the resurrection of satire as a genre at the Nineteenth Congress.[96] The cultural thaw faded as Malenkov's political fortunes declined.

The conservative counterattack began in early 1954, taking Pomerantsev as its principal target.[97] It grew more intense in the summer, as other liberal writers came under fire, including Grossman, Ehrenburg and Panova.[98] The editor-in-chief of the liberal literary journal *Novyi Mir*, Aleksandr Tvardovskii, was summoned to a meeting with Khrushchev in late July at which the First Secretary stated that there was no need for a party resolution on literature; four days later Tvardovskii was summoned back to the Central Committee building and shown the text of just such a resolution. In early August the official Writers' Union passed its own resolution criticising *Novyi Mir*.[99]

In December of that year a Second Congress of Soviet Writers was convened, some thirty years after the first. Writers were attacked for such sins as cosmopolitanism and bourgeois nationalism, and the editors of *Novyi Mir* were accused of 'attempts to attack the basic position of our literature from a nihilistic platform'.[100] The greetings of the Central Committee to the Congress set the tone for cultural policy for the next few years:

> The duty of Soviet writers is to create truthful art, an art of great thoughts and feelings which shows the rich spiritual world of Soviet people; it is to incarnate in literary heroes all the diversity of their work, their social and private lives, in unbroken unity. Our literature is called on not only to reflect that which is new, but to aid its victory in every way.[101]

This statement undoubtedly reflected Khrushchev's own

views; he was riding high in December 1954 and his grip on the Central Committee Secretariat was firm.

The harvest of 1953 was poor, but Khrushchev, who had staked his reputation and his political future to the Soviet Union's chronically ill agricultural sector, was undaunted. His September proposals were still being implemented, so he could scarcely be blamed for the 1953 harvest. On the contrary, he seized on poor agricultural performance as proof of the need for further initiatives. In January he addressed a memorandum to his Presidium colleagues calling for an expansion of the sown area devoted to grain by assimilating 13 million hectares of idle land. Six days later – before the matter had been decided by the leadership – he publicly called for this to be done by the end of 1955. Just over a week after that he spoke publicly of assimilating 13 million hectares by the end of 1954. On 15 February this figure was raised to 15 million hectares, and a week later Khrushchev stated that the figure of 15 million hectares was to be regarded as a minimum and that the target should be 25 million.[102] By making public commitments before a decision had been taken, Khrushchev hoped to ensure that he would be identified as the initiator of the Virgin Lands Programme and that his Presidium colleagues would be constrained by his public promises to agree to the proposals.

The decision to launch the programme was taken by a Central Committee plenum in February and March. Khrushchev's choice of this forum is itself significant. Every plenum called between Beria's fall and Malenkov's resignation was devoted to agriculture, and Khrushchev addressed them all. No other Soviet leader followed this example; Khrushchev alone explained his decisions to the Central Committee, acknowledged his accountability to it and treated it as more than an honorific body. He defended the Central Committee's prerogatives against proposals to limit its jurisdiction to 'cadres and propaganda'.[103] His aim was to revive the CC and use it to compensate for his relative weakness in the Presidium and Secretariat. This clearly seems to have been the case with the Virgin Lands initiative. None of his Presidium colleagues showed any enthusiasm for the scheme, yet Khrushchev carried the day at the February–March plenum.[104]

Khrushchev's efforts to channel unresolved policy disputes into the Central Committee enhanced his standing among the members of that body, since he was the Presidium member most inclined to respect the committee's institutional interests. Moreover, his defence of the interests of the party apparatus on a range of issues won him the support of the largest single constituency in the Central Committee. It is unlikely that Khrushchev at this stage could have used the committee to force through initiatives against the determined opposition of his Presidium colleagues, but their acquiescence was not difficult to obtain. None of the other members of the leadership showed much interest in agriculture, let alone had an alternative policy. Responsibility for agriculture was considered a poisoned chalice, and Khrushchev's rivals probably believed that by letting him have his head in this area (while distancing themselves from his crazy schemes) they were merely giving him the rope with which he would hang himself.

The Virgin Lands Programme was indeed vintage Khrushchev: massive in scope, mobilisational in character and aimed at achieving quick results on the cheap. By June 1954 the stated goal was 30 million hectares by 1956. The party and the Communist Youth League (*Komsomol*) were called on to mobilise tens of thousands of young people to move to the Virgin Lands as pioneers, even before housing and necessary social amenities had been built. The programme was also high-risk. Khrushchev's aim was to solve the USSR's grain problem virtually overnight; because of the diversion of resources from traditional farming areas to the Virgin Lands, failure would represent a major setback to Soviet agriculture.

Khrushchev's alternative to Malenkov was now clear. In hindsight it is easy to see how he had outmanoeuvred the premier. The consumer goods drive would not have affected the living standards of the great majority of the population for years to come; it was a measure that would in the short-term benefit only the urban middle class. Malenkov's farming policies would likewise have taken longer to bear fruit. Khrushchev's programme promised faster, more widely felt results – and it promised to achieve them cheaply. Moreover, his proposals required neither doctrinal revisions concerning the relative priority of heavy industry nor defence cuts. Some defence cuts had been made at the end of the Korean War, but the premier hoped to make further reductions by relying more heavily on nuclear weapons for Soviet security. His programme thus placed him on a collision course with defence and heavy industrial interests.

The differences between Khrushchev and Malenkov were crystallised in their speeches before the Supreme Soviet elections of 1954 and to the first session of the new Supreme Soviet.[105] Khrushchev appealed to supporters of heavy industry and the armed forces, two extremely powerful constituencies, with his calls for further modernisation and strengthening of the armed forces and for an expansion of machine-building to support the Virgin Lands Programme. Malenkov's alternative, by contrast, required the diversion of resources away from heavy industry, which he did not mention at all, and the defence budget. In addressing defence, Malenkov made two points which would later come back to haunt him: first, he denied that the armed forces required further modernisation in order to perform their duties; secondly, he stated that a new world war would mean 'the destruction of world civilisation'. Malenkov was alone in this position; Bulganin, Voroshilov, Molotov and Kaganovich all called for the further strengthening of Soviet defences. By late April Malenkov was compelled to acknowledge that only capitalism would be annihilated in the event of a world war.[106]

In early 1954 a new round of ministerial reorganisations began. The amalgamation of ministries undertaken the year before was reversed, and the number of ministries began to grow rapidly. Moreover, an increasing proportion of the new ministries were either reorganised into joint union–republican ministries or abolished at the all-union level and replaced by ministries in the republics. These changes represented a perfectly rational retreat from the hyper-centralisation of the Stalin years, but they were used by Khrushchev to his own political advantage. First, the union republics which gained most from this limited decentralisation of the ministerial structure were those with leaders who were close associates of Khrushchev. Secondly, Khrushchev emerged as a champion of local leaders against the mighty Moscow ministries, a position which reflected both his rivalry with Malenkov and his understanding of the point of view of local and republican officials.

On 17 August a joint party–government decree on the Virgin Lands appeared in the press; it was the first decree in years in which the Central Committee took precedence over the Council of Ministers.[107] The press campaign calling for more aggressive party oversight of non-party bodies was renewed shortly thereafter. The scope of the party's rights in this area steadily expanded, ultimately encompassing even the security organs. The party was called on to become a partner in management, not only drawing attention to shortcomings but devising remedies.[108]

Khrushchev's advantage was further confirmed when he rather than Malenkov led the Soviet delegation to Beijing for the celebrations marking the fifth anniversary of the establishment of the People's Republic of China. Still a novice in foreign affairs, Khrushchev was extremely anxious to secure the goodwill of the Chinese, and in the Sino-Soviet negotiations on trade and aid which preceded the trip he put himself and his colleagues in an awkward position by promising to Zhou Enlai that the Soviet side would fulfil obligations which it had yet to assume. Zhou led Khrushchev to believe that the Soviets had made greater commitments to China in Stalin's time than was in fact the case. Determined to conclude an agreement with Zhou in time for the Chinese anniversary and to lead the Soviet delegation to the festivities, Khrushchev refused to back down in the face of arguments concerning the feasibility of the proposals or their impact on the Soviet economy. He became, in effect, Zhou's most powerful advocate in Moscow, pressing for a massive programme of aid to China and for the return of certain Chinese territories then under Soviet control.[109]

Khrushchev's colleagues finally agreed to a package which was similar in scope to that originally proposed but which was stretched out over a longer period of time. Presidium member Kliment Voroshilov objected at the last

moment. The exchange that ensued says much about the
change of atmosphere which followed Stalin's death.
Khrushchev, exasperated with Voroshilov, asked, 'Klim,
what are you up to? It seems that all was agreed, and now,
just before our departure for Beijing, you've become
stubborn and spoken against this. That's not on. What is
the matter and what do you object to?' Before explaining
his position Voroshilov remarked,

> First of all, permit me to thank the party and its Central
> Committee for the fact that people are no longer arrested
> and thrown in prison for having unusual views, and that
> one can now say what one thinks.[110]

Khrushchev saw the agreement as critical to building the
Sino-Soviet relationship and saw no point in going to
Beijing without it. His awareness of the effort he had made
to secure it increased his later bitterness at the Chinese
after relations with Beijing soured.

In the end Voroshilov gave way and Khrushchev travelled
to China, where the Soviets committed a major breach of
protocol on arrival. KGB chief Serov flew into Beijing
ahead of the delegation; he and his team were whisked off
to meet the Chinese leaders, who were expecting Khrushchev and his colleagues. The actual delegation arrived some
time later. The advance plane was intended to be a van-
guard for the delegation in case an ambush or some other
trap awaited the Soviet leaders in Beijing; the Chinese, who
understood this, were deeply offended.[111] Khrushchev later
recalled the trip as a success, although he remembered
himself as a much tougher negotiator than he appears to
have been.[112] Having little experience abroad and none in
the Orient, he was impressed by Chinese customs but found
some rather difficult to adjust to:

> the Chinese served tea every time we turned around –
> tea, tea, tea. . . . if you didn't drink it up right away,
> they'd take that cup away and put another one in front
> of you – over and over again. . . . after awhile I refused
> to drink any more tea – first, because it was green tea,

which I'm not accustomed to, and second, because I can't take that much liquid.[113]

Bulganin, by contrast, continued to drink the tea in order not to offend his hosts and consequently developed insomnia.[114]

The struggle with Malenkov came to a head shortly after Khrushchev's return from Beijing. The beleaguered premier's work and personal life had suffered all year on account of his preoccupation with his deteriorating position. He had been publicly out of step with his colleagues over defence policy and investment priorities since March and was under attack over his involvement in the fabrication of the Leningrad Case. The Presidium had discussed the case on 3 May, and on 6–7 May Khrushchev and Procurator-General Rudenko had gone to Leningrad to discuss it with local party activists; the trial of V. S. Abakumov, the former Minister of State Security who had fabricated the case, was being prepared. In June Malenkov lost his pride of place in the listing of Presidium members in official statements and decrees; the names of the leaders thenceforth appeared in alphabetical order. By November, Khrushchev was chairing Presidium meetings and Bulganin was signing documents on behalf of the Council of Ministers.[115]

Khrushchev had the party apparatus firmly behind him at this stage. While on holiday in Crimea during August and September he had met with Mikoian, Bulganin and the party chiefs of Leningrad, Moscow and Ukraine; according to some accounts it was there and then that Malenkov's fate was decided.[116] Khrushchev also met with party leaders in Vladivostok, Sakhalin, Khabarovsk, Chita, Irkutsk and Sverdlovsk on stopovers *en route* to and from Beijing.[117] The battle with Malenkov was to be fought over investment priorities. Khrushchev, as the champion of heavy industry and defence interests, was thus able to present himself as the defender of Stalinist orthodoxy against the revisionism of the premier.

Khrushchev further underscored his orthodox credentials by calling for a 'decisive offensive' against 'religious foolishness'.[118] The resolution of 10 November appeared under Khrushchev's own name rather than that of the

Central Committee as a whole. It criticised anti-religious propaganda which offended believers by questioning their political loyalty and called for propaganda based on accurate presentations of scientific data and historical facts. Khrushchev affirmed his belief in the loyalty to the Soviet state of the majority of the clergy and condemned administrative interference in the activities of religious organisations.[119] As passionate an opponent of religion as he was a believer in socialism, Khrushchev was convinced that the struggle against religion could and would be won at the level of ideas, without resort to force. Later in his tenure he would incline towards tougher measures, however.

There was as yet little basis for accusing Malenkov of revisionism. The heavy industry proportion of Soviet industrial production actually rose slightly during the two years of Malenkov's premiership, despite his exertions on behalf of light industry and consumer goods. Production of consumer goods did rise appreciably, however: the production of refrigerators trebled, and substantial increases were registered for textiles, shoes, hosiery and sewing machines. The targets for 1955, however, required a significant shift in investment to light industry, and it was this prospect which activated Malenkov's opponents.[120] Ironically, the counterattack of the heavy industry lobby began with a speech by Malenkov's client Saburov on 6 November. Saburov spoke at length about the importance of Lenin's dictum that heavy industry is 'the cornerstone of a socialist economy'.[121] For the next six weeks a debate over investment priorities took place in academic quarters.[122]

On 21 December the conflict broke into the open with contradictory articles in *Pravda* and *Izvestiia* commemorating the seventy-fifth anniversary of Stalin's birth. Both newspapers addressed the issue of industrial investment; *Pravda* stressed the Stalinist orthodoxy of the priority of heavy industry, while *Izvestiia* praised the party and government for measures taken to develop light industry and increase consumer goods production.[123] The difference in emphases between the two papers continued into the new year; the debate ended on 5 January, when *Izvestiia*'s lead editorial stated that 'only by the all-out development of all branches of heavy industry can our country successfully fulfil the great historic tasks before it'.[124] In the midst of this debate *Pravda* reported on the trial of Abakumov; the mere mention of the Leningrad Case in the press was a blow to Malenkov. On 24 January *Pravda* carried an article by its editor, Dmitrii Shepilov, entitled 'The General Line of the Party and the Vulgarisers of Marxism'. Shepilov attacked the ideas of 'some economists', who had called into question the priority of heavy industry. His real target was, of course, Malenkov, and the article was reprinted in many republican newspapers the following day.[125]

On 25 January a plenary meeting of the Central Committee was convened in Moscow to hear the First Secretary's report on the production of animal products. The report included a blistering attack on the right deviation over the question of investment priorities. Caricaturing his opponents' position as Shepilov had done, he attacked this 'belching forth of the right deviation . . . of views hostile to Leninism which were preached in their time by Rykov, Bukharin and their ilk'.[126] Khrushchev also reported to the plenum on an 'organisational question', telling the Central Committee that the Presidium was dissatisfied with Malenkov's performance as premier. The First Secretary reminded his audience of Malenkov's close ties to Beria and his responsibility for the Leningrad Case, and criticised Malenkov for his attempts to lead not only the government but also the Presidium, a party body in which the premier, as head of government, enjoyed no special authority. Khrushchev reserved his severest criticism for Malenkov's attempt to buy 'cheap popularity' with the consumer goods campaign and his contention that a world war would mean the end of civilisation.[127]

Malenkov spoke twice at the plenum, as his first *mea culpa* did not satisfy the Khrushchev faction. He resigned the premiership at the Supreme Soviet session on 8 February and was replaced by Nikolai Bulganin. Malenkov was not removed from the Presidium, however, and was given the post of Minister for Electric Power Stations. Bulganin, who had been a friend and colleague of Khrushchev's since the mid-1930s, was unquestionably the second man in the leadership; he remained head of government for more than three years, but never emerged as an independent political force. Khrushchev's position as first among the members of the collective leadership was now beyond any reasonable doubt.

6 Dethroning Stalin
The Secret Speech and its Aftermath, 1955-7

> *Though indulgence in terrorist action against any section of the population may corrupt the entire personality . . . nevertheless, the contrary is also true – that the preservation of more or less humanist attitudes, even if only in a limited field, may, when the particular motives for terror against others have lapsed, spread out again and rehumanise the rest.*
>
> Robert Conquest, *The Great Terror*[1]

Khrushchev had defeated Malenkov by casting himself as defender of the true faith and attacking Malenkov as a rightist, but their ideological conflict must be seen in context: the disagreements between them, though real, were limited. Malenkov's revisionism was rather mild, while Khrushchev's brand of orthodoxy was far less rigid than Stalin's. Neither man challenged the institutional or ideological bases of the Soviet system, and both were agreed on the need to raise living standards, to keep the secret police under party control and to achieve some relaxation in tensions with the outside world. Khrushchev's relative conservatism was largely tactical: he occupied the only political ground which Malenkov, by occupying the right, had left open to him.

Khrushchev, like Stalin before him, had no qualms about adopting much of his fallen rival's agenda, particularly in foreign affairs. Despite the bellicose rhetoric he had employed against Malenkov, Khrushchev pressed for further relaxation of tensions in Europe in 1955. His first step was a shift in the Soviet position on the Austrian question, which Moscow had previously maintained could be resolved only as part of a larger settlement with Germany. The Soviets indicated in January 1955 that they would agree to the withdrawal of occupying forces from Austria in return for guarantees of Austrian neutrality. Though he still occupied no government post, Khrushchev participated in the negotiations which led to the Austrian State Treaty on exactly these lines. According to Khrushchev, the costs of administering the Soviet zone in Austria were great and the benefits meagre. Khrushchev was also keenly aware of the propaganda value of withdrawing Soviet troops from Austria, a move which cost Moscow nothing in strategic terms and left a neutral wedge between NATO members Germany and Italy.[2] Khrushchev took great pride in the treaty, which was signed on 15 May 1955:

> It was the European debut for a country bumpkin, and it did us a lot of good. The bumpkin had learned a thing or two. We could orient ourselves without directives from Stalin. We had exchanged our knee pants for long trousers in international politics.[3]

The Austrian State Treaty was also intended as a demonstration to Germany of the benefits of neutrality. The Soviets had tried for several years to prevent West German rearmament, going so far as to propose the creation of a unified, disarmed and neutral Germany in early 1954 – the very idea for which Beria had been attacked in 1953. The West had rejected this out of hand. For a time Moscow pinned its hopes on French opposition to a rearmed Germany, but this was finally overcome, and on 5 May 1955 West Germany ratified the Paris Agreements, under which the western allies confirmed the end of their occupation of West Germany and acknowledged its sovereignty; on 6 May Germany joined NATO. Moscow responded by cancelling war-time treaties of friendship with France and Britain on 7 May; a week later, the USSR and its European satellite states formed the Warsaw Treaty Organisation as a counterweight to NATO. Nevertheless, only a month later German Chancellor Adenauer was invited to Moscow to discuss the normalisation of relations between the two countries. The Soviet leaders were aware of the potential benefits of economic ties with Bonn, and were coming to hope that West Germany might be 'decoupled' from the western alliance if a strong Soviet–West German relationship developed.

The visit took place in September and resulted in the establishment of diplomatic and commerical ties and the repatriation of 10 000 German POWs. When Adenauer insisted that there were more than 100 000 German prisoners still in Russia, Khrushchev subjected him to a torrent of verbal abuse.[4] The Soviets rejected Adenauer's offer of massive German financial assistance in return for reunification – in effect, an offer to buy the GDR from the Kremlin. Khrushchev saw the situation in terms of a domino theory; Adenauer's proposals

> would have meant for us to retreat to the borders of Poland. . . . It would have been the beginning of a chain reaction, and it would have encouraged aggressive forces in the West to put more and more pressure on us. Once you start retreating, it's difficult to stop.[5]

Khrushchev and Adenauer did find one thing in common during the Chancellor's visit: a love of wine. The two men sent one another their countries' wines for some time thereafter.[6]

The next item on Khrushchev's agenda was Yugoslavia. Diplomatic links between the two countries had been restored soon after Stalin's death, but little else had been done to repair the breach which had opened in 1948, when Stalin, unable to tolerate a communist leader whom he could not control, had excommunicated Tito from the communist bloc. Unauthorised pursuit of a *rapprochement* with Belgrade had been one of the charges against Beria in 1953. By 1955, however, Khrushchev had decided that he must come to terms with Tito. Indeed Khrushchev wanted more than simply courteous diplomatic relations – he wished to re-establish formal ties between the League of Communists of Yugoslavia (LCY) and the CPSU. Tito's independence was an affront to Moscow's claim to leadership of the world socialist movement and, in Moscow's view, a threat to the stability of Eastern Europe. *Rapprochement* with him would strengthen the socialist bloc and demonstrate Moscow's commitment to allowing each communist party to develop socialism in its own way.

Khrushchev, Bulganin, Mikoian, Shepilov and Andrei

Gromyko travelled to Yugoslavia on a fence-mending visit at the end of May 1955; Molotov, though Foreign Minister, remained in Moscow, stubbornly opposed to the whole venture. Tito was known to be cool towards the idea of renewed ties between the two parties, but Khrushchev was not to be deterred, and in his arrival speech at Belgrade airport he made a pitch for closer relations between the LCY and the CPSU as well as between the two governments. He blamed the rift between Moscow and Belgrade entirely on Beria and Abakumov.[7] Tito, who had made it clear in advance that he would not agree simply to pin the blame on Beria, cut Khrushchev's interpreter off in mid-speech and motioned his guests to a waiting automobile.[8]

The rest of the trip was full of petty humiliations for Khrushchev and his colleagues. Tito did everything he could to make his guests look foolish, and they sometimes co-operated. Khrushchev and Bulganin became drunk more than once during the trip (so did their host), the last time at a Soviet embassy reception attended by the western press. The Yugoslav visit was the western world's first close-up look at the man who had emerged as first among the new Soviet leaders; what it saw did not impress: a short, fat, balding extrovert whose baggy summer suits looked all the more ridiculous alongside the splendid uniforms and dinner jackets of his hosts. He radiated energy but not intellect, and many observers quickly dismissed him as loud-mouthed buffoon who would not last long. The trip was by no means a failure, however, and Soviet–Yugoslav relations continued to improve.

Khrushchev's new course in foreign policy was opposed at every turn by Viacheslav Molotov, the Foreign Minister. Molotov had no institutional power base, but he had been closer to Stalin than any of his colleagues. He was popular among party conservatives and respected by the public. He posed no threat to Khrushchev's power, but he was capable of obstruction within the Presidium, and his fidelity to Stalinist orthodoxy made it difficult for Khrushchev to free himself from old dogmas without appearing to be a revisionist. To move further with his planned innovations in domestic and foreign policy, Khrushchev had to put Molotov in his place. The issue was Yugoslavia, but this was in many ways a surrogate for the Stalin question. Khrushchev was aware of the link between the two issues:

> I first sensed the falsity of our position when we went to Yugoslavia and talked with Comrade Tito in 1955. When we . . . mentioned Beria as the culprit behind the crimes of the Stalin period, the Yugoslav comrades smiled scornfully and made sarcastic remarks. We were irritated and we launched into a long argument in defence of Stalin. Later I spoke out publicly in defence of Stalin when the Yugoslavs criticised him. It's now clear to me that my position was wrong.[9]

It is in this light that the discussion of Yugoslavia at the July 1955 plenum must be seen. Molotov, who alone in the Presidium opposed Khrushchev on the Yugoslav question, also realised that acceptance of the Yugoslavs would sooner or later necessitate a downgrading of Stalin.[10] Nineteen orators, including all the other Presidium members, criticised Molotov at the plenum, but he did not budge from his position. He did, however, assure the plenum that he would respect its decision and obey the will of the party.[11]

Molotov was subjected to a further humiliation in October, when he was forced to apologise publicly for a minor ideological mistake.[12] In November former secret police officials in Georgia were charged with having persecuted Ordzhonikidze; Molotov had been Ordzhonikidze's bitter enemy and the driving force behind Ordzhonikidze's fall and the purge of his associates.[13] The mention of Ordzhonikidze was thus a sign of political trouble for Molotov, even as the Leningrad Case was for Malenkov. Ordzhonikidze's fate was raised again at the Twentieth Congress (when Khrushchev revealed that he had committed suicide) and in a trial in Azerbaijan shortly before Molotov was replaced as foreign minister.[14]

The July plenum also announced that the Twentieth Congress of the CPSU would take place in February 1956 and elected three new Central Committee secretaries, all of whom were Khrushchev protégés. The Secretariat, which ran the party's central bureaucracy, was now firmly under Khrushchev's control. His client Kirichenko was elevated to full membership of the Presidium, as was the ideologist and Central Committee Secretary Mikhail Suslov. Suslov's elevation at this time is somewhat surprising, since, like Molotov, he held that Yugoslavia was not a socialist country.[15]

The relaxation in tensions brought about by the Austrian treaty, together with the decline in the debate over German rearmament opened the way to a summit meeting of the war-time allies later in the summer. With Malenkov demoted and Molotov in decline, Khrushchev was determined to make the most of it. The Geneva summit, attended by the leaders of the USSR, the United States, France and the United Kingdom was his most important international venture up to that time. He and his colleagues approached the meeting with feelings of nervousness and even inferiority: 'The Geneva meeting was a crucial test for us: Would we be able to represent our country competently? Would we approach the meeting soberly, without unrealistic hopes, and would we be able to keep the other side from intimidating us? I would say we passed the test.'[16] Khrushchev was concerned less with the substance of the meeting than with impressing his western counterparts. Thus he found it 'somewhat embarrassing' when the Soviet delegation arrived in Geneva aboard a two-engine Iliushin, while the other delegations arrived in four-engine aircraft; he was offended when the Swiss government refused to allow him to join Bulganin in reviewing the honour guard, since Bulganin, as premier, was formally the head of the delegation.[17]

The Soviet side proposed the liquidation of both NATO and the Warsaw Pact, a comprehensive security treaty among the states of Europe and the withdrawal of 'foreign' (US) troops from the continent. The proposal was not taken seriously by the western allies, but it demonstrated the propaganda value of the new symmetry of alliances in Europe. Khrushchev, for his part, regarded the principal western proposal, Eisenhower's 'Open Skies' plan, as a transparent attempt to legitimate US aerial espionage in the Soviet Union. The plan would have allowed each side to fly over and photograph the other's military facilities, but US technical capabilities in the field of aerial surveillance were so much greater that Khrushchev rejected it out of hand.[18]

Khrushchev liked Eisenhower personally but believed
him to be 'soft' and 'much too dependent on his advisors',
particularly Secretary of State John Foster Dulles, the
'chained cur of imperialism' whom Khrushchev believed to
be the real architect of US policy. Eisenhower was 'like a
dutiful schoolboy taking his lead from his teacher. . . . It
certainly appeared that Eisenhower was letting Dulles do his
thinking for him.' Khrushchev also took a liking to French
premier Edgar Faure, whom he delighted in calling 'Edgar
Fedorovich'; he realised, however, that French governments
turned over so rapidly that it was not worth paying them
too much attention.[19] Western statesmen, by contrast, were
generally unimpressed with Khrushchev. British Foreign
Secretary Harold Macmillan privately wondered, 'How can
this fat, vulgar man with his pig eyes and ceaseless flow of
talk be the head – the aspirant Tsar of all those millions of
people . . . ?'[20]

The summit produced no concrete results, but it created
the impression on all sides that tensions on the continent
were easing. The Soviets had scored a propaganda success
by demonstrating their commitment to coexistence. For
Khrushchev, its most significant result was the realisation
that 'our enemies probably feared us as much as we feared
them'. Khrushchev was acutely aware that the USSR was
weaker and less influential than the United States, and the
discovery that his adversaries feared him as much as he
feared them was thus something of a revelation.[21]

In the autumn Khrushchev and Bulganin rounded out
the year's travels with a trip to India, Burma and
Afghanistan. This was the first indication that Khrushchev
understood the opportunities for the USSR represented by
the break-up of European colonial empires. Moscow had
supported communists in North Vietnam and elsewhere,
but Stalin, believing that 'he who is not with us is against
us', had been extremely wary of courting non-communist
nationalists in the Third World. Khrushchev, by contrast,
preferred to think that 'he who is not against us is with us'.
During his travels in the Indian subcontinent he emphasised that the Soviet Union did not wish to impose its
system on other countries but that it was prepared, indeed
eager, to share its experience of socialist development. For

Khrushchev there was no need to discuss communism, which he scarcely mentioned, or to impose anything. Soviet aid and Soviet achievements would demonstrate to non-aligned countries the benefits of close relations with Moscow and the attractions of the Soviet model of development.

Nineteen fifty-five was the year in which Khrushchev himself became an instrument as well as a shaper of Soviet foreign policy. For the next nine years, his face and voice were the face and voice of the Soviet Union; his personality was bound up with the international image of the USSR. He was the medium of Soviet foreign policy, and, to a considerable degree, the message as well. He could be charming or vulgar, ebullient or sullen; he was given to public displays of rage (often contrived) and to soaring hyperbole in his rhetoric. But whatever he was, however he came across, he was more human than his predecessor or even than most of his foreign counterparts, and for much of the world that was enough to make the USSR seem less mysterious or menacing.

Khrushchev was also active at home. Immediately after Malenkov's demotion a campaign of criticism aimed at the economic ministries which had been his power base began in the press.[22] The campaign culminated in an all-union conference in May which discussed the guidance of industry which both Khrushchev and Bulganin addressed. The First Secretary continued to emphasise regional planning, the devolution of economic authority and the role of local and republican party organs in the guidance of enterprises.[23] A series of decrees issued in 1955 expanded the rights of the USSR's constituent republics over economic planning and budgetary policy,[24] and the campaign for expanding party oversight of economic enterprises resumed.[25] Khrushchev's commitment to party activism in industrial management reached a peak in early 1956:

The work of a party official should be evaluated primarily by those results attained in the development of the economy for which he is responsible. . . . Evidently it is necessary, comrades, to raise the material responsibility of officials for the jobs entrusted to them. If the plan is fulfilled or overfulfilled – more pay; if it is not fulfilled, earnings should be reduced.[26]

Khrushchev's proposal was bad news for managers, ministerial officials and party functionaries alike; nothing more was ever heard of it.

Khrushchev's choice of themes was entirely in keeping with his belief in party activism and his reliance on the party's territorial bosses for political support. Of equal significance were the themes he chose not to address: enterprise autonomy and managerial power. Khrushchev understood the need to decentralise the Stalinist command economy, but both his experience and his political needs led him to favour administrative decentralisation of authority to any real economic reform. Economic reform required a loosening of controls over enterprises and the creation of conditions in which they could respond to economic rather than administrative signals. Khrushchev's emphasis on party activism and devolution merely subjected enterprise managers to greater interference from local officials without freeing them from the *diktat* of the central ministries.

Early 1955 also brought a renewal of Khrushchev's war of attrition against the USSR Ministry of Agriculture. The minister was dismissed, and for most of 1955 the post was left vacant; one observer suggested that Khrushchev himself had taken direct control of the ministry.[27] A decree of 9 March attacked the State Planning Committee (Gosplan) and the ministries concerned with agriculture for excessive centralisation and arbitrariness in planning. They were criticised for imposing too many planning indicators on the farms and for obstructing Khrushchev's campaign to extend the cultivation of maize. The maize campaign had by now become one of Khrushchev's *idées fixes*; he pushed for its cultivation everywhere from Sukhumi on the Black Sea to Yakutia in Siberia.

Under the new system of agricultural administration established by the decree the state plan was to specify only the volume of MTS tractor work on the kolkhozes and the volume of agricultural procurements. The agricultural ministries were excluded from this process and instructed to concentrate on research and development.[28] In theory the new reforms put the key decisions of what, when and where to sow into the hands of farm directors. In practice procurement quotas were as great a constraint on their freedom as production targets. MTS and local party officials supervised the farm's plans and made frequent (and sometimes arbitrary) changes in them.[29] As in industry, the upshot of Khrushchev's policies was to decentralise administrative power to local party bodies rather than to increase the freedom of producing units, be they farms or factories, to run themselves.

Khrushchev's expansion of the powers of local party organs suited his political needs perfectly, securing for him the strong support of the provincial and republican party bosses who made up the single largest bloc of votes in the Central Committee. His reliance on party activism to achieve results in every sphere caused him no end of frustration, however. Khrushchev's plans for advancing Soviet industrial and agricultural development on the cheap required local party officials who shared his energy, drive and willingness to become involved even in detailed technical issues. This was utterly unrealistic; Khrushchev's style of party work was even more out of the ordinary in the 1950s than it had been in the 1920s. He found himself waging an unending and unsuccessful verbal campaign against 'leadership from the desk', 'administrative fiat' and leadership 'overall'. He constantly urged local party officials to visit farms, to master the technical aspects of agricultural issues and to become involved in the resolution of specific problems.[30] The First Secretary remained sensitive to his political reliance on the territorial party apparatus, however, and never subjected its officials to the intense criticism he directed at ministerial officials. He also defended party bureaucrats against attacks from other quarters; when Malenkov spoke out sharply against corruption and moral degradation in the party apparatus, Khrushchev replied, 'All that is, of course, true, Georgii Maksimilianovich. But the apparatus is our buttress.' The party officials who made up the audience answered Khrushchev with a thunderous ovation.[31]

The year between Malenkov's resignation and the Twentieth Congress was a crucial period from the point of view of personnel policy. The Congress would elect a new

Central Committee, the membership of which would be drawn primarily from among high-ranking party and state officials. Khrushchev's ability to install his supporters in key positions would thus determine the extent to which he could influence the composition of the new Central Committee. Success would not endow him with the dictatorial powers which Stalin had enjoyed, but it would enable him to escape to a greater extent the remaining constraints of collective leadership. A number of ministers associated with Malenkov were sacked shortly after his resignation.[32] An estimated thirty-one provincial party secretaries were replaced on account of links to Malenkov.[33] At least ten officials from the Ukrainian party apparatus were transferred to important party posts in other republics. Khrushchev also took steps to bring the security services still more firmly under party control. By the time of the Twentieth Congress, the positions of Minister of the Interior, Chairman of the KGB and Procurator-General of the USSR were all occupied by men who had worked for Khrushchev in either the Ukrainian or Moscow party organisations.[34]

Khrushchev opened the Twentieth Congress on 14 February 1956, downgrading Stalin in his first breath: 'Comrades! During the period between the Nineteenth and Twentieth congresses we lost three of the best-known leaders of the communist movement: Iosif Vissarionovich Stalin, Klement Gottwald and Kiutsi Tokuda. I ask that you honour their memory by standing.'[35] The late vozhd' received no greater tribute than the drunken Gottwald or the unknown Tokuda. In the General Report of the Central Committee which he delivered on the same day, Khrushchev had nothing to say about Stalin. He touched only briefly on the personality cult and even then mentioned no names:

The CC has decisively condemned as alien to Marxism-Leninism the cult of personality, which transforms this or that leader into a hero-miracle worker and simultaneously plays down the role of the party and the popular masses, leading to a reduction in their creative activity. The propagation of the cult of personality reduced the role of collective leadership in the party and led at times to serious errors in our work.[36]

Privately, however, Khrushchev knew that he could not pass over the Stalin question in silence. He had already recognised that he and his colleagues were 'trapped' by the 'Beria version' of the repressions which they had concocted in 1953.[37] Moreover, a steady stream of of Stalin's victims was now returning to Soviet cities. The pace of rehabilitation was still quite slow, but thousands more were returning home after the completion of their sentences. Unless the regime wished to keep everyone in the camps indefinitely, it could not prevent the spread of knowledge about the repressions and the GULAG which the returnees brought with them.[38]

There was also a pressing need to accelerate the rehabilitation process. People returning from the camps at the end of their sentences continued to suffer discrimination on account of their status as 'enemies of the people'. The Pospelov Commission, the Party Control Committee and the Military Collegium of the Supreme Court were all rehabilitating people, but they lacked the resources and the information to do so rapidly and on a large scale. In some cases this lack of information led to bizarre results. A letter informing the poet Osip Mandel'shtam of his rehabilitation was sent to his address in Cheboksary, notwithstanding that he had been shot in 1938.[39] Despite the growing number of rehabilitations, there was no public criticism of Stalin prior to the Congress. He was mentioned as little as possible in the press. Articles devoted to his life and work in reference books and elsewhere were gradually pruned, so that edition by edition his reputation was diminished, but the silence concerning his crimes remained unbroken.

Khrushchev genuinely believed that the truth about Stalin's crimes could not be covered up indefinitely and that the party's authority at home and abroad would be strengthened rather than weakened if it confronted the issue before it was compelled by events to do so. Power politics also played a role. Many of the members of the ruling group in 1956 had been senior to Khrushchev in the

1930s. They thus bore a greater share of the responsibility for the bloodbaths of 1936–8 than did he. By forcing the issue of Stalin's crimes onto the agenda, Khrushchev would acquire a powerful weapon against men like Molotov, Kaganovich and Malenkov.

The question of what, if anything, to say about Stalin at the Congress was not resolved until after it began. Khrushchev's initial suggestion that the repressions of the 1930s and 1940s be discussed at the Congress met with stiff opposition from Molotov, Kaganovich and Voroshilov, who were understandably concerned about the impact of such a discussion on their own political standing.[40] Unable to persuade them, Khrushchev presented his colleagues with an ultimatum. The mandates of the party's leading organs had formally expired at the beginning of the Congress, and a new Central Committee had yet to be chosen. Strictly speaking this meant that he was no longer subject to the discipline of the Presidium in his public statements. He had said nothing about Stalin in the General Report, which was delivered in the name of the Central Committee, but he could under party statutes say anything he wished on the matter when speaking as a simple delegate.[41] The implied threat was clear: if his colleagues agreed to the report, they would have some influence over its content and would avoid the appearance of a divided leadership; if not, there was no telling what Khrushchev might say on his own.

A compromise was quickly agreed. The issue would be addressed at a closed session of the Congress *after* the election of the new Central Committee; this would ensure that it would not threaten anyone's position in the balloting for the new committee. The Presidium already had in its possession the findings of the Pospelov commission on the repressions, and Khrushchev suggested that Pospelov deliver a report based on them. Khrushchev's colleagues argued that this would create the appearance of a split within the leadership, since Khrushchev had not touched on the issue in the General Report. They insisted that Khrushchev himself deliver the report.[42] In reality all present understood the risks involved; Khrushchev, therefore, preferred to have someone else deliver the report, while the others were determined that he would assume these risks himself. Some doubtless hoped that it would prove his undoing.

Khrushchev's speech was hurriedly drafted on the basis of Pospelov's report to the Presidium; this haste was reflected in its disjointed structure and numerous factual errors, which might have been avoided in a more carefully prepared text. The closed session took place on the morning of 25 February, the last day of the Congress. By that time, however, the crimes of the Stalin era had already been raised. On 16 February, Anastas Mikoian had spoken of 'wrongly declared enemies of the people' and had called Kosior and Antonov-Ovseenko, two of the most prominent victims of the purges, 'comrades'. He told the Congress that 'for roughly 20 years we did not really have collective leadership' and that 'a cult of personality . . . flourished'. Mikoian also criticised Stalin's last major theoretical work, *Economic Problems of Socialism in the USSR*.[43] The speech struck the Congress like a thunderbolt; the commotion in the hall was such that no one even heard the next speaker. It would be easier to evaluate Mikoian's performance if it were known when the decision to present Pospelov's findings to the Congress was taken. If Mikoian spoke before a decision, then his speech must have been intended to force the Presidium's hand; the leadership could not have left Mikoian's words hanging in the air without some more authoritative comment. If he spoke after the decision was made, then he may have been testing the waters for Khrushchev himself.

Khrushchev delivered what became known as the Secret Speech in the early hours of 25 February. He began speaking just after midnight, and over the next four hours he demolished the reputation of the man to whom he had offered absolute loyalty and slavish obedience for thirty years. The devoted tiger at last turned on his master. The version of party history he presented was incomplete and often self-serving, but the significance of the speech should not for this reason be underestimated, nor should Khrushchev's courage. He delivered his report to an audience of powerful officials who were overwhelmingly opposed to confronting the past. Khrushchev alluded to such opposition when he stated that 'not everyone as yet appreciates the practical consequences of the cult of personality, the great harm caused by violation of the principle of collective leadership in the party'.[44] In other words, the speech was an answer to those who wished to leave the horrors of the past in the past and maintain the conspiracy of silence around them. Although he discussed at length such issues as Stalin's relations with Lenin and Stalin's record as a war leader, the primary focus of the speech was on the late dictator's repression of leading party officials. This choice of emphasis was both an attempt to make the speech more palatable to Khrushchev's listeners and an assurance that there would be no recurrence of such abuses.

Khrushchev's explanation of the evils of Stalinism was far from complete. Italian communist leader Palmiro Togliatti observed,

> Previously all good was due to the superhuman qualities of one man; now all the evil is attributed to his equally exceptional and shocking defects. . . . The real problems are skipped over – how and why Soviet society . . . could and did depart from the self-chosen path of democracy and legality to the point of degeneration.[45]

Even Togliatti's remarks show a failure to grasp the deeper roots of the Stalin phenomenon; his reference to the 'self-chosen path of democracy and legality' ignores both the nature of the Bolshevik seizure of power and the character of the early communist regime. Togliatti did, however, recognise Khrushchev's failure to undertake a serious examination of the ideological and structural roots of Stalinism. The terror and autocracy of Stalin's rule were explained almost entirely in terms of Stalin's own personality.

In fairness to Khrushchev, a more extensive analysis of the problem was probably beyond him. His passionate belief in the essential soundness and justice of the Soviet system, a belief born of his whole life experience, effectively precluded any admission that the system itself might in some fundamental way be flawed. This belief in the system was the source of much of the ambivalence with which Khrushchev spoke of Stalin then and later. The system to which he was committed had, after all, been built by Stalin, not by Lenin. Thus no mention was made of the millions who had perished during collectivisation: Khrushchev approved of the party's ruthlessness towards its enemies and was committed to the maintenance of the collective farm system in the countryside.

Other lines of analysis were off-limits for political reasons. Khrushchev could not trace the roots of the terror back into Lenin's time without raising questions about the legitimacy of the regime. He later stated that he could not address the cases of those like Bukharin, Rykov, Zinoviev and Kamenev, who had been tried in open court, because many of the foreign communist leaders present at the Twentieth Congress had been at the show trials and had then returned home and reported favourably on them to their parties.[46] This was disingenuous: men like Thorez of France and Togliatti of Italy would have been far less embarrassed by a renunciation of the show trials than would Khrushchev, who had agitated publicly and at length against the defendants, or his Presidium colleagues, some of whom had been involved in fabricating these cases.

The First Secretary did try to use the speech to damage the reputations of his 'guiltier' colleagues, like Molotov, but Khrushchev's references to his rivals had to be carefully tempered so as to avoid provoking a backlash or puncturing the myth that Stalin alone was responsible for what happened. Of the Presidium members in office at the time of the Twentieth Congress, Khrushchev mentioned himself, Molotov, Mikoian, Kaganovich, Malenkov, Voroshilov and Bulganin. In each instance they are cast in one of three roles: powerless witnesses to Stalin's abuses, recipients of his orders or prospective victims of his wrath. Many of these episodes appear to have been Khrushchev's personal emendations to the text prepared by Pospelov.

In closing, Khrushchev warned his audience that 'we must not let this matter get out of the party, especially to the press . . . we should not feed our enemies; we should not expose our sores to them'.[47] The speech did not long remain a secret, however. Moscow was abuzz with rumours about it within twenty-four hours, and the 1430 voting and non-voting delegates who listened to the speech soon returned to their homes, taking with them news of the bombshell detonated by Khrushchev on the last day of the Congress. Even Mikoian failed to keep the secret; at the end of February he summoned Stalin's daughter, Svetlana Alliluyeva, to his office and gave her a copy of the speech to read.[48] Foreign communist leaders were allowed to listen to a tape recording of the speech, and a copy of the text was even sent to Tito.[49] In the spring a copy circulated in the Polish party reached the West, where translations appeared in *Le Monde* and the *New York Times*. Neither Khrushchev nor his colleagues would acknowledge the authenticity of the text which appeared in the western press, but they stopped short of denying it. When asked about it by US Ambassador Charles Bohlen, Khrushchev replied, 'Those translations which have been published abroad do not correspond to reality.'[50]

When it became clear that the secret could not be kept, it was decided that the speech should be read to all primary party organisations. Special PPO meetings were convened for this purpose. The text of the speech was read without commentary, and, as a rule, no discussion of its contents followed. Party members recounted it to non-members, as the unpublished, unacknowledged report became an open secret in the Soviet Union.

The Twentieth Congress was more than a forum for posthumously dethroning Stalin; Khrushchev also proposed doctrinal innovations of his own. In the General Report of the Central Committee, he sought to establish himself as the representative of a middle course between the extremes of dogmatism and revisionism represented by Molotov and Malenkov. He attacked those (Malenkov) who 'assure us that the predominant development of heavy industry was essential only in the early stages of Soviet economic development' as well as the 'erroneous formulations' of 'some people' (Molotov), including the assertion that 'so far only the foundations of socialism have been built in our country'.[51]

Khrushchev's most significant innovations were in the section of the General Report devoted to foreign affairs. First, he rejected Lenin's theses concerning the inevitability of war and the role of war as the 'midwife of the

revolution', arguing that these had been formulated at a
time when imperialism was an all-embracing world system.
The expansion of socialism and the creation of a world
socialist system, Khrushchev maintained, meant that the
forces for peace in the world had been greatly strengthened. In place of these Leninist theses Khrushchev took up
the principle of peaceful coexistence between states with
differing social systems. The alternatives, he argued, were
'either peaceful coexistence or the most destructive war in
history. There is no third option.' Khrushchev thus appropriated yet another of the themes for which he had
castigated Malenkov in 1954. Khrushchev articulated a
theory of deterrence, but not mutual deterrence. There was
no reason for a socialist state to wage aggressive war, he
said; therefore it is only the imperialists who must be
deterred.[52]

As a corollary to his doctrine of peaceful coexistence,
Khrushchev advanced the thesis that communism could
be achieved by peaceful – even parliamentary – means.
Violence was no longer the only, or even the principal, way
to remake society. He was quick to stress, however, that
peaceful coexistence applied only to relations between
states, not between *classes*. The Soviet Union was therefore
justified in supporting 'wars of national liberation' in the
ex-colonial countries of the developing world. Khrushchev
laid great stress on the potential for developing the Soviet
Union's relations with the emerging new states of Africa
and Asia. Khrushchev's final innovation in foreign affairs
was to elaborate on his belief that there were 'different
paths to socialism' and that countries like Yugoslavia and
China (both of which he mentioned) were no less socialist
for having adapted their systems to suit local conditions
rather than mimicking the USSR.[53]

In the portions of his report devoted to domestic issues,
Khrushchev's most significant departures from the policies
of the Nineteenth Congress concerned nationality policy.
He spoke at length of the expansion of the powers of the
union republics since 1953 and called for this to continue.
In contrast to the Russian chauvinist tone of nationality
policy statements at the previous Congress, Khrushchev
quoted Lenin on the compatibility of national pride with

both socialist internationalism and Soviet patriotism. He stated flatly that socialism would not and should not obliterate national differences.[54] He reinforced his commitment to the rights of the non-Russian nationalities in the Secret Speech twelve days later, attacking Stalin's treatment of five small nations which had been deported from their lands in the 1940s for alleged collaboration with the Nazis. They had been exiled in toto to remote regions of the USSR.[55] Khrushchev omitted any mention of the deportations of Germans and Crimean Tatars.

The Central Committee elected at the Twentieth Congress and the Presidium and Secretariat elected by the new Committee immediately afterwards reflected the continued shift in the locus of political power from the central state machinery to the territorial party apparatus, Khrushchev's principal power base: regional and republican officials made up 56 per cent of the full membership of the new Committee and just under 46 per cent of the candidates. Khrushchev enjoyed the strong support of roughly a third of the new Central Committee, with another third more likely to lean to him than to anyone else. The full membership of the Presidium remained unchanged, but Malenkov's client Ponomarenko was dropped from candidate membership and four close Khrushchev associates were elected as candidates; three of them were local party bosses.[56] In addition, Khrushchev seems to have been close to the Defence Minister, Marshal Georgii Zhukov, who was raised to candidate membership. Leonid Brezhnev and Ekaterina Furtseva, both Khrushchev clients, were elected to the Secretariat.[57] (Furtseva, the highest-ranking woman in the political hierarchy was widely and, it would appear, incorrectly rumoured to be Khrushchev's lover.[58])

For four and a half months after the Congress Khrushchev rode the storm his words had unleashed. Stalin's posthumous dethronement triggered riots in Tbilisi, the capital of his native Georgia, on the anniversary of his death.[59] Across the country the effect of the speech was to loosen the tongues of the long silent populace; political discussions began to take place in public, and in the Lenin–Stalin mausoleum, the holy of holies of the Soviet regime, visitors were overheard muttering curses at Stalin. Writers took the report as a cue to begin addressing long-forbidden themes, often moving far beyond Khrushchev's carefully qualified criticism of Stalin's personal qualities. Khrushchev pressed the East European regimes to follow the Soviet lead and undertake de-Stalinisation, but it was of cardinal importance that local communist parties remain in control of the process and direct it in such a way as to enhance rather than undermine their own authority. This was not always possible; foreign communist parties were in a ferment, and many of them felt free for the first time to criticise the CPSU and its leaders.

Khrushchev had intended the speech to remain an internal party matter, but in the Soviet Union and abroad it had moved beyond the party and, as it did so, beyond the issue of Stalin's faults to the larger failings of the system. Foreign anti-communists were having a field day with the speech, and even foreign communists openly criticised the Soviet system. Within the Soviet party the privileges and abuses of officials came under attack from below. The secretary of the Vladimir provincial party committee complained that he could scarcely show his face at any party gathering. Rank-and-file communists raised issues such as multi-party democracy and free elections. The party officialdom, raised under Stalin, was frightened and confused.[60]

In late March and early April *Pravda* attempted to channel the wave of de-Stalinisation along lines approved by the Party. A pair of editorials stressed Stalin's achievements as well as his faults and drew conclusions for readers as to the appropriate steps to be taken: communists were to struggle both against the bureaucratic work methods which had grown up in conjunction with the cult of personality and against any attempts to advance 'slanderous' and 'anti-party' statements under the guise of criticism of the cult. The paper attacked those 'rotten elements' who 'under the guise of condemning the cult of personality are trying to raise doubts about the correctness of the party's policies'.[61]

Nevertheless, the changes continued. The abolition of the special tribunals operated by the security services was announced on 19 April. Experiments with workers' councils were initiated in factories, and there was even discussion of allowing multiple candidates in elections to local soviets. The most notorious of pre-war labour laws were relaxed, and a commission of jurists was appointed to examine the legal code.[62] The most significant internal change was the acceleration of the rehabilitation process. At Khrushchev's suggestion more than ninety special commissions were established to re-examine convictions in prison camps and settlements established for internal exiles. By the end of the summer several million people had been released, some after serving thirty years in the camps or in internal exile.[63]

The new line of the Twentieth Congress was also reflected in foreign policy. In April the Communist Information Bureau, the organisation used by Stalin to excommunicate Tito, was dissolved. Khrushchev also attempted to engage western social democratic parties in discussions concerning the formation of a united front of communist and social democratic parties in Europe; the latter were unimpressed, and the bureau of the Socialist International stated that the condemnation of Stalin at the Twentieth Congress had not altered fundamentally the character of the Soviet regime.[64] Undaunted, Khrushchev raised his united front proposal with British Labour Party leader Hugh Gaitskell while on a state visit to Britain. The meeting was not a success. Khrushchev annoyed his hosts with talk of the Soviet H-bomb and hints of a Soviet–West German alliance against the rest of Europe; he in turn was offended when Gaitskell handed him a list of 200 political prisoners in the communist countries whom the Labour Party wished to see released. The First Secretary found Labour politician George Brown's criticisms of Soviet policy so offensive that he and Bulganin left before dinner was over. Khrushchev is said to have complained the following day that if this was British socialism, he preferred to be a Tory.[65] Nevertheless, he made similar (likewise unsuccessful) attempts to encourage anti-American, neutralist sentiment in talks with French socialists on the way home from London.

Khrushchev's purpose in going to the United Kingdom had been to persuade the Eden government to allow the Soviets to buy embargoed strategic goods. Eden saw this as a Soviet attempt to obtain economic favours from Britain while simultaneously sowing discord between London and Washington. The proposal came to nothing, and little of substance was said on other questions under discussion. Khrushchev and Bulganin were received by the Queen, after being assured that they could wear ordinary business suits to meet her; Khrushchev had made it clear that he and Bulganin were unwilling to 'get all dressed up in tails and top hats or anything else they might have insisted on'. Khrushchev, whose image of royalty was still rooted in the Bolshevik propaganda of the 1920s, was surprised to discover that Elizabeth II

> looked exactly like the sort of young woman you'd be likely to meet walking along Gorky Street on a balmy summer afternoon. . . . She was completely unpretentious, completely without the haughtiness that you'd expect of royalty.[66]

He presented her with a tiger cub.

The de-Stalinisation campaign reached a crescendo in June before coming to an abrupt halt. Tito arrived on 2 June, the day Molotov was replaced by Dmitri Shepilov as Minister of Foreign Affairs. His visit received extensive coverage in the Soviet press. On 27 June a *Pravda* article by American communist leader Eugene Dennis went further than any author in the Soviet press had yet done in criticising Stalin and made the first reference to the Secret Speech published in the USSR. Three days later, however, the regime retreated. The Central Committee resolution of 30 June, 'On Overcoming the Cult of Personality and its Consequences', criticised certain of Stalin's theoretical mistakes and the repressions of the 1930s, but defended his achievements as a statesman and confirmed his status as a great Marxist-Leninist theoretician. His 'merciless struggle against the enemies of Leninism' was approved, as was his war-time leadership. The resolution explicitly condemned Togliatti's suggestion that the cult was related to 'certain forms of degeneration' in Soviet society.[67] *Pravda* retreated further in July, and by the end of the month criticism was reserved almost exclusively for those who had carried de-Stalinisation too far.[68]

Among the chief sinners in this respect were Soviet writers and artists. The ideological basis for literary policy was still the resolution 'On the Journals *Zvezda* and *Leningrad*' with which Zhdanov had initiated his cultural crackdown a decade before. The resolution had lost much of its force, but formally it remained party doctrine. In June the prominent writer Ol'ga Berggol'ts called for its annulment. Other writers, composers and artists soon joined her, including the influential Konstantin Simonov, then editor of *Novyi Mir* and a member of the Central Revision Commission of the CPSU. Even more radical demands were made by university students, who called for the separation of art from politics. Intellectuals, writers and artists had begun to raise the issue of creative freedom in the discussions which followed the Congress; party meetings in the writers' unions and other artistic organisations became especially heated.[69] Works such as Dudintsev's controversial *Not by Bread Alone* began to appear, drawing attention to the moral deformation of Soviet society during the Stalin era.

This was unacceptable to Khrushchev; he could not yield on the matter of party guidance of the arts, because he did not believe that art could be apolitical:

> Creative work . . . has a tendency to interfere in the political sphere because it is part of the artistic process to analyse relations among people, including relations between those in power on the one hand and common workers on the other. Writers are forever delving into questions of philosophy and ideology – questions on which any ruling party . . . would like to have a monopoly. You can't accomplish much unless you cultivate people's minds and guide them in the right direction. . . . We wanted to guide the progress of the thaw so that it would stimulate only those creative forces which would contribute to the strengthening of socialism.[70]

In the General Report to the Twentieth Congress, he stated that

> Creative activity in the field of literature and the arts should be permeated with the spirit of struggle for

communism; it should inspire cheerfulness of heart and firmness of convictions; it should develop socialist consciousness and comradely discipline.[71]

Far more serious than the problem of the writers was the impact of the de-Stalinisation campaign in Eastern Europe. The most serious problems were in Poland and Hungary. Poland had gone furthest of all, largely on account of the death of the Polish party leader, Boleslav Bierut, on 12 March. The change of leadership which ensued opened the way for an amnesty for thousands of political prisoners and a purge of Stalinists in the Polish security services. When a workers' strike developed into a rising in Poznan in late June, the Polish authorities refused to follow Moscow in blaming the events on western interference; they instead acknowledged that the causes of the rising were social and economic conditions in the region and made concessions to the workers. Moscow was more upset by the Polish regime's reaction than by the disturbances themselves.[72]

Hungary presented a different problem. Hungarian communist leader Mathias Rakosi was attempting to yield as little as possible to the pressures for change. Opposition to him continued to grow within both the ruling Hungarian Party of Labour and the society at large, as Rakosi himself admitted to Mikhail Suslov, who travelled to Budapest in June. Suslov stressed the need to maintain the unity of the Hungarian party and told his hosts that the removal of Rakosi or a split in the Hungarian Central Committee would be 'such a gift to hostile forces that they could not hope for anything better'.[73] The Soviet embassy in Budapest reported to Moscow in June that the situation was explosive; Rakosi was hated not only by intellectuals but also by the workers. Mikoian, dispatched to Budapest by Khrushchev in July, concluded that Rakosi must go.[74] His removal in July bought time for the regime but failed to address the deeper causes of its unpopularity or its internal divisions.

By October events in Poland and Hungary were coming to a head. The rising in Poznan had been put down at the cost of 53 dead, more than 300 wounded and 323 arrests. The Polish authorities, however, did not stop at the restoration of order. Ignoring Moscow's blame-the-imperialists line, the government made a series of financial concessions designed to improve workers' living standards; those arrested in connection with the rising were quickly released. By mid-October it was clear that Wladislaw Gomulka, a prominent party official who had been imprisoned as a Titoist, was to replace Bierut's successor, Edvard Ochab, as party leader.

Khrushchev and his colleagues were concerned about the Polish party's independence, and about increasingly public displays of anti-Soviet sentiment in Poland. Khrushchev was offended that the Poles seemed so quickly to have forgotten the Soviet liberation of Poland from the Nazis (rather as he was quick to forget the Soviet–German partition of Poland in 1939) and worried that an anti-Soviet leadership was about to be installed; his principal concern was the prospect of Polish withdrawal from the Warsaw Pact.[75] On the eve of the Polish Central Committee plenum which was to replace Ochab, Khrushchev requested permission to send a delegation from the Soviet leadership to the plenum. Gomulka's negative reply only made Khrushchev all the more determined to go.

He arrived uninvited on 19 October along with Mikoian, Molotov, Kaganovich and the Warsaw Pact commander, Marshal Konev. The Soviets were refused admission to the Polish plenum but conducted lengthy discussions with the Polish Politburo. Khrushchev instructed Marshal Konev to move Soviet units in Silesia toward Warsaw, where, he claimed, an anti-Soviet rising was imminent. It is unclear whether Khrushchev actually believed this; the troop movements may simply have been a means of intimidating the Polish leaders. After receiving assurances from Gomulka that the changes in Poland would not affect the Polish–Soviet relationship, Khrushchev and his colleagues returned to Moscow on 20 October.[76]

Returning home, Khrushchev had reason to view the resolution of the Polish crisis with satisfaction. The Polish United Workers' Party under Gomulka was popular, united and in firm control of the country, and Gomulka had assured him that the new leadership in Warsaw would pose no threat to Soviet security. Gomulka kept his word, and

Khrushchev never again faced a political crisis in Poland. In Moscow the Presidium devoted four sessions to relations with the East European states before inviting the leaders of Bulgaria, East Germany and Czechoslovakia to Moscow to discuss Soviet–East European relations on 24 October. The Soviets promised not to interfere in their neighbours' affairs and offered to withdraw their troops from Eastern Europe and to reduce the number of Soviet 'advisers' attached to local military and security establishments. Far from being a concession, this offer was a grave threat to the East European communists, who knew that they had no hope of survival without Soviet military backing.[77]

Khrushchev's handling of the crisis in Warsaw secured Soviet interests in Poland without bloodshed, but its effect on the Hungarian situation was catastrophic. Hungarian reformists, taking heart from the Poles' successful defiance of Moscow, renewed the pressure for radical change. A mass demonstration in Budapest on 23 October quickly turned into a popular uprising, forcing Hungarian party leaders to replace Prime Minister Hegedüs with the reformist ex-premier Imre Nagy. With Nagy's consent, the government requested that Soviet troops enter Budapest. Their presence inflamed the resistance and they spent four days in a vain attempt to restore order. On 28 October Nagy negotiated a ceasefire and the withdrawal of Soviet troops from Budapest. He conceded the rebels' major demands, including the demand for a multi-party system. The government's authority had all but collapsed by this time and the party was disintegrating.

Some time before 30 October Khrushchev and his colleagues decided that the Hungarian rising was a counter-revolution and must be crushed. On 31 October Mikoian and Suslov, who had been in Budapest for some days, returned; the former, when confronted with the decision to use armed force, threatened suicide if it were carried out. Khrushchev himself was strongly in favour of intervention.[78] Soviet troops withdrawing from Budapest in accordance with the agreement of 28 October took up positions around the capital; other Soviet units entered the country from Ukraine on the pretext of arranging the safe evacuation of Soviet dependents. Nagy was outraged by these developments and for three days demanded an explanation from the Soviet ambassador in Budapest, Yuri Andropov. On 1 November, Nagy declared Hungary's intention to leave the Warsaw Pact and become a neutral power. He appealed to the United Nations and the four great powers to secure Hungarian neutrality and the withdrawal of Soviet forces.

Khrushchev in the meantime was explaining his decision to other East European communist leaders, including Tito. Tito had earlier been sympathetic to Nagy but was by now upset by the turn which events had taken; communists were being lynched and Nagy seemed to have become an agent of the imperialists. Khrushchev understandably stressed the ideological rather than the security dimension of Soviet concerns to Tito, but he also alluded to the implications for Soviet domestic politics of a successful counter-revolution in Hungary. Stalinists, he said, would use it to discredit the line of the Twentieth Congress. According to Tito's ambassador in Moscow at the time, the Yugoslav leader agreed on the need to intervene but stressed that reliance on Soviet military might alone was not enough; a political solution was needed for Hungary, said Tito, who recommended Janos Kadar as the next leader rather than Ferenc Munnich, the candidate favoured by Khrushchev. It was agreed that the Yugoslavs would neutralise Nagy by inviting him to seek refuge in their embassy.[79]

On 2 November Kadar and Munnich, both members of Nagy's government, disappeared from Budapest; they turned up the following day in Ukraine at the head of a self-proclaimed provisional revolutionary government which requested Soviet intervention. The Soviet offensive began in earnest early on 4 November with the arrest of Nagy's Minister of Defence, Pal Maleter, who had gone under a promise of safe conduct to negotiate a Soviet withdrawal with Marshal Malinin. The pacification of Hungary was quick and bloody; at least 4000 Hungarians died, as did 669 Soviet troops. Kadar was installed in Budapest. On 22 November Nagy, after receiving assurances of his personal safety from the government, left his refuge in the Yugoslav embassy to go home. He was arrested immediately. On the whole, Kadar attempted to keep the number of post-invasion executions to a minimum and asked the Soviet leaders to take a soft line: only about 300 death sentences were carried out, far fewer than had been expected.[80] Nagy was among them; in 1957, after much hesitation and discussion with Moscow and Belgrade, the Hungarian regime condemned and executed him.[81]

Khrushchev defended his actions in Hungary for the rest of his life. He regarded Nagy's government as counter-revolutionary and was unwilling to allow Hungary to leave the Warsaw Pact or abandon one-party socialism. A change in the status of Hungary would have undermined the post-war status quo in Europe, and the potential ripple effects on other East European countries were extremely serious. If the Polish example had ignited Hungary, who could say what a successful Hungarian revolution would set off elsewhere in the bloc? Khrushchev was also aware that his own chances of remaining in power would have been slender indeed had he not crushed the Hungarian revolution. Nevertheless, the Hungarian events undid in a fortnight much of what Khrushchev had achieved over the previous three and a half years. His talk of peace, non-interference and 'different paths' to socialism, his 'twentieth-century Canossa' at Belgrade and his constant attempts to present the world with a new image of the Soviet Union all fell victim to the Soviet tanks in Budapest.

The costs to Khrushchev of smashing the uprising would have been much greater had it not been for the bungling of the western powers. Angered by Nasser's nationalisation of the Suez Canal, France and Britain plotted with Israel to take back control of it. On 29 October, Israel, which had been alarmed by Nasser's bellicose rhetoric, invaded the Sinai peninsula. Within 100 hours Israeli forces were on the east bank of the canal. At this point France and Britain, allegedly acting to defuse the crisis, demanded that both sides withdraw ten miles from the canal; Israel complied but Egypt refused. The two European states then used Nasser's refusal as a pretext for intervention and seized control of the canal. The United States strongly condemned its allies' actions and exerted enormous financial pressure on Britain in particular in order to force a withdrawal. Moscow was delighted with the crisis, which distracted attention from Hungary, but did little more than lodge protests and exploit the propaganda value of the conflict until 5 November, by which time US pressure was forcing Britain and France to withdraw. At that point Khrushchev rattled his nuclear sabre in a diplomatic note to Britain, France, Israel and the United States:

> If missile weapons were used against Britain and France, you would doubtless call that a barbarous deed. But how does it differ from the inhuman attack conducted by the armed forces of Britain and France against a practically unarmed Egypt? . . . We are fully resolved to use force to crush the aggressors and restore peace in the East.[82]

Khrushchev later claimed that it was the Soviet threat rather than Eisenhower's speech ('just a gesture for the sake of public appearances') which brought about a withdrawal.[83] It is impossible to know if he believed this or if he knew when the threat was made that the danger was already past. In any case, the threat was damaging as well as unnecessary. It had a certain propaganda value in some developing countries – especially in the Arab world – but it precluded any Soviet attempts to play on the friction which had arisen between America and her allies over the crisis.

East–West relations remained extremely tense in the months following the twin crises, and it was in this atmosphere that Khrushchev uttered the phrase for which he is best remembered in the West. On 18 November western diplomats left the room when he rose to speak at an embassy reception in Moscow; it was the second such walkout in as many days. In response to this gesture, Khrushchev remarked,

> About the capitalist states, it doesn't depend on you whether or not we exist. If you don't like us, don't accept our invitations and don't invite us to come see you. Whether you like it or not, history is on our side. We will bury you.[84]

Ironically, the remark came in the midst of a generally conciliatory speech, full of references to the need for *détente* which were overlooked or quickly forgotten. Khrushchev himself was frustrated for the rest of his life by the fact that this was taken as a military threat; he repeatedly emphasised that what he had in mind was the victory of socialism in a peaceful economic competition with capitalism.[85] In the tense atmosphere following Suez and Hungary, however, such pacific interpretations were not the first to spring to mind in the West.

Shaken by events in Hungary, the Soviet leaders put the post-Congress literary thaw on ice. The writers had largely ignored the party's change of course in July. Simonov had – apparently with approval from above – called for a revision of the party's line in the arts as late as October, but in December the Zhdanovite resolutions of 1946 were reaffirmed. A closed letter of the Central Committee circulated to party organs stated, 'All communists who are employed in literature, the arts or scientific institutions are obligated . . . to demonstrate a high degree of party spirit and principle in their activity and to give a decisive rebuff to any attempts to reexamine the party's line in the field of literature and the arts.'[86] The secretary of the Moscow party writers' organisation stated that 'We should have in our armoury the decisions of the CC on ideological questions from 1946–48. They are only outdated in certain particulars, but in the main they correctly direct people working in the arts and literature.'[87]

Khrushchev's mounting political troubles at home and abroad were compounded by problems with the newly inaugurated Sixth Five-Year Plan. Its overly ambitious goals led to a capital investment crisis by the end of 1956; the available capital fell short of plan requirements by more than 25 per cent. Under Stalin such crises had occurred frequently and had always been solved at the expense of housing and consumer interests; heavy industrial growth was maintained no matter what. In the wake of events in Hungary, such a solution could no longer be considered safe.[88] The ambitious targets of the plan were largely Khrushchev's doing, and its failure came at a time when he was already politically vulnerable. In late December his rivals struck back.

On 25 December *Pravda* reported that a Central Committee meeting had just revised both the Five-Year Plan and the annual plan for 1957. The volume of capital investments was reduced and plan targets were lowered accordingly. Control over both current and long-term planning was given to the State Economic Commission (*Gosekonom-komissiia*), which was placed under the control of Presidium member M. G. Pervukhin; a number of high-powered industrial administrators were appointed to serve as his deputies.[89] The centralisation of economic power in the hands of Pervukhin and his deputies represented a repudiation of the policies of regionalisation and decentralisation which Khrushchev had been pursuing. None of the leading members of Pervukhin's team could be identified as a close associate of Khrushchev, and at least two had been in conflict with him. Khrushchev's name was not even mentioned in official accounts of the plenum, and his protégé Shepilov, who had been appointed foreign minister in June, was dropped from the Secretariat. To all appearances, the First Secretary had been cut off from any significant involvement in economic policy.

As 1957 opened Khrushchev's political future looked uncertain indeed. In every sphere from foreign policy to culture the regime had retreated from the innovations of the Twentieth Congress and the challenges posed by the Secret Speech. Khrushchev himself had retreated as well, frightened by the effect of his own words. When Central Committee Secretary Dmitrii Shepilov suggested renaming the Stalin prizes which were awarded in the arts, Khrushchev replied, 'Why? If I had a Stalin prize I would wear it with pride.'[90] At a Chinese reception in Moscow in January 1957 the First Secretary told his hosts that 'the term "Stalinist", like Stalin himself, is inseparable from the high title of communist'.[91] It had been a year of struggles since Khrushchev had turned on his late master, and Stalin's ghost appeared to be gaining the upper hand.

7 Khrushchev Triumphant
The Drive for Supremacy, 1957–8

I tried not to occupy two posts, but, after all, it was you who gave me these two posts! And despite the fact that I am a talented person, I consider this incorrect. My mistake was that I failed to raise this question at the Twenty-Second Congress of the CPSU.

N. S. Khrushchev, 13 October 1964[1]

By the time the USSR Supreme Soviet convened to confirm the revised Plan worked out in December, there were signs that Khrushchev's star was again rising. Pervukhin declared the Virgin Lands scheme a 'striking success', and his report to the Supreme Soviet was much less critical of the economic decisions made at the Twentieth Congress than the resolution of the December plenum had been.[2] Pervukhin's reference to the Virgin Lands points to the basis for the revival of Khrushchev's fortunes. Between the December plenum and the February Supreme Soviet session it had become clear that the 1956 harvest from the Virgin Lands was a tremendous success. The importance of this development was all the greater in light of the drought that had occurred in the traditional grain-growing areas of the western Soviet Union. Khrushchev's scheme had saved the country from a serious shortage of grain.[3]

The February Supreme Soviet session confirmed Pervukhin's plan revisions and gave no indication that he would not retain the enormous authority he had been given by the Central Committee in December. No sooner had the deputies gone home, however, than yet another Central Committee plenum was convened, this time to discuss a report by Khrushchev on 'the further perfection of the guidance of industry and construction'. The approach of the December plenum was reversed. The resolution based on Khrushchev's report called for Gosekonomkomissiia to be confined to long-term planning and severely criticised the industrial ministries for waste, inefficiency, remoteness from actual production and, most significantly, for limiting 'the opportunities of local party, soviet and trade union organs in direct economic construction'. The resolution declared it 'expedient to organise the management of industry and construction according to the major economic regions'.[4]

The meaning of the vaguely phrased resolution did not become clear for six weeks. On 19 February Khrushchev explained that 'we mean to do away with the industrial ministries altogether, both at the centre and in the republics. Instead, all industrial enterprises . . . will be directed by territorial departments',[5] but the exact nature of the reform was made public only at the end of March, when the major newspapers published Khrushchev's 'theses' on industrial reorganisation and opened a nationwide discussion on the issue.[6] Khrushchev proposed nothing less than the abolition of all branch economic ministries and their replacement by councils of the national economy, or sovnarkhozes. He justified this shift to territorially based economic administration primarily on the grounds that it would lead to closer ties between different branches of the economy, greater attention to regional considerations in planning and closer relations between key economic administrators (now the sovnarkhoz chairmen in the locales rather than ministers in Moscow) and enterprises.

The theses were advanced in Khrushchev's own name rather than in the name of the Central Committee, the Presidium or any other body. That they were his initiative was underscored by the silence of his fellow Presidium members during the month of discussion which followed their publication. The delay in publishing the theses was indicative of stiff opposition to the plan, and Khrushchev himself referred to the unfounded fears of 'some comrades' about its effects.[7] The root of their opposition was obvious. Khrushchev proposed to abolish the very institutions which formed their principal base of support: seven of the eleven full members of the Presidium held ministerial positions. The plan was designed to strengthen Khrushchev's traditional supporters, the leaders of the territorial party apparatus, who would oversee the new sovnarkhozes, while simultaneously smashing once and for all the powerful industrial ministries which had been bastions of support for his opponents.

The proposals provoked one of the bitterest fights of Khrushchev's career. The nationwide discussion of the theses was remarkably open for the time, and opposition to the reforms was only thinly veiled.[8] No one publicly questioned the desirability of the reform 'in principle', but enterprise directors and economists were remarkably frank in criticising the specifics of the proposals; often their remedies amounted to nothing less than gutting the scheme altogether.[9] Ministerial officials, who were overwhelmingly opposed to the reform, maintained an almost unbroken silence; none of those who did address the issue publicly indicted the ministerial system.[10]

Regional and republican officials also criticised the proposals, in one of the most successful public lobbying campaigns conducted in the USSR up to that time. Khrushchev's original theses were intended to pursue regionalisation of management with only limited decentralisation. He intended to destroy the ministries and increase the role of the union republics while still maintaining strong central direction of the economy. This reflected his vision of Soviet federalism: central decision-making and local implementation. The reform which was implemented in the summer of 1957, however, differed from the original proposals on a number of key points. In each instance the effect of the changes was to weaken the powers of the centre in the new system and to effect a degree of decentralisation far greater than what Khrushchev had intended.[11] The impetus for these changes came not from Moscow but from the provinces and republics. Local leaders pressed openly and aggressively for changes in the proposed reforms which would enhance their control over the new sovnarkhozes. Khrushchev, facing powerful opposition from his Presidium colleagues and their supporters, needed the support of provincial and republican party leaders more than ever. The price of their support was a much more radical decentralisation of management than he had envisioned, but he willingly paid it.

Economically, the sovnarkhoz reform turned out to present even more problems than the ministerial system. The departmental barriers between ministries were replaced by no less irrational barriers between economic regions, a danger of which Khrushchev himself was aware:

> Under the new structure of management, where local organs are granted extensive rights, there may appear tendencies toward autarky, attempts to build a closed economy within a region or republic. . . . The exposure and struggle against these harmful localist tendencies, which run counter to the interest of the whole state, should always be kept in view by party, soviet, economic and trade union organs.[12]

Yet despite the awareness that the reorganisation might simply replace departmental barriers with territorial ones, Khrushchev pressed ahead with the reforms. His decision to do so reflected political expedience rather than economic rationality. The problems which the reorganisation addressed were not even on the political agenda prior to February 1957; they were well-known defects of the system, and there is no reason to believe that they had suddenly reached crisis proportions or that they required a solution as radical as Khrushchev's.

Yet if the problems of industrial management had not yet reached crisis proportions in early 1957, Khrushchev's political difficulties had. The decisions of the December plenum threatened to cut him off completely from the making of economic policy. The sovnarkhoz reform was his attempt to keep that from happening. Initially, he proposed a reorganisation which would rid him of the ministries while leaving effective control of the economy at the centre. In the political struggle that followed he was forced to make the reform much more radical in order to win the support of local party élites.

The system of economic councils established by the reform was designed to put party officials directly in charge of industry by placing the sovnarkhozes in each area under the authority of local party committees. This party activist approach to industrial management required party officials at lower levels who were competent industrial administrators. The adoption of the sovnarkhoz reform thus coincided with a reorganisation of the party schools which trained up-and-coming party officials; Khrushchev himself oversaw this reorganisation. The term of study in the schools was doubled to four years, and the curriculum was restructured to emphasise 'practical' economic subjects rather than 'theoretical' political ones. Some 1800 hours were devoted to topics like book-keeping, production methods and animal husbandry, as against 1400 hours of instruction in political economy, dialectical materialism and related political topics.[13]

Passage of the sovnarkhoz reform was a major defeat for Khrushchev's opponents. Less than a fortnight later he provoked them again. On 22 May the First Secretary, without having consulted his Presidium colleagues, publicly called for the USSR to surpass the United States in the per capita production of meat, milk and butter within three years.[14] This would have required a 40 per cent increase in the production of milk and a trebling of meat output. It was not the first time that Khrushchev had attempted to tie his colleagues' hands by making public promises he had not discussed with them in advance, and it angered them greatly. When Khrushchev repeated the pledge in Moscow a few days later, Bulganin led them in a walkout.[15]

By this time Molotov no longer stood alone in the Presidium, as he had often done prior to the Twentieth Congress. The upheavals of 1956 had frightened even Bulganin, the comparatively moderate premier, to say nothing of conservatives like Kaganovich and Voroshilov. Malenkov, Saburov and Pervukhin were opposed to the growing power of the party apparatus, which threatened their own 'technocratic' vision of a Soviet future guided by expert managers and administrators rather than party hacks. No less worrisome than the consequences of Khrushchev's new course was his drive for personal dominance. The presence of five Khrushchev clients among the candidate members of the Presidium raised fears in the minds of full members that Khrushchev was preparing to replace them. By May 1957 an anti-Khrushchev group within the Presidium had formed, headed by Molotov, Kaganovich and Malenkov.[16]

The group's unity stemmed entirely from opposition to Khrushchev and his policies. Molotov and Malenkov, in particular, represented very different political positions and were ill-disposed towards one another personally. The group's 'platform' consisted of opposition to a range of Khrushchev policies: the sovnarkhoz scheme, material incentives for kolkhozes, the break up of the Machine and Tractor Stations and the campaign to overtake the United States in agricultural production. Ironically, this last issue raised the spectre of the investment priorities question over which Malenkov had fallen, this time placing Khrushchev in the revisionist position and aligning the ex-premier with Stalinist conservatives like Molotov.[17]

The anti-Khrushchev faction, by then a majority of the Presidium's voting members, made its move at a Presidium meeting on 18 June. Khrushchev's position was all the weaker on account of the absence of both Kirichenko, the one Presidium member who was his undoubted client, and Suslov, who had not been drawn into the conspiracy. As soon as the meeting opened, Malenkov proposed that Khrushchev be replaced in the chair by Bulganin. Malenkov, Molotov and Kaganovich then spoke in turn, bitterly criticising the First Secretary. Khrushchev's protégé Shepilov supported them, as did Bulganin, Voroshilov, Saburov and Pervukhin. The opposition proposed to eliminate the post of First Secretary and to elect themselves to the Secretariat. The group hoped to resolve the issue quickly, so as to present the Central Committee with a *fait accompli*. Khrushchev, however, stalled for time on procedural grounds, threatening to boycott the meeting unless and until all Presidium members and candidates and all Central Committee Secretaries were summoned to participate. He was supported by Mikoian, Brezhnev, Furtseva and, perhaps most importantly, Minister of Defence Zhukov, who controlled the armed forces. Khrushchev's procedural objections carried weight largely because the armed forces under Zhukov, the KGB under Serov and the MVD under Dudorov were all loyal to him, a fact which prevented the conspirators from announcing or implementing their decisions.

On 19 June the full Presidium and the Secretariat met together. Malenkov, Molotov and Kaganovich again led the attack. The presence of the Presidium candidates and the Central Committee secretaries shifted the balance of forces in Khrushchev's favour, however, and the opposition were not allowed to resolve the issue by means of a simple vote of full members of the Presidium, among whom they still had a majority. On the following day the opposition faction limited their demand to the abolition of the post of First Secretary 'with the goal of preventing the appearance of a Khrushchev personality cult'; they made no mention of actually removing Khrushchev from the Secretariat.

By this time word that the Presidium was in constant session had leaked out to members of the Central Committee, more and more of whom were coming to the capital to investigate – often on air-force planes provided on Zhukov's orders. On 21 June eighty members of the Committee who were in Moscow signed a letter to the Presidium complaining that they were not being informed about what was taking place and requesting that a plenum be convened immediately; a delegation of twenty of the signatories took the letter to the Kremlin, but was refused admission to the meeting. Bulganin instead promised them that the CC would meet within two weeks. The delegation rejected this and demanded that the Presidium refrain from taking any decisions concerning the First Secretary and call a plenum immediately. The two sides agreed to meet again at 6 p.m. that day. By evening, however, it was too late for the opposition to avoid a plenum: more than a third of the Committee had already gathered in Moscow. Under the party rules, this would have been sufficient to force the calling of an extraordinary party congress if the opposition had not backed down.[18]

The convening of the Central Committee was itself a Khrushchev victory, for several reasons. First, he had assiduously courted that body for four years and had promoted many of its newer members to high office. The anti-Khrushchev faction in the Presidium, by contrast, had attempted to remove the party's leader without even consulting the CC. Kaganovich had openly attacked the pressure being placed on the Presidium by Central Committee members, dismissing that body's prerogatives in scornful tones.[19] A vote for the Presidium majority at this stage would thus have been a vote against the collective rights and status of the Central Committee itself. The anti-Khrushchev opposition wished to limit the role of the Central Committee to intra-party affairs, ideology and culture. Both their tactics and their policies were seen as heralding a return to Stalinism.[20] Secondly, representatives of republican and provincial bodies, the principal beneficiaries of Khrushchev's attack on the ministries, formed the largest bloc of votes on the Committee; they stood to lose a great deal if the reform were overturned. Finally, the plenum allowed Khrushchev to make use of his most potent weapon: Stalin. His own past meant that he himself could not bring his rivals to account for their activities during the 1930s and 1940s, but many of the younger Khrushchevites had not been involved in the repressions and therefore had no such scruples.

The plenum opened on 22 June with a report by Suslov, who attacked the group for trying to take over the party; he then took the chair. Zhukov spoke next and addressed the issue of the repressions and the role played in them by Molotov, Malenkov and Kaganovich. Brezhnev linked the opposition's attempt to seize power to fear of the accelerating process of rehabilitation. Many other speakers addressed the complicity of Khrushchev's opponents in the terror. Statistics were presented on the number of executions which Molotov and Kaganovich had sanctioned; one speaker reported that on 12 November 1938 Stalin and Molotov had approved the shooting of 3167 people. According to the figures presented at the plenum, there were more than 1.5 million arrests in 1937–8, leading to 681 692 executions.

This was only one prong of Khrushchev's plenum strategy. While most of the speakers concentrated their fire on the three principals, Mikoian, Shvernik and others introduced a second line of attack, referring to the whole of the opposition as an 'anti-party group'. Such a label implied a charge of factionalism, supported by the admissions of Bulganin, Saburov and Pervukhin that the group had met together for several months. The opposition's united front crumbled. One by one Saburov, Pervukhin, Voroshilov and finally Bulganin began to distance themselves from Molotov, Malenkov and

Kaganovich, minimising the extent of their involvement in the group's activities. Then the three leaders began to yield. Kaganovich acknowledged that 'of course, there were consultations, there was collusion'. 'Undoubtedly', admitted Malenkov, 'there was collusion.' Molotov was more cautious: 'We met with each other, we talked . . . there was that which is now being called factionalism.' All three denied the anti-party character of their activities, however, and Molotov and Kaganovich stoutly defended Stalin. They attacked Khrushchev for undermining collective leadership, arbitrariness in making appointments and errors in policy.

Finally, Khrushchev spoke. He accused his enemies of attempting to reverse the decisions of the Twentieth Congress and described their activities in the 1930s in terms which made them look even guiltier than Stalin himself. The image of Stalin in his speech closely resembled the Stalin presented to the July 1953 plenum: a leader cut off from the people and manipulated by his unscrupulous lieutenants. In presenting matters thus Khrushchev carried a step further his own retreat from the Secret Speech. The published text of the plenary resolution passed over the whole issue in silence.[21]

The plenum was a major victory for Khrushchev. The Central Committee condemned the anti-party group and expressed its confidence in Khrushchev as First Secretary. Molotov, Malenkov and Kaganovich were removed from the Presidium and expelled from the Central Committee, as was Shepilov. Although little attention was paid to him at the plenum, Shepilov was the object of special abuse in public discussions of the affair for years afterward. To emphasise his disloyalty to his patron, he was referred to always as 'Shepilov who joined them' – a practice which gave rise to jokes about his having the longest surname in the Russian language. Ironically, the abuse heaped on Shepilov was proof that factionalism, though formally condemned by the party, was practised by all: his sin was that he had switched sides in the course of the conflict. Saburov was removed from the Presidium and Pervukhin was demoted to candidate status. Bulganin and Voroshilov retained their positions for the time being, apparently because Khrushchev wished to maintain the fiction that the anti-party group commanded only minority support within the Presidium.

The plenum promoted the Finnish communist Otto Kuusinen to the Secretariat and elected a new Presidium which was heavily stacked with Khrushchev supporters drawn from the party apparatus. Central Committee secretaries Aristov, Beliaev, Brezhnev and Kuusinen were made full Presidium members, as were the party bosses of Moscow (Furtseva) and Leningrad (Kozlov). The party leaders of Georgia, Belorussia, Uzbekistan, Latvia and Sverdlovsk[22] were elevated to candidate membership, as was Khrushchev's old friend Korotchenko, then the Chairman of the Council of Ministers of Ukraine. P. N. Pospelov, the author of the Secret Speech, was made a candidate member, as was Aleksei Kosygin. Shvernik and Zhukov were made full members of the Presidium. Zhukov's promotion was unprecedented; no professional soldier had ever held such a high position in the party. It was a reflection of his authority in the armed forces and of the key role he had played on Khrushchev's behalf during the crisis.

Zhukov's support for Khrushchev was the product of a long courtship. The First Secretary had cultivated the military in general, and Zhukov in particular, for some time. In 1954–5 his position on the investment priorities question had made him preferable to Malenkov in the eyes of the military, and he had played an active role in the rehabilitation of officers who had fallen victim either to the terror of the 1930s or to Stalin's jealousy after the war. A considerable portion of the Secret Speech had been devoted to the military commanders annihilated in the pre-war purges and to absolving the military establishment of blame for Soviet reverses in the early days after Barbarossa, clearly a gesture to Zhukov and other top military men.[23] Soon after the June crisis had passed, however, Zhukov found that he was unwelcome in Khrushchev's Presidium.

Khrushchev's victory over the opposition vindicated the political strategy he had pursued since Stalin's death. His resuscitation of the Central Committee, his consistent defence of the interests of the party officialdom, his expansion of the authority of local officials and his denunciation of Stalin all contributed to the Central Committee's support

for him in June 1957. His treatment of defeated rivals further
underscored the extent to which Soviet politics had changed
since March 1953; there were no arrests, no executions and,
at this point, no expulsions from the party; Kaganovich
allegedly telephoned Khrushchev after the plenum pleading
for mercy. Khrushchev is said to have replied,

> Comrade Kaganovich, your words confirm once again
> what methods you wanted to use to achieve your vile
> aims. You wanted the country to return to the order that
> existed during the cult of personality. You wanted to kill
> people. You measure others by your own yardstick, but
> you are mistaken. We adhere to Leninist principles and
> will continue to do so. You will be given work. You will
> be able to work and live peacefully if you work honestly
> like all Soviet people.[24]

Kaganovich was appointed manager of a cement works in
Sverdlovsk, Molotov was dispatched to Outer Mongolia as
ambassador, and Malenkov was sent to run a power station
in Central Asia.

The removal of the most committed Stalinists from the
Presidium did not lead to a renewal of de-Stalinisation. On
the contrary, Khrushchev's pronouncements concerning
Stalin remained guardedly favourable, and his statements
on cultural policy continued to emphasise the need for
strict party control over literature.[25] The party's view of the
Zhdanovite cultural resolutions of 1946–8 was revised only
slightly; the fundamental positions of the resolutions were
affirmed, and only the crudest forms of persecution and
repression were condemned. Simonov and Berggol'ts,
among others, acknowledged the errors they had committed in 1956 and submitted to the will of the party.[26]
Writers were haunted by Khrushchev's remark at a party-
government reception for writers in May that 'there would
have been no revolt in Hungary if they had tossed two or
three windbags into prison in time'.[27]

Soon after the fall of the anti-party group Khrushchev
decided that he must be rid of Marshal Zhukov. There

were a number of reasons for the marshal's rapid fall from grace. Zhukov's important role in the defeat of the anti-party group clearly worried Khrushchev in so far as it demonstrated the marshal's very considerable authority. Khrushchev's concerns about Zhukov's power were evident in the accusations of Bonapartism which followed Zhukov's removal. According to Suslov, Zhukov claimed that he had warned the leaders of the anti-party group that he could appeal to the army and the people, who would support him against them. Zhukov himself quibbled over the form of words used but admitted having made a statement along these lines.[28] Zhukov was also the only member of the leadership to mention publicly the 'offences against legality' committed by Molotov, Malenkov and Kaganovich under Stalin. This was a charge to which Khrushchev himself was vulnerable and about which the party wished to keep quiet; Zhukov's remarks were censored in *Pravda* when he raised it publicly.[29]

Yet there was more at issue than political tactics and Khrushchev's fear of Zhukov's power. The First Secretary and the Marshal had different political views on several key subjects, including investment priorities and the sovnarkhoz reform, and Khrushchev must have seen his erstwhile ally as a potential obstacle in the Presidium. The day after the reportage on the June plenum appeared in the press, *Krasnaia zvezda*, the military newspaper, warned against any weakening of the commitment to heavy industry and defence needs.[30] The military's reservations about the sovnarkhoz reforms were linked to the issue of investment priorities. Military leaders and officials of the defence industries went to Khrushchev personally to press for the retention of direct central control of defence enterprises; they feared that local control would lead to the diversion of resources from defence production to civilian production for local needs.[31] These ministries were retained at the time of the sovnarkhoz reform only to be abolished after Zhukov's removal, when their enterprises were placed under sovnarkhoz management.[32] As part of his compromise with defence industry leaders, Khrushchev agreed to establish state committees to oversee research and development in defence sectors.[33]

Zhukov and Khrushchev also disagreed about the role of the party in the armed forces. At the time of Zhukov's removal he was accused of having proposed the abolition of the Military Council of the Ministry of Defence, which consisted of Presidium members, fleet commanders and the commanders of the military districts of the USSR, and of the military councils of the military districts themselves, on which local party leaders and local commanders were represented. These councils were intended to facilitate party leaders' oversight of military affairs, and their abolition would have represented a step towards making the armed forces independent of the party. Suslov also accused Zhukov of trying to end the discussion of military questions in party organisations in the armed forces and to limit the role of these organisations to political indoctrination and education.

In answering Suslov's report, Zhukov admitted that he had underestimated the role of the political organs in the military and relied too heavily on military commanders to be party as well as military leaders. Nevertheless, Zhukov insisted that the position of military commanders in relation to political organs was in need of a re-examination; the great majority of commanders were now communists, he said, and they had to be viewed differently from the way they had been viewed twenty-five years earlier. This reference to history and to the party membership of senior officers suggests that Zhukov wished to remind his listeners of the original rationale for creating the political organs in the armed forces. They had been formed during the civil war, largely on account of the unreliability of both the Red Army's conscripts and its officers, many of whom had previously served the Tsar. Professional military men detested the interference of the 'politicals', and Zhukov seems to have been suggesting that the latter no longer needed to watch over the former; the senior professional officers were not ex-tsarist commanders but party members of proletarian origin who had made their careers in *Soviet* military academies and the *Soviet* armed forces. Such a position was utterly unacceptable to the party activist Khrushchev, especially given his own career as a political officer and his suspicions concerning the Minister of Defence.

Zhukov was dispatched on an extended visit to Albania and Yugoslavia in October while his demotion was arranged. By the time he was summoned back to Moscow to answer his accusers he had been replaced by Marshal Rodion Malinovskii, an apolitical soldier who had served with Khrushchev in Ukraine during the war. The Central Committee met on 29 October to discuss the case. Zhukov was accused of attempting to downgrade the role of party organs in the armed forces, fostering his own cult of personality and a host of other sins. Apart from those discussed above, the most serious accusation was that Zhukov had proposed replacing Serov and Dudorov, the KGB and MVD chiefs, with military men. According to Adhzubei, Zhukov had once told Serov, in Khrushchev's presence, that the KGB was 'the eyes and ears of the army'; Khrushchev angrily snapped that the KGB was 'the eyes and ears of the party'. He did not forget Zhukov's words.[34] The plenary resolution repeated Suslov's criticisms of Zhukov and dropped him from the Presidium.[35]

The removal of Zhukov was not the only good news for Khrushchev in October 1957. On 4 October the USSR launched the world's first artificial earth satellite, Sputnik 1. Khrushchev was an enthusiastic proponent of rocket technology, primarily because he believed that it would in future provide the foundation for an inexpensive, secure defence for the Soviet Union. Sputnik 1 also provided him with a propaganda tool for foreign policy purposes. He was delighted, and for several years Soviet launches were frequently timed to precede his major trips abroad, a practice that his western hosts occasionally found quite discomfiting. Sputnik 1 took the rest of the world completely by surprise, and many in the West, including US Vice-President Richard Nixon, believed it to be a hoax. There was considerable consternation in western capitals when it became clear that the launch had indeed taken place, for Sputnik suggested that the Soviet ICBM programme must be further along than had been suspected. Khrushchev reinforced this impression a few days later, telling the American journalist James Reston, 'We now have all the rockets we need: long-range rockets, intermediate-range rockets and short-range rockets.'[36]

This was the beginning of several years of deception by Khrushchev, who sought political concessions and psychological advantage in the widespread perception that Moscow was well ahead of Washington in its ICBM programme. The actual strategic balance at the time was extremely unfavourable to the USSR, and Khrushchev's decision to forego massive expenditures on first-generation ICBMs in favour of waiting to invest in more reliable later technologies meant that this balance would not change soon. Khrushchev's missile deception made life difficult for the Eisenhower administration, which knew on the basis of its U-2 surveillance flights that the missile gap was a hoax. The administration was criticised at home for falling behind in the ICBM race but was unable to rebut the charges without compromising the secrecy of the U-2 programme. In the end, the deception backfired; Khrushchev's mythical 'missile gap' triggered a US defence build-up which created an actual missile gap in Washington's favour.

The Sputnik launch and Zhukov's removal were followed by the fortieth anniversary of the Bolshevik Revolution on 7 November. For Khrushchev it was a celebration not only of the achievements of forty years of socialism but also of the recovery of his own political fortunes. The anniversary celebrations provided the occasion for a gathering of the leaders of sixty-six communist parties from around the world which gave Khrushchev the endorsement he so desired of Soviet leadership of the world communist movement. It was a hollow victory. China's endorsement came only at the price of a thundering condemnation of 'revisionism' in the final communiqué and a pledge by a reluctant Khrushchev to assist China's nuclear weapons programme. Khrushchev did not want China to become a nuclear power, and the condemnation of revisionism, moreover, angered the Yugoslavs, who refused to sign the communiqué. This was a setback for Khrushchev, who had been trying to repair the damage done to Soviet–Yugoslav relations by the invasion of Hungary.

The November meeting underscored the dilemma Khrushchev faced in his policies towards the socialist countries. He was still trying at this point to keep the

Chinese within the fold, although he had known for several years that it would be difficult if not impossible to avoid conflict with China. His differences with Beijing over de-Stalinisation and relations with the West were growing wider every day, and Mao Zedong, whom Khrushchev increasingly regarded as somewhat mad, did not respect Khrushchev as a theoretician or a statesman. Mao saw himself, not Khrushchev, as the doyen of the world communist movement. Attempts to conciliate Beijing, moreover, alienated Belgrade. Yugoslavia was much less influential than China, but its location made it of vital importance. Failure to achieve *rapprochement* with Tito would threaten the Soviet grip on other East European states. Much of the zigzag course of Soviet foreign policy in the late 1950s reflected Khrushchev's refusal to give up on either Mao or Tito. Thus in December 1957, only six weeks after condemning Yugoslav revisionism to please Beijing, Khrushchev was at pains to play down his differences with Tito and speak well of Yugoslavia.[37]

Khrushchev completed his consolidation of power in March 1958, when Bulganin was removed from office and made head of the State Bank. Khrushchev assumed the office of Chairman of the USSR Council of Ministers and appointed a new government. Shortly thereafter the USSR Defence Council was formed with Khrushchev as its chairman, making him in effect the commander-in-chief. Five years after Stalin's death, he stood triumphant at the summit of Soviet politics, having taken firm control of the party and used it as a base from which to defeat rivals and potential rivals in each of the other major institutions of the Soviet party-state: the security organs, the economic bureaucracy and the military. Khrushchev was not, however, another Stalin. Although clearly pre-eminent within the leadership, he did not enjoy absolute power. Many of his policies provoked fierce and sometimes successful resistance within the élite. Exercising power from the top offices of party and government was in many ways a greater challenge than winning them.

The successful political strategy which Khrushchev had employed since Stalin's death confronted him with a major problem in this connection: the very constituency on which his power was based had a vested interest in limiting that power. The territorial party bosses who had supported Khrushchev against his rivals were interested in maximum autonomy for themselves, while Khrushchev remained committed to central direction of political and economic development. Moreover, Khrushchev's destruction of the central ministries left him reliant on these same territorial bosses for the implementation of his policies, while his renunciation of terror limited his ability to discipline them or to frighten them into submission. Whereas Stalin had been able to rule through the party apparatus or over it, according to his needs, Khrushchev had in effect made it his partner. In the struggle to succeed Stalin this had made political sense, but once that struggle was over, Khrushchev's interest lay in reducing his reliance on the party machine for both the possession and the exercise of his power.

Khrushchev's first major initiative of 1958 was to break up the Machine and Tractor Stations and sell their machinery to the kolkhozes. He had favoured such a move since the early 1950s but was unable to push it through until after the fall of the anti-party group.[38] The MTS had been established at the time of collectivisation because the small kolkhozes then being created could not have purchased, maintained and operated modern agricultural machinery. A generation later, the kolkhozes were larger and their workers better trained; Khrushchev decided that the time had come to break up the MTS.

Even after the defeat of the anti-party group Khrushchev's plans for the MTS met with opposition from conservatives.[39] The MTS had been one of the foundations of Stalinist agricultural policy, and many regarded their abolition as a retreat from communism. The collective farms, after all, were not state enterprises; they were (in theory) voluntary peasants' collectives. The transfer of MTS machinery to the farms thus meant that non-state entities would become owners of the means of production. The MTS had also been a political control mechanism in rural areas where the party had been weak and where forced collectivisation had generated hostility towards the regime. Khrushchev's willingness to break up the MTS was a sign of his confidence in the loyalty of the peasants, a confidence some of his conservative colleagues did not share. It was also a reflection of the increased party presence on the farms. According to Khrushchev, the sell-off was to unfold gradually, with particular care being taken in those areas in which kolkhozes were relatively small and would not have been capable of assuming responsibility for all of their machinery.[40]

In March 1958 Khrushchev disregarded his own advice and launched a crash programme to break up the MTS and sell their equipment to the farms as quickly as possible. Within three months a majority of the MTS were abolished; by the end of the year only 20 per cent of them remained to be liquidated. The result was catastrophic for the farms' finances. Many poorer kolkhozes were already in debt and could make the required purchases only with additional credit from the state. Prices were the same for all types of machinery, so that some farms were forced to pay the same prices for old and worn-out equipment as more fortunate farms paid for new. Moreover, in addition to the cost of the machinery, the farms had to construct fuel storage facilities, warehouses and workshops. Pressure was placed on the farms to pay for the equipment within a year, rather than within the three to five years stipulated by law. As a result even prosperous kolkhozes were forced to postpone needed investments in their own facilities. MTS technicians did not wish to join the kolkhozes, where they would lose the pay and privileges that they enjoyed as state employees; roughly half of them found other work, leaving the countryside with a shortage of needed specialists.

After assuming the premiership Khrushchev also began to rebuild the power of the central government, much of which he had himself helped to dismantle in the struggles with his rivals. His aim in so doing had not been to decentralise political authority but to enable the party to replace the state machinery as the effective agent of central control. His co-optation of many regional and republican leaders into the Presidium was intended as a centralising measure as well as a reward for political support. If the sovnarkhozes were to strengthen central control by 'bringing centralism right down to where the direct economic process is going on', as Khrushchev asserted,[41] then the co-optation of local leaders into the all-union Presidium was an attempt to bring the localities closer to the centre. By including local leaders in central decision-making bodies, Khrushchev intended to prevent 'localism' and provide a mechanism whereby local interests could be harmonised with those of the whole state. By early 1958, however, it was evident that relying on the party alone was insufficient.

The localist impulse was built into the territorial structure of the party apparatus: officials charged with responsibility for a region naturally gave its needs priority. They would not, after all, be held accountable for conditions elsewhere. The abolition of the central ministries and the weakening of the USSR State Planning Commission (*Gosplan*) had removed important checks on these localist tendencies. Aggressive campaigns against localism were waged by the press, and in early 1958 Khrushchev began to curb the autonomy of the economic councils. It was decreed that no plant could be considered to have fulfilled its plan tasks if it had not met its obligations to enterprises in other regions.[42] Gosplan's powers were strengthened even as Khrushchev was forming his first government.[43] On 24 April criminal sanctions were imposed on party and economic officials who failed to meet their obligations for inter-regional deliveries.[44] In May the powers of the Commission for Soviet Control, charged with overseeing local compliance with central decisions, were strengthened. These were only the first moves in a six-year campaign by Khrushchev to strengthen central authority over the economy without actually abandoning the sovnarkhoz reform.

In July Khrushchev launched his second major reform of 1958 with a memorandum to the Presidium containing his ideas for a reform of Soviet secondary education.[45] He proposed to revive the technical and vocational emphasis which had been dropped in the 1930s. Since that time most schools had been oriented towards preparing their students for higher education, an opportunity which was afforded only to a small minority. Khrushchev proposed to re-structure general secondary education so that vocational training became its principal concern. Part of this training could be provided within the schools, but students were also to work in factories or serve apprenticeships as part of their education. Khrushchev proposed that within five years almost all general secondary schools be abolished. Full-time schooling would end after eight years, at which point students would enter industrial or agricultural enterprises for a combination of training and work experience, and would complete their general secondary education by studying two or three days a week in schools which operated in 'shifts' to accommodate students' work schedules.

As with the MTS reform, Khrushchev was in a hurry. In November the Central Committee's 'theses' on education reform were published in the press.[46] A month later, after a nationwide press discussion, the reforms were adopted by the Supreme Soviet. Many of the planned reforms were never implemented, however. The liquidation of general secondary schools, which was supposed to take place over five years, never occurred. Instead, schools developed links to nearby enterprises and students went to work instead of school one or two days a week. The reforms won Khrushchev few friends. Academic performance in traditional subjects declined, students and their families complained that they were unable in most cases to choose the trade to be learned, and enterprises resented the imposition of a pedagogic function on top of production tasks.

Khrushchev redoubled his efforts to avert a split with China in the summer of 1958. In July Moscow attacked the revisionism of the new Yugoslav party programme just before Khrushchev travelled to Beijing for talks with Mao. There was much to discuss; Khrushchev and his Soviet colleagues were upset by the Great Leap Forward, Mao's attempt to find a shortcut to communism, and the Chinese were angered by the apparent timidity of Khrushchev's policies towards the West. In response to US and British intervention in the Middle East, Khrushchev had proposed a summit conference involving the USSR, the United States, Great Britain, France and *India* to resolve the crisis. As if that were not enough to offend Mao, Khrushchev had then agreed to President Eisenhower's counterproposal: a conference under the aegis of the UN Security Council, on which the Chinese seat was still held by Chiang Kai-shek's nationalist regime.

Chinese dissatisfaction with Khrushchev grew in the autumn, when communist Chinese bombardment of two nationalist-held islands in the Straits of Formosa led to a US deployment in the Pacific and an American promise to defend Taiwan. Beijing found Moscow too cautious in its support for the Chinese stand against the Americans. Khrushchev was to some degree a victim of his own missile deception: Chinese leaders believed in the Soviet strategic advantage no less than the rest of the world, and they could not understand why Khrushchev, who claimed that the USSR was cranking out missiles 'like sausages', was so timid in dealing with the West.

Khrushchev, for his part, was disturbed by both the Great Leap Forward and Mao's cavalier approach to the question of nuclear war. Khrushchev later claimed that Mao had pressed him to help China accelerate its nuclear weapons programme, but that he had refused, limiting himself to a promise to use Soviet nuclear weapons against America in the event of a 'serious' US–Chinese conflict. Khrushchev also complained that the Chinese were excessively sensitive on questions of sovereignty, refusing to allow Soviet ships or planes to use Chinese facilities, even when these were offered as support for China against the United States. He was dismayed by the Chinese refusal to allow Soviet experts to examine a late-model US missile which had been given to the Nationalist forces and had fallen into communist China's hands.[47]

According to N. T. Fedorenko, who was Moscow's ambassador in Beijing at the time, Khrushchev and Mao also discussed the Twentieth Congress's condemnation of Stalin at length. Mao argued that Khrushchev had gone too far in condemning Stalin's crimes without giving due credit to his achievements and that the Soviets in any case had no right to address this issue unilaterally. Stalin, Mao argued, was a figure of such international significance that a re-evaluation of his role should have involved consideration of the positions of other communist parties. The most interesting point recalled by Fedorenko is that both Khrushchev and Mao agreed that Stalin was responsible for the starvation and bloodshed which accompanied forced collectivisation. Khrushchev expressed this view only in private. Committed as he was to maintaining the kolkhoz system, he never dared to question publicly collectivisation or Stalin's role in it.[48]

The need to refute Chinese accusations of Soviet cowardice may have been a part of Khrushchev's decision to attack the western allies' position in Berlin. In November 1958 he announced that the 'abnormal' situation in West Berlin had to change and demanded the withdrawal of allied troops from Berlin.[49] On 27 November he called the situation in West Berlin 'a sort of malignant tumour. If that tumour is not removed, the situation is fraught with such danger that there might be some undesirable consequences. Therefore we have decided to do some surgery.'[50] He gave the West six months to conclude a German peace treaty; otherwise, the Soviet Union would sign a peace treaty with the GDR on its own, giving the East Germans the right to govern access to West Berlin. The treaty he proposed was to be signed by the four victorious allies of World War II and the two Germanies. It would have confirmed the existence of two German states, limited the size of their armed forces and proscribed German access to certain types of weapons. Berlin was to become a free city, which meant that allied forces stationed there since the war would have to be removed.

Although China may have been a factor in Khrushchev's decision to issue such an ultimatum over Berlin, it was by no means the most important one. The desire for a German peace treaty was genuine. A treaty would provide the Soviets with western ratification of post-war borders, including the division of Germany, which Moscow had decided must not be reversed. It would also provide an opportunity for the Soviet Union to become a party to agreements limiting West German rearmament. Moscow's fear of a rearmed West Germany was shared by some of Bonn's NATO allies, but the Soviet Union could not rely on them to 'hold the line' forever on this issue. Limitations enshrined in a peace treaty to which Moscow was a signatory would give the USSR a veto over any revision of those limits. The ultimatum over Berlin, a significant but secondary issue, was an attempt to force the West to agree to a four-power summit on the German question, for which Khrushchev had been pressing since January.[51]

By threatening to alter the status quo in Berlin, Khrushchev nearly split the western alliance. None of Bonn's allies were pleased at having to conduct negotiations when faced with a Soviet ultimatum, but neither were they prepared to start a world war over 'whether a passport was stamped by a Russian soldier or an East German bureaucrat'. Even the hawkish US Secretary of State, John Foster Dulles, acknowledged that American public opinion would never support war over such a trivial issue; he could accept the idea of East Germans acting as 'agents' for the Russians. For the Adenauer government in Bonn, however, the issue was of cardinal importance. Recognition of East German bureaucrats for any purpose whatsoever could only lead to eventual recognition of the German Democratic Republic. So opposed was Adenauer to any admission of the legitimacy of the East German state that West Germany broke diplomatic ties with any country which established relations with the GDR.[52]

Having set the cat among the NATO pigeons, Khrushchev sat back to wait. At the very least he had sown doubts in the West Germans' minds about the reliability of their allies, a worthwhile achievement in itself. The Eisenhower administration ordered the reinforcement of US troops in Europe and began drafting plans of action in the event of an attempt to seal off West Berlin after Khrushchev's 27 May deadline. Nothing was done to break the impasse until the next year, however; in the meantime, Khrushchev's threat was left hanging in the air.

The most infamous literary scandal of Khrushchev's career erupted on 23 October 1958, when, to Khrushchev's acute embarrassment, the Nobel Committee announced that the Russian writer Boris Pasternak was to be awarded the Nobel Prize for Literature, primarily in recognition of his novel about the Russian Revolution, *Doctor Zhivago*. Pasternak sent the Swedish Academy of Sciences a telegram which read simply: 'Am eternally grateful, touched, proud, surprised, confused.'[53] Pasternak had completed *Doctor Zhivago* in 1956, but it had been rejected by the censors. In 1957 he became the first Soviet writer to circumvent Soviet censorship by publishing a work abroad; *Doctor Zhivago* appeared in a number of western countries and became a best-seller. The Soviet authorities were enraged, and the Nobel Prize, which added insult to their sense of injury, triggered an intense press campaign against Pasternak, who was expelled from the Union of Soviet Writers.[54]

Communist Youth League (*Komsomol*) chief Vladimir Semichastnyi said that the writer had 'spit in the face' of Soviet society. In the crudest of terms, Semichastnyi argued that Pasternak was not even worthy to be compared to a pig:

> A pig . . . never shits where it eats, it never shits where it sleeps. . . . But Pasternak, who counts himself one of the leading members of our society, has done this. He shat where he ate, he shat on those by whose labours he lives and breathes.[55]

Threatened with expulsion from the USSR, Pasternak rejected the award and published an apology,[56] but the attacks on him continued.[57]

Khrushchev himself later acknowledged that he had not read *Doctor Zhivago* but had nevertheless supported Suslov's decision to forbid its publication. (When Khrushchev finally did read it in retirement, he found it boring rather than anti-Soviet.[58]) According to Khrushchev, Suslov had not read the book either. Khrushchev was aware of the impact which the Pasternak scandal had on the regime's relationship with Soviet artists and on the Soviet Union's international reputation and later regretted the role he had played in the affair.[59] In early 1959 he indicated that he was unhappy with the way in which subordinates like Semichastnyi had handled the case.[60] Semichastnyi, however, claims that he was simply following Suslov's instructions. Suslov told him, in Khrushchev's presence, to 'work over' Pasternak in his report to the plenum and proceeded to dictate two pages of sometimes vulgar remarks on the subject. When Semichastnyi pointed out that as a Komsomol official he could not pretend to speak for the government, Khrushchev replied, 'You say it, and we will applaud. Everyone will understand.'[61] Semichastnyi's crude pig metaphor was also one which Khrushchev himself used in public on another occasion, a fact that lends credence to Semichastnyi's claims.[62] Whether Semichastnyi's version is true or not, Khrushchev could not have been too displeased: Semichastnyi remained in his post and was later promoted to head the KGB.

The harvest of 1958 turned out to be the best on record. The grain harvest of 134.7 million tonnes was 30 per cent above the poor harvest of 1957 and almost 70 per cent above the 1949–53 average. Much of this increase was a result of Khrushchev's Virgin Lands Programme, although the excellent weather conditions of 1958 concealed the unreliability of the new grain-growing regions: the Virgin Lands in the Urals were hit by droughts in 1955, 1957 and 1958, and the new grain regions of the Volga and Kazakhstan were likewise prone to droughts.[63] Khrushchev, however, did not choose to see 1958 as an exceptional year. Although he remarked in December that in Soviet agriculture 'good years alternate with bad', he viewed the 1958 harvest as a base from which to plan further rapid growth in the Seven-Year Plan which he was to present at the Twenty-first Congress in early 1959. Thus in December he called a Central Committee plenum to discuss agricultural issues.

Substantively the December 1958 Central Committee meeting was of no real significance; the agricultural questions under discussion were relatively unimportant. The main purpose of the plenum was actually to provide a forum for renewed attacks on the anti-party group (Bulganin's membership had been revealed in November[64]) and a propaganda preview for the Twenty-first Congress. The conduct of the plenum was more important than its content. Hundreds of functionaries who were neither members nor candidates of the Central Committee or of the Central Revision Commission were invited to attend; many of them even spoke. For the first time the transcript of a plenum was published in book form.[65] Both of these practices were continued at future plena, which were increasingly publicised in advance, often in conjunction with press campaigns intended to settle the issue in question ahead of time. Secret voting was subsequently abolished.[66] In the chair Khrushchev reverted to old habits, interrupting speakers and treating many of them quite rudely. The CC also met less frequently: whereas in the two years from December 1956 to December 1958 it met eleven times, from the beginning of 1959 to the fall of Khrushchev in October 1964 it was convened only fourteen times – just over the twice-yearly minimum mandated by the party statutes. The agenda were broadened to cover entire fields, such as industry or ideology, and were therefore less concerned with the resolution of specific issues.

Khrushchev, who had worked to revive the Committee after 1953, was now determined to downgrade it. The 'openness' which he imposed on the plena lent Central Committee proceedings the character of theatre and reduced the freedom of internal debate. The external openness provided by stenographic records and the inclusion of outsiders in the Committee's work reduced its internal openness as a body. This 'democratisation' of the Central Committee was resented by its members and was discontinued after Khrushchev fell.[67] Khrushchev's concern for the status and rights of the Central Committee had strengthened his position as the champion of the party apparatus in the mid 1950s; his willingness to treat it with contempt after 1958 suggests that he felt that his position was secure and that he no longer needed it. This was a mistake Khrushchev would later regret, for it contributed to his fall in 1964.[68] That was all to come, however. As 1958 drew to a close, the notion that he might be removed from office against his will was far from Khrushchev's mind. His thoughts were occupied with the upcoming Twenty-first Congress, at which he would celebrate his victories and advance his vision of the Soviet future.

8 Frustration
High Hopes and Bitter Disappointments, 1959–60

*There is nothing more difficult to take in hand, more
perilous to conduct, or more uncertain in its success,
than to take the lead in the introduction of a new order
of things.*

Niccolo Machiavelli

The Extraordinary Twenty-first Congress of the CPSU
opened on 27 January 1959 with only one item on the
agenda: the Seven-Year Plan covering 1959–65. The plan's
ambitious targets were to be the 'decisive step' towards
Khrushchev's goal of overtaking the United States in per
capita industrial and agricultural production by 1970. Both
plan and Congress were, strictly speaking, unnecessary.
There was neither precedent nor need for the adoption of
a seven-year plan, although some attempt was made to
provide an economic justification for the shift from seven-
year to five-year planning periods. The convening of the
Twenty-first Congress a year ahead of schedule (hence its
'extraordinary' status) was also unnecessary. Khrushchev
simply did not wish to wait until 1960 to convene his own
'Congress of the Victors'; he had seized the political initiative and was determined to press his advantage rather
than to risk losing his momentum by waiting.

On the opening day of the Congress Khrushchev presented the details of the Seven-Year Plan, which was to
provide the basis for a rapid transition to a fully communist
society in which living standards exceeded those of the
West, and wealth was distributed according to need. Gross
output was to rise 80 per cent by 1965. Although Khrushchev spoke of sharply rising living standards for the
population, the new plan continued to give priority to
heavy industry, which was to grow at a rate of 9.8 per cent
per year, as against 7.3 per cent for consumer goods

production. Indeed, growth rates for light industry and consumer goods were lower than those posited by the Sixth Five-Year Plan, despite the fact that the new plan was on the whole more ambitious than its predecessor. Improvements in living standards were to come not from rising individual consumption, but from gains in agriculture and from the development of *collective* institutions, such as housing, schools, cultural facilities, medical services and communal dining facilities.[1] Such an approach was more in keeping with Khrushchev's collectivist vision of the Soviet future. It was also much less expensive.

The plan's ambitious targets were based on Khrushchev's belief that the economic performance of 1958, an exceptionally good year for both industry and agriculture, could be maintained indefinitely. His faith in the continuing success of the Virgin Lands in particular was underscored by the decision to shift a number of grain-growing areas in Transcaucasia, Central Asia and Ukraine into the production of other crops.[2] Such optimism was without foundation. The Virgin Lands on which Khrushchev staked so much were prone to drought, and his constant pressure to expand the sown area meant that increasingly marginal lands were being assimilated; while his original goal of 13 million hectares had been reasonable, he eventually demanded some 28–30 million hectares. Nor could industry keep pace with Khrushchev's ambitions. Soviet economic development had reached the stage where each additional step forward required more investment than the one before it. Khrushchev himself implicitly acknowledged this fact when he stressed that the key to further advances lay in the automation of production, an issue to which great attention was devoted during and after the Twenty-first Congress.

Khrushchev and the Chinese continued to play down their differences at the Congress. Although seventy foreign communist delegations attended, the Yugoslavs were not invited. Zhou Enlai, who headed the Chinese delegation, acknowledged the 'leading role' of the USSR in the socialist camp and did not mention China's claim to have found a shortcut to communism via the organisation of people's communes, a claim which posed an ideological challenge to Moscow.[3] Khrushchev criticised the communes, albeit obliquely, but stressed that there were no major differences of opinion between the Soviet and Chinese parties, directing his fire instead against Yugoslav revisionism. Khrushchev was moving further down a path which the Chinese leaders could not accept, however. His declaration that the USSR was no longer beset by 'capitalist encirclement' and could not be overthrown from within or without opened the way to a measure of accommodation with the West and a concomitant relaxation at home, but it won him no friends in Beijing.[4]

The doctrinal basis for the Stalinist police state had rested on two pillars: Stalin's contention that the class struggle in the USSR would intensify during the construction of socialism, and his continual warnings about the dangers of capitalist encirclement of the Soviet Union. Khrushchev had already rejected the first of these dogmas at the Twentieth Congress; by abandoning the second, he opened the way to a declining role for state coercion in the management of society. His attempts to show that the 'withering away of the state' was already under way in the USSR – the establishment of voluntary militias and informal 'comrades' courts', and the transfer of some state activities to social organisations – were trivial and unconvincing, but the abandonment of the capitalist encirclement dogma represented a further retreat from Stalinist methods of rule. The role of the party, by contrast, was increasing, and would continue to do so even under communism.

The anti-party group was also widely discussed at the Congress, during which Pervukhin and Saburov were exposed as members. In December Khrushchev had demanded their expulsion from the party, and USSR Procurator-General Rudenko had implied that criminal charges might be brought against them in connections with 'violations of legality' committed under Stalin.[5] There were no trials or expulsions, however, and Khrushchev barely mentioned the group at the Congress. His subordinates did; sixty-seven of the eighty-six Soviet speakers at the Congress attacked the group with varying degrees of intensity. Khrushchev's closest Presidium-level supporters attacked the group fiercely, but none called for further action against them, which suggests that Khrushchev had agreed to let the matter rest there. His plans for further action against the anti-party group may have been blocked by resistance from Suslov, Mikoian and other of his more independent Presidium colleagues, who were clearly unenthusiastic about the idea. Khrushchev himself may also have recognised that such measures as show trials would make him look like another Stalin. Moreover, he had little to gain by further persecution of his ex-colleagues.

The Twenty-first Congress also brought the Khrushchev cult to full flower. Collective leadership, the praise of which had been on the lips of every major leader after Stalin's death, vanished from the speeches of senior politicians; in its place was 'the Central Committee with N. S. Khrushchev at its head', 'the Central Committee of the party under the leadership of N. S. Khrushchev', 'the untiring activity of the Presidium of the Central Committee and Comrade N. S. Khrushchev personally' and so on. Collective leadership did, however, get one memorable mention from Omsk party chief Kolushchinskii: 'Nobody will forget the enormous merits of and efforts of the indomitable Leninist, the First Secretary of the Central Committee of the party, Nikita Sergeevich Khrushchev, in restoring Leninist collective leadership.'[6] This was faint praise compared with the Stalin cult, but it accurately reflected Khrushchev's new status: he was less than another Stalin but more than simply first among equals. Closely related to the development of the cult was the growth in the size and power of Khrushchev's personal staff. This personal secretariat, staffed for the most part by young men like his son-in-law Aleksei Adzhubei and the publicist Fedor Burlatsky, reduced Khrushchev's reliance on the Central Committee apparatus when it came to drafting speeches, developing policy initiatives and managing Khrushchev's publicity at home and abroad.

Shortly after the congress, British Prime Minister Harold Macmillan arrived in Moscow in an attempt to defuse the crisis over Berlin. Khrushchev had already softened his stance in January, lifting the six-month deadline he had imposed in November.[7] Macmillan's initial offer came as a great disappointment to Khrushchev; by agreement with President Eisenhower, the Prime Minister offered only a meeting of the foreign ministers of the four powers to discuss Berlin and other issues. Khrushchev wanted a summit and expressed his irritation by withdrawing a public invitation to escort Macmillan to Kiev and Leningrad. Khrushchev claimed that he could not travel because a filling had fallen out of his tooth, and he needed to visit the dentist. On his return to Moscow from Leningrad, Macmillan indicated that the foreign ministers' meeting might lead to a summit. Khrushchev responded by stressing that he had not intended 'to put pressure on anybody' and that 27 May ought not to be regarded as some sort of deadline. For the time being matters went no further; Khrushchev was prepared to engage in serious negotiation only at a summit, and Eisenhower would agree to a summit only if the foreign ministers made significant progress. On 30 March Khrushchev agreed to the foreign ministers' conference.[8] The conference took place in May and June in Geneva; when it recessed on 20 June after seven weeks of talks, the two sides were as far apart as ever.

Macmillan, who had been thoroughly put off by Khrushchev in 1955, now found him

> a curious study. Impulsive, sensitive of his own dignity and insensitive to anyone else's feelings, quick in argument, never missing or overlooking a point; with an extraodinary memory and encyclopedic information at his command; vulgar, and yet capable of a certain dignity when he is simple and forgets to 'show off'. Ruthless but sentimental – Khrushchev is a sort of mixture between Peter the Great and Lord Beaverbrook.[9]

The Third Congress of Soviet Writers convened in May amid signs that the party line on literature and the arts was again softening. In the run-up to the congress Paustovskii, Ehrenburg, Tvardovskii and others criticised the use of administrative methods to direct literature and urged writers to write the truth as they saw it. The conservative writers Surkov and Kochetov were replaced by more liberal men as head of the Union of Soviet Writers and editor of *Literaturnaia Gazeta* respectively, and Khrushchev himself delivered a remarkably conciliatory speech to the congress.

While still criticising writers who placed too much stress on negative aspects of Soviet life, he found positive things to say about their work and even acknowledged that their motivation was to help the party. He spoke favourably, though not uncritically, of Dudintsev and praised certain aspects of *Not by Bread Alone*, which had been harshly attacked in 1957. Khrushchev criticised those who continued attacking deviant writers who had yielded and expressed a willingness to 'adopt a correct position', thereby implicitly rebuking those who had persecuted Pasternak the year before. Khrushchev also rejected administrative censorship and said that banning books was stupid. This was not a call for a free press; Khrushchev simply felt that the writers themselves, together with the party, should resolve such questions.[10]

Khrushchev may have feared that he had gone too far at the congress, for a month later he attacked writers who did not wish to accept party direction of literature. Party guidance, he said, represented 'the will of millions of people', and writers who did not wish to submit their subjective views to the will of the masses were guilty of establishing their own cults of personality. In August he cited Sholokhov as proof that acceptance of party positions did not deprive a writer of his individuality. If a writer were truly involved with the life of the people, Khrushchev argued, then the party spirit would be the essence and meaning of his life and work.[11]

In June Khrushchev also addressed a Central Committee meeting on the automation of industry. Perhaps no other plenum of his career so clearly illustrated the gap between his view of industrial management and the requirements of Soviet industry. The speakers at the plenum criticised the 'technical conservatism' of many managers when it came to enterprise modernisation. The red tape involved in winning approval of new methods and machinery was complex and time-consuming. Changes in production processes were risky for managers, under constant pressure from above to fulfil current plans, and undesirable for workers, who often suffered wage cuts when new equipment was introduced.[12] The solution to these problems lay in greater material incentives for enterprise modernisation and greater enterprise autonomy. Khrushchev, however, again sacrificed economic reform in favour of party activism. The resolution adopted by the plenum blamed the problems on the failure of primary party organisations in industry to exercise their right of *kontrol'* and ordered the creation of special party commissions within enterprises to supervise managerial and administrative tasks and to propose ways of improving performance.[13]

In late July Khrushchev played host to US Vice-President Richard Nixon, who travelled to Moscow to open the American National Exhibition; the two did not get along, although they developed a measure of respect for one another. They argued about the merits of their respective social systems wherever they went together, with the best-known exchange coming in the model American kitchen at the US exhibition. Khrushchev disregarded both diplomatic niceties and simple hospitality, launching into an attack on American consumer gimmickry and US foreign policy. Nixon gave as good as he got and both men afterwards regarded themselves as victors in the debate. Worse than the consumer gadgets, in Khrushchev's view, were the works of art at the exhibiton, which he found 'revolting. Some of them were downright perverted. I was especially upset by one statue of a woman [*Standing Woman* by Gaston Lachaise]. I'm simply not eloquent enough to express in words how disgusting it was. It was a monster-woman, all out of proportion, with a huge behind and grotesque in every other way.' What did impress Khrushchev was the actual construction of the US pavilion, which was built by assembling prefabricated sections that had been manufactured in America.[14]

Khrushchev had hinted since 1955 that he wished to visit the United States. In July 1959 he at last received the invitation he so desired. He was stunned:

> I must say, I couldn't believe my eyes. We had no reason to expect such an invitation – not then, or ever for that matter. Our relations had been extremely strained. . . . And now, suddenly, this invitation. What did it mean? A shift of some kind? It was hard to believe.[15]

Although Khrushchev could not have known it, Eisenhower was no less surprised. US State Department official Robert Murphy had misunderstood the President's instructions; the invitation he conveyed to Presidium member Frol Kozlov, who visited the United States in July, was supposed to have been contingent on progress in the foreign ministers' talks, but Murphy made no such link. Eisenhower first learned that an unconditional invitation had been extended in his name when Khrushchev communicated his acceptance to the Americans.[16]

The preparations for the trip once again cast light on Khrushchev's persistent fear that the American President would not deal with him as an equal. Khrushchev's position as Chairman of the USSR Council of Ministers meant that he was head of government, but the Soviets insisted that, for protocol purposes, he be treated as a head of state; the Americans acquiesced. Many other demands were made in this vein; Khrushchev later acknowledged that 'on some points' the Soviets 'may have gone a little overboard', but he wished to prevent any 'discrimination' against himself and his delegation by their hosts. When the Soviets learned that Khrushchev was to meet with Eisenhower at a place called Camp David, a frantic investigation was conducted to find out where – and what – Camp David was; neither the Ministry of Foreign Affairs nor the embassy in Washington knew, and Khrushchev feared that it might be a place which would for some reason be degrading for him to visit.[17] The trip was the greatest foreign test of Khrushchev's career, and he was taking no chances.

Khrushchev arrived in Washington on 15 September and lost no time in annoying his host. After discussing the latest Soviet space successes at the airport, Khrushchev, at their first White House meeting, gave Eisenhower replicas of the spheres and pennants carried by the Soviet rocket which had landed on the moon the day before. Khrushchev's gesture confused the President: the Americans had all assumed that the airport remarks were intended to taunt them; they could scarcely believe Khrushchev's tactlessness in raising the issue a second time that same day. Eisenhower began to think that 'the fellow *might* have been sincere'.[18]

Khrushchev, for his part, was pleased with the pomp and

ceremony of his initial reception. He later recalled, 'I was terribly impressed. . . . We didn't do such things in our country; we always did things in a proletarian way, which sometimes, I'm afraid, meant that they were done a bit carelessly. Those Americans really know how to lay on a reception.'[19] The initial meetings between Khrushchev and Eisenhower produced no results, and even the purely symbolic aspects of the visit sometimes had unexpected outcomes. The President had specifically arranged for Khrushchev to be given a helicopter ride over Washington at rush hour, so that he could see all the automobiles in the streets – the best possible evidence of American prosperity. Khrushchev drew his own conclusions: 'We're never going to have automobiles like you have in this country, jamming up the roads. Absolutely uneconomic.'[20] And indeed it was Khrushchev who determined that the USSR would not pursue the mass production of automobiles.

Khrushchev's itinerary in Washington included a state dinner, a rather rocky press conference, a meeting with members of the Senate Foreign Relations Committee and a trip to the Lincoln Memorial, where he removed his hat and bowed his head in homage. He then set off on a coast-to-coast tour of America. His first stop was New York, where, he remembered, 'I wasn't very impressed. If you've seen one skyscraper you've seen them all. One thing I'll say for climbing to the top of the highest skyscraper in New York: at least the air is fresh up there. On the whole New York has a humid, unpleasant climate, and the air is filthy.'[21] Mayor Wagner gave a luncheon in his honour, and Khrushchev was invited to meet with a number of important businessmen at a reception hosted by Averell Harriman. Khrushchev was keenly interested in developing US–Soviet trade, but his first few conversations at the reception convinced him that his expectations were premature. He visited Harlem, addressed the United Nations on disarmament and spoke to the New York Economic Club at the Waldorf-Astoria. The questioning at the club was more aggressive than he had expected, and Khrushchev became rather testy in his replies.

From New York Khrushchev and his entourage flew to Los Angeles, where he was bemused to find himself accompanied by a city official who was the son of a factory owner from Rostov-on-Don in southern Russia. In Hollywood Khrushchev and his party were guests of honour at a luncheon hosted by Twentieth Century–Fox; Bob Hope, Henry Fonda, Elizabeth Taylor and several hundred other stars attended. (Ronald Reagan boycotted it.) Khrushchev was especially taken with Marilyn Monroe, but his feelings were unrequited; she found him repulsive.

The visit to Los Angeles did, however, have its less pleasant moments. Khrushchev was annoyed that he could not go to Disneyland for security reasons and was disgusted by the dancing he was taken to see on the set of *Can-Can*, which was then being filmed at the Twentieth Century–Fox studios. He was even more embarrassed when he and Nina Petrovna were photographed with some of the film's scantily clad (by Soviet standards, at any rate) dancers. At a dinner given in Khrushchev's honour, Los Angeles Mayor Norris Poulson denounced Khrushchev's policies and chided him for, among other things, his 'we will bury you remark'. Khrushchev was so enraged that he threatened to cut short his visit and return to Moscow. He later admitted that his threat was a bluff, but it succeeded in rattling Ambassador Henry Cabot Lodge, who was accompanying Khrushchev on his trip.

On the whole, the trip went much better after Khrushchev left Los Angeles. He was generally well-received – more, perhaps, out of curiosity than friendship – and was keenly interested in much of what he saw. Everywhere he went, he encountered anti-Soviet demonstrations, many of them denouncing him as the butcher of Hungary; but most of those who turned out to see him simply wanted to have a look. As the trip progressed, he became more aggressive in his insistence that he be allowed to work the crowds along his route, so that he might have a chance to speak with ordinary citizens. Ironically, the real star of the show in the eyes of the US public turned out to be Nina Petrovna.

The decision to take her, as well as Foreign Minister Gromyko's wife Lidiia, was unprecedented and not without controversy; Soviet leaders had always travelled abroad without their wives. In part this was a legacy of Stalin's belief that no one who left with a spouse could be trusted to return, and in part it reflected the view that travelling with spouses would be 'unbusinesslike – and a petit-bourgeois luxury'. Mikoian, who had been to the United States, was quick to see the public-relations advantages of sending Nina Petrovna with her husband, and Khrushchev agreed.[22] Mikoian was right; Khrushchev's wife was a hit. Her pleasant manner, halting English and smiling face created the impression of a kind-hearted mother and house-wife, an image she reinforced by showing off pictures of her grandchildren wherever she went. Nina Petrovna charmed many who remained hostile to Nikita Sergeevich and helped to allay American suspicions about him.

From Los Angeles, Khrushchev travelled to San Francisco before returning to Washington by way of Des Moines, Iowa, and Pittsburgh, Pennsylvania. Ironically, his sharpest encounters after leaving Los Angeles were with American labour leaders, with whom he met and sparred in San Francisco. In Iowa he went to visit an American farmer whom he had met in the 1950s and with whom he had corresponded about corn and livestock breeding. In Pittsburgh Khrushchev was given the key to the city; he assured his audience that the key would never be used without the hosts' permission. Finally Khrushchev reached Washington and retired with Eisenhower to the presidential retreat at Camp David.

Their negotiations did not at first go smoothly. Khrushchev had gone to Camp David expecting some sort of dramatic new proposals from his host and was disappointed when none were forthcoming. According to Eisenhower, Khrushchev was quite convivial and inclined to play down their differences when they were alone together but extremely cautious around Gromyko, in whose presence Khrushchev repeatedly insisted that this or that would have to be cleared with the Presidium. This may have been a genuine reflection of limitations on Khrushchev's power or the First Secretary's way of acknowledging his colleagues' right to be consulted. Khrushchev may also have done it as a negotiating tactic, much as Eisenhower constantly emphasised the limits on his ability to negotiate without France and Britain. In the end Khrushchev dropped his threat of unilateral action over Berlin, and Eisenhower agreed to the four-power summit which Khrushchev had long sought. Khrushchev also invited Eisenhower to visit the USSR in the spring or summer of 1960.[23]

Khrushchev concluded his trip with an hour-long television broadcast to the American people and returned to Moscow on 27 September. He had every reason to regard the visit as a success. The immediate diplomatic results of the trip were modest enough, but it had brought about a lasting change in American perceptions of him and of the Soviet Union. He had not won his hosts over, to be sure, but he had shown them that the 'Russian bear' was not such an alien or threatening creature as they had thought. His own perceptions of America, by contrast, changed remarkably little. It would, of course, be unreasonable to expect that a fortnight in the United States would shake his Bolshevik faith, but his recollections of the trip show the extent to which Khrushchev was able to interpret everything he saw and heard in a way that reinforced the image of capitalist society which he had formed in pre-revolutionary Iuzovka. Everyone and everything was carefully assigned its proper Marxist-Leninist label and placed in the correct intellectual pigeonhole. Nevertheless, Khrushchev returned to Moscow convinced that he could achieve *détente* with America.

This optimism was based principally on his favourable impression of Eisenhower. After the tension of their early meetings the two men had developed a measure of rapport. This was largely one-sided: Khrushchev's opinion of Eisenhower was far better than the President's view of him. The First Secretary was delighted when Eisenhower referred to him as 'my friend'. He was convinced that Eisenhower personally was committed to peaceful coexistence and could be trusted, although he believed that America was still dominated by monopoly capital and military interests which were implacably hostile to the Soviet Union. In his public statements after the trip Khrushchev repeatedly stressed Eisenhower's 'wise statesmanship' and his commitment to peaceful coexistence.[24] Subsequent events were to show how imprudent was Khrushchev's decision to stake so much on his personal relationship with the President. In the autumn of 1959, however, Khrushchev was full of optimism, as was the Soviet press, which celebrated his trip for some time afterwards. A team of journalists under the direction of his son-in-law Adzhubei produced a 700-page account of Khrushchev's journey called *Face to Face with America*.[25]

Khrushchev himself, however, did not have time to celebrate his triumph; on 29 September, the day after his arrival in Moscow, the jet-lagged premier boarded a plane for Beijing, where he was to attend the celebrations marking the tenth anniversary of the People's Republic. Relations with the Chinese were at a low ebb. In June Moscow had unilaterally abrogated the 1957 agreement under which the USSR was to provide technical assistance to China's nuclear programme. Beijing was further irritated by Khrushchev's trip to America and by his decision to remain neutral in a border conflict between China and India which had led to skirmishes along the Sino-Indian frontier. Mao also suspected that Khrushchev had been in close contact with Chinese Defence Minister Peng Teh-huia, who had mounted a challenge to Mao's domestic and foreign policies in mid-1959; many external observers believed that Mao's suspicions were well-founded.[26]

Khrushchev later recalled, 'The warmth had gone out of our relations with China, and it had been replaced by a chill that I could sense as soon as I arrived.' Despite the observance of diplomatic formalities, he found his hosts 'seething with resentment against the Soviet Union and against me personally'.[27] He saw little of Mao, who claimed to be too busy to spend much time with him, and their discussions were fruitless anyway. Khrushchev is reported to have suggested that Beijing accept the *de facto* independence of Taiwan and adopt a 'Two-China' policy.[28] He could not have formulated a proposal more offensive to Mao and his colleagues if he had tried.

Khrushchev made no further attempt to conciliate his Chinese comrades; the price of keeping China at least formally within a Soviet-led socialist camp had become too high. Broadly speaking, Khrushchev was pursuing three distinct foreign policy aims: maintaining the unity of the world communist movement under Soviet leadership; achieving a reduction in tensions with the West, which would include recognition of the post-war status quo in

Europe and would ease the Soviet defence burden; and exploiting opportunities for increasing Soviet influence in the Third World at the expense of the West. These aims were not always compatible with one another, and Khrushchev was sometimes slow to recognise the trade-offs he had to make, but by 1959 it was clear that he could not pursue any of these goals while still avoiding a rift between Moscow and Beijing.

A split with Beijing would, of course, represent a blow to Khrushchev's pretensions to be the leader of world communism, but conciliating China meant alienating Yugoslavia. The events of 1956 left Khrushchev convinced that good relations with Tito were critical to the stability of the other East European states, and Moscow was in many ways politically closer to Belgrade than to Beijing anyway. Khrushchev's attempts to come to terms with the West were repugnant to the Chinese leadership, and Chinese belligerence threatened his chances of achieving this end, particularly if Moscow continued to aid China in the development of nuclear weapons. Finally, Mao and his colleagues resented Khrushchev's courting of the non-communist rulers of certain developing states, particularly India. Khrushchev was in any case convinced that, even had he accommodated Mao on all of these issues, he would not have had a reliable ally on his hands.

The deterioration of relations with China coincided in 1959, as before, with a gradual improvement in Soviet–Yugoslav relations. The propaganda campaign against Belgrade died out by the late spring and Khrushchev on 24 May congratulated Tito on his sixty-seventh birthday. This was a particularly telling gesture, for it came shortly before Khrushchev travelled to Albania. The Albanians were second to none in their vilification of Tito and were particularly angry over the imprisonment in Yugoslavia of more than twenty ethnic Albanians charged with espionage. Albania's hard-line communist leader, Enver Hoxha, sympathised with the Chinese in the Sino-Soviet quarrel, and when the final rupture took place, Hoxha stuck with Mao.

At the end of 1959 Khrushchev again turned his attention to domestic affairs. The first item on his agenda was agriculture, which was performing well below his expectations.

Drought in Ukraine, excessive rain in much of Russia and early snows east of the Urals all contributed to a poor harvest. Grain output was in fact only 10 per cent below the level of 1958 and well above the 1954–8 average, but this was far short of the Seven-Year Plan targets. Khrushchev may have taken some comfort from his belief that bad years alternate with good and from the fact that the Virgin Lands performed slightly better than the traditional grain-growing regions, but it was nevertheless clear that both his plans for shifting certain regions out of grain production and the targets set for 1959–65 were in jeopardy.

Khrushchev's immediate response was increased pressure on party officials. The December 1959 Central Committee plenum reaffirmed the goal of overtaking the United States in per capita production of milk, meat and butter. Indeed the Union Republics were instructed to fulfil their Seven-Year Plan commitments by the end of 1963 – two years early. Even higher targets were set for 1965. Procurement prices for kolkhoz produce were reduced, thereby increasing the economic pressure on the farms themselves, many of which were still in disastrous financial shape as a result of the MTS sell-off. In order to concentrate the minds of officials, Khrushchev identified a hero and a goat for the 1959 harvest. The goat was N. I. Beliaev, the party chief of Kazakhstan and a Khrushchev client. At the Twenty-first Congress Beliaev had promised a record crop from the new grain regions in his republic.[29] He failed to deliver and was sharply criticised by Khrushchev, who concluded his rebuke of Beliaev by noting, 'Friendship is friendship; service is service.'[30] In other words, Beliaev would not be spared on account of his ties to Khrushchev; *Pravda* announced his dismissal in January.[31] This was a warning to the entire party apparatus – especially to Khrushchev clients who believed that their personal connections would shield them from criticism.

The hero of the 1959 harvest was A. N. Larionov, the party boss of Riazan' Province. In late 1958 Larionov had promised that his province would treble its sales of meat to the state from 48 000 tonnes in 1958 to 150 000 tonnes in 1959.[32] Khrushchev praised Larionov's initiative at the Twenty-first Congress and used it to pressure other provincial officials into making similar pledges of 150–200 per cent increases in meat output in a single year.[33] This was the kind of great stride forward which Khrushchev believed could be achieved by heightened party activism combined with mass enthusiasm. On 16 December 1959 the authorities of Riazan' Province announced that they had fulfilled their promises.[34] Larionov was made a Hero of Socialist Labour and his achievement was celebrated at the December plenum. He promised to raise output even further in 1960, and once again other provincial and republican leaders came under pressure to follow suit. For a time the slogan 'Three plans a year!' was widely used in propaganda.

The reality behind Larionov's 'achievement' was a catastrophe. Milk cows and breeding stock had been slaughtered in the province, taxes which were payable only in meat had been levied on non-farm institutions, and livestock purchases in other provinces reached such high levels that the authorities in neighbouring provinces, fearing that they would not be able to meet their own plan obligations, set up police blockades to prevent the smuggling of cattle to Riazan'. Much of the meat 'procured' by the state had been purchased by the farms in state stores and then sold (at a loss) to the procurement agencies a second time. In other cases there was straightforward falsification of accounts. Other types of farm production suffered from neglect as a result of the meat campaign. In 1960 the province was able to produce only 30 000 tonnes of meat and 50 per cent of its grain quota. Larionov committed suicide. Khrushchev received reports of what was going on in Riazan' but chose to ignore them until it was too late.[35]

The Riazan' campaign was symptomatic of Khrushchev's approach to agriculture after 1958. The share of state investment devoted to agriculture, which had risen steadily after Stalin's death, began to decline in 1958. This was no accident; the agricultural successes of 1954–8 had convinced Khrushchev that the farming sector was at last on its feet and that investment resources could be shifted elsewhere. When agricultural performance began to falter, Khrushchev's response was a series of campaigns to change cropping patterns, in a vain attempt to improve agricultural performance without increasing investment. The corn campaign was intensified, and Khrushchev, on the advice of the charlatan agronomist T. D. Lysenko, began pushing for earlier sowing in an effort to avoid a repetition of the 1959 harvest, when the early arrival of winter had destroyed much of the crop. This led to lower yields. In the early 1960s Khrushchev began pressing for a reduction in the area given over to unproductive grasses or clean fallow. In the absence of the necessary fertiliser, weedkiller and equipment, this intensification of land use led to wind erosion, weed infestation and other problems.

This approach to agriculture brought to the fore Khrushchev's tendency to meddle directly in scientific and technical issues which were beyond his grasp. It also exposed his tendency to use specialist expertise as a means of overcoming opposition to his policies rather than as a means of improving the determination of policy in the first place. Khrushchev suppressed the views of specialists whose conclusions he found unpalatable and advanced those who supported his pet nostrums. The worst of these was the agronomist Lysenko, who rejected both the methods and concepts of modern genetics. Lysenko had remained in Stalin's favour until 1953 but had suffered a decline under Khrushchev until 1956-7, after which he again returned to prominence. Lysenko's power retarded the development of genetics, cytology, plant physiology and biochemistry in the Soviet Union and wrought enormous damage in agriculture.

Lysenko promised that his prescriptions would achieve rapid and spectacular results on the cheap, and this was precisely what Khrushchev wished to hear. Lysenko's schemes were introduced across the country without serious laboratory research or testing. By the time any given panacea had failed, Lysenko had already moved on to the next one, and he was able to maintain his influence until the end of the Khrushchev era. Support for Lysenko brought Khrushchev into conflict with the USSR Academy of Sciences in 1963-4 and was one of the reasons for his removal from office in 1964.

In January 1960 Khrushchev took advantage of the thaw in relations with the United States to announce a unilateral reduction of one-third in the size of the Soviet armed forces by the autumn of 1961. Khrushchev stressed that the troop cuts would not lead to any reduction in the firepower of the armed forces, as they would be more than offset by the development of advanced weapons systems. Indeed, so great was his faith in the strategic revolution wrought by the coming of the missile age that he anticipated even more radical changes in the future:

> Our state has powerful missiles at its disposal. The air force and the navy have lost their former importance in view of the contemporary development of military technology. Such armaments are not being reduced but replaced. Almost the entire air force is being replaced by rockets. We have now cut sharply, and will continue to cut or perhaps even end, production of bombers and other obsolete equipment. In the navy the submarine fleet assumes great importance, while surface ships can no longer play the part they once did. In our country the armed forces have to a significant extent been transformed into rocket forces.[36]

Soviet military men were not so quick to be carried away by visions of future wars waged entirely with rockets. On the day of Khrushchev's announcement Minister of Defence Malinovskii warned against overreliance on rocket forces, or any single branch of the armed forces, stressing the need to maintain all branches 'at a definite strength and in relevant, sound proportions'.[37]

The belief that the USSR could be defended cheaply by reliance on rocket forces was critical to Khrushchev's entire domestic strategy. Unless the burden of Soviet defence spending could be reduced, the goals of the Seven-Year Plan, to say nothing of his longer-term aims, could never be reached. Although the Seven-Year Plan's growth rates were higher for heavy industry than for light industry, Khrushchev was keen to accelerate development of the latter. In March 1959 Aleksei Kosygin, whose background was in the light and consumer goods industries, had been appointed Chairman of the State Planning Commission, an indication that Khrushchev intended to give this sector greater attention. Throughout the summer and autumn the press carried numerous discussions of shortages of consumer goods. On 16 October a joint party–government decree outlined plans for increasing consumer goods production well above the targets specified by the Seven-Year Plan.[38] These targets could not be realised without a shift in investment patterns, and Khrushchev's defence cuts were to be the answer. Yet because neither the troop cuts nor the additional consumer goods investment was in the Seven-Year Plan, Khrushchev had avoided adopting an openly 'revisionist' position on the issue of investment priorities.

Khrushchev was aware of opposition to the cuts. He had been anxious to convene the four-power summit as soon as possible after his trip to America and certainly by the end of the year – before the troop cuts were announced. A successful summit would further demonstrate that the relaxation in international tensions which he and Eisenhower had achieved was secure enough to permit defence cuts. French President Charles de Gaulle, however, insisted on postponing the meeting until 1960; he was already under attack from the French right over his retreat from Algeria and was not enthusiastic about the idea in any case.

In February 1960 Khrushchev set off on an extended trip to Asia, visiting India, Burma, Indonesia and Afghanistan. His aim on this trip, as it had been on his previous trip to Asia in 1955, was to advertise the achievements of Soviet socialism to non-communist developing countries; ideology took a back seat to technical assistance. He provided the Indians with a team of agronomists and agricultural engineers, as well as the agricultural machinery, to establish a model state farm. Khrushchev later remarked,

> As far as I'm concerned, the best way to propagandise for socialism is to set concrete examples. By giving the Indians the farm, we showed them how well our socialist method of agriculture works and strengthened our friendly relations with them.[39]

In Jakarta he repeated the call for universal and total disarmament which he had made at the UN in September.

The speech was pure propaganda, and Khrushchev said nothing about verification or enforcement.[40]

The trip to Asia was, however, a relatively minor matter on Khrushchev's foreign policy agenda in the spring of 1960. With the four-power summit coming up in May and Eisenhower's visit planned for June, Khrushchev was bound to concentrate on East–West relations. In March he travelled to Paris for preliminary meetings with de Gaulle, who seems to have known just how to handle his guest. Khrushchev was delighted when de Gaulle called him *mon ami*, and attached great significance to his host's words. The Frenchman assured Khrushchev that France would never fight the Soviet Union as an ally of Germany, and repeatedly expressed his belief that Europe should free itself from US guardianship. He also confirmed French mistrust of Germany and opposition to German reunification, half seriously telling the Soviet premier, 'Two Germanies is not enough; our preference has always been for a larger number of independent Germanies.' These were mere sentiments, however; de Gaulle offered no concessions on issues of substance. He opposed any alteration of the status quo in Europe, seeing maintenance of the two alliances as the best way to keep Germany divided and in check. Khrushchev left Paris convinced that the French President was, despite his 'class affiliation', more in sympathy with Moscow than with Washington on the major questions of European politics but could not say so publicly.[41]

During April the positions of the two superpowers stiffened noticeably in anticipation of the summit. Statements on both sides reflected the leaders' desire to silence criticism from more hawkish elements at home and to stake out tough negotiating positions before going to Paris.[42] On 9 April the United States resumed U-2 espionage flights over the Soviet Union after a lengthy hiatus. America's U-2 spy planes had flown missions over the USSR since 1956, much to the annoyance of Khrushchev and his colleagues. Three Soviet protests were issued in 1956 and 1958, but all were rejected by the US government. Moscow then dropped the issue, recognising that nothing could be done unless and until a plane was actually downed. Washington would simply reject the charges of border violations, and any publicity given to the issue would be embarrassing to the Soviet Union. Khrushchev did not even raise the U-2 problem on his visit to America, and his silence may have convinced Eisenhower that the Soviet Union did not regard the flights as a serious provocation.[43] Khrushchev was bewildered and enraged by the resumption of the flights, and concluded that CIA chief Allen Dulles was ordering them without Eisenhower's knowledge, in an attempt to sabotage the summit.

On 1 May Soviet forces managed for the first time to shoot down a U-2; the plane was brought down over Sverdlovsk, deep inside the USSR, and the pilot, Francis Gary Powers, was captured alive. Khrushchev faced a dilemma. If he prevented the incident from being made public, he would look weak in the eyes of his own military and security forces, but if he were to turn it into a propaganda weapon with which to attack the Americans, he would jeopardise the summit for which he had laboured so long. He took his time in deciding how to play the issue, saying nothing about it in public for several days. In the meantime, there were no signs that Khrushchev intended to shift course: the visit of Soviet Marshal Vershinin to America was announced, and the Soviets moved closer to the US position in negotiations on a nuclear test-ban treaty which Khrushchev hoped would be concluded in time for the summit.

The U-2 crisis coincided with a major shake-up of the party's leading organs. N. I. Beliaev, the former party leader of Kazakhstan, and A. I. Kirichenko, the Ukrainian party boss who for several years had appeared to be Khrushchev's heir-apparent, were dropped from the Presidium. The size of the Secretariat was halved; six secretaries known to be close to Khrushchev were demoted. Leningrad party chief Frol Kozlov was promoted into the Secretariat, and three candidate members of the Presidium, Podgornyi, Polianskii and Kosygin, were elevated to full membership.[44] Some western scholars have linked this upheaval to the U-2 affair, arguing that Soviet 'conservatives' had become increasingly outspoken on foreign policy prior to the shootdown and that the incident had strengthened their position. The demotion of so many Khrushchev clients at one time would appear to confirm this view, as does the promotion of Kozlov, a representative of the party's conservative wing, into the Secretariat.[45]

This interpretation goes too far; the U-2 incident was indeed a setback for Khrushchev, but the personnel changes of May 1960 were not the result of a weak Khrushchev suffering a defeat at the hands of party conservatives. In April 1960 hard-line foreign policy statements were a part of Khrushchev's pre-summit strategy, not a sign of his weakness; Khrushchev himself revived his threat of unilateral action on Berlin.[46] The personnel changes ratified by the Central Committee do not suggest that Khrushchev had lost control of events; they appear to have been planned long before the U-2 incident. Beliaev's case has already been discussed above, and many of the other demotions were of a similar type: Khrushchev was prepared to demote his clients and supporters not because he was weak, but because he felt strong enough to assign greater importance to performance than he had in the past. During the struggles of the 1950s, his main concern had been the promotion of officials on whom he could rely for political support. With his grip on the leadership secure, loyalty was no longer at such a premium, and Khrushchev was free to replace clients who were not up to their jobs with more capable officials. Beliaev, Furtseva, Ignatov and Kirichenko fell because they had incurred Khrushchev's displeasure, not because he had been forced to drop them.[47]

The halving of the Secretariat was in any case part of a larger strategy by Khrushchev to reduce his reliance on that body and to build up alternative sources of political authority for himself. For reasons of both political security and policy effectiveness, Khrushchev sought to avoid dependence on any one institution for his power, but after the dismantling of much of the central government in 1956–7, he had no powerful executive organ on which to rely except the Secretariat. By 1960 he had made considerable headway in rebuilding the central government and in strengthening the Central Committee Bureau for the RSFSR; the Bureau for the RSFSR, of which Khrushchev was chairman, gradually assumed many of the functions of the Secretariat in managing the largest Soviet republic,

Russia. Podgornyi and Polyanskii, moreover, were both Khrushchev men from Ukraine, and the rise of Kosygin, who was promoted along with them, appears to be a result of Khrushchev's consumer goods drive, which scarcely would have made Kosygin the darling of party conservatives. This leaves Kozlov's promotion as the only evidence of a conservative advance, but Kozlov is known to have been well-regarded by Khrushchev and to have had good relations with him, despite the Leningrader's more conservative orientation.[48]

Further evidence of Khrushchev's political strength came at the Supreme Soviet session which opened on 5 May. There was no evidence of a retreat from his policies of *détente*, defence cuts and greater attention to the needs of Soviet consumers, although he did allude to the concerns of 'some comrades', who thought certain of these measures premature. In his opening speech Khrushchev confirmed increases in spending on consumer goods over and above the Seven-Year Plan and announced the introduction of a 42-hour work-week in 1960 (down from a 48-hour week in 1958). By 1962 the work-week was to fall to 40 hours, and it would be cut to 35 hours soon thereafter. Khrushchev also announced the 'abolition' of taxes on the population; in reality, taxes were to be phased out by increasing tax exemptions and simultaneously cutting wages and salaries.[49] This was supposed to be a further step in the 'withering away of the state' as part of the transition to full communism; in practice its only effect would be a minor reduction in the disparities between the best- and worst-paid workers. Khrushchev was opposed to a 'levelling' approach to wage policy, but he maintained that a gradual equalisation of wages would accompany the transition to communism; in a communist society all working people would receive equal pay.[50]

Khrushchev reaffirmed his goals for the Paris summit: disarmament, the conclusion of a peace treaty with Germany and agreement over Berlin. Finally, some two hours into his speech, he revealed to the deputies and the world that an American U-2 had been shot down over the USSR; he said nothing about Powers or the location of the shootdown. While maximising the propaganda value of the affair, Khrushchev was careful never to accuse Eisenhower himself of having ordered the flight; the guilty parties were 'imperialist circles and militarists, whose stronghold is the Pentagon', 'aggressive circles, which wish to torpedo the Paris summit, or at least prevent an agreement which the whole world awaits'. A born agitator, Khrushchev, once under way, was unstoppable:

> Just imagine what would happen if a Soviet aircraft appeared over New York, Chicago or Detroit. . . . How would the United States react? . . . What was this? A May Day greeting?

Then he addressed what was for him the key issue:

> The question arises: who sent this aircraft across the Soviet border? Was it sent by the Commander-in-Chief of the Armed Forces of the United States, who, as everyone knows, is the President? Or was this aggressive action taken by Pentagon militarists without the President's knowledge? . . . I do not doubt President Eisenhower's sincere desire for peace.[51]

Khrushchev in his memoirs described the anger and frustration that each successive U-2 mission aroused in the Kremlin:

> On several occasions we'd protested [the U-2s'] violations of our airspace, but each time the US brushed our protest aside. . . . We were more infuriated and disgusted every time a violation occurred. . . . We were sick and tired of these unpleasant surprises, sick and tired of being subjected to these indignities. They were making these flights to show up our impotence.[52]

Once again the central issue was the sense that the Soviets were not being treated as equals by the United States; Washington seemed to view the USSR as a country whose sovereignty need not be respected. The irony of Khrushchev's reaction is that the U-2 flights were one of the principal reasons Eisenhower was able to restrain the growth of the US defence budget. The President knew on the basis of U-2 data that Khrushchev was bluffing about Soviet strategic superiority. While Khrushchev certainly did not want the President to see through his deception, the alternative would have been for Eisenhower to undertake a massive missile build-up, thereby weakening Khrushchev and undermining support for his domestic agenda.

Khrushchev apparently believed that, by avoiding direct accusations, he was leaving the President a way out. Eisenhower, however, could not have admitted that his military and security forces were so completely out of control as to conduct such operations behind his back. Moreover, Khrushchev's determination to extract maximum propaganda leverage from the episode added to Eisenhower's difficulties. The decision to conceal the location of the shootdown and the survival of Powers ensured, as Khrushchev knew it would, that the United States would elaborate on the story it had fabricated after 1 May, when Washington claimed that a weather research plane had disappeared over Turkey; on 7 May Khrushchev compounded the Americans' embarrassment, telling the Supreme Soviet that the US pilot, who had been shot down over Sverdlovsk, was 'alive and well' and in Soviet hands.[53]

A few days later the remains of the plane and of Powers's equipment were put on display in Gorky Park; Khrushchev turned up at the exhibition and launched into another diatribe against the United States. By this time, the United States had admitted its deception and Eisenhower, much to Khrushchev's consternation, had taken responsibility for ordering the flights. The President refused to apologise or to promise to end the flights, which he described as 'distasteful' but 'a vital necessity'. Khrushchev knew that dissociating Eisenhower from the affair was crucial to salvaging US–Soviet *détente*, and the Soviet leader therefore chose to reject Eisenhower's confession. He insisted that Dulles had blackmailed the President into taking responsibility and indicated that Eisenhower would visit the USSR as planned.[54] Vershinin's trip was cancelled, however, and Khrushchev invited Mao to Moscow for the first time in years; Mao, who was doubtless enjoying the whole spectacle, declined.

Eisenhower's unapologetic assumption of responsibility for the flights had been an unmitigated disaster for the Soviet premier. While it was obvious that the President could not possibly make use of the 'escape route' which Khrushchev had left him, Khrushchev himself genuinely seems to have expected that Eisenhower would at least remain silent about the issue; the President's statement left him flabbergasted.[55] Khrushchev had thought that he could have it both ways, maximising the propaganda value of the Americans' humiliation, while continuing to move towards *détente* (from a position of even greater strength). He now told US Ambassador Llewellyn Thompson, 'This U-2 thing has put me in a terrible spot. You have to get me off it.'[56] By this time Khrushchev and his colleagues seem to have been confused as to how they ought to handle the summit; the extent of their indecision is revealed by the fact that the Soviet summit position was worked out on the way to Paris.[57]

On the plane to the summit – a four-engine Iliushin 18 selected in order to avoid the embarrassment Khrushchev had felt at Geneva in 1955 – the Soviet delegation, in consultation with Presidium members in Moscow, decided to present an ultimatum. If Eisenhower did not apologise officially for the flights and promise to end them, the Soviets would withdraw their invitation for him to visit Moscow.[58] Khrushchev probably had little doubt that his demands would mean the break-up of the summit, but, faced with the prospect of only modest progress in Paris and under pressure from China, East Germany and Soviet hardliners, he concluded that he could not afford to go ahead with the meeting unless Eisenhower gave way on the U-2 issue. The political price would otherwise be too high for what Khrushchev might hope to achieve at the summit.

Khrushchev arrived in Paris on 14 May, two days before the summit was to start; on the following day another Soviet rocket was launched into space. *Pravda* told its readers,

In Paris in recent years people constantly await the latest miraculous achievements of the Soviet Union. Today we heard such a conversation here: 'The latest Russian rocket is great. But one had to expect such an event, given that Khrushchev has come for the summit'. Perhaps that statement sounds naive, but it expresses the conviction that Moscow can do anything, that she can create miracles as though to order, for a day which has been designated in advance.[59]

A successful summit, however, turned out to be a miracle beyond Moscow's abilities. In the days prior to the meeting, Khrushchev met with de Gaulle and Macmillan and explained his demands, warning that if they were not met, the summit could not proceed. Both men tried unsuccessfully to persuade him to soften his position. Khrushchev left these meetings in the belief that Eisenhower's allies – particularly the proud nationalist de Gaulle – sympathised with Moscow on the U-2 issue. De Gaulle later claimed that Khrushchev had threatened to bomb US U-2 bases in Turkey, Japan and elsewhere.[60] Eisenhower and Khrushchev both expected to meet ahead of the summit, and the President was prepared to end the U-2 programme, but no meeting took place. Khrushchev was offended that the Americans did not approach him, the injured party, and request a meeting, while Eisenhower was puzzled by Khrushchev's failure to do the same and angered that the Russian had presented written demands to de Gaulle and Macmillan but not to him.[61]

On 16 May at 11 a.m. the four leaders finally met. Khrushchev and Eisenhower both asked to make preliminary statements; de Gaulle, as chairman, ruled that Eisenhower, as a head of state, should be given precedence over Khrushchev, a head of government. Khrushchev objected to this on the grounds that he had demanded the floor first and began to read the statement which he and his colleagues had agreed; forty-five minutes later he had torpedoed the entire meeting, demanding an apology from Eisenhower and recommending that the conference be postponed for six to eight months, that is, until after the US elections. Eisenhower would leave office in January 1961 and Khrushchev meant to have nothing more to do with him, preferring to await his successor. According to Khrushchev, the Soviet translator saw the President pass a note to Secretary of State Christian Herter suggesting that he, the President, apologise, but Herter overruled him, thus confirming Khrushchev's belief that the State Department dictated policy to Eisenhower. The story is almost certainly pure invention.[62]

Eisenhower then spoke; he refused to apologise, but assured Khrushchev that the flights had been suspended and would not be renewed. The President revived his Open Skies proposal, under which surveillance missions would be flown over both countries under UN auspices and recommended that the Soviets and Americans confine any further discussion to bilateral talks, so that the summit conference might proceed. Macmillan then pleaded with Khrushchev not to disrupt the summit in view of Eisenhower's promise that there would be no more flights; he more than any of his western colleagues had wanted a summit and had worked to bring it about. Finally de Gaulle rose and gave Khrushchev an undiplomatic dressing-down, pointing out that he had only days before received Khrushchev's assurances that the meeting would take place as scheduled. Now Macmillan had come, Eisenhower had come, and he, de Gaulle, had been 'put to serious inconvenience' to organise and attend the meeting which Khrushchev was now breaking up. De Gaulle also pointed out that the Soviet satellite launched the day before passed over France eighteen times a day, making Khrushchev's concern about the inviolability of Soviet airspace both hypocritical and obsolete.[63]

Khrushchev remained in Paris until 18 May; he met again with both Macmillan and de Gaulle but had no further contact with Eisenhower. His final performance in Paris was a fist-thumping, red-faced, two-and-a-half-hour denunciation of America, Eisenhower and his French audience, whom he called 'lackeys of imperialism'. The intensity of his rhetoric far surpassed anything he had said in years and was reminiscent of his philippics against the show-trial defendants in the 1930s. Significantly, although he threatened to attack U-2 bases in neighbouring countries, he did not threaten to scuttle the test-ban talks in Geneva or to sign a peace treaty with the GDR. The summit would take place in due course – after Eisenhower was gone. Khrushchev concluded that 'in the end it will be necessary to overcome [the flight's] consequences and digest all of this. Relations must be normalised so the American and Soviet peoples can live not only in peace but friendship.' He raised a glass of mineral water and added, '*Vive la paix!*'[64]

But the summit did not take place in 1961 or ever. East–West relations remained tense for two and a half more years, during which a second crisis occurred over Berlin, and the superpowers went to the brink of war over Cuba. The partial test ban, which was very nearly agreed by May 1960, was not signed until 1963. The renewed cold war hindered Khrushchev's drive for domestic change as well, and, although the crisis did not lead directly to any challenges to his rule at home, his authority was damaged by the perception that he had allowed himself to be suckered by Eisenhower. A *Pravda* article quoting the American columnist Walter Lippmann made an unprecedented reference to 'those in the Soviet Union who criticise [Khrushchev]', and *Pravda Ukrainy* flatly stated that the President knew 'everything, absolutely everything', despite the fact that Khrushchev himself continued to argue that Eisenhower had been manipulated by the CIA and the Pentagon.[65] The Powers shootdown proved to be the beginning of the end of Khrushchev's grand design for the Soviet Union.

9 From Crisis to Crisis
The Cold War Renewed, 1960-2

He who thinks that he can charm the workers with nice revolutionary phrases is mistaken. . . . If one does not show concern for the growth of material and spiritual wealth, then people will listen today, they will listen tomorrow, and then they will say: 'Why do you always promise us everything in the future, talking, so to speak, about life beyond the grave? The priest has already talked to us about that.'

N. S. Khrushchev, Moscow, 1964[1]

The scuttling of the Paris summit was followed in short order by the final rupture with China. Mao Zedong had watched with pleasure as the U-2 crisis disrupted the best-laid plans of both Eisenhower and Khrushchev; from Mao's perspective, Khrushchev had gotten what he deserved for entering into such a close relationship with the leader of the imperialist camp. The stiffening of Soviet policy towards the West which followed the summit did nothing to repair the breach in Sino-Soviet relations; on the contrary, China stepped up its criticism of the Soviet Union, and Moscow responded in kind.[2] Bitter exchanges at a Romanian party congress in Bucharest later in the month led to the withdrawal of Soviet specialists from China, which thenceforth received no Soviet economic assistance.[3] Beijing responded by cancelling trade agreements with Czechoslovakia, Moscow's loyal client, and the Soviets were compelled to purchase Czechoslovak goods which had been earmarked for China.[4]

In November a conference of eighty-one communist parties in Moscow provided the forum for another round of mudslinging between the two communist giants, chiefly over the question of peaceful coexistence with capitalist states; Beijing also attacked Soviet aid to Egypt and India.

The East European parties, with the exception of Albania, backed Moscow; altogether only about a dozen communist parties supported Beijing.[5] The final break with China did not, however, lead to a swing back towards Tito. Khrushchev's ideological orthodoxy was under attack and he responded by taking a tough line against both 'revisionism' (Tito) and 'dogmatism' (Mao) in order to demonstrate that the Soviet path was a middle course between these extremes.

In September Khrushchev travelled to New York for the opening of the UN General Assembly, apparently in order to annoy Eisenhower. He spent three weeks there, wooing Third World states, attacking the United States and generating plenty of coverage of himself in the US press. On 23 September he delivered a scathing attack on western governments, UN Secretary-General Dag Hammarskjöld and the UN Security Council, which he described as a 'spittoon'. Khrushchev called for the replacement of the Secretary-General by a troika including representatives of East, West and the neutral states. In vain he demanded a General Assembly debate of the U-2 affair.[6] When British Prime Minister Macmillan mentioned Khrushchev's destruction of the Paris summit, the Soviet premier shouted, 'Yes, let's talk about Powers! Don't send your spy planes to our country.'[7] The members of the Soviet delegation began pounding their fists on the table; Khrushchev himself began to beat the tabletop with his shoe. The Assembly's presiding officer broke his gavel attempting to restore order, but the unflappable Macmillan simply requested a translation.[8]

Khrushchev's programme was in trouble at home as well as abroad. Nineteen sixty produced another disappointing harvest. Though better than 1959 – and in the Virgin Lands the best since 1956 – the 1960 grain harvest was more than 25 million tonnes short of the plan target for that year, which had already been revised downwards by almost 30 million tonnes.[9] Late in the year Larionov's fraud in Riazan' Province was exposed. This was particularly embarrassing to Khrushchev, who had been publicly identified with the 'three plans' campaign.[10]

He took this setback in stride, and at the January 1961

Central Committee plenum he went on the offensive, charging that the falsification of data which had taken place in Riazan' was typical of many other provinces.[11] There was some truth to this claim: the unrealistic pledges he had extracted from other provincial leaders had led to similar falsification of data, albeit on a smaller scale, across the country.[12] Khrushchev criticised and heckled a number of speakers at the plenum, interrupting even Presidium members Podgornyi and Polianskii. Khrushchev then spent much of the early spring on an inspection tour of farming regions, during which he continued to increase the pressure on local officials, whom he blamed for the previous year's poor agricultural performance.[13] By late October 1961 more than a third of the provincial party secretaries in Russia had been replaced, many of them for their failures in agriculture.[14] Those who remained were frequently berated about agricultural performance in their domains; some were interrogated weekly over the telephone by the First Secretary.[15]

A number of ill-conceived administrative 'reforms' were hastily adopted in order to prevent future 'hoodwinking' in agriculture. The agriculture ministries were stripped of all managerial and planning powers, which were transferred to the State Planning Commission, and ordered to concentrate on research, development and propagation of new methods. Procurements were to be managed by a newly created USSR State Procurements Committee in conjunction with a new system of party purchasing inspectors, whose salaries depended on the volume of procurements in their area. The reforms left unanswered basic questions about co-ordination between Gosplan, the State Procurements Committee, the purchasing inspectors and local party organs.

Although he maintained intense pressure on local party leaders, Khrushchev was at last coming to realise that party activism alone was not enough; new investment in the farming sector was urgently required. In February 1960, he had said that the Seven-Year Plan targets for agriculture, which required a 35 per cent increase over the record 1958 cereals harvest, would be reached 'by raising even higher the enthusiasm of the masses for work'.[16] In a note to the

Presidium on 29 October 1960, however, he acknowledged that additional investment funds for agriculture had to be drawn from surpluses created by the over-fulfilment of plan targets by industry.[17] Such a revolutionary step was bound to generate opposition. The Stalinist system of collective agriculture had been devised to ensure that the state could squeeze the rural sector in order to finance industrialisation; now Khrushchev was proposing to finance agricultural investment with the surpluses provided by industry. The proposals were quickly watered down; surpluses were divided between industry and agriculture.[18] Khrushchev was, however, able to thwart attempts to increase the steel targets in the Seven-Year Plan; raising the targets would have eliminated above-plan surpluses (and additional investment in agriculture) at the stroke of a pen.[19]

Over the longer term, agriculture could be provided with the needed investment only if Khrushchev were able to achieve a relaxation in tensions with the West. To his great relief, the victor in the 1960 US presidential election had been the Democrat, John F. Kennedy, whom Khrushchev had met in Washington in 1959. Khrushchev considered Kennedy's rival, Richard Nixon, a McCarthyite whose election would have been a catastrophe. Though careful not to meddle in the US campaign, Khrushchev did his bit for Kennedy by refusing to release the crew of an American RB-47 spy plane shot down over the Barents Sea until after the election.

Khrushchev, who was eager for an early summit with Kennedy, was taken aback by the tough rhetoric of the new administration. Kennedy was determined to show both domestic and foreign audiences that he would be as tough as his predecessor; ironically, he was reacting to a hard-line Khrushchev speech published on 18 January, just two days before the inauguration. The speech was actually aimed at the Chinese, but it made more of an impact on Kennedy's thinking than gestures and statements calculated to convey Khrushchev's desire for better relations, such as the release of the RB-47 crew.

Kennedy suffered his first international setback in April, when a US-backed attempt to invade Cuba and overthrow the Castro regime met with defeat at the Bay of Pigs. The

Cuban fiasco came just five days after the Soviet cosmonaut Yurii Gagarin had made the first manned space flight in history. The two events gave Khrushchev a good month for propaganda bluster, but his most aggressive remarks about Cuba (as about Suez in 1956) came only after the danger was past. The failure of the US-backed invasion meant that Khrushchev's 1960 pledges to defend Cuba with Soviet missiles were not put to the test. The Bay of Pigs did not prevent agreement on a summit, which was set for Vienna in June, but, unfortunately for Khrushchev, it reinforced Kennedy's determination to make no concessions. The President's advisers feared that a dovish line so soon after the failure in Cuba would look like a show of weakness on Kennedy's part.

The two leaders met in Vienna on 3–4 June. The agenda included a test-ban treaty, which the US side had been led to believe would be completed at the summit, and conflicts in Berlin, Laos and the Congo.[20] Khrushchev's refusal to budge on the remaining obstacles to a test-ban agreement came as a rude shock to the Americans, but the most difficult question on the agenda was Berlin. At the beginning of the year Khrushchev had told the West German ambassador to Moscow that the status of Berlin and the GDR must be addressed in 1961.[21] He had warned Ambassador Thompson that if a deal was not reached in Vienna, then Moscow would sign a treaty with the GDR.[22] In Vienna he repeated his proposals for a peace treaty recognising two Germanies and according Berlin the status of a free city; otherwise, he would by the end of the year conclude a peace treaty with the GDR which would render existing agreements concerning access to Berlin invalid. Kennedy, however, insisted that East–West tensions would have to be eased before any deal concerning Berlin could be struck; the tense international environment made any alteration of the status quo unacceptably dangerous.[23]

This was Kennedy's principal theme in Vienna. In all his discussions with Khrushchev he repeatedly stressed that the international environment was too tense for either side to risk unilateral attempts to change the existing balance of power. Khrushchev found this line of reasoning utterly unacceptable. He regarded the international status quo as

dynamic, not static: communist influence was gaining
ground the world over, in accordance with irreversible
historical processes. Kennedy was asking him to help hold
back the march of history, which Khrushchev genuinely
believed to be in the direction of socialism.[24] Moreover,
both men knew that the global balance, which Kennedy was
so keen to preserve in the name of peace, happened to give
the United States a substantial economic, political and
strategic advantage. Such rhetoric must have seemed rich
indeed to Khrushchev, coming just weeks after Kennedy
had tried and failed to alter the status quo in Cuba. Despite
their deep disagreements and sometimes heated exchanges,
both men were at pains to stress their commitment to
avoiding war.

The summit's principal significance turned out to be the
effect it had in shaping the two leaders' impressions of one
another. Kennedy went away exhausted by Khrushchev's
aggressive, ideological attacks on the United States and his
complete stubbornness as a negotiator; he later told his
brother Robert that dealing with Khrushchev was 'like
dealing with Dad. All give and no take.'[25] Kennedy had
erred in allowing himself to be drawn into an extended
discussion of Marxism for which he was ill-prepared and in
which Khrushchev easily bested him. When Kennedy
warned of the dangers of 'miscalculation' setting off a
nuclear war, Khrushchev exploded, enraged by the President's apparent condescension. Khrushchev's harsh tone
was a product of Kennedy's refusal to accept any negotiations over Berlin, which Khrushchev saw as a retreat from
Eisenhower's acceptance in 1959 of the need for talks.
Macmillan, who met with Kennedy after the summit, found
the President 'rather stunned – baffled would perhaps be
fairer . . . completely overwhelmed by the ruthlessness and
barbarity of the Russian premier'.[26]

Khrushchev's view of Kennedy at this time is difficult to
pin down. It was reported that on returning from Vienna
he told an aide, 'I guess we scared that young man',[27] but
Khrushchev and his son Sergei later claimed that the Soviet
leader had held Kennedy in high regard; this may reflect a
later revision of his opinion in the wake of the Berlin and
Cuban missile crises.[28] G. M. Kornienko, who was then

Counsellor in the Soviet embassy in Washington, has claimed that Khrushchev came to view Kennedy as a strong and capable leader during the autumn 1960 presidential campaign.[29] Khrushchev aide Fedor Burlatsky, however, believes that Kennedy's flexibility and lack of apparent ideological convictions may have led Khrushchev to believe that the President lacked the backbone to be a strong leader; Burlatsky suggests that Khrushchev considered Kennedy an able man but one who might well fold in a crisis.[30] Khrushchev also knew that Kennedy was the son of a millionaire and remarked upon this fact more than once; as an older, self-made man, the Russian may have assumed that he would be more than a match for the rich young heir.[31]

Khrushchev was aware even before Vienna that Kennedy's slender majority in the 1960 elections would make it difficult for the new president to concede anything on Berlin even if he wanted to. Kennedy's performance at Vienna, taken together with his proposal to increase the US defence budget, left Khrushchev little hope of forcing Kennedy to the negotiating table over Berlin in 1961. Khrushchev's best hope of gaining a settlement was to step up the pressure on America's European allies, who might be easier to intimidate. His attempts to threaten them were so crude as to be almost comic: at a Moscow reception on 2 July he remarked to the British ambassador that it would take only six Soviet hydrogen bombs to demolish the United Kingdom; France would require nine.

Khrushchev could not afford the prolonged period of tension required to drive a wedge between America and Western Europe, however. Kennedy's defence proposals had already compelled him to increase the Soviet defence budget and suspend the 1960 troop reductions. The Soviet leader could not back down without looking weak, but neither could he maintain such a confrontational stance without putting his domestic investment plans on hold indefinitely. Nor could he accept an indefinite postponement of action over Berlin: the continuing flood of East Germans into West Berlin was an embarrassment to the entire socialist bloc and an economically damaging 'brain drain' for the GDR.

In late July the Americans offered him a way out. US diplomat Charles Bohlen and Senator J. William Fulbright both stated that East Germany had the right to close its borders. Fulbright went so far as to say that he did not understand why the GDR did not exercise this right; when asked about Fulbright's statement, Kennedy refused to disavow it. As early as March Ambassador Thompson had foreseen the possibility that the East Germans might close the inter-sector border in Berlin. Kennedy, who thought Khrushchev's concerns on this score understandable, stated that the US could not keep East Berlin open.[32] On 13 August Khrushchev and his East German allies took the hint, closing the inter-sector border and beginning the construction of what was to become Khrushchev's most enduring monument in Europe, the Berlin Wall. Khrushchev was aware that the wall – built to keep German workers from leaving their workers' paradise – was a propaganda disaster, but felt he had no choice: the GDR had 'yet to reach a level of moral and material development where competition with the West is possible'.[33] He claimed that the economic performance of the GDR improved markedly as a result of the closing of the border.[34]

In order to cover what was in fact a retreat on the Berlin question, Khrushchev left his ultimatum hanging over the West for some time after the wall was built. He also resumed Soviet nuclear weapons tests, which had been suspended in 1958; the tests were 'to provide support for the USSR's policy on the German question'.[35] Khrushchev's decision to resume testing reflected his economic priorities as well as the need to look tough on Berlin; nuclear tests were a cheap way of demonstrating Soviet power, and nuclear weapons provided his least expensive hope of establishing Soviet parity with the United States. The thirty tests in the series lasted until late October, when a 60-megaton device was detonated.

Meanwhile, Soviet policy on Berlin softened. At the end of September Foreign Minister Andrei Gromyko privately informed Washington that Moscow would not insist on the 31 December deadline.[36] On 17 October Khrushchev, reporting to the Twenty-second Congress of the CPSU, publicly played down the significance of his deadline, just as he had done in 1959.[37] It was a humiliating climb-down. Khrushchev's second attempt to force the Berlin issue had achieved less than his earlier efforts in 1958-9. He had instead strengthened western unity, helped Kennedy justify increases in the US defence budget and convinced many in the West that he was a bluffer who would not follow through on his threats.

The Twenty-second Congress, which opened on 17 October, was a study in contrasts; the launching of the Third Party Programme, with its description of the bright Soviet future, was accompanied by an unexpected return to the Stalin issue and the horrors of the Soviet past. The official Programme of the Communist Party of the Soviet Union in early 1961 was a document authored by Lenin in 1919 and long out of date. The need to draft a new programme had been discussed since 1939, but work had actually begun only in 1958. The new programme would not only encapsulate Khrushchev's vision for the Soviet future, it would also raise his stature as a theoretician: Lenin had been the theorist of revolutionary socialism; now Khrushchev would become the theorist of a new epoch in Soviet development, the period of 'full-scale communist construction'. The draft programme had been prepared by a team of specialists in the Central Committee apparatus (albeit with considerable input from Khrushchev), and in the spring and summer of 1961 the First Secretary dictated forty-six pages of comments and alterations to the text.[38]

On the face of it, the document was optimistic to the point of utopianism. The original draft promised that by 1980 the 'foundations of a communist society' would be built in the USSR; the final text was even more upbeat, stating that communism in the USSR would have been constructed 'in the main' by 1980.[39] The socialist principle of distribution, 'from each according to his abilities to each according to his work', would give way to the communist principle, 'from each according to his abilities to each according to his need'. Khrushchev's colleague Otto Kuusinen worried that the programme was too utopian and warned of the need to distinguish clearly in the programme between the tasks and developments of the coming two decades and longer-term elements of the communist transformation, such as the complete withering away of the state, the disappearance of linguistic and cultural differences between nationalities, and so on. Kuusinen stressed that only the 'foundation and some important component parts' of the 'majestic communist building' would be built by 1980, and that the programme ought not to confuse this with the coming of full communism in its highest form.[40] Khrushchev took some of Kuusinen's advice. The 'withering away of the state' disappeared from the programme, as did the 'merger of the nations' and certain other excessive claims. Nevertheless, the final programme asserted that 'the construction of a communist society' would be completed 'in the main' by 1980, and Khrushchev himself promised that 'the present generation of Soviet people will live under communism'.[41]

Khrushchev's willingness to make such promises reflected his belief that the party could not go on indefinitely asking the people to make sacrifices today for the sake of a future which never came; such an approach would make communism seem as unreal to the masses as the church's promises of life after death.[42] Secondly, by generating high popular expectations, Khrushchev hoped to generate pressure on Soviet officials from below as well as from above for the achievement of his ambitious goals for economic development. Finally, Khrushchev's vision of a communist society was far less utopian than that of Marx and his disciples. Communism for Khrushchev meant little more than achieving a western level of material abundance, but in a much more collectivist and egalitarian society. In his view 'the main thing' in a communist society would be 'labour and discipline' – scarcely a formula for utopia in the minds of most people:

> society will be highly organised, with a high degree of discipline, and that discipline will depend not on any coercive means, but on fostering a feeling of duty to fulfil one's obligations . . . the discipline in communist society will not be a burden for people, because every member of society will be brought up in the spirit of the necessity for everyone to participate in work.[43]

This was not a vision of a liberal society, but of a highly disciplined collectivism in which compliance no longer depended on state coercion. Khrushchev was at pains to stress that there would be no 'unlimited "freedom of the individual"' under communism.[44]

Khrushchev went on to elaborate several stages in the development of a communist society, of which only the most basic would be realised by 1980.[45] His notion of communism was far from being a realistic goal for Soviet society in 1961, but it was much less fantastic than the utopia described by earlier Marxists. As if to underscore the modesty of his claims, Khrushchev insisted that the phrase 'in the main' be inserted into passages referring to the resolution of Soviet housing problems by the 1980s.[46] Apparently the housing shortage would not be completely eliminated even after the arrival of the first stage of communism.

Khrushchev also insisted on a reformulation of the nature of the Soviet state. He argued that the dictatorship of the proletariat no longer existed in the Soviet Union, since all exploiting classes had been liquidated. Dictatorship, according to Khrushchev, was a form of class oppression. In the early years after the revolution, the working class took power and suppressed the exploiters; now that there were no more exploiters, there was no object of oppression. Ergo, there could be no dictatorship. The USSR, he said, had become an all-people's state. This change of formula removed the last basis for arguing that people of non-proletarian origins were second-class citzens or for using class struggle as a justification for internal repression. Khrushchev also discussed at length the significance of the change for international propaganda. As long as the USSR proclaimed itself a dictatorship of any sort, it was handing its enemies a powerful propaganda weapon.[47]

Internal opposition and international tensions conspired to block one of Khrushchev's major innovations. During his examination of the draft programme in April, Khrushchev had considered at length a possible reformulation of the investment priorities question. Although he stopped far short of suggesting even privately that the priority of heavy industry could yet be overturned, he did attempt to specify the conditions which, once achieved, would permit a decisive shift in priorities in favour of the consumer.[48] The draft published in the summer implied that such a shift was in the making.[49] By the time of the Congress in October, however, Khrushchev said only that the leadership was 'considering' some convergence of the growth rates of heavy and light industry over the next twenty years, adding that 'heavy industry has always played the leading role . . . and will continue to do so'.[50]

Ironically, it was during the Congress that Khrushchev's last hope of restraining defence spending while remaining on an equal footing with the United States disappeared. In his opening speech Khrushchev had masked his disavowal of the 31 December Berlin deadline with aggressive rhetoric. In response, Kennedy decided that the time had come to expose Khrushchev's four-year-old missile deception. During the campaign Kennedy had made extensive use of the 'missile gap' which Eisenhower had allegedly allowed to open up in the ICBM race; Eisenhower had refused to allow Nixon to rebut these charges by exposing the deception and revealing the true extent of US superiority. Eisenhower reckoned that such a revelation might compel Khrushchev to initiate a crash ICBM programme. Khrushchev's Congress report convinced Kennedy that the greater danger lay in continuing to let Khrushchev go on making serious threats on the basis of a mythical strategic edge. He authorised Roswell Gilpatric, a senior Defense Department official, to reveal for the first time the true extent of US strategic superiority. Khrushchev's cover was blown.

The exposure of his fantastic bluff deprived Khrushchev of any hope of preserving both his foreign policy ambitions and his domestic agenda; it also made him look positively foolish in the eyes of the world at a moment when his conflict with Mao was heating up again. Khrushchev had been publicly criticised and then snubbed by Zhou Enlai at the Congress, not least for his failure to stand up to the West. Now he was exposed as even more of a 'paper tiger' than the Americans. So serious was the issue that Defence Minister Malinovskii took time at the Congress to rebut the claims made in Gilpatric's speech. The Soviets also detonated another enormous atomic device in order to demonstrate their capabilities. But this was only short-term damage control; Khrushchev began to search for the cheapest, fastest possible means of shifting the strategic balance in Moscow's favour so as to restore its political parity with Washington.

The feud with China was related to the Stalin question as well as to Khrushchev's policies towards the West, and it was one of the reasons for the unexpected prominence of de-Stalinisation at the Twenty-second Congress. In his private remarks back in April Khrushchev had agreed to Kuusinen's suggestion that a section of the new programme be devoted to the cult of personality and its effects, but no such discussion was ever included in any of the drafts.[51] The fact that there was no mention of it in the draft which Khrushchev presented to his Presidium colleagues suggests that he himself changed his mind and decided that the party's description of the glowing future ought not be marred by a discussion of past terrors.[52] The final version said only that Leninism was incompatible with personality cults.[53] In his two-day opening address to the Congress Khrushchev barely mentioned the issue.

It was therefore something of a shock to most of the delegates when Khrushchev's subordinates began to attack the members of the anti-party group for abuses committed during Stalin's time. Khrushchev in his General Report had revealed Voroshilov's support for the opposition in 1957, but other than that he left the dirty work to his lieutenants for several days. Only on 27 October did he speak to the issue again, this time going further than he had gone in the Secret Speech in addressing Stalin's responsibility for the abuses committed in the 1930s and 1940s.[54] What Khrushchev presented was largely a rehashing of material from the Secret Speech, albeit with more information about certain questions; unlike the Secret Speech, however, it was delivered at an open session of the Congress and published in the press afterwards.

The reasons for this new attack on Stalin are far from clear. It would be a mistake, of course, to discount completely the role of guilt and genuine idealism in Khrushchev's decision, but this was far from the whole story. Khrushchev's new programme represented a break with important Stalinist dogmas in a number of areas, and Khrushchev may have felt that this break with the past could be completed only by a more serious attempt to grapple with the history of Stalin's rule. Thus he promised the Congress that a monument to Stalin's victims would be set up and that more information on the Kirov assassination and other mysteries would be brought to light. He stressed the need to uncover the truth and tell it to the party and people. The most dramatic moment of the Congress came when former prison inmate D. A. Lazurkina, an old Bolshevik who had known Lenin himself, seconded a proposal 'from the floor' (which had, of course, been orchestrated by Khrushchev) to remove Stalin's body from public display in the Lenin Mausoleum on Red Square. Lazurkina told the Congress that she had consulted Lenin 'as if he were alive in front of me' and that he had told her that it was 'unpleasant' for him to lie there next to Stalin.[55] The Congress agreed. Late on the night of 30 October Stalin's body was removed from the mausoleum and buried behind it, beneath the walls of the Kremlin.[56]

The de-Stalinisation campaign of the Twenty-second Congress turned out to be more promise than performance. The Congress resolutions were softer on Stalin, China and the anti-party group than the rhetoric at the actual sessions. Although there was pressure to bring the members of the anti-party group to trial for their part in the repressions, this was never done; it would have set a precedent which threatened many senior officials, including Khrushchev and Mikoian. Cities, towns and public institutions named for Stalin were renamed, but the promised monument to Stalin's victims never materialised, and there were no further revelations concerning the Kirov assassination or other infamous events of the period.

In addition to the new programme, the Twenty-second Congress adopted extensive revisions to the party statutes. The most significant of these concerned the 'systematic renewal of cadres'. The new rules mandated minimum levels of turnover in party bodies and limitations on the number of terms which individuals in 'elective' party posts could serve. These rules did not apply to secretaries above the PPO level or to the Central Committee, and they allowed exceptions to be made for those with 'recognised authority and . . . outstanding political, organisational or other qualities'.[57] Khrushchev himself advanced three reasons for the changes. First, he stressed the need for the 'constant renewal of cadres' and the introduction of 'new forces' into leading party bodies; in other words, he wished to institutionalise and extend the purge of the party apparatus which had been under way since January. Secondly, the new rules were linked to de-Stalinisation, as they would facilitate the removal of autocratic Stalinists from party executive bodies. The threat to conservative officials was explicit:

> It is no secret that we have comrades who in their time were thought worthy and elected to executive posts. . . . Since then, some of them have lost the ability to conduct business creatively and lost their sense of the new; they have become an obstacle.

Finally, the new rules would help eradicate the practice of building up 'family groups' in party organisations, which involved 'elements of nepotism and of mutual concealment of shortcomings and mistakes'.[58]

Not surprisingly, the new rule was unpopular with party officials. Older officials were faced with the constant threat of replacement by younger men, while younger officials believed that the rules would prevent them from enjoying long careers at the top as men like Khrushchev and Mikoian had already done.[59] The threat was in fact more apparent than real: the targets outlined actually involved lower rates of turnover than had obtained in the eight years since Stalin's death. The purpose of the rule may have been not to enhance the utility of Khrushchev's control over appointments, but to preserve it, by enshrining minimum levels beneath which personnel turnover in party organs could not fall. The danger was that a gradual freezing of personnel policy would 'block up' the system, and stagnation would occur.[60]

Despite the setbacks and the resistance which many of his policies encountered, Khrushchev remained firmly entrenched as leader of the Soviet Union. Most Soviet observers, including some of Khrushchev's aides and colleagues in the leadership regarded the Twenty-second Congress as the apogee of his career.[61] According to Adzhubei, Khrushchev's was the decisive voice in determining the make-up of the Central Committee and other leading organs. The composition of the Presidium was resolved by him alone, possibly in consultation with Mikoian; the list of names he proposed to the Congress for election to the new Presidium was written in pencil in Khrushchev's own hand; he had not even entrusted it to a typist.[62] Those Presidium members dropped at the Congress also believed that their demotions were Khrushchev's doing.[63]

In March 1962 Khrushchev returned to the question of agricultural administration, pushing through yet another major reorganisation. The farming sector was reorganised into a network of Territorial Production Associations (TPAs) which encompassed several districts each. The network was guided at the all-union level by the new State Committee for Agriculture. The new entities irritated district officials, on whose prerogatives they encroached, and duplicated the work of a range of central and local bodies involved in agriculture. To make matters worse, Khrushchev told provincial party bosses that they would be held personally responsible for agricultural production in their regions.[64] The resulting tangle of jurisdictions further eroded what little independence the farms enjoyed.

Khrushchev also suffered the acute embarrassment of performing a public *volte-face* on price policy. His opening report to the March CC plenum discussed in considerable detail the inadequate supply of machinery to the farms and the need for new investment in agriculture.[65] Four days later, however, he stated that there would be no diversion of resources from industry and defence to agriculture.[66] The pressure to reverse course appears to have come from the military; in the months following the plenum, military leaders were at pains to stress the dangers of over-reliance on rocket forces and the need to build up all branches of the armed forces.[67]

Unable to divert resources from the defence complex or other branches of industry, Khrushchev sought to pass a greater share of the burden of supporting agriculture onto Soviet consumers. On 1 June retail prices on many basic food products were raised by 25–30 per cent in order to offset necessary rises in the state purchase prices paid to the farms for produce. The price rises came as a shock to Soviet citizens, who had long taken stable or even falling prices in the state stores for granted. For many workers in the southern Russian town of Novocherkassk this blow to their already low standard of living was the last straw; they went on strike. Troops were brought into the city to restore order under the supervision of Presidium members Frol Kozlov, Anastas Mikoian and A. I. Kirilenko. The demonstrators occupied the town's central square and the buildings of the city soviet and party committee. When the protestors refused to disperse, the commanders on the scene, acting on orders from Defence Minister Malinovskii, ordered their troops to fire on the crowd; several demonstrators were killed and a number of others wounded.[68] In comparison with similar episodes in other countries, the events in Novocherkassk were not especially serious, but this was the Soviet Union, where strikes and public demonstrations were all but unheard of. The message of Novocherkassk to party leaders was that Khrushchev was becoming a political liability; his bungles and failures threatened to turn the populace against the regime.

In the spring Khrushchev renewed his anti-Stalin drive. Even the very modest acknowledgement of Stalin's virtues which had characterised his remarks at the Twenty-second Congress disappeared. In the arts this third wave of de-Stalinisation brought significant results. Nineteen sixty-two witnessed the height of the literary and artistic thaw; of particular importance was Khrushchev's decision to permit publication of Solzhenitsyn's account of life in a labour camp, *One Day in the Life of Ivan Denisovich*.[69]

Ivan Denisovich was preceded by Evgenii Evtushenko's poem 'Stalin's Heirs', which appeared in *Pravda* on 21 October. Referring to Stalin's new resting place, he wrote:

> And I turn to our government with a petition
> to double
>   and triple the sentries by that slab,

       so that Stalin does not rise
          and with Stalin – the past. . . .
       We removed
          him from within the Mausoleum,
       But how can we remove Stalin
          from within the heirs of Stalin?

Thinly veiled allusions to the fallen premier, Bulganin, and
to Khrushchev's own number two in the Secretariat, Frol
Kozlov, followed. Evtushenko concluded:

       While the heirs of Stalin
          are still alive on the earth,
       it will seem to me
          that Stalin is still in the Mausoleum.

   From his summer holiday on the Black Sea Khrushchev
launched his last major attempt to refashion the party
apparatus into an effective instrument of his rule. He had
not yet come to understand that his endless reorganisations could not achieve the economic renewal he desired.
Constant rearrangements of bureaucratic flow charts
angered managers and administrators but did nothing to
change either their work habits or the pressures which
gave rise to the most destructive practices. Nevertheless,
Khrushchev continued to believe that if he could simply
arrange the boxes on the flow chart in just the right way,
then all would be well. His latest solution was to split the
entire party apparatus from the provincial level on down
into two parallel structures, one for agriculture and one for
industry. He advanced the proposal in a memorandum to
the Presidium on 10 September.[70]
   Khrushchev's stated objective was to rectify what he
perceived to be the conflict between the party's involvement in agriculture and its role in industrial management.
Attention to the needs of agriculture meant that industry
tended to be neglected, and party officials adopted a
'campaign style of work', concentrating intensively on one
issue for a short period, only to forget about it when attention shifted to the next campaign, which might concern an

altogether different sector.[71] This neglect of industry reflected both the pressure Khrushchev placed on party officials with his agricultural schemes and the limited education of most provincial party officials, who were 'more at home in running agricultural "campaigns" than in attempting to raise industrial productivity'.[72] Khrushchev's unstated aim was to open the way to the appointment virtually overnight of a whole new corps of younger, better-educated party officials, who could manage industry effectively. The need for 'new blood' in the party apparatus was as obvious to Khrushchev as it was dangerous to incumbent officials. The decision to split the party organs was mute testimony to the inadequacy of the turnover rules adopted in 1961. Had Khrushchev been able to replace large segments of the party apparatus with fresh blood, he might never have been attracted to the bifurcation scheme.

Before this latest reorganisation could be pushed through, however, Khrushchev found himself faced with the greatest foreign policy crisis of his career. On 22 October President Kennedy announced that the United States had discovered that Moscow was deploying offensive missiles in Cuba and warned that Washington would regard any attack from Cuba as an attack by the USSR. He declared a naval quarantine of Cuba to prevent the shipment of Soviet missiles to Cuba. So began the public phase of the Cuban missile crisis. The confrontation had its origins in Khrushchev's visit to Bulgaria the preceding May. As the two men were walking along the beach at Varna, Defence Minister Malinovskii drew Khrushchev's attention to the fact that on the opposite shore were US missile bases capable of launching strikes against Kiev, Moscow and other major Soviet cities. The missiles were in fact the progeny of Khrushchev's own missile deception, having been deployed in late 1957 to ease European fears of a missile gap aroused by Sputnik 1. Khrushchev, angered by the imbalance of power which American Jupiter missiles in Turkey represented, asked why the USSR could not have bases close to the United States. The two men began to discuss the possibility of deploying Soviet missiles in Cuba, which Malinovskii assured Khrushchev could be done without detection.[73]

Such a deployment would allow Khrushchev to alter the

strategic balance at a stroke, recouping the authority he had
lost when Gilpatric had exposed his missile deception. The
actual strategic balance was even more lopsided than the
Kennedy administration realised: the USSR in 1962 had
only twenty ICBMs capable of hitting the United States, far
fewer than the seventy-five or more that the administration
estimated.[74] The Cuban deployment would provide Khrushchev with a basis for pressing Soviet demands on Berlin and
other issues. Soviet missiles in Cuba would also be an
additional source of security for Cuba, which Khrushchev
believed the Kennedy administration was planning to
invade.[75] Finally, the missiles would demonstrate Soviet
equality with the United States, an issue of great importance to Khrushchev, who found it galling that US bases
surrounded the USSR while there were no Soviet bases in
the western hemisphere.[76]

Back in Moscow the proposal was discussed with the
Presidium members, all of whom favoured deployment,
although Mikoian expressed reservations about the Cubans'
willingness to accept the missiles and about plans to deploy
them secretly.[77] The Cubans were indeed reluctant to accept
the missiles, and, once persuaded, they, like Mikoian,
argued that they should not be deployed in secret.[78] In
January 1992 Castro stated,

> We had a sovereign right to accept missiles. We were not
> violating international law. Why do it secretly – as if we
> had no right to do it? I warned Nikita that secrecy would
> give the imperialists the advantage.[79]

Castro turned out to be right. The secrecy of the operation provoked Kennedy as much as the deployment itself
and made it much easier for Washington to secure allied
support during the crisis. If Khrushchev had cited US
missiles in Turkey and declared publicly his aims in Cuba,
Kennedy's position would have been morally much weaker.
Khrushchev, however, feared that such a declaration would
trigger an immediate US attack on Cuba. His views prevailed.

A secret defence co-operation agreement between the

USSR and Cuba was signed by Raul Castro and Marshal Malinovskii in September; it was agreed that in November, after the deployment and the US midterm congressional elections, Khrushchev would travel to Cuba to sign the agreement with Fidel Castro. Kennedy would then be presented with a *fait accompli*.[80] This would be followed by a US–Soviet summit at which Khrushchev would be in a much stronger position to press his demands on Berlin and other matters. It did not enter the Soviet premier's head that Kennedy would react as he did to the Cuban missiles. Khrushchev had sounded the President out in May, telling him that the USSR had no plans to deploy missiles in Cuba but noting that it would be acting within its rights if it did so, since the United States had deployed such weapons in countries around the Soviet Union. Kennedy did not respond to this blatant hint, and Khrushchev took his silence as an indication that Kennedy would not react strongly to such a move.[81] Khrushchev may have believed that in Cuba, as in Berlin, Kennedy would be more likely to accept a *fait accompli* than advance notification of Soviet intentions.

The missiles were spotted by a U-2 on 14 October. Although the missiles had been transported in total secrecy, no effort had been made to camouflage the construction sites. The Soviet troops on the sites simply followed standard operating procedures; since previous deployments had been in the USSR, these made no allowance for camouflaging the operation.[82] On 22 October Kennedy made his broadcast. The President also wrote directly to Khrushchev, reminding the Soviet premier of previous US warnings against placing offensive weapons in Cuba and demanding their removal.[83]

The two men had exchanged a number of letters since Khrushchev had first written to Kennedy in September 1961 and had also passed messages through a number of informal channels, using as intermediaries journalists and intelligence operatives, as well as Kennedy's brother Robert, the US Attorney-General, and Khrushchev's son-in-law, *Izvestiia* editor Aleksei Adzhubei. These channels suited both leaders, since neither fully trusted his foreign minister and both had a liking for personal diplomacy, and they were important throughout the crisis.[84] This multiplicity of channels of communication proved useful at times, but, as the crisis showed, it also increased the chances of misunderstanding and confusion between the two sides. Khrushchev's penchant for using Adzhubei as a personal emissary would come back to haunt him two years later.

Khrushchev replied to Kennedy's letter on 23 October, assuring the President that the weapons in Cuba were exclusively defensive and accusing the US of violating international law with its quarantine. He ordered an acceleration of the work in Cuba and instructed Soviet ships to ignore the quarantine; this latter order was rescinded before it was put to the test, however, and an early confrontation was thus avoided. For the next three days neither side budged from its position, but both avoided further escalation of the crisis, and secret negotiations continued. Khrushchev pressed for a summit, but this was interpreted by Kennedy as an attempt to buy time while construction in Cuba continued. A letter to Kennedy offering a withdrawal of the missiles from Cuba in return for withdrawal of the Jupiters from Italy and Turkey was prepared on 25 October. Each side would pledge not to invade the other's allies after the withdrawal.

Khrushchev, however, was unnerved by Soviet intelligence reports suggesting that a US move against Cuba was imminent and decided to drop the demand concerning the Jupiters. The offer was transmitted on 26 October. The letter of 26 October was less of a capitulation than it appeared at first glance. Its tone suggested that Khrushchev was frightened and eager to come to terms, but there was in fact *no explicit offer* to withdraw the missiles. Khrushchev implied that they would be withdrawn but offered only to halt further arms shipments to Cuba in return for an end to the quarantine and the opening of negotiations. Since there were already at least thirty-six Soviet nuclear warheads in Cuba,[85] anything which would prolong the crisis until the missiles were operational was to Khrushchev's advantage. The letter, far from being the panicky surrender many thought it to be, was an attempt to buy time and forestall a US attack. As it became clear that no US attack was about to take place, Khrushchev raised the stakes; on 27 October, before the US had responded to the letter of 26 October, the Soviets sent and broadcast a second letter, incorporating their demands on the Jupiters, which had already been discussed through informal channels. Kennedy chose to reply to the first letter and ignore the second, a move which upset Khrushchev.

The Soviet leader's worries were compounded by the unauthorised downing by Soviet forces of an American U-2 over Cuba; the incident drove home to Khrushchev the limits on his ability to control even Soviet actions in the crisis. On 28 October he and Kennedy agreed to the withdrawal of the missiles in exchange for a US pledge not to invade Cuba; Washington also agreed to withdraw the Jupiters (something Kennedy had intended to do anyway) but insisted that this part of the agreement be kept secret, as the Jupiters were NATO weapons which Kennedy was not entitled to bargain away. Khrushchev accepted the secrecy of this aspect of their agreement, despite the fact that it meant that he was making much greater public concessions than Kennedy. Khrushchev knew that Cuba would be upset at being treated as a bargaining chip on a par with a minor US ally like Turkey; and Kennedy had warned him that if the Turkey deal were publicised, it would not be honoured by the United States.[86] The entire deal was cut without consulting Castro, who was enraged; Khrushchev claimed that there had not been time for consultations. Ironically, this impression may have been reinforced by the urgent tone of Castro's 26 October letter to Khrushchev, which predicted US aggression against Cuba within 24–72 hours.[87] Whatever the truth of the matter, Moscow's other friends and clients could not fail to notice Khrushchev's readiness to sacrifice the interests of his ally in order to reach agreement with Washington.

With the most dangerous phase of the crisis past, Kennedy pressed his advantage over Khrushchev, while the Russian sought to make up for his losses by pressing ahead as rapidly as possible with his own post-crisis agenda. Kennedy attached to his no-invasion pledge conditions which Castro himself rejected; as a result, Kennedy never considered the pledge binding. He could not, however, point this out to his conservative critics, who attacked him for selling out Cuba to the communists, without running

the risk that Khrushchev would expose the agreement on
the Jupiters. It would then be clear that more than one
superpower had negotiated the fate of a smaller ally
without consulting it. Kennedy also raised the issue of
Soviet Il-28 bombers in Cuba. Khrushchev had left himself
open on this point by refusing to acknowledge in correspondence that there were missiles or warheads in Cuba,
referring only to 'the weapons you describe as "offensive"'.
Kennedy insisted that this must include the Il-28s; he was
supported by Ambassador Thompson, who believed that
'Khrushchev, having swallowed a camel, would not strain at
a gnat.'[88] Thompson was right; after protest and some
hesitation Khrushchev agreed to withdraw these obsolete
short-range bombers on 19 November. In return Kennedy
at last lifted the quarantine. Castro, who maintained that
the bombers were Cuban and was attempting to use them
as bargaining chips to win a UN-brokered no-invasion
pledge from Kennedy, was livid. Once again he was informed of an agreement only after the fact.[89]

Khrushchev attempted to regain the initiative and move
beyond the crisis as quickly as possible. On 30 October
he wrote to Kennedy to urge not only the lifting of the
quarantine but also US evacuation of the Guantanamo Bay
naval base in Cuba, a non-aggression treaty between the two
blocs, a disarmament treaty, resolution of the German
issue, the seating of the People's Republic of China at the
UN and a summit meeting between himself and Kennedy.
He concluded by observing, 'I understand that I have raised
a great number of questions. Therefore, if we were to begin
after breakfast, we probably would not be able to resolve all
these issues before lunch.' He also expressed his genuine
belief that Kennedy was operating under intense pressure
from right-wing militarists: 'I take the liberty to think [sic]
that you evidently held to a restraining position with regard
to those forces which suffered from militaristic itching . . .
my role was simpler than yours because there were no
people around me who wanted to unleash war.'

For the next several months Khrushchev persisted in his
attempts to draw Kennedy into a broader discussion of
East–West relations, but the American remained stubbornly
focused on his immediate concerns in Cuba and simply

ignored the rest of Khrushchev's proposals until the crisis was resolved in late November. The President was in no hurry to move on to these other matters. This was a problem for Khrushchev, who believed that he could justify the risks he had taken in Cuba if he were able to show that Kennedy, having been to the brink of war, was now more willing to negotiate on the other issues. Khrushchev himself was shaken by the crisis, noting in his letter of 11 November that 'we were very close to that abyss'. His letters took on an almost pleading tone, as he reflected on the horrors which had so narrowly been averted and urged the President to act with him in moving towards a broader *détente*. Kennedy's letters, by contrast, became stiffer, almost condescending at times, once the danger was past. He had come out of the crisis in good shape politically and was unwilling to give ammunition to conservative critics by rushing into new agreements with Khrushchev.

Although it is now known that Khrushchev got more from Kennedy than was acknowledged at the time, the Cuban crisis was an unmitigated disaster for the Soviet leader, for it put an end to his hopes of finding a quick, inexpensive way to establish Soviet strategic parity with the United States. American nuclear superiority could neither be disguised by bluff and deception nor overcome by a single bold gamble; nuclear equality would require time and money, and Khrushchev had too little of both. Moreover, nuclear parity would not be enough. Khrushchev's belief that reliance on rockets and nuclear warheads alone could assure Soviet security and underpin Soviet foreign policy around the world was exposed as folly in October 1962; the risks of reliance on nuclear blackmail alone were too great. Military equality would require a conventional build-up as well as a major ICBM programme. Khrushchev could realise his ambition to be treated by the Americans as an equal only at the expense of his plans for domestic prosperity.

In November Khrushchev at last pushed the bifurcation of the party apparatus through the Central Committee. The bifurcation was the first of Khrushchev's 'hare-brained schemes' to be reversed by his successors in 1964, but the fact that he was able to push it through in the wake of Cuba suggests that his initiative enjoyed broad support within the Presidium; Brezhnev, Podgornyi and Polianskii, at least, were all enthusiastically in favour.[90] There was, however, considerable opposition to the plan. The ideologically orthodox objected that the reorganisation would make the party's primary political function secondary to economic tasks and that the agricultural–industrial division of labour would rupture the 'alliance of workers and peasants' on which Soviet power was based.[91] So serious were the ideological objections that *Pravda* carried a 'newly discovered' (fraudulent) article by Lenin which defended the priority of economics over politics in the party's tasks.[92] An intensive propaganda campaign was conducted at the local level after the plan was adopted, a further sign of widespread opposition.[93]

The most intense opposition to the scheme came from provincial party bosses, who, having run their provinces alone for many years, were loath to see their authority cut in half. Moreover, those provincial bosses who were also Central Committee members feared that they would lose their committee seats to their new colleagues at the next party congress. (There is reason to believe that this was indeed Khrushchev's intention.) Some of these officials were bold enough to voice their objections at the time of the reorganisation,[94] and more than one-third of provincial committees never did implement it, remaining united under the control of a single secretary throughout the two years until the bifurcation was reversed.[95]

The reform was one of Khrushchev's greatest domestic failures. It angered provincial party officials, and triggered intense local rivalries between the new and old secretaries over investment funds, budgetary allocations and control of those areas of party activity which could not be identified as 'industrial' or 'agricultural' tasks: law enforcement, justice, public health, education and so on. The impact on agriculture was disastrous. The rural sector lacked the resources to operate independently and had traditionally relied on assistance from the towns; local conflicts between party officials often resulted in the loss of crops, which rotted in the fields because industrial party committees refused to allow urban workers to be employed as temporary agricultural labourers during the harvest. Nor did industry flourish under the new system, which simply generated additional bureaucracy and party interference in the affairs of enterprises.

An extensive reorganisation of the sovnarkhoz system followed soon after the bifurcation of the party. A series of decrees issued since 1958 had steadily eroded the powers of the economic councils in an attempt to curb localism and restore central authority, but these had proved to be insufficient.[96] In late 1962 the number of sovnarkhozes was cut in half by an enlargement of the economic regions, and the number and powers of the all-union state committees were sharply increased. In January 1963 a USSR Council of the National Economy was established to guide the work of the sovnarkhozes. A further series of centralising measures was adopted in March 1963. Many of the state committees at this time were reorganised into state *production* committees, which enjoyed direct managerial power over enterprises; they differed from pre-1957 industrial ministries in name only. The restructuring of the sovnarkhozes was accompanied by the creation of powerful new organs of party and state control, which were placed under the direction of former KGB chief Aleksandr Shelepin; the new control bureaucracy was the latest in a series of attempts to devise an effective system for monitoring the fulfilment of central decisions in the locales.

The cumulative result of these changes was to abandon the central principles of the original sovnarkhoz reform of 1957. Economic management increasingly emphasised branch rather than territorial considerations, and the devolution of economic authority to the provinces and republics had been almost completely reversed. This was a further blow to provincial party secretaries, since the enlarged sovnarkhozes now encompassed several provinces and were therefore no longer subordinate to provincial authorities. Khrushchev was unable simply to reverse the sovnarkhoz reforms, however, for he had staked too much of his personal prestige to the new system; as a result, changes in industrial management after 1957 simply created additional layers of bureaucracy above the sovnarkhozes.

The creation of this bureaucratic leviathan was all but

inevitable, given Khrushchev's approach to economic reform. The First Secretary was prone to view all economic problems entirely in administrative terms and never evinced much enthusiasm for the reformist ideas of economists who advocated greater enterprise autonomy and greater reliance on economic, as opposed to administrative, levers.[97] In 1957 the economic reformists, who had been gaining ground in 1955–6, were caught in the crossfire between the ministries on the one hand and Khrushchev and the territorial apparatus on the other. The sovnarkhoz reform was, if anything, worse than the ministerial system from the point of view of managerial rights and enterprise autonomy. In the autumn of 1962 it again appeared that many of the proposals of the reformist economists were about to be adopted, and again Khrushchev pre-empted such changes with a scheme of his own which enhanced the role of the party apparatus at the expense of the managers. The resulting structure was so cumbersome and unwieldy as to make the pre-1957 system look positively sleek by comparison. Never before had there been so many officials of ministerial rank – there were nearly a hundred in 1963 – and never before had their duties and powers been so ill-defined.

10 The Fall
Removal and Retirement, 1962–71

A Leninist party is the enemy of subjectivism and drift in communist construction. Harebrained scheming; premature conclusions; hasty decisions and actions divorced from reality; bragging and bluster; a penchant for management by fiat; an unwillingness to take into account the conclusions of science and practical experience; these are alien to the party.
Pravda, 17 October 1964

The thaw in the arts which had accompanied Khrushchev's late 1962 anti-Stalin drive came to an abrupt end on 1 December. On that day Khrushchev, in the company of the conservative painter Alexander Gerasimov, Minister of Culture Furtseva and Leonid Il'ichev, the party's chief ideologist, visited an exhibit at the Manezh Gallery devoted to the thirtieth anniversary of the Moscow branch of the Artists' Union. After looking over the exhibit, which consisted of the works of a number of officially approved artists, Khrushchev was taken up to the second floor of the gallery to see the works of the avant-gardists of Eli Beliutin's Moscow studio. Khrushchev, who detested modern art and music (he once said that jazz made him feel as if he had 'gas on the stomach'), exploded. To the painter Zheltovskii he said

We should take your pants down and set you down in a clump of nettles until you understand your mistakes. . . . Are you a pederast or a normal man? Do you want to live abroad? Go on, then; we'll take you free as far as the border. Live out there in the 'free world'. Study in the school of capitalism. . . . But we aren't going to spend a kopeck on this dog shit.

257

To another artist he remarked,

> It's a pity, of course, that your mother's dead, but maybe
> it's lucky for her that she can't see how her son is
> spending his time. What master are you serving
> anyway? . . . You've got to get out or paint differently. As
> you are, there is no future for you on our soil.

He addressed similar comments to a number of other
artists.[1] Within hours of Khrushchev's outburst, *Pravda*
issued a call for purity in the arts.[2]

The Manezh visit was a set-up: although the main exhibit
had been open for over a month, the avant-gardists had
suddenly and unexpectedly been invited to display their
works just days before Khrushchev's visit. Since April party
conservatives had been struggling unsuccessfully to bring
heterodox writers and artists to heel; the unexpected avant-
garde exhibition was a manoeuvre to bring Khrushchev
himself into the conflict. Against conservative opposition
Khrushchev had favoured liberal writers like Evtushenko
and even praised some modern architecture,[3] but those who
knew him well were aware that he could not abide abstract
painting.[4] The exhibit was thus a perfect provocation.[5]

The press attacks on the artists were followed by a
meeting of writers and artists with the party leadership on
17 December, at which the writers rose to the defence of
the abstractionists. When Evtushenko argued that the
'formalist tendencies' in the abstractionists' work would be
'straightened out with time', Khrushchev snapped, 'The
grave straightens out the hunchback.' Evtushenko was
appalled: 'Nikita Sergeevich, the times when only the grave
straightened out hunchbacks have passed; really, there are
other ways.'[6] The hall broke into applause at Evtushenko's
words, and Khrushchev himself joined in. But he did not
back down. The campaign against the artists continued and
was now widened to include literature.

The reversal of course in cultural policy was a product of
more than simply the Manezh incident. The Cuban crisis
and Beijing's attacks on Khrushchev's 'revisionism' played
a role, as did the unrest of the preceding summer, when disturbances similar to those in Novocherkassk had occurred

in Kemerovo and the North Caucasus. The most important factor, however, was the growing sense that the party was losing control over the arts. There were calls in the Cinematographers' Union for an end to censorship, and an increasing number of writers were circumventing the censors by taking works rejected in Moscow and Leningrad to little-known publishing houses in the provinces.[7] This was a serious matter; Khrushchev's line on art and literature changed frequently during his years in power, but he never wavered on the principle of party control. He rejected official attempts to micro-manage the creative process but insisted that it was the prerogative of the party, not the writers and artists themselves, to determine 'the main aim of creative work'.[8] In other words, Khrushchev wished to be able to use liberal writers and artists for his own ends, defining and redefining their 'mission' as his political needs changed.

Despite signs that the literary thaw was getting out of control, Khrushchev had seemed unmoved when a group of conservatives appealed to the November 1962 Central Committee plenum for party intervention in the arts.[9] His remarks on cultural policy at the plenum were relatively liberal; indeed he openly confirmed that he had personally approved *One Day in the Life of Ivan Denisovich*[10] and made no move to block the publication of five poems on the Terror just days after the plenum.[11] It took the Manezh episode to turn the tide.

The pressure on the writers and artists intensified in early 1963. Khrushchev publicly attacked a number of writers himself, sometimes with embarrassing results. At another meeting with leading cultural figures in early March, the young prose-writer Vasilii Aksenov came under attack. Khrushchev angrily summoned Aksenov out of the audience to address the charges; unfortunately, the man he ordered to the rostrum was not Aksenov but the artist Illarion Golitsyn. When at last Aksenov himself was found and called forward, Khrushchev, who had been incorrectly briefed on the writer's background, thundered, 'I know, Aksenov, that you are avenging yourself on us for the death of your father!' Aksenov replied that his father was alive and that his parents, who had indeed been repressed under

Stalin, had been rehabilitated after the Twentieth Congress, for which Aksenov and his family were grateful to Khrushchev.[12] Aksenov's words did nothing to mollify the First Secretary, who in June demanded Aksenov's expulsion from the party. Khrushchev made an ominous reference to Gogol's hero Taras Bulba, 'who killed his own son for going over to the side of the enemy'.[13]

Although the political and psychological pressure on writers and artists such as Ehrenburg, Aksenov and Neizvestnyi was intense, there were no arrests, exiles or show trials in connection with the campaign; this relative restraint distinguished Khrushchev's approach from that of both his predecessor and his successors. Moreover, many heterodox writers continued to publish throughout the period; only the principal targets of the campaign disappeared from print.[14] The Manezh exhibit which had sparked the whole furore remained open for some time after Khrushchev's visit, and attendance increased markedly after *Pravda*'s condemnation of the avant-gardists.

The campaign in the arts coincided with (and was largely a by-product of) a retreat from the aggressive anti-Stalinism of the previous year. In March Khrushchev complained that, after the publication of *Ivan Denisovich*, the publishing houses had been 'flooded' with manuscripts about the repressions, which could only 'delight' the enemies of the Soviet Union.[15] Khrushchev was especially sensitive to the question of his own complicity in Stalin's crimes. He insisted that the 'leading cadres of the party' had not known that innocent people were being arrested in the purges but then contradicted himself almost immediately, claiming that he had successfully prevented the fabrication of political cases in Moscow and Ukraine. Resurrecting the lies of 1953, he sought to blame as much as possible on Beria's manipulation of an ailing Stalin and stated that Stalin's abuses had come to light only after Beria's fall. He praised Stalin's commitment to communism and his crushing of the enemies of the Revolution.[16] Khrushchev's defensiveness may have been a reaction to an attack by the conservative writer Galina Serebriakova, herself a victim of the camps, on the liberal Ehrenburg, whom she accused of having been Stalin's mouthpiece.[17] Serebriakova's attack revealed that de-Stalinisation was a two-edged sword; many of the 'de-Stalinisers', Khrushchev among them, were as vulnerable as their opponents to questions about their activities before 1953.

During February and March 1963 there were also noticeable shifts in foreign policy and investment priorities. The polemic with China, which had heated up in late 1962,[18] was brought to a halt in mid-February, and the two sides exchanged letters in preparation for a meeting at which their differences could be ironed out.[19] Soviet statements on East–West relations became tougher at the same time, and Moscow broke off the test ban talks. Khrushchev was angered by Kennedy's rejection of a proposal for a comprehensive test-ban agreement which included two to four on-site inspections per year. This was far fewer inspections than Kennedy wanted, but the mere acceptance of any on-site inspections was a major concession for the Soviets, and Khrushchev resented Kennedy's failure to accept it. The worsening of East–West relations served in turn as the justification for a reassertion of traditional investment priorities favouring defence and heavy industry. In late February Khrushchev himself all but acknowledged that international realities had, for the time being at least, scuttled his plans for improving the lot of the Soviet consumer. He sought to dampen popular expectations of rising living standards in the near future.[20]

There is no doubt that Khrushchev, who was politically vulnerable after the Cuban fiasco, was under pressure from more conservative elements within the leadership at this time. Frol Kozlov, Khrushchev's heir-apparent and the leading spokesman of the party's conservative wing, was unusually prominent in the press between February and early April. This conservative pressure eased when Kozlov was incapacitated by a stroke in April. It would, however, be a mistake to suggest that Khrushchev was simply a hostage of conservatives in the Presidium and was opposed to all of the measures being taken. Thwarted in Cuba and rebuffed in his efforts to talk Kennedy into moving quickly towards *détente*, Khrushchev himself may reluctantly have concluded that *rapprochement* with China, higher defence spending and a tough line in East–West relations were for the moment his only possible course of action. Khrushchev had performed such changes of course before, in response to adverse developments at home or abroad.

This new course could not last, however, for Khrushchev knew that his real interests would be better served by an accommodation with America than with China. After Cuba there could be no doubt that peaceful coexistence with the United States mattered more than leadership of a superficially united socialist camp. The half-hearted attempt to reopen the dialogue with Beijing merely underscored how insurmountable were their differences. In a Central Committee letter of 30 March to the Chinese leaders, the Soviet side listed peaceful coexistence, which the Chinese regarded as nothing more than a tactical manoeuvre, as the first priority of the socialist camp's foreign policy, and affirmed Yugoslavia's status as a socialist state.[21] The letter made it clear that these positions were not negotiable; Khrushchev was not prepared to sacrifice his relations with Washington or Belgrade to please Beijing. At the same time China aggravated matters by raising its claims to certain disputed lands on the Soviet side of the Sino-Soviet border.

In East–West relations, the harder line of early 1963 found little expression other than in words. Even as Soviet rhetoric was at its most belligerent, Moscow was privately assuring the Kennedy administration that it was withdrawing several thousand troops from Cuba, and negotiations were under way on the establishment of a Kremlin–White House hotline; agreement was reached on 5 April. In early June Khrushchev accepted US and British proposals for an agreement to end atmospheric testing; the treaty was signed on 2 August. Khrushchev's refusal to accept any on-site inspections, which he had earlier indicated he might accept on a limited basis, made controls on underground testing impossible.[22] The test-ban agreement was accompanied by (and doubtless contributed to) the renewal of the Sino-Soviet polemic. A Central Committee plenum in mid-June upheld Khrushchev's position against the Chinese.

As he moved towards a thaw with the United States, Khrushchev began to revive his battered domestic agenda. At the June plenum he eased up on the writers and criticised Stalin for being mistrustful and out of touch with the people, and for deluding himself about the real state of affairs in the countryside. Revealing yet again his sensitivity to the question of complicity in Stalin's crimes, Khrushchev presented himself as a man who had been prepared to stand up to Stalin and to tell the dictator unpleasant truths about the real life of ordinary people.[23] This claim may have some truth to it, not least because Khrushchev probably knew more about the lives of rank-and-file workers and peasants than any other member of Stalin's inner circle. Adzhubei's attempt to demonstrate that Khrushchev had spoken out against the Stalin cult in 1937, however, was a ludicrous falsification of history.[24]

On 19 July Khrushchev delivered his sharpest attack ever on both Stalin and the Chinese, whom he accused of having rehabilitated the late dictator. Khrushchev numbered Stalin among the 'tyrants in the history of mankind', who stayed in power with the aid of the 'executioner's axe'. So intense was this attack, which was broadcast live to the country, that the version which appeared in *Pravda* the following day was heavily censored. Khrushchev also spoke at length of the need to improve living standards and stated in connection with the test ban that a reduction in defence costs would contribute to a better deal for consumers.[25]

Khrushchev's major domestic emphasis for the rest of 1963 was the drive to increase chemicals production, his latest panacea for the needs of both agriculture and Soviet consumers. He had periodically raised the issue since early 1958, when he had stated that chemicals had replaced steel as the 'decisive' branch of heavy industry.[26] The production of chemicals for use in plastics, fertilisers and so on would enable Khrushchev to address consumer and agricultural needs without calling into question the priority of heavy industry. Little had been done, however, and by June 1963 Khrushchev had been pushing for a Central Committee plenum on chemicals for some time. The First Secretary told the June plenum that he would report to the next plenum on the development of the chemical industry.[27] In a July memorandum to the Presidium he proposed a target of 100 million tonnes of chemical fertiliser for 1970, a near quadrupling of production in seven years.[28]

A compromise of sorts on the literary front emerged in

August. A State Committee for the Press was established under the leadership of Pavel Romanov, the former censor-in-chief.[29] It was intended to centralise control over publishing operations and thereby to keep writers from circumventing Moscow and Leningrad censors by taking their works to provincial publishers. Fortunately for the writers, Khrushchev ignored proposals to abolish the existing writers' and artists' organisations and establish a single centralised institution to govern all creative activity.[30] In mid-August Khrushchev met with sixteen foreign and twelve Soviet writers at his Black Sea retreat in Gagra. He took a strong line against 'cultural' coexistence, stating that compromises for the sake of peace could be made in politics, but that there were no compromises in the war of ideas. He then told a stunned Aleksandr Tvardovskii to recite his long poem 'Terkin in the Other World', a bitter satire in which Hell is described as a sort of Stalinist bureaucracy. Tvardovskii was Khrushchev's favourite contemporary poet, but he had for six years been unable to publish the poem. A few days after the Gagra recital, 'Terkin in the Other World' appeared in *Izvestiia*. Shortly thereafter Ehrenburg, Evtushenko and Voznesenskii, three of the conservatives' principal targets, were all back in print.[31]

By autumn Khrushchev's summer offensive had run into trouble. His main problem was the failure of the 1963 harvest, which came in at only 107.5 million tonnes (as against 134.7 million in 1958) owing to drought. Of the USSR's major grain-growing regions, the North Caucasus produced the best harvest, and even there production fell 10 per cent from the levels of 1962. Khrushchev's cherished Virgin Lands produced their smallest crop in eight years, despite the fact that the sown area was 10 million hectares larger than it had been in 1955.[32] The disastrous harvest presented Khrushchev with a choice: he must either spend scarce hard currency on wheat imports from abroad or accept a sharp drop in the living standards of the population. With memories of Novocherkassk no doubt in mind, Khrushchev opted for the first course, a decision opposed by party conservatives, who rejected both the expenditure of vital currency reserves and the economic dependency on the West implied by the purchases. Khrushchev accused them of preferring to let the population starve, as Stalin and Molotov had done.[33]

Khrushchev pointed to the poor harvest as evidence of the necessity of his chemicals programme, arguing that greater use of chemical fertilisers would insure the Soviet Union against such crises in the future. Nevertheless, his plans for the chemical industry had to be scaled back, and the targets which he presented to the December 1963 plenum were about 25 per cent lower than those he had proposed in July.[34] Even the revised target of 70–80 million tonnes – a trebling of output in seven years – represented an unrealistic goal; the economy as a whole could not have sustained the diversion of resources needed to meet such a target, nor could the chemical industry have absorbed such an enormous increase in investment. The reasons for the scaling back of Khrushchev's original targets are unclear; the lower targets may have been a political defeat for the premier, but it is entirely possible that they represented a compromise with economic reality on his part.

The investment funds needed for the chemicals industry were to come mainly from the defence budget, or so Khrushchev intended.[35] In fact, Khrushchev's proposed troop cut was never acted on, and the reduction in the 1964 defence budget which followed the December plenum was, at only 600 million roubles, purely symbolic. Even this small cut generated so much opposition that Khrushchev felt obliged to defend it to the Central Committee and to reassure the military brass that consumer needs would not be addressed at the expense of national security.[36] Nevertheless, the military was taking no chances; a number of leading officers argued publicly for expanding Soviet ground forces and attacked over-reliance on rocket forces at the expense of conventional capabilities.[37]

Khrushchev's willingness to undertake defence cuts in 1963–4 suggests that he was prepared to accept that the Soviet Union would remain for the indefinite future in a position of military inferiority to the United States. The Cuban crisis and the economic problems of 1962–3 had put paid to his hopes of avoiding painful trade-offs by finding inexpensive shortcuts to strategic parity and higher living standards, and Khrushchev was unwilling to sacrifice the

latter goal to achieve the former. To the end of his life he
remained firm in his conviction that superior living
standards rather than military might would ensure the
ultimate victory of socialism.[38] It would be a mistake to
exaggerate the reallocation of investment resources from
defence to consumer-oriented industries which he now
advocated, but even a modest redistribution of investment
funds was enough to provoke intense opposition, especially
given America's superior and growing strategic power.
Détente with Washington was thus more important than
ever.

In the summer of 1963, everything seemed to be going
smoothly on this front; agreement over the partial test ban
led to a softening of Kennedy's rhetoric and the hope that
further agreements would soon follow. In October, however,
Khrushchev's correspondence with Kennedy came to a
sudden and unexpected end. On 20 October Kennedy
answered a conciliatory letter from Khrushchev which had
been transmitted ten days earlier; Kennedy's reply was
never sent, however, owing to a clerical error in the State
Department.[39] Khrushchev believed that he had been
snubbed and refused to renew the correspondence. His
Revolution Day speech was tough on America and conciliatory to the Chinese,[40] and early November saw friction
between Moscow and Washington over western access to
Berlin and the arrest (authorised by Brezhnev in Khrushchev's absence) of a visiting American scholar on charges
of espionage. By the time the loss of Kennedy's letter was
discovered in December, Kennedy was dead, and Khrushchev was left to deal with President Lyndon Johnson, whom
he feared would turn out to be a reactionary southerner.
Johnson moved quickly to allay these fears, and in early
1964 the two men agreed to reductions in the production
of enriched uranium for the manufacture of nuclear warheads. Cuts in the production of fissile material were
anathema to those in the élite who favoured a rapid nuclear
build-up.

On 17 April 1964 Khrushchev reached his seventieth
birthday. The press carried congratulatory messages from
across the country and the world, and the premier was
awarded the title 'Hero of the Soviet Union' for his services

to party and state. The eighth volume of *The Construction of Communism in the USSR and the Development of Agriculture*, which consisted of Khrushchev's speeches and writings on economic and agricultural themes, was released to coincide with the occasion, and a reception and banquet were held in the Kremlin. Soviet newspapers and magazines were full of tributes to the premier; many established a special rubric, *Velikoe desiatiletie* ('The Great Decade'), for articles celebrating the achievements of Khrushchev's ten years as First Secretary. Such was the public façade. In reality, the Great Decade was drawing to a close amid economic failure and political intrigue.

Agricultural output had grown at a rate of only 2.4 per cent per year since 1960, as against 7.6 per cent in 1955–9. This was well below the rates required by the targets of the Seven-Year Plan (8 per cent) and the Third Party Programme (7.2 per cent). Industrial performance had held up much better, but the 7.3 per cent growth rate since 1960 was well below both plan targets and the levels of the late 1950s; it was also too little to permit much of a redirection of investment into the light and food industries, which grew by only 3.9 per cent annually after 1960.[41] As has been seen, Khrushchev's response to this declining performance was a series of hasty administrative reorganisations and ill-advised agricultural panaceas; the failure of each successive scheme to achieve the promised miracles led Khrushchev merely to intensify his frantic search for a new cure-all.

As his frustration increased, Khrushchev's temper grew shorter. His surviving associates agree that prior to about 1961 colleagues and subordinates could argue freely with Khrushchev and criticise his schemes. Voronov speaks of the 'absolutely free character of discussion' within the Presidium; he, Shelest, Mazurov and others confirm that Khrushchev would listen to points of view at odds with his own. After the Twenty-second Congress, however, Khrushchev's lieutenants found him ever more sensitive to any hint of criticism. His tendency to throw his weight around – even to bully his subordinates – increased. Many have gone so far as to suggest that there were 'two Khrushchevs': one before the Twenty-second Congress and another after it. While some have linked this change to the arrogance which comes of remaining in power too long, it seems more likely to have been a product of frustration, disillusionment and failure.[42]

The flowery toasts and laudatory speeches pronounced by Khrushchev's most senior lieutenants in honour of his birthday concealed their true intentions. Since March, Brezhnev and Podgornyi, who had jointly replaced Kozlov in the role of heirs-apparent, had been actively soliciting the support of Central Committee members for a move to oust Khrushchev.[43] Having learned the lessons of 1957, when Khrushchev had turned to the Central Committee to overturn the decision of a hostile Presidium majority, Brezhnev and his supporters were determined to secure the support of the bulk of the CC before making their move; everyone drawn into the plot was to 'work on' certain CC members. Usually this meant that the senior party officials in each region were recruited first and were then responsible for bringing their subordinates on board.[44] Virtually the entire Central Committee, apart from a few Khrushchev loyalists, were approached by the plotters. Their task was made easier by the fact that many Central Committee members elected in 1961 had by 1964 been removed from high office by Khrushchev; others were in danger of being demoted.[45] These men consituted a substantial bloc prepared to support any move against the First Secretary.

There were leaks in the process. More than one attempt was made to warn Khrushchev of the impending danger. Several were blocked by the KGB, and one was even intercepted by Khrushchev's long-time personal assistant, G. T. Shuiskii, who had joined the plot. Shuiskii had worked for Khrushchev for twenty-two years, and his loyalty was thought to be beyond question. Khrushchev's other personal assistant, V. S. Lebedev, was regarded as a hard-liner with close ties to Suslov and was therefore never completely trusted; ironically, it was he who remained loyal to the end.[46] Khrushchev's daughter Rada received more than one warning about what was afoot but did not believe her informers.[47] When at last word of the plot reached Khrushchev himself, he miscalculated badly. On learning that N. G. Ignatov, the Chairman of the Presidium of the RSFSR

Supreme Soviet, was plotting against him, Khrushchev failed to guess that Ignatov was not acting on his own initiative. He therefore made the mistake of telling Podgornyi and others what he knew, promising to 'clear everything up' after his holiday in Pitsunda.[48] Khrushchev thereby gave notice to his opponents that they must act quickly and then left Moscow for an extended period, giving them ample opportunity to make their move.

Khrushchev unwittingly played into his opponents' hands in other ways as well. During the first nine months of 1964 the peripatetic premier was away from the capital a total of 135 days. Sergei Khrushchev believes that his father allowed himself to be manoeuvred into a number of unpopular positions in 1964, including decisions to delay the planned introduction of a five-day working week and the adoption of economic reforms along the lines proposed by the Khar'kov economist Evsei Liberman and others. In April he ordered a 45 per cent cut in capital investment for housing construction in Moscow. The 'Khrushchev cult' boomed in 1964, chiefly thanks to the efforts of Brezhnev, Podgornyi and Shelepin, whose praise of the leader masked their disloyalty and left Khrushchev vulnerable to charges of fostering his own cult. The food supply problems of 1964, which arose despite a record harvest, have also been seen as part of a sabotage campaign intended to undermine Khrushchev's popularity.[49]

Khrushchev also renewed his eight-year-old war of attrition against the peasants' private plots and private livestock holdings, which had been subjected to a series of new restrictions since 1956. In early 1964, Khrushchev began pressing for the adoption of industrial management methods on the farms, which would have included further restrictions on the size of private plots.[50] When, on a visit to his native Kalinovka, Khrushchev suggested that private livestock holdings should be eliminated altogether, one of the farm workers in the audience cried, 'Nikita! Have you lost your mind or what?'[51]

At a Central Committee plenum in July Khrushchev proposed a major reorganisation of agricultural administration which he had not previously discussed with the Presidium. The proposal, which was accompanied by a stinging attack (including some threats) on local party officials, would have concentrated agricultural management in Moscow.[52] The July plenum also witnessed a bitter attack by Khrushchev against the USSR Academy of Sciences, with which he had been in conflict over Lysenko and other issues since the previous year. Khrushchev questioned the need for the Academy's existence and suggested that a future plenum might consider liquidating it. The issue was a relatively minor one, but this apparently spontaneous outburst reinforced the impression that Khrushchev was in some sense 'out of control'.[53] His impulsive and authoritarian style aggravated his colleagues, who were 'stuffed to the throats' with ill-considered reorganisations and wanted, above all else, stable leadership.

Khrushchev's final 'policy offensive' in the autumn of 1964 further alienated conservative and even middle-of-the-road members of the ruling élite. Khrushchev had finally dropped his long-standing opposition to enterprise autonomy and economic reform.[54] Reformist economists returned to prominence in the press,[55] and elements of their thinking found their way into Khrushchev's own speeches.[56] In July he unveiled plans for an Eighth Five-Year Plan (the Seven-Year Plan was to be scrapped), which was to bring about a long-term shift in economic policy in favour of the consumer. What he envisioned was not a short-term increase in consumption but a shift in investment to producing capital goods for light industry, agriculture and those branches of heavy industry which served consumer-oriented sectors. He dropped the assurances given the previous winter that consumer needs would be subordinated to the requirements of defence.[57] This decisive shift to what Khrushchev had less than a decade before called 'a belching forth of the right deviation' was to be accompanied by further steps towards an East–West *détente*. Adzhubei had been dispatched to Bonn in July to lay the groundwork for the normalisation of relations with West Germany, which Khrushchev himself planned to visit. It was hoped that this would provide the basis for a badly needed economic relationship with Bonn.

Although these proposals were unpopular with the armed forces, the evidence suggests that the military did not play a major role in the plot.[58] Malinovskii reportedly told the plotters that the military was outside politics and would support neither Khrushchev nor his enemies.[59] The KGB, by contrast, was deeply involved from the beginning. Under Semichastnyi's guidance the secret police intercepted attempts to warn Khrushchev, kept him under constant surveillance and monitored the actions of the military in order to prevent any last-minute action in support of Khrushchev from that quarter.[60] In the event, none was forthcoming.

The plotters decided to make their move on 12 October, while Khrushchev was still on holiday at his Black Sea retreat in Pitsunda. There was no time to lose, for the First Secretary was growing suspicious and had promised to toss them out 'like whelps' if he found them up to no good when he returned.[61] On the evening of 12 October Brezhnev telephoned Khrushchev in Pitsunda and called him back to Moscow for an urgent meeting to discuss the agricultural reorganisation which was to be adopted in November. Khrushchev initially refused to interrupt his holiday, but after a second phone call and a threat by his colleagues to meet without him, he relented and promised to return to the capital. Brezhnev's insistent tone aroused Khrushchev's suspicions.[62] He understood that the Presidium would discuss something other than agriculture. 'If I'm the issue, I won't make a fight', he told Mikoian, who had joined him on holiday.[63]

In Moscow, Khrushchev's colleagues anxiously awaited his arrival. Early in the evening Khrushchev ordered a plane for the return journey to Moscow, but Semichastnyi, who was monitoring the situation in Moscow, learned of the order only at midnight. In the meantime, the KGB chief received hourly telephone calls from a nervous Brezhnev, who feared that Khrushchev had changed his mind and would not return.[64] Although Khrushchev was both physically and politically isolated, his adversaries feared that he might yet take some sort of retaliatory action. The plotters could, of course, have brought the First Secretary back from Pitsunda by force, but they were anxious to avoid creating the appearance of a coup. Arrest and assassination had been considered, but it was decided that everything should be done according to rule and that Khrushchev must be removed 'democratically' by a Central Committee plenum. Khrushchev's own co-operation was therefore required.[65]

Khrushchev, to his credit, was largely responsible for creating the conditions within the party which made it possible to plot his overthrow in this manner. In addition to restoring the authority of the Central Committee, he played a key role in repudiating the use of terror in Soviet politics, a change that greatly reduced the risks his colleagues ran when they plotted his removal in 1964. Having done so much to set the stage for the drama which was unfolding, he did not fail to play the part assigned to him. On 13 October he returned to Moscow and was driven directly to the Kremlin, where the Presidium was waiting. Semichastnyi meanwhile replaced the security details at Khrushchev's home and dacha.[66] At the Kremlin an appearance of total normality was maintained; there were no additional troops deployed on the Kremlin grounds, which remained open to tourists all day. The Presidium adhered to normal procedures as well: Khrushchev himself, as First Secretary, chaired the meeting called to discuss his removal.[67]

Suslov and Shelepin raised the question of Khrushchev's removal and were the most outspoken representatives of the prosecution. Ukrainian party leader Petr Shelest was also quite forceful, as was Gennadii Voronov. Brezhnev and Podgornyi remained silent. The issues raised against Khrushchev included questions of policy as well as criticisms of his leadership style and insinuations of nepotism and petty corruption. Khrushchev's rude treatment of both his colleagues and local party officials was discussed. Shelepin claimed that Sergei Khrushchev had been awarded a doctorate which he had not earned, and the First Secretary was criticised for taking members of his family on overseas trips.[68]

Remarkably little attention was paid to the complaints of the military, which further confirms the belief that the armed forces were not involved in the plot.[69] Nor was foreign affairs at the centre of the debate, although the Suez, Berlin and Cuba crises were all discussed, as were relations with China.[70] The fact that these issues received so little emphasis suggests that Khrushchev spoke the truth when he reminded his colleagues that the decisions in these crises had been reached collectively.[71] The foreign policy issue which generated the most discussion was Adzhubei's trip to Bonn in July. He was reported to have promised the West Germans that the Berlin Wall would disappear after Khrushchev visited the Federal Republic. This triggered a crisis for the East German leadership, which still harboured fears of being sold out by Moscow. Adzhubei denied having said any such thing,[72] but Gromyko told a visitor in late 1964, 'Why was Khrushchev removed? Because he sent Adzhubei to Bonn, of course.'[73] At issue was neither Adzhubei nor Soviet policy on the German question but rather Khrushchev's leadership style. Professional diplomats had long been irritated by Adzhubei's role as Khrushchev's personal emissary. The incident epitomised the problems created by Khrushchev's concentration of power in his own hands and his reliance on a few close personal advisers.[74]

The most important issues were those which concerned the interests of the party officials who constituted the great bulk of the Central Committee membership and who had been Khrushchev's strongest supporters in the power struggles that followed Stalin's death. Dissatisfaction with the huge and unwieldy bureaucracy which had grown up over the sovnarkhozes after 1960 and irritation with Khrushchev's frequent circumvention of local party officials when dealing with other local organs played a role, as did Committee members' irritation at Khrushchev's attempts to downgrade the Central Committee after 1958 and his often rude and high-handed conduct of CC plena. By far the most important issues, however, were the bifurcation of the party apparatus (which in November became the first of Khrushchev's major innovations to be reversed) and the rules adopted at the Twenty-second Congress concerning mandatory levels of turnover in party bodies. These two reforms undermined senior officials' security of tenure, as did Khrushchev's constant 'leapfrogging' of cadres.[75] With the Twenty-third Congress expected to take place in 1965, many members' prospects for re-election were far from certain.

There is a great deal of evidence to suggest that Khrushchev's colleagues were also concerned about his declining popularity with the Soviet public.[76] This concern with popular opinion reflected the ruling élite's insecurity rather than any genuine desire to allow ordinary citizens a voice in how the state should be run. Khrushchev's utopian promises had raised popular expectations; now the failure of his policies was alienating large sections of the public, and (as the events in Novocherkassk seemed to demonstrate) raising the risk of social unrest. Moreover, Khrushchev remained unwilling to moderate his statements or to acknowledge that many of his goals were unrealistic. The growing gap between Khrushchev's rhetoric and the regime's performance raised the spectre of a social explosion.

Mikoian alone dissented from the majority's demand that Khrushchev leave political life altogether, urging that he be allowed to retain one of his two posts.[77] At the end of the first day of the Presidium meeting, the members went home to prepare for the next round. The plotters agreed not to answer their telephones, in case Khrushchev began calling around in an effort to win them back one by one. Adzhubei attempted to get in touch with Shelepin, Polianskii and others, but got no answer.[78] Brezhnev continued to worry that Khrushchev might 'call in help' from somewhere, but Semichastnyi assured him that the Khrushchev could do nothing without the KGB's knowledge.[79] Unbeknownst to the others, Khrushchev decided that he could not carry on the struggle; he informed Mikoian that he would resign all his posts the following day.

A tearful Khrushchev delivered his final address to the Presidium on 14 October. Although he rejected the validity of much of his colleagues' criticism, he accepted their decision. He apologised for his mistakes and his rudeness towards other members of the leadership but pointed out that they too had participated in the decisions for which he alone was now being called to account. He also accused them of failing to be honest with him and of having lacked the 'principles and boldness' to speak to him of their grievances. Then he turned to the subject of his removal:

I rejoice that the time has come when the members of

the Presidium have begun to control the activity of the First Secretary and speak with a full voice. . . . Today's meeting of the CC Presidium is a victory for the party. I thought that I would have to leave. . . . I have lost touch with you. You have criticised me vigorously for that today and I myself have suffered from it. I thank you for the opportunity which you are granting me to resign.[80]

Khrushchev later repeated his thanks to his colleagues for being allowed to retire, which suggests that he may have feared more serious measures. At the same time, he still harboured some hope that they would offer him more than just a safe retirement: 'I thought that you perhaps would consider it possible to create some sort of honorary post for me, but I will not ask that of you.'[81] He then offered to leave Moscow if his successors so desired; someone replied, 'Why do that?' Brezhnev rejected Khrushchev's request to address the Central Committee, fearing that the First Secretary might yet try to turn the tables.[82]

The speed of Khrushchev's capitulation came as a surprise to many. His passivity in October 1964 was largely a product of age; he had hinted at retirement off and on since early 1963, and many believed at the time that he was preparing to step aside in favour of younger men. He was tired and frustrated, disillusioned by his own inability to make good on his promises to the people. Some of his remarks, moreover, suggest that he planned to purge the leadership in order to introduce 'new blood' prior to his retirement; if his colleagues believed that he was preparing such a purge, then their fears can only have hastened Khrushchev's demise.[83] Khrushchev's enemies, moreover, had acquired, and were prepared to use, documents from the Stalin era concerning Khrushchev's complicity in the repressions.[84] The fear that the Stalin weapon might at last be turned on him may be what prompted Khrushchev to thank his colleagues for allowing him to resign.

While the second Presidium meeting was going on, the tension outside the Kremlin increased. Semichastnyi telephoned Brezhnev to warn him that the meeting was going on too long. The KGB chairman was being bombarded with calls from Central Committee members and other high officials demanding to know what was happening; some wished to save Khrushchev, others to support the opposition. Brezhnev told Semichastnyi to stall a bit longer; the Presidium would soon complete its deliberations and a Central Committee plenum would be convened at 6.00 p.m. The members of the Committee had already been summoned to Moscow on false pretences so that they would be available for a plenum at short notice.[85] After the Presidium meeting ended, Khrushchev returned home and informed his family that he had retired. After a pause he added, 'I didn't want to have lunch with them any more.'[86]

The plenum that evening was opened by Brezhnev and chaired by Mikoian. In order to eliminate any risk of a mishap, the new leaders barred several well-known Khrushchev supporters from attending. Khrushchev sat to one side while Suslov read the hour-long report on the Presidium's decision. Most of the Committee simply sat in silence; a few interrupted Suslov with demands for Khrushchev's expulsion from the party, or even his arrest and trial. A resolution releasing Khrushchev from his duties on account of his age and health was put to the Committee and adopted unanimously. It was also resolved that the posts of First Secretary of the Central Committee and Chairman of the Council of Ministers would never again be united in one person. Brezhnev and Kosygin were chosen to replace Khrushchev as party leader and premier respectively. Brezhnev gave a short speech and the plenum was adjourned; the Khrushchev era had come to an end.[87]

That its end was both bloodless and orderly was testimony to the dramatic changes in Soviet political life in the eleven years since Stalin's death. Not everything had changed, to be sure; Soviet leadership politics remained a rough-and-tumble game in which the rules were unclear and the composition of the opposing sides constantly changed. But the October plenum demonstrated how much *had* changed. As Khrushchev put it,

Perhaps the most important thing I did was just this – that they were able to get rid of me simply by voting; Stalin would have had them all arrested.[88]

Khrushchev must also have known that in an earlier time he would undoubtedly have been shot after his removal from office.

On the evening of 14 October Mikoian came to see Khrushchev at home. He explained that the new leaders had decided to allow Khrushchev to keep both his house in Moscow and his government dacha at Gorky-2. His domestic staff and security detail would be replaced, and he would be given a pension of 500 roubles a month and an automobile. Mikoian said that he had tried to persuade the Presidium to appoint Khrushchev 'consultant' to the Presidium of the Supreme Soviet but that this had been rejected. Khrushchev thanked him for this gesture and saw him to the door. Mikoian embraced Khrushchev, kissed him on both cheeks and disappeared out the gate. The two men never saw one another again.[89]

The plenum was not announced until late on 15 October. Georgian party leader V. P. Mzhavanadze, returning to Tbilisi after the plenum, stepped off his train to buy a newspaper at one of the stations along the way. He was frightened when he found that it contained no mention of the plenum. Only when he heard the announcement on the radio did he at last relax.[90] The announcement which appeared in the press gave no details other than that Khrushchev had been released from his duties in connection with his advanced age and deteriorating health.[91] From that point on, he became an 'un-person' in the Soviet Union. His name appeared in the central press only once more before his death, when he pronounced the volume of his memoirs published abroad to be a fake. There were no show trials, no ritual attacks at party congresses, no public confessions and no expulsion from the party. Even the denunciations of 'subjectivism' and 'hare-brained scheming' which followed his removal did not mention him by name.[92] His successors wished to forget that he existed, and clearly they hoped that the public would forget him as well.

Khrushchev was devastated by his forced retirement, and never fully recovered from the emotional shock of it. He found the idleness of his pensioner's life almost as difficult to bear as his sense of failure and frustration at being unable to finish his life's work. Years later he remarked,

A pensioner's lot is simply to exist from one day to the next – and to wait for the end. An idle old age isn't easy for anyone. It's especially difficult for someone who's lived through as tumultuous a career as mine. Now, after a lifetime of weathering storms, I've run aground.[93]

In the days following the October plenum, Khrushchev's life was turned upside-down. His bodyguard was changed, and Khrushchev knew that its function had changed also, from security to surveillance. His Zil limousine was replaced by a less impressive Chaika, which in turn was withdrawn after only a few hours and replaced by a still more modest Volga.[94] Khrushchev believed that his life had lost all purpose and meaning; he was listless and depressed for months and wept much of the time.[95]

The new leaders' sensitivity concerning Khrushchev's presence was exposed on 23 October, when the latest Soviet cosmonauts were feted on Red Square. Khrushchev could not bear to watch the proceedings on television and decided to go to his dacha. Brezhnev and his colleagues were notified as soon as he left home and feared that he was trying to come to Red Square. They were greatly relieved when word came that Khrushchev was leaving town, but the incident led them to ask Khrushchev to stay out of Moscow until further notice.[96] At the end of November, after recovering from a bout of the flu, Khrushchev was summoned to the Central Committee to meet with Brezhnev, Kosygin and their colleagues, who outlined new arrangements for his retirement, reneging on certain of the promises they had made through Mikoian. The dacha in Gorky-2 was replaced with a smaller one in Petrovo-Dal'nee, some 20 miles from Moscow, and the Khrushchevs were given a flat in Moscow in place of their government house on the Lenin Hills. Khrushchev worried that Nina Petrovna, who had always minded the family's finances, would be unable to meet all their needs on the 400-rouble monthly pension provided by the new leaders.[97] It was, by Soviet standards, a comfortable, if unhappy, retirement, although Khrushchev was annoyed by the bugging and surveillance to which he was subjected by the authorities.

In August 1966 Khrushchev began the composition of his

memoirs, which he recorded on tape – he would never have set pen to paper to write them. The memoirs soon became his principal occupation, and Khrushchev spent many hours sitting alone or with friends recounting his memories of years gone by. Before each recording session he would stroll about the countryside near the dacha and collect his thoughts, deciding what to discuss and how best to express himself. His son Sergei took charge of having the tapes transcribed and edited them himself. After early attempts to record outside proved unsatisfactory because of airplanes overhead and other background noise, Khrushchev began to record indoors, knowing full well that everything he said could also be recorded by the KGB. Nevertheless, the work continued without interference from the authorities for two years.[98]

Khrushchev also found other outlets for some of his lifelong passions. He put a great deal of energy into his gardening, testing various agricultural theories himself and following closely the latest developments in agronomy. He was particularly interested in hydroponics.[99] His fascination with things mechanical also remained undiminished, and, quite apart from the memoir project, Khrushchev derived considerable pleasure from his tape recorder, which he used for recording bird calls.[100] He was also fond of his Hasselblad camera. Khrushchev's hatred of solitude made him especially happy to receive (and, inevitably, to photograph) visitors, although many of those who had been closest to him prior to 1964 were unwilling to see him. Abandoned by lifelong friends and associates, he was visited and treated with respect by many of the writers and artists with whom he had clashed in the past. As the conservatism of the new leaders in domestic affairs became apparent, the creative intelligentsia came to view the erratic Khrushchev in a more favourable light. One visitor Khrushchev particularly regretted missing was Richard Nixon, who visited Moscow in the late 1960s and attempted to find his old sparring partner. The Khrushchevs were at their dacha, however, and found Nixon's note at their apartment only after he had returned home. Nixon's gesture puzzled but also touched Khrushchev.[101]

In 1968 the authorities decided that Khrushchev's recording of his memoirs had to stop. He was summoned to the Central Committee building to meet with Politburo[102] member A. P. Kirilenko, Central Committee Secretary Petr Demichev and Party Control Commission chairman Arvid Pel'she. Khrushchev was ordered to stop recording and to hand over the tapes to the Central Committee. He refused, insisting that he was acting within his rights as a Soviet citizen. When Kirilenko told Khrushchev that he was obliged as a communist to obey, Khrushchev exploded, telling his former protégé,

> You are behaving in a way no government allowed itself to behave even under the Tsars. . . . You can take everything away from me; my pension, the dacha, my apartment. That's all within your power, and it wouldn't surprise me if you did. So what – I can still make a living. I'll go to work as a metalworker – I still remember how it's done. If that doesn't work out, I'll take my knapsack and go begging. People will give me what I need. But no one would give you a crust of bread. You'd starve.

In an angry reference to KGB surveillance of his home, he added that the new leaders had 'violated the consitution again when you stuck listening devices all over the dacha. Even in the bathroom – you spend the people's money to eavesdrop on my farts.'[103]

Despite his defiant stance at the meeting with Kirilenko, Khrushchev recorded considerably less in the months following the interview. The encounter was far from a victory for the new leaders, however, for it was at this time that Khrushchev and his son Sergei began to entertain the idea of having the memoirs published abroad.[104] This was an extremely serious matter; the Pasternak affair had been only a decade earlier, and in 1965 two other Soviet writers had been tried for 'anti-Soviet propaganda' and sent to a labour camp after publishing their works abroad. Nevertheless, Khrushchev and his son reached agreement with the US publisher Little, Brown and Company; they would hand over part of the tapes and transcripts to the publisher, but the book would not be released until they signalled from Moscow that it was time to do so.

That time came sooner than anyone had expected. With his father in hospital suffering from heart trouble, Sergei found himself under pressure to hand the tapes and transcripts over to the KGB, which claimed that there was a risk of their theft by foreign agents. Sergei was aware that he could be punished if he did not co-operate; he also knew that the KGB could steal the materials, claim that the theft was the work of foreign spies and blame him for their disappearance. Either way, the authorities would come out ahead. He therefore agreed to hand over 3700 pages of typescript and thirty-four tapes on condition that they be returned to Nikita Sergeevich after his release from hospital. Knowing that this promise would not be honoured, Sergei decided that the moment had come to signal Little, Brown. The memoirs, under the title *Khrushchev Remembers*, began to appear in serial form in the late autumn, much to the consternation of the authorities.[105]

After he had more or less recovered from his illness, the elder Khrushchev was informed of all that had transpired. He never forgave his son for handing over the memoirs to the KGB, but he supported the decision to publish the material which was in the West. It was a costly decision for Khrushchev and his family. Nikita Sergeevich, Sergei and Aleksei Adzhubei were summoned to the Central Committee to be disciplined. The younger men were transferred to new jobs, which were much less desirable than those they then held; Adzhubei was forced to leave Moscow altogether.[106] Nikita Sergeevich met with Party Control Commission chairman Pel'she, who handed him a statement that he, Khrushchev, had never written any memoirs or given such materials to anyone and that the book published in America was a fake. He refused to sign it. According to Sergei Khrushchev, Nikita Sergeevich told Pel'she,

It's a lie and to lie is a sin, especially at my age. It's time to think of the next world. It wouldn't hurt you to think about that either.

After some haggling, however, he signed a statement to the effect that he had never given memoirs or similar materials to any publishing house in the USSR or abroad and that the book published by Little, Brown was a fabrication. The first part of the statement was, strictly speaking true, since it was Sergei who had handled the relationship with the publishers; the second part was not.

Khrushchev then asked Pel'she for the return of the memoir materials surrendered by Sergei in July, insisting that he had a right to work on his memoirs. According to one account, he told Pel'she that if he were not allowed to do so, he would find himself in the position of Tsar Aleksandr I, who, according to legend, rose from the grave and travelled across Russia in the guise of a peasant, telling his story to the people.[107] Pel'she apparently knew nothing about the materials in question. Nikita Sergeevich then launched into an extended critique of the new leaders' record, pointing out that although they had blamed him for all the country's problems in 1964, they had made little or no progress in solving those problems after six years without him. Pel'she rose to the defence of the Brezhnev–Kosygin leadership, but Khrushchev was not interested in listening. 'I've done what you asked', he said. 'I signed. Now I want to go home. My chest hurts.'[108]

The strain of the affair took its toll on Khrushchev's already poor health. By the time of his seventy-seventh birthday in April 1971 his doctor had forbidden him even to tend his beloved garden. In July he was in such a black depression that he spoke of suicide.[109] On 5 September Nikita Sergeevich paid a surprise visit to the Adzhubeis. According to Aleksei Adzhubei, his father-in-law knew that he would not live much longer and had come to say farewell to his daughter and her family. To his son-in-law and former aide he said, 'Never regret that you lived in stormy times and worked with me in the Central Committee. We will yet be remembered!'[110] That night he suffered a massive heart attack; a second attack followed on the next day. Less than a week later, on 11 September 1971, Nikita Sergeevich Khrushchev died in a Moscow hospital.

Even in death Khrushchev was a source of worry to his erstwhile protégés in the Kremlin. Fearful that his funeral might become an occasion for the expression of views critical of his successors, the authorities decided not to announce Khrushchev's death until 10 a.m. on 13 September, the hour at which the wake would begin at the hospital and only two hours before the funeral in Novodevichii cemetery. In this way they hoped to ensure that few people would know to turn up for the funeral. Word leaked out, however, and a number of Moscow's artists and writers joined the family at the cemetery. There, too, the authorities had taken every precaution: a sign was posted saying that the cemetery was closed for the day, only to be removed once the funeral was over. There were buses and lorries full of internal security troops everywhere around the cemetery, and the mourners had to pass through three police cordons to reach the gravesite.[111] A wreath arrived from the Central Committee and the Council of Ministers, and, at the last minute, one from Anastas Mikoian, the only one of Khrushchev's ex-colleagues who took the trouble to remember him in death.

When the former leader's death was made public, condolences poured in from all over the world. Nina Petrovna received messages from many Soviet citizens and foreign dignitaries, including former US Ambassador Llewellyn Thompson and former first lady Jacqueline Kennedy Onassis. From the men with whom Khrushchev had governed the Soviet Union for more than a decade, many of whom owed their careers to him, there came not a word. And although Khrushchev's obituaries abroad were long and often laudatory, his successors at home found little to say:

The Central Committee of the CPSU and the USSR Council of Ministers announce with regret the death on 11 September 1971, after a protracted, painful illness, of the former First Secretary of the Central Committee of the CPSU and the Chairman of the USSR Council of Ministers, personal pensioner Nikita Sergeevich Khrushchev, at the age of 78.[112]

For twenty years the silence surrounding Khrushchev's name in the Soviet Union remained unbroken. The final word, however, belonged to Nikita Sergeevich; he was at last remembered, as he promised Adzhubei he would be. In fact, he was never forgotten. Throughout the Brezhnev years and the lengthy interregnum that followed, the generation which had come of age during the 'first Russian spring' of the 1950s awaited its turn in power. As Brezhnev and his colleagues died or were pensioned off, they were replaced by men and women for whom the Secret Speech and the first wave of de-Stalinisation had been a formative experience, and these 'Children of Twentieth Congress' took up the reins of power under the leadership of Mikhail Gorbachev and his colleagues. The Khrushchev era provided this second generation of reformers with both an inspiration and a cautionary tale. Academics and policy-makers studied Khrushchev and his policies in search of insights which might help shape the evolution of *perestroika*, while the wider public eagerly devoured memoirs, interviews and popular articles about Khrushchev and his times.

The treatment Khrushchev received was far from uncritical, but most observers acknowledged his courage and his vision in launching the first attempt to free the Soviet Union from its Stalinist past. Neither Khrushchev's flaws nor his ultimate defeat can conceal his very real achievements. He was all that his critics said he was: hare-brained schemes there were, and subjectivism and voluntarism and hasty decisions. Yet after eleven years in power he left his fellow citizens freer and more prosperous than they were before; Soviet influence in the world had increased, and the first steps towards a *détente* with the West had been taken.

In the end Khrushchev's fundamental faith in the system that he inherited – and had helped to build – prevented him from seeing the extent of its deformity. His diagnosis of its ills was superficial, and his remedies were insufficient, but it is difficult to judge Khrushchev too harshly in the wake of the Gorbachev experience. The failure of Gorbachev's much more ambitious attempt to transform the Soviet system underscores the enormity of the task that both he and Khrushchev undertook in trying to reform the Soviet system without destroying it. Khrushchev was removed from office for his labours and became a virtual un-person in his own country; his successors reversed many of his policies and brought the process of de-Stalinisation to a grinding halt. The Secret Speech, however, could not be reversed; the Terror could never again be buried under official silence. In the early morning hours of 25 February 1956 Khrushchev the chatterbox changed the Soviet Union forever with his words. Had he known what those words would unleash, he would likely have remained silent, but speak he did.

The system never really recovered.

Notes

References are given in full at their first citation in each chapter, and are thereafter referred to by author only, with a short title where there is potential ambiguity.

1 THE DONBASS BOLSHEVIK

1. *Pravda*, 22 September 1959.
2. *Pravda*, 18 October 1961.
3. N. S. Khrushchev, *Khrushchev Remembers* (London, 1971) p. 403.
4. Iu. I. Shapoval, *M. S. Khrushchov na Ukraini* (Kiev, 1990) p. 6.
5. Until the 1860s, peasants and common town-dwellers were subject to conscription; the unfortunates so drafted had to serve for twenty-five years.
6. N. S. Khrushchev, *Khrushchev Remembers: The Glasnost Tapes* (Boston, 1990) pp. 4–5.
7. Khrushchev, *Glasnost Tapes*, p. 4.
8. T. H. Friedgut, *Iuzovka and Revolution, Vol. 1: Life and Work in Russia's Donbass, 1869–1924* (Princeton, 1989) pp. 208–9.
9. Khrushchev, *Glasnost Tapes*, p. 5.
10. F. A. Brokgauz and I. A. Efron, *Entsiklopedicheskii slovar'* (St Petersburg, 1903) XXA, p. 765.
11. Khrushchev, *Glasnost Tapes*, pp. 5–6.
12. Khrushchev, *Khrushchev Remembers*, p. 22.
13. Khrushchev, *Glasnost Tapes*, pp. 5–6.
14. Japanese author Takasu Hirose claims that Khrushchev was undoubtedly of princely blood (*Izvestiia*, 7 April 1993).
15. A. G. Malenkov, *O moem ottse Georgii Malenkove* (Moscow, 1992) pp. 8–9.
16. This family was descended from a Pole named Chruszcz (Khrushch) who went to Moscow in 1453, converted to Russian Orthodoxy and was christened Ivan Ivanovich Khrushchev (Brokgauz and Efron, *Entsiklopedicheskii slovar'* XXXVIIA, p. 753).
17. G. Paloczi-Horvath, *Khrushchev: The Road to Power* (London, 1960) pp. 14–15.
18. A. I. Adzhubei, *Krushenie illiuzii: vremia v litsakh i sobytiiakh* (Moscow, 1991) p. 52. Aksiniia Ivanovna's death was noted by the Soviet press in 1945 (*Pravda Ukrainy*, 27 February 1945).
19. Khrushchev, *Glasnost Tapes*, p. 6.
20. Friedgut, p. 216.
21. Friedgut, pp. xii, 3, 329–31.
22. Friedgut, pp. 128–30, 328–9.

23. P. Bogdanov, *Rasskaz o pochetnom shakhtere: N. S. Khrushchev v Donbasse* (Stalino, 1961) p. 24.
24. K. Paustovskii, *Slow Approach of Thunder* (trans. M. Harari and M. Duncan) (London, 1965) p. 197.
25. Khrushchev, *Glasnost Tapes*, p. 6.
26. Adzhubei, pp. 122–3, 152.
27. Friedgut, pp. 304–5.
28. Adzhubei, pp. 89, 152.
29. Khrushchev, *Glasnost Tapes*, pp. 6–7.
30. Friedgut, pp. xiii, 331.
31. P. Surozhskii, 'Krai uglia i zheleza', *Sovremennik*, no. 4 (1913) p. 297; cited in Friedgut, p. 92.
32. Khrushchev, *Khrushchev Remembers*, p. 23; see also *Pravda*, 27 March 1958.
33. V. Modestov, *Rabochee i professional'noe dvizhenie v Donbasse do Velikoi Oktiabr'skoi Sotsialisticheskoi Revoliutsii* (Moscow, 1957) p. 65.
34. N. S. Khrushchev, 'Vospominaniia rutchenkovtsa', *Diktatura truda*, 12 March 1922; Shapoval, p. 6.
35. R. Medvedev, *Khrushchev: politicheskaia biografiia* (Moscow, 1990) p. 15; Bogdanov, p. 17.
36. Medvedev, p. 16.
37. Shapoval, p. 6.
38. Growing strike activity in the war-time Donbass is recorded by Modestov, pp. 81, 87, 95.
39. Adzhubei, p. 50.
40. A. N. Kolesnik, 'Letchik L. N. Khrushchev', *Voenno-istoricheskii zhurnal* 11 (November 1989) p. 91.
41. Shapoval, p. 6; Medvedev, p. 16.
42. See, for example, Molotov's comments in F. Chuev, *Sto sorok besed s Molotovym* (Moscow, 1991) p. 352; also E. Crankshaw, *Khrushchev: A Biography* (London, 1966) pp. 29–30; and L. Pistrak, *The Grand Tactician: Khrushchev's Rise to Power* (London, 1961) p. 3.
43. S. Kyleshov, 'On zakonov ishchet v bezzakon'i', in Chuev, p. 555.
44. Khrushchev, *Glasnost Tapes*, p. 11.
45. Shapoval, p. 6; Medvedev, p. 17.
46. Bogdanov, p. 33.
47. Shapoval, p. 6; Medvedev, p. 17.
48. Bogdanov, p. 39.
49. Khrushchev, *Glasnost Tapes*, pp. 8–9.
50. S. Fitzpatrick, *The Russian Revolution, 1917–1932* (Oxford, 1982) p. 61.
51. Khrushchev, *Glasnost Tapes*, p. 11. The uezd was the lowest administrative unit in tsarist Russia.
52. I. P. Kozhukalo and Iu. I. Shapoval, 'N. S. Khrushchev na Ukraine', *Voprosy istorii KPSS* 9 (September 1989) p. 87; and *Polytika* (Warsaw) no. 28 (11 July 1959) p. 3 (cited in Pistrak, p. 10).
53. Khrushchev, *Glasnost Tapes*, p. 11; Kozhukalo and Shapoval, p. 87.
54. Kozhukalo and Shapoval, p. 87.
55. Adzhubei, p. 50.

56. Kolesnik, p. 91.
57. Khrushchev, *Khrushchev Remembers*, p. 17.
58. Khrushchev, *Khrushchev Remembers*, pp. 20–1.
59. Shapoval, p. 7.
60. Adzhubei, p. 48; Adzhubei here reproduces a short autobiography written by Khrushchev's second wife, Nina Petrovna, for their daughter Rada.
61. Adzhubei, p. 89.
62. TsGAODgM (former Moscow Party Archive) f. 160, op. 1, k. 1, d. 4, l. 71.
63. TsGAODgM, f. 3, op. 8, k. 80, d. 1, p. 51; N. S. Khrushchev, *Otchetnyi doklad na moskovskoi X oblastnoi partiinoi konferentsii o rabote MK VKP(b)* (Moscow, 1952) p. 15.
64. Adzhubei, p. 48.
65. Shapoval, p. 7; .
66. TsGAODgM, f. 4, op. 8, d. 3, k. 80, l. 3.
67. Adzhubei, p. 49.
68. Shapoval, p. 7.
69. Adzhubei, p. 49.
70. Shapoval, p. 9.
71. Shapoval, p. 9.
72. RTsKhIDNI (former Central Party Archive) f. 17, op. 26, d. 770, l. 147.
73. Shapoval, p. 9.
74. Khrushchev, *Khrushchev Remembers*, pp. 18–20.
75. *Pravda*, 25 October 1959.
76. RTsKhIDNI, f. 17, op. 26, d. 768, ll. 32, 62, 67, 78.
77. RTsKhIDNI, f. 17, op. 26, d. 769, ll. 4–6.
78. RTsKhIDNI, f. 17, op. 26, d. 769, l. 10.
79. He began attending bureau meetings as a member in November 1926 (RTsKhIDNI, f. 17, op. 26, d. 770, l. 97) but this membership was formally confirmed only in January 1927 (RTsKhIDNI, f. 17, op. 26, d. 776, l. 7).
80. RTsKhIDNI, f. 17, op. 26, d. 777, ll. 17, 83, 166–9.
81. RTsKhIDNI, f. 17, op. 26, d. 775, ll. 31, 34, 37, 38, 96–103; d. 776, l. 12; and d. 777, l. 19.
82. RTsKhIDNI, f. 17, op. 26, d. 776, l. 34; d. 777, ll. 23, 65, 85, 104–5, 107–10, 121–2; d. 779, l. 56.
83. Adzhubei, pp. 49–50.
84. *XIV S"ezd Vsesoiuznoi Kommunisticheskoi Partii (Bol'shevikov): stenograficheskii otchet* (Moscow, 1926).
85. Quotation from Shapoval, p. 12; see also RTsKhIDNI, f. 17, op. 26, d. 767, l. 5.
86. *Persha vceukrains'ka konferentsiia KP(b)U (17–21 zhovtnia 1926 roku): stenografichnii zvit* (Khar'kov, 1926) pp. 87–93.
87. *Persha vceukrains'ka...*, pp. 93–5.
88. *Persha vceukrains'ka...*, pp. 85 (Gvozdev), 87 (Tarapurov), 369–70 (resolution).
89. For a discussion of this transformation, see Eric van Ree, 'Stalin's

289

Organic Theory of the Party', *Russian Review*, vol. 52, no. 1 (January 1993) pp. 43–57.
90. *Pravda*, 17 October 1926.
91. *Desiatii z'izd Komunistichnoi Partii (Bil'shovikiv) Ukraini: stenografichnii zvit* (Khar'kov, 1928) p. 236.
92. Khrushchev, *Khrushchev Remembers*, p. 39.
93. RTsKhIDNI, f. 17, op. 26, d. 11, ll. 197, 224, 232, 239.
94. RTsKhIDNI, f. 17, op. 26, d. 776, l. 53.
95. RTsKhIDNI, f. 17, op. 26, d. 775, l. 133.
96. G. Malenkov, 'V bor'be za tempy', *Partiinoe stroitel'stvo*, 2(4) (February 1930) pp. 35-40.
97. RTsKhIDNI, f. 17, op. 26, d. 777, ll. 131-5.
98. Shapoval, p. 10; RTsKhIDNI, f. 17, op. 26, d. 776, ll. 53-4.
99. RTsKhIDNI, f. 17, op. 26, d. 776, l. 53.
100. RTsKhIDNI, f. 17, op. 26, d. 776, l. 56.
101. Khrushchev, *Khrushchev Remembers*, p. 25.
102. Khrushchev, *Khrushchev Remembers*, p. 32.
103. The Russian historian Roy Medvedev presents a very different account of this transfer, based on the testimony of A. V. Snegov, who served in the apparatus of the Ukrainian Central Committee at this time. Snegov credits Kosior, Kaganovich's successor as Ukrainian First Secretary, with bringing Khrushchev to Khar'kov, but Kosior became First Secretary only after Khrushchev's transfer. See Medvedev, p. 23.
104. Khrushchev, *Khrushchev Remembers*, pp. 32-3.
105. RTsKhIDNI, f. 17, op. 26, d. 405, ll. 221.
106. Khrushchev, *Khrushchev Remembers*, p. 34.
107. Friedgut, p. 331.
108. Khrushchev, *Khrushchev Remembers*, pp. 33-4.
109. RTsKhIDNI, f. 17, op. 26, d. 405, ll. 251-3, 257-60, 273-6, 296; d. 406, l. 129; d. 407, ll. 108, 128, 131, 136, 142, 150-4, 179; d. 417, l. 34; d. 418, l. 34.
110. RTsKhIDNI, f. 17, op. 26, d. 405, l. 253; d. 406, ll. 172, 187, 193, 200, 204-5, 214. Khrushchev, *Khrushchev Remembers*, pp. 33-4.
111. RTsKhIDNI, f. 17, op. 26, d. 411, ll. 25-6.
112. RTsKhIDNI, f. 17, op. 26, d. 411, ll. 25-33.
113. *Visti VTsVK*, 12 April 1929.
114. *Visti VTsVK*, 11 January 1928.
115. RTsKhIDNI, f. 17, op. 26, d. 416, l. 98; d. 418, l. 34.

2 THE CITY FATHER

1. N. S. Khrushchev, 'O kul'te lichnosti i ego posledstviiakh', *Izvestiia TsK KPSS* 3 (March 1989) p. 133.
2. Rada Khrushcheva Adzhubei, who was born in mid-1929, has stated that she was Nina Petrovna's second daughter, and that an older daughter, Nadezhda, had died. It is not clear when Nadezhda was

born or if Nikita Khrushchev was her father (L. Vasil'eva, *Kremlevskie zheny* [Moscow, 1993] p. 437).
3. N. S. Khrushchev, *Khrushchev Remembers* (Boston, 1971) pp. 36-7.
4. D. Filtzer, *Soviet Workers and Stalinist Industrialisation* (London, 1986) pp. 81-91; C. Merridale, *Moscow Politics and the Rise of Stalin* (Basingstoke, 1990) p. 88.
5. TsGAODgM, (former Moscow Party Archive) f. 160, op. 1, k. 1, d. 4, ll. 67, 95.
6. TsGAODgM, f. 160, op. 1, k. 1, d. 3, ll. 30-2.
7. *Rabochaia Moskva*, 3 November 1929.
8. TsGAODgM, f. 160, op. 1, k. 1, d. 3, ll. 43-5, 49; d. 4, l. 68.
9. TsGAODgM, f. 160, op. 1, k. 1, d. 3, l. 43.
10. *Pravda*, 26 April 1930.
11. Khrushchev, *Khrushchev Remembers*, p. 39.
12. Khrushchev, *Khrushchev Remembers*, pp. 38-9.
13. TsGAODgM, f. 160, op. 1, k. 1, d. 3, l. 40.
14. Khrushchev, *Khrushchev Remembers*, p. 37.
15. TsGAODgM, f. 160, op. 1, k. 1, d. 8, l. 45; *Pravda*, 3 June 1930.
16. Khrushchev, *Khrushchev Remembers*, p. 40.
17. TsGAODgM, f. 160, op. 1, k. 1, d. 8, l. 45; d. 9, ll. 133-6.
18. TsGAODgM, f. 160, op. 1, k. 1, d. 9, ll. 133, 138; *Pravda*, 29 May 1930.
19. TsGAODgM, f. 160, op. 1, k. 1, d. 9, ll. 144-5; d. 8, ll. 46, 50; *Pravda*, 29 May 1930.
20. *Pravda*, 31 May 1930.
21. *Pravda*, 31 May, 2 June and 3 June 1930.
22. TsGAODgM, f. 160, op. 1, k. 1, d. 8, ll. 48, 62, 87-8, 92-3; d. 9, l. 119; d. 10, ll. 16, 43, 56-7.
23. TsGAODgM, f. 63, op. 1, k. 23, d. 393, ll. 109-12.
24. TsGAODgM, f. 160, op. 1, k. 1, d. 8, l. 106
25. *Pravda*, 22 November 1930.
26. TsGAODgM, f. 160, op. 1, k. 1, d. 8, ll. 108-9; d. 9, l. 98.
27. TsGAODgM, f. 160, op. 1, k. 1, d. 9, ll. 96-7.
28. TsGAODgM, f. 160, op. 1, k. 1, d. 9, ll.12, 102, 119.
29. RTsKhIDNI, f. 17, op. 20, d. 221, l. 102.
30. *Rabochaia Moskva*, 29 January 1931; *Pravda*, 26 February 1931.
31. Khrushchev, *Khrushchev Remembers*, pp. 43-4.
32. L. Pistrak, *The Grand Tactician: Khrushchev's Rise to Power* (London, 1961) pp. 62, 65-6; E. Crankshaw, *Khrushchev: A Biography* (London, 1966) pp. 67-72; A. N. Ponomarev, *N. S. Khrushchev: put' k liderstvu* (Moscow, 1990) p. 11; R. Medvedev, *Khrushchev: politicheskaia biografiia* (Moscow, 1990) pp. 24-5.
33. Crankshaw, p. 70; G. Paloczi-Horvath, *Khrushchev: The Road to Power* (London, 1960) p. 63.
34. Merridale, pp. 88, 109.
35. Merridale, pp. 87-8.
36. The term 'shapelessness' in this context is borrowed from Seweryn Bialer; S. Bialer, *Stalin's Successors: Leadership, Stability and Change in the Soviet Union* (Cambridge, 1980) pp. 10, 16-17.

37. Ponomarev, p. 18.
38. RTsKhIDNI, f. 17, op. 20, d. 221, l. 102.
39. Ponomarev, p. 19.
40. *Pravda*, 13 July 1931.
41. *Pravda*, 16 July 1931.
42. TsGAODgM, f. 69, op. 1, d. 750, l. 80; Ponomarev, p. 20.
43. *Pravda*, 16 July 1931.
44. Goreva's account of the meeting is in Ponomarev, p. 19.
45. TsGAODgM, f. 69, op. 1, d. 750, l. 80; Ponomarev, p. 20.
46. Ponomarev, p. 20.
47. RTsKhIDNI (former Central Party Archive) f. 17, op. 24, d. 344, l. 262-5.
48. *Pravda*, 15 December 1931; *Rabochaia Moskva*, 6 and 8 January 1932.
49. I. V. Stalin, *Sochineniia* (Moscow, 1949) vol. XIII, p. 101.
50. *Pravda*, 15 December 1931.
51. *Rabochaia Moskva*, 8 January 1932.
52. Pistrak, pp. 76-7.
53. *Pravda*, 5 January 1932.
54. *Pravda*, 4 January 1933.
55. TsGAODgM, f. 69, op. 1, d. 797, k. 43, ll. 41, 42.
56. *Rabochaia Moskva*, 6 and 8 January 1932.
57. RTsKhIDNI, f. 17, op. 24, d. 244, l. 5.
58. Merridale, p. 208.
59. *Tret'ia Moskovskaia oblastnaia i vtoraia gorodskaia konferentsii VKP(b): Biulleten' no. 4* (Moscow, 1932) pp. 30-5.
60. He repeated the proposal in 1935; N. S. Khrushchev, *Stroit' prochno, bystro, krasivo i deshevo* (Moscow, 1935) pp. 7-8; the measure was finally adopted when he was CPSU First Secretary (*Rezoliutsii XX S"ezda Kommunisticheskoi Partii* (Moscow, 1956) p. 14.
61. *Tret'ia Moskovskaia ... Biulleten' no. 4*, pp. 30-5.
62. *XVII S"ezd Vsesoiuznoi Kommunisticheskoi Partii (b): stenograficheskii otchet* (Moscow, 1934) pp. 145-7.
63. Moscow Province (*oblast'*) at that time was considerably larger than it is now and included the present day provinces of Kaluga, Tula, Riazan' and Kalinin.
64. Khrushchev, *Khrushchev Remembers*, p. 49.
65. Ponomarev, p. 32.
66. See, for example, *XVII S"ezd*, p. 145; *Pravda*, 22 November 1936.
67. Adzhubei, pp. 50-2.
68. *IV Moskovskaia oblastnaia i III gorodskaia konferentsii VKP(b): stenograficheskii otchet* (Moscow, 1934) p. 302.
69. See *XVII S"ezd*, p. 145: 'We officials of the Moscow organisation have experienced the leadership of the Leninist Central Committee and of Comrade Stalin personally especially directly, from day to day, in connection with all of the matters on which Moscow Bolsheviks were working.'
70. Khrushchev, *Khrushchev Remembers*, pp. 57-61.
71. *Moskovskaia pravda*, 9 April 1989.

72. Khrushchev, *Khrushchev Remembers*, p. 45.
73. RTsKhIDNI, f. 17, op. 2, d. 612, vyp. III, ll. 67–8.
74. Ponomarev, p. 38.
75. *Moskovskaia pravda*, 9 April 1989.
76. Ponomarev, p. 37.
77. *IV Moskovskaia oblastnaia i III gorodskaia konferentsii VKP(b): stenograficheskii otchet* (Moscow, 1934) pp. 276, 278, 281; Khrushchev, *Khrushchev Remembers*, pp. 62–3.
78. *IV Moskovskaia...*, p. 281;
79. *XVII S"ezd*, p. 146.
80. *Pravda*, 6 September 1933.
81. Ponomarev, p. 25.
82. Crankshaw, p. 91.
83. Khrushchev, *Khrushchev Remembers*, p. 64.
84. Khrushchev, *Khrushchev Remembers*, pp. 64–5.
85. *Pravda*, 7 February 1935.
86. Khrushchev, *Khrushchev Remembers*, p. 68.
87. *Rasskazy stroitelei metro* (Moscow, 1935) pp. 33; *Piat' let moskovskogo metro* (Moscow, 1940) p. 33; Khrushchev, *Khrushchev Remembers*, pp. 69–70.
88. *Rasskazy*, pp. 62–3.
89. *Pravda*, 16 March 1935.
90. *Kak my stroili metro* (Moscow, 1935) pp. 649–50; *Rasskazy*, p. 257.
91. *Piat' let*, p. 33; *Rasskazy*, pp. 86–8, 226–31.
92. *Rasskazy*, p. 94.
93. *Rasskazy*, pp. 34, 113, 130; *Pravda*, 16 March 1935.
94. *Kak my stroili*, p. 24.
95. *Pravda*, 6 April 1935; *Rasskazy*, p. 42.
96. *Rasskazy*, pp. 481.
97. V. Gonzalez and J. Gorkin, *Life and Death in Soviet Russia* (New York, 1952) p. 80.
98. *Rasskazy*, p. 44.
99. Z. Troitskaia, *The L. M. Kaganovich Metropolitan Railway of Moscow: Moscow's Metro* (Moscow, 1955).
100. *Moskovskii Komsomol na metro* (Moscow/Leningrad, 1934) p. 17; *XVII S"ezd*, p. 504; Pistrak, p. 97.
101. Ponomarev, pp. 34–5.
102. Ponomarev, pp. 34–5.
103. J. A. Getty, *Origins of the Great Purges: The Soviet Communist Party Reconsidered, 1933–1938* (Cambridge, 1985) pp. 198–9.
104. RTsKhIDNI, f. 17, op. 2, d. 561, l. 131.
105. RTsKhIDNI, f. 17, op. 120, r. 108, d. 240, l. 129.
106. RTsKhIDNI, f. 17, op. 2, d. 612, vyp. III, ll. 35–7.
107. RTsKhIDNI, f. 17, op. 2, d. 612, vyp. III, ll. 67–8.
108. RTsKhIDNI, f. 17, op. 2, d. 612, vyp. III, l. 36.
109. RTsKhIDNI, f. 17, op. 2, d. 612, vyp. III, l. 68.
110. Ponomarev, p. 37.
111. Getty, pp. 12–20.
112. See, for example, K. B. Bailes, *Technology and Society under Lenin*

and *Stalin: Origins of the Soviet Technical Intelligentsia, 1917–1941* (Princeton, 1978) pp. 154–5.

113. Getty, pp. 14–16.
114. RTsKhIDNI, f. 17, op. 2, d. 514, vyp. 1, ch. 1, ll. 9–10; *Pravda*, 10 January 1933.
115. *XVII S"ezd*, pp. 354, 435–6.
116. *Pravda*, 6 September 1933.
117. *Itogi dekabr'skogo Plenuma TsK VKP(b) i zadachi moskovskikh bol'shevikov* (Moscow, 1936) pp. 7, 13–18.
118. The history of the movement and its significance for Soviet politics are recounted in L. Siegelbaum, *Stakhanovism and the Politics of Productivity in the USSR* (Cambridge, 1988).
119. Siegelbaum, pp. 81–6, 90.
120. N. S. Khrushchev, *Rech' tovarishcha N. S. Khrushcheva na pervom Vsesoiuznom soveshchanii rabochikh i rabotnits stakhanovtsev* (Iakutsk, 1935) pp. 3–12.
121. *Pravda*, 27 December 1935.
122. Khrushchev, *Itogi dekabr'skogo Plenuma...*, pp. 5–7, 13–27.
123. Ponomarev, pp. 33–4.
124. *XVII S"ezd*, p. 35.
125. *IV oblastnaia...*, p. 300.
126. *XVII S"ezd*, p. 145.
127. *Pravda*, 1 February 1934.
128. For differing views of the case see R. Conquest, *Stalin and the Kirov Murder* (New York, 1989); Getty, pp. 207–10; A. Ulam, *Stalin: The Man and His Era* (New York, 1973) pp. 375–88. Khrushchev believed that Stalin was behind the plot (*Khrushchev Remembers: The Glasnost Tapes* [Boston, 1990] pp. 24–5) but a commission appointed by him in the 1950s to investigate the case was unable to demonstrate this; see 'Zapiska P. N. Pospelova ob ubiistve Kirova', *Svobodnaia mysl'* 8 (April, 1992) pp. 64–71.
129. 'Skol'ko delegatov XVII S"ezda golosovali protiv Stalina?', *Izvestiia TsK KPSS* 7 (July 1991) pp. 114–21.
130. For an account of this period see R. Conquest, *The Great Terror: A Reassessment* (New York, 1990); Getty, *Origins*, provides a view sharply at odds with Conquest.
131. See, for example, N. S. Khrushchev, *Itogi iiunskogo Plenuma TsK VKP(b) i zadachi moskovskoi partiinoi organizatsii* (Moscow, 1935) pp. 22–4; Khrushchev, *Itogi dekabr'skogo Plenuma...*, pp. 44–5; *Pravda*, 10 June 1936.
132. *Rabochaia Moskva*, 17 March 1937; see also similar statements in *Pravda*, 24 May 1937.
133. *Pravda*, 30 January 1937.
134. *Pravda*, 2, 5, 6 and 7 June 1937.
135. *Pravda*, 30 May 1937.
136. Khrushchev, 'O kul'te lichnosti', p. 157.
137. *Tret'ia Moskovskaia oblastnaia i vtoraia gorodskaia konferentsii VKP(b): Biulleten'* no. 4 (Moscow, 1932) pp. 30–5.
138. *XVII S"ezd*, p. 145; *Pravda* 26 January 1934.

139. *Pravda* 24 May 1937.
140. Conquest, pp. 485–7, reckons the toll at about 8 million arrests and 3.5 million deaths. For much lower estimates, see J. Hough and M. Fainsod, *How the Soviet Union is Governed* (Cambridge, Mass., 1979) pp. 176–7; see also Getty, p. 176, n. 16.
141. 'Sud'ba chlenov i kandidatov v chleny TsK VKP(b) izbrannogo XVII S"ezdom partii', *Izvestiia TsK KPSS* 12 (December 1989) pp. 86–7. The figures for the Central Committee do not include the assassinated Kirov or Politburo member Valerian Kuibyshev, who Conquest believes may have been murdered (Conquest, pp. 72–3, 387–8).
142. RTsKhIDNI, f. 17, op. 2, d. 630, l. 43; d. 640, l. 99.
143. *Kolomenskaia pravda*, 19 September 1989.
144. TsGAODgM, f. 3, op. 150, d. 1, l. 159.
145. TsGAODgM, f. 3, op. 24, k. 345, d. 128, l. 16.
146. TsGAODgM, f. 4, op. 8, k. 80, ll. 33–4, 52.
147. TsGAODgM, f. 4, op. 8, k. 80, ll. 33–4.
148. TsGAODgM, f. 4, op. 8, k. 80, ll. 3–4.
149. Khrushchev, *Glasnost Tapes*, pp. 36–8.
150. *Znamia* 10 (October) 1989, p. 25; see also RTsKhIDNI, f. 17, op. 21, d. 3023, ll. 3, 4, 128–9, 220, 226–7; d. 3024, ll. 3–6, 78; d. 3025, ll. 11, 13, 16, 105–19, 201.
151. TsGAODgM, f. 3, op. 19, k. 233, d. 15, l. 2.
152. See, for example, RTsKhIDNI, f. 17, op. 21, d. 3026, ll. 11, 108–9; d. 3027, ll. 57–9.
153. RTsKhIDNI, f. 17, op. 20, d. 221, l. 102; Khrushchev, *Khrushchev Remembers*, p. 83.
154. RTsKhIDNI, f. 17, op. 21, d. 3023, ll. 128, 220.
155. L. Kolodnyi, 'Pervyi Sekretar'', in L. Kirshner (ed.), *Svet i teni velikogo desiatiletiia: N. S. Khrushchev i ego vremia* (Leningrad, 1989) pp. 268–9, 275. Kolodnyi states that his source on this point was Rosa Treivas herself.
156. A. I. Adzhubei, *Krushenie illiuzii: vremia v sobytiiakh i litsakh* (Moscow, 1991) p. 36.
157. TsGAODgM, f. 3, op. 24, k. 348, d. 150, l. 35.

3 THE VICEROY

1. *Pravda*, 14 December 1944; translated in L. Pistrak, *The Grand Tactician: Khrushchev's Rise to Power* (London, 1961) p. 165.
2. N. S. Khrushchev, 'O kul'te lichnosti i ego posledstviiakh', *Izvestiia TsK KPSS* 3 (March 1989) p. 144; R. Conquest, *The Great Terror: A Reassessment* (New York, 1990) p. 248.
3. Iu. I. Shapoval, *M. S. Khrushchov na Ukraini* (Kiev, 1990) p. 21.
4. *Pravda*, 19 January 1938.
5. RTsKhIDNI (former Central Party Archive) f. 17, op. 21, d. 4670, l. 1.
6. RTsKhIDNI, f. 17, op. 21, d. 4670, l. 2; d. 4686, l. 6.

Notes   295

7. RTsKhIDNI, f. 17, op. 21, d. 4670, l. 5.
8. Shapoval, p. 18.
9. *Visti VTsVK*, 22 and 27 February, 9, 17 and 28 April, 30 May and 5, 8 and 10 June 1938; also RTsKhIDNI, f. 17, op. 21, d. 4686, ll. 108, 164–70; d. 4687, ll. 67–70.
10. RTsKhIDNI, f. 17, op. 21, d. 4686, ll. 6–10; d. 4687, ll. 34–5.
11. *Visti VTsVK*, 15 May and 13 June 1938.
12. TsGASA (Archive of the Soviet Army) f. 25 880, op. 4, d. 1, ll. 2–3; cited in D. Volkogonov, *Stalin: Triumph and Tragedy* (trans. H. Shukman) (Rocklin, Calif., 1992) p. 318.
13. Shapoval, p. 19.
14. *XIV z'izd Komunistichnoi Partii (Bil'shovikiv) Ukraini: stenografichnii zvit* (Kiev, 1938) pp. 169–70.
15. *Pravda*, 16 June 1938.
16. *Visti VTsVK* 27 May1938.
17. N. S. Khrushchev, *Rech' na obshchegorodskom mitinge trudiashchikhsia Kieva; rech' na IV Kievskoi oblastnoi partiinoi konferentsii* (Kiev, 1938) pp. 8–11.
18. *Pravda*, 7 June 1938.
19. *Pravda*, 16 June 1938.
20. Shapoval, p. 22.
21. *Trud*, 14 March 1991; Shapoval, p. 23.
22. G. I. Voronov, 'Nemnogo vospominanii', *Druzhba narodov* 1 (January 1989) p. 201; A. I. Adzhubei, 'Po sledam odnogo iubileia', *Ogonek* 41 (October 1989) p. 9.
23. 'Problemy istorii i sovremennosti', *Voprosy istorii KPSS* 2 (February 1989) p. 53.
24. RTsKhIDNI, f. 17, op. 2, d. 630, l. 34; d. 640, l. 33.
25. RTsKhIDNI, f. 17, op. 2, d. 577, ll. 5–20; Volkogonov, *Triumph*, pp. 285–7.
26. J. A. Getty, *Origins of the Great Purges: The Soviet Communist Party Reconsidered, 1933–1938* (Cambridge, 1985) pp. 175–6.
27. K. B. Bailles, *Technology and Society under Lenin and Stalin: Origins of the Soviet Technical Intelligentsia, 1917–1941* (Princeton, 1978) p. 270.
28. Getty, p. 184, n. 51.
29. N. S. Khrushchev, *Khrushchev Remembers: The Last Testament* (Boston, 1974) p. 438.
30. N. Machiavelli, *Discourses*, III.2.1.
31. The phrase is Winston Churchill's.
32. Volkogonov, p. 330. Volkogonov attributed Ezhov's fall to alcoholism, which Stalin interpreted as a sign of a weak will.
33. RTsKhIDNI, f. 17, op. 21, d. 4687, ll. 63–4; d. 4691, ll. 6–7.
34. *Pravda*, 18 May 1940; R. S. Sullivant, *Soviet Politics and the Ukraine, 1917–1957* (New York, 1962) p. 236.
35. RTsKhIDNI, f. 17, op. 21, d. 4686, l. 96.
36. RTsKhIDNI, f. 17, op. 21, d. 4670, l. 1;
37. RTsKhIDNI, f. 17, op. 21, d. 4686, ll. 97, 108; d. 4691, l. 23; d. 4692, l. 82.

38. Y. Bilinsky, *The Second Soviet Republic: The Ukraine after World War II* (New Brunswick, NJ, 1964) p. 85.
39. See, for example, *Pravda*, 7, 13 and 16 June 1938; *Vtoraia sessiia Verkhovnogo Soveta SSSR I sozyva: stenograficheskii otchet* (Moscow, 1938) pp. 715–24; Khrushchev, *Rech' na obshchegorodskom...*, pp. 3, 5, 7–9.
40. 'O tak nazyvaemom natsional-uklonizme', *Izvestiia TsK KPSS* 9 (September 1990) pp. 80–2.
41. Shapoval, p. 21.
42. RTsKhIDNI, f. 17, op. 21, d. 4686, l. 6.
43. RTsKhIDNI, f. 17, op. 21, d. 4686, ll. 189–91.
44. V. Turetskii, 'Pravo na obrazovanie v sovetskom gosudarstve', *Sovetskoe gosudarstvo i pravo* 9 (September 1936) p. 45.
45. RTsKhIDNI, f. 17, op. 21, d. 4686, ll. 189–91.
46. 'Ob obiazatel'nom izuchenii russkogo iazyka v shkolakh natsional'nykh respublik i oblastei', *Izvestiia TsK KPSS* 3 (March 1989) p. 179.
47. *Visti VTsVK*, 29 July 1938.
48. RTsKhIDNI, f. 17, op. 21, d. 4690, l. 20.
49. *Pravda*, 16 June 1938.
50. *Visti VTsVK*, 15 July 1938.
51. RTsKhIDNI, f. 17, op. 21, d. 4687, l. 11; d. 4693, ll. 19, 133.
52. RTsKhIDNI, f. 17, op. 21, d. 4686, l. 133.
53. *Visti VTsVK*, 2 October 1938.
54. *Visti VTsVK*, 29 August and 20 November 1938; V. Kirpotin, 'Russkaia kul'tura', *Bol'shevik* 12 (June 1938) pp. 59–60.
55. RTsKhIDNI, f. 17, op. 21, d. 4687, l. 65.
56. See R. Conquest, *Harvest of Sorrow: Soviet Collectivisation and the Terror-Famine* (London, 1988).
57. RTsKhIDNI, f. 17, op. 21, d. 4792, ll. 43, 85–6, 88.
58. RTsKhIDNI, f. 17, op. 21, d. 4692, l. 87; *Pravda*, 9 June 1939.
59. *Visti VTsVK*, 3, 8 and 18 August 1938, 29 September 1940.
60. Khrushchev's promotion to the status of full member of the Politburo appeared in *Pravda*, 11 March 1939.
61. *Visti VTsVK*, 3 March 1939; *XVIII S"ezd Vsesoiuznoi Kommunisticheskoi Partii (Bol'shevikov): stenographicheskii otchet* (Moscow, 1939) p. 174; *Pravda*, 21 December 1939.
62. N. S. Khrushchev, *Khrushchev Remembers* (London, 1971) pp. 126–35.
63. *Krasnaia zvezda*, 29 September 1939.
64. D. R. Marples, *Stalinism in Ukraine in the 1940s* (Basingstoke, 1992) pp. 43–4.
65. Marples, pp. 44–5.
66. *Krasnaia zvezda*, 20 and 27 September and 2 October 1939.
67. A. I. Adzhubei, *Krushenie Illiuzii: vremia v sobytiiakh i litsakh* (Moscow, 1991) pp. 56–9.
68. *Stalinskoe plemia* 26 October 1939; cited in Pistrak, p. 198.
69. *Pravda*, 15 November 1939.
70. *Pravda*, 26 March and 17 December 1940.

71. RTsKhIDNI, f. 17, op. 21, d. 4697, ll. 233-7, 241-4.
72. Shapoval, p. 29.
73. Shapoval, p. 30.
74. V. S. Parsadanova, 'Deportatsiia naseleniia iz zapadnoi Ukrainy i zapadnoi Belorussii v 1939-1941gg', *Novaia i noveishaia istoriia* 2 (March-April 1989) pp. 28, 32.
75. RTsKhIDNI, f. 17, op. 21, d. 2965, l. 127.
76. Marples, pp. 27-30, 35-40.
77. RTsKhIDNI, f. 17, op. 21, d. 3271, l. 47.
78. RTsKhIDNI, f. 17, op. 21, d. 2961, l. 38.
79. Khrushchev, *Khrushchev Remembers*, pp. 137-8; Khrushchev, 'O kul'te lichnosti', pp. 147-8.
80. J. Erickson, *The Road to Stalingrad: Stalin's War with Germany* (London, 1975) vol. 1, p. 79; *Narisi istorii Komunistichnoi Partii Ukraini* (Kiev, 1964) p. 499; R. Medvedev, *N. S. Khrushchev: politicheskaia biografiia* (Moscow,1990) pp. 38-9.
81. G. K. Zhukov, *Vospominaniia i razmyshleniia*, 11th edn (Moscow, 1992) vol. 2, pp. 292, 317. The 11th edn of Zhukov's memoirs includes (in italics) material censored from the Brezhnev-era editions.
82. A. M. Vasil'evskii, *Delo vsei zhizni* (Moscow, 1978) p. 246.
83. 'Vozglavlial li N. S. Khrushchev nelegal'nyi TsK KP(b) Ukrainy?' *Izvestiia TsK KPSS* 2 (February 1990) pp. 109-11.
84. Erickson, p. 458.
85. *Pravda*, 7 August 1961.
86. 'O zashchite pravoberezh'ia Dnepra', *Izvestiia TsK KPSS* 7 (July 1990) p. 209.
87. Khrushchev, *Khrushchev Remembers*, pp. 168-9; Vasil'evskii, pp. 123-4; *Izvestiia TsK KPSS* 9 (September 1990) p. 202.
88. 'Telegramma iz Khar'kova. 13 sentiabria 1941 g.', *Izvestiia TsK KPSS* 10 (October 1990) p. 222.
89. 'O poriadke evakuatsii i unichtozhenii imushchestva', *Izvestiia TsK KPSS* 7 (July 1990) pp. 206-8.
90. 'Telegramma komandovaniia Iuzhnogo fronta I. V. Stalinu i S. M. Budennomu', *Izvestiia TsK KPSS* 9 (September 1990) p. 195.
91. 'O sozdanii oboronitel'noi linii na levom beregu Dnepra' *Izvestiia TsK KPSS* 9 (September 1990) pp. 196-7.
92. 'Ob organizatsii oborony Kievskogo ukrepraiona', *Izvestiia TsK KPSS* 9 (September 1990) pp. 199-200.
93. Zhukov, vol. 2, p. 119.
94. Khrushchev, *Khrushchev Remembers*, pp. 168-71.
95. A. Werth, *Russia at War* (London, 1964) pp. 203ff.
96. Erickson, p. 243.
97. Sullivant, p. 238.
98. Sullivant, p. 238.
99. 'Ob organizatsii partizanskikh otriadov i diversionnykh grupp dlia deistvii v tylu protivnika', *Izvestiia TsK KPSS* 9 (September 1990) pp. 197-8.

100. J. A. Armstrong, *Soviet Partisans in World War II* (Madison, 1964) p. 51.
101. 'Vozglavlial li Khruschev...', pp. 109–11.
102. I. Kh. Bagramian, *Tak nachalas' voina* (Moscow, 1977) pp. 48–9; 'Nekotorye voprosy rukovodstva vooruzhennoi bor'boi letom 1942 goda', *Voenno-istoricheskii zhurnal* 8 (August 1965) p. 4; 'Vot gde pravda, Nikita Sergeevich!' (Part 2) *Voenno-istoricheskii zhurnal* 1 (January 1990) p. 9.
103. Erickson, p. 347.
104. 'Vot gde pravda' (Part 2) pp. 13–18; 'Vot gde pravda, Nikita Sergeevich!' (Part 3) *Voenno-istoricheskii zhurnal* 2 (February 1990) pp. 35–6.
105. Khrushchev, *Khrushchev Remembers*, pp. 184–7.
106. Zhukov, p. 256–7.
107. Vasil'evskii, p. 196.
108. Bagramian, pp. 116–17.
109. 'Vot gde pravda' (Part 2) p. 12.
110. 'Vot gde pravda' (Part 3) pp. 44-6.
111. Erickson, p. 360.
112. Chuikov said this to Alexander Werth in February 1943; Werth, pp. xiii, 557.
113. V. I. Chuikov, *Nachalo puti* (Moscow, 1962) p. 246.
114. Erickson, p. 458.
115. Chuikov, pp. 101, 173, 184, 220.
116. Khrushchev, *Khrushchev Remembers*, pp. 193–6.
117. *Pravda*, 13 February 1943, 11 April 1943.
118. *Pravda*, 6 February 1944.
119. B. E. Pestov, 'Pogib? Popal bez vesti? Zhiv?', *Voenno-istoricheskii zhurnal* 4 (April 1990) p. 79.
120. Pestov, p. 79; A. N. Kolesnik, 'Letchik L. N. Khrushchev', *Voenno-istoricheskii zhurnal* 11 (November 1989) p. 93.
121. Pestov, p. 79; Kolesnik, p. 94.
122. Pestov, pp. 78–9.
123. Kolesnik, p. 93.
124. F. Chuev, *Sto sorok besed s Molotovym* (Moscow, 1991) p. 351.
125. L. Vasil'eva, *Kremlevskie zheny* (Moscow, 1993) p. 437.
126. RTsKhIDNI, f. 17, op. 45, d. 1967, l. 206.
127. *Vos'maia sessiia Verkhovnogo Soveta USSR 1ogo sozyva* (Kiev, 1947) p.88.
128. RTsKhIDNI, f. 17, op. 45, d. 1967, ll. 271–2, 293–6.

4 THE COUNTER-HEIR

1. *Khrushchev Remembers* (London, 1971) p. 307.
2. RTsKhIDNI, f. 17, op. 45, d. 1966, l. 96; see also ll. 97–109.
3. RTsKhIDNI, f. 17, op. 45, d. 1967, ll. 4, 17–20, 26, 29, 47–50.
4. N. S. Khrushchev, *Nashi zadachi v vosstanovlenii i blagoustroistve gorodov i stroitel'stve v selakh i kolkhozakh* (Moscow, 1945) p. 12.

5. RTsKhIDNI, f. 17, op. 45, d. 1967, ll. 47–50.
6. I. P. Kozhukalo and Iu. I. Shapoval, 'Khrushchev na Ukraine', *Voprosy istorii KPSS* 9 (September 1989) pp. 97–8.
7. *Pravda Ukrainy,* 30 January 1946.
8. D. R. Marples, *Stalinism in Ukraine in the 1940s* (Basingstoke, 1992) pp. 86–7.
9. B. Nahaylo and V. Swoboda, *Soviet Disunion: A History of the Nationalities Problem in the USSR* (London, 1990) pp. 99–100.
10. Marples, pp. 87–8.
11. RTsKhIDNI, f. 17, op. 44, d. 1628, ll. 68, 10–14, 17; op. 45, d. 1967, ll. 192–3.
12. Iu. I. Shapoval, *M. S. Khrushchov na Ukraini* (Kiev, 1990) p. 34;
13. *Pravda,* 23 August 1946.
14. *Pravda,* 25 November 1944.
15. RTsKhIDNI, f. 17, op. 45, d. 1967, l. 201.
16. R. S. Sullivant, *Soviet Politics and Ukraine, 1917–1957* (New York, 1962) p. 240. See, for example, *Pravda,* 17 and 21 July 1941, 25 December 1942, 17 February and 3 and 20 October 1943.
17. *Pravda,* 16 and 17 March 1944.
18. *Pravda,* 21 August 1946
19. Sullivant, pp. 257–67.
20. *Pravda,* 23 August 1946.
21. See *Pravda Ukrainy,* 20 November 1947; *Literaturnaia gazeta,* 24 November 1947.
22. *Pravda Ukrainy,* 2 August 1947; *XVI z'izd Komunistichnoi Partii (Bil'shovikiv) Ukraini: stenografichnii zvit* (Kiev, 1949) pp. 73–4.
23. *Pravda,* 23 August 1946.
24. *Pravda Ukrainy,* 8 June and 6 July 1946.
25. *Pravda,* 23 August 1946.
26. V. F. Zima, 'Golod v Rossii 1946–47 godov', *Otechestvennaia istoriia* 1 (January 1993) p. 35.
27. TsGANKh, f. 8040, op. 8, d. 360, ll. 21–3.
28. Zima, p. 35.
29. Khrushchev, *Khrushchev Remembers,* pp. 234–5.
30. Khrushchev, *Khrushchev Remembers,* pp. 233–4, 240–1.
31. See, for examples, *Pravda,* 14 December 1944; *Sed'maia sessiia Verkhovnogo Soveta USSR 1-go sozyva: stenograficheskii otchet* (Kiev, 1945) pp. 41–2, 67, 84; *Vos'maia sessiia Verkhovnogo Soveta USSR 1-go sozyva: stenograficheskii otchet* (Kiev, 1946) pp. 30, 55, 149, 159, 185.
32. *Pravda,* 28 February and 7 March 1947; Khrushchev, *Khrushchev Remembers,* p. 237–9.
33. Khrushchev, *Khrushchev Remembers,* p. 240.
34. *Pravda Ukrainy,* 4 and 5 March 1947.
35. *Pravda Ukrainy,* 25 and 26 March 1947.
36. *Pravda Ukrainy,* 23 March 1947.
37. Khrushchev, *Khrushchev Remembers,* p. 240; A. I. Adzhubei, *Krushenie Illiuzii: vremia v sobytiiakh i litsakh* (Moscow, 1991) p. 30.
38. Marples, pp. 94–5.
39. Adzhubei, pp. 30–1.

40. Khrushchev, *Khrushchev Remembers*, pp. 241-4; *Pravda*, 3 July 1957, 20 and 24 October 1961.
41. Adzhubei, pp. 30-1.
42. Khrushchev, *Khrushchev Remembers*, p. 285; Iu. I. Shapoval, 'Stalinskyi poslanets na Ukraini', *Pid praporom leninizmu* 20 (October 1989) pp. 82-3.
43. Khrushchev, *Khrushchev Remembers*, pp. 243-4.
44. Khrushchev, *Khrushchev Remembers*, pp. 241-3.
45. Marples, p. 91.
46. Adzhubei, p. 31.
47. The last vestiges of armed resistance were not eliminated until 1952; Nahaylo and Swoboda, p. 99.
48. Adzhubei, pp. 31, 36, 41, 87.
49. Marples, pp. 121-2.
50. *Pravda Ukrainy*, 27 January 1949.
51. N. Jasny, 'Kolkhozy, the Achilles Heel of the Soviet Regime', *Soviet Studies* III, no. 2 (October 1951) p. 158.
52. Khrushchev, *Khrushchev Remembers* (Boston, 1971) p. 250.
53. Khrushchev, *Khrushchev Remembers*, pp. 246-50; Adzhubei, pp. 24, 29, 33, 38.
54. *Pravda*, 21 December 1949.
55. A. N. Ponomarev, *N. S. Khrushchev: put' k liderstvu* (Moscow, 1990) p. 52.
56. Popov himself made reference to the case in his own unpublished memoirs, which are now in the Central State Archive for Social Movements of the City of Moscow (the former Moscow Party Archives); Ponomarev, p. 50.
57. Khrushchev, *Khrushchev Remembers*, pp. 249-50.
58. TsGAODgM, f. 3, op. 117, d. 1, l. 7.
59. Ponomarev, p. 53.
60. Adzhubei, p. 137.
61. *Pravda*, 19 February 1950.
62. Marples, p. 144.
63. *Pravda*, 25 February 1950.
64. *Pravda*, 8 March and 25 April 1950.
65. H. Carrére d'Encausse, *Stalin: Order Through Terror* (London, 1981) pp. 141, 145.
66. *Kommunisticheskoi Partii Sovetskogo Soiuza v resoliutsiiakh i resheniiakh s"ezdov, konferentsii i plenumov TsK* (Moscow, 1971) vol. 6, pp. 304-7.
67. Ponomarev, p. 54.
68. *Moskovskaia pravda*, 28 June 1950.
69. *Moskovskaia pravda*, 28 June 1950.
70. *Izvestiia*, 13 February 1951.
71. *Pravda*, 4 March 1951.
72. TsGAODgM f. 3, op 137, d. 4, l. 84; cited in L. A. Openkin, *Ottepel': kak eto bylo* (Moscow, 1991) p. 28.
73. TsGAODgM, f. 3, op. 124, d. 24, l. 51; Ponomarev, p. 57.
74. *Pravda*, 5 March 1951.

75. RTsKhIDNI, f. 17, op. 133, d. 41, ll. 99-115.
76. *Molodaia gvardiia* 4 (April 1989) p. 58.
77. TsGAODgM, f. 3, op. 138, d. 12, ll. 4-6; Openkin, p. 29.
78. N. S. Khrushchev, *Otchetnyi doklad na moskovskoi X oblastnoi partiinoi konferentsii o rabote MK VKP(b)* (Moscow, 1952) pp. 14-15.
79. *Pravda*, 6 October 1952.
80. Khrushchev, *Otchetnyi doklad*, pp. 18-19.
81. Khrushchev, *Otchetnyi doklad*, p. 23.
82. Khrushchev, *Otchetnyi doklad*, p. 15.
83. TsGAODgM, f. 3, op. 129, d. 188; Ponomarev, pp. 55-6.
84. Khrushchev, *Khrushchev Remembers*, pp. 296-306.
85. Openkin, p. 47.
86. R. Conquest, *Power and Policy in the USSR: The Study of Soviet Dynastics* (London, 1961) pp. 95-100.
87. N. S. Khrushchev, 'O kul'te lichnosti i ego posledstviiakh', *Izvestiia TsK KPSS* 3 (March 1989) p. 153; Khrushchev, *Khrushchev Remembers*, p. 312; Conquest, pp. 129-53.
88. Khrushchev, *Khrushchev Remembers*, p. 256.
89. *Pravda*, 13 January 1953.
90. *Pravda*, 20 August 1952.
91. The report appeared in *Pravda*, 13 October 1952; for Khrushchev's account of its writing see Khrushchev, *Khrushchev Remembers*, pp. 277-8.
92. Khrushchev, *Otchetnyi doklad*, pp. 3-4, 23-4, 45, 47-8, 54-5.
93. Khrushchev, *Otchetnyi doklad*, p. 4.
94. *Pravda*, 13 October 1952.
95. *Pravda*, 25 May 1945.
96. *Zaria Vostoka*, 16 September 1952; *Pravda Ukrainy*, 25 September 1952; *Pravda* 2 and 9 October 1952.
97. *Pravda*, 6-13 October 1952.
98. *Pravda*, 16 October 1952; Khrushchev, *Khrushchev Remembers*, p. 279.
99. The members with ties to Malenkov were Ignat'ev, Malyshev, Mel'nikov, Mikhailov, Pervukhin, Ponomarenko and Saburov; the candidates were Patolichev, Pegov and Tevosian. Korotchenko (member) and Brezhnev (candidate) were clearly Khrushchev men. Aristov, Ignatov and Kosygin were later to find favour with Khrushchev. Minister of State Security S. D. Ignatiev has been identified as a possible Khrushchev client in the 1950s, but Malenkov's son Andrei asserts that he was a Malenkov man (A. G. Malenkov, *O moem ottse Georgii Malenkove* [Moscow, 1992] p. 64).
100. Khrushchev, *Khrushchev Remembers*, pp. 279-80.
101. *Pravda*, 24 December 1952, 22 and 23 January, and 6 February 1953
102. F. R. Kozlov, 'Politicheskaia bditel'nost' - obiazannost' chlena partii', *Kommunist* 1 (January 1953) pp. 46-58.
103. Khrushchev makes no such claims in either his memoirs or the Secret Speech; Andrei Malenkov does not mention any threat to his father, stressing instead that Georgii Maksimilianovich enjoyed the dictator's full confidence (Malenkov, pp. 60-1.)

104. *Pravda* and *Izvestiia*, 6 April 1953.
105. Conquest, pp. 232–3, 322.
106. Conquest, p. 190.
107. Malenkov, pp. 61, 64.
108. Khrushchev, *Khrushchev Remembers*, pp. 286–7.
109. *Pravda*, 23 July 1954.
110. Conquest, pp. 178–9, 190–1.
111. Unless indicated otherwise, the account of Stalin's last days is based on D. Volkogonov, *Stalin: Triumph and Tragedy* (trans. Harry Shukman) (Rocklin, Calif., 1992) pp. 570–4.
112. Khrushchev, *Khrushchev Remembers*, p. 318.
113. S. I. Alliluyeva, *Twenty Letters to a Friend* (London, 1967) pp. 16–18; Shepilov also noted this (Volkogonov, p. 574).

5 FIRST AMONG EQUALS

1. N. S. Khrushchev, *Khrushchev Remembers: The Last Testament* (Boston, 1974) p. 79.
2. *Pravda*, 6 March 1953.
3. *Pravda*, 7 March 1953.
4. *Pravda*, 7 March 1953.
5. Secretaries Mikhailov, Ignat'ev and Shatalin; Presidium members Saburov and Pervukhin; and Presidium candidates Mel'nikov and Ponomarenko. There is also good reason to believe that Azerbaijani party leader M. D. Bagirov, a candidate member who is generally reckoned a Beria client, was by then in Malenkov's camp, not Beria's. See W. J. Tompson, *Nikita Khrushchev and the Territorial Apparatus, 1957–1964* (D.Phil. thesis, University of Oxford, 1991) pp. 59–63.
6. This charge was first directed at Malenkov at the January 1955 plenum (Iu. V. Aksiutin and O. V. Volobuev, *XX S"ezd KPSS: novatsii i dogmy* [Moscow, 1991] p. 34); see also Khrushchev, *Khrushchev Remembers* (London, 1971) pp. 323–4.
7. 'Plenum TsK KPSS: iiul' 1953 goda: stenograficheskii otchet', *Izvestiia TsK KPSS* 1 (January 1991) p. 150.
8. *Pravda*, 7 March 1953.
9. R. Medvedev, *Khrushchev: politicheskaia biografiia* (Moscow, 1990) p. 67.
10. *Pravda*, 10 March 1953.
11. *Pravda*, 16 March 1953.
12. *Pravda*, 8, 9 and 10 March 1953. The original of the Stalin–Malenkov–Mao shot appeared in *Pravda*, 14 February 1950.
13. RTsKhIDNI (former Central Party Archive) f. 629, op. 1, d. 54, l. 69; *Pravda*, 27 October 1989.
14. *Literaturnaia gazeta*, 19 March 1953; K. Simonov, 'On okazalsia printsipial'nee i energichnee, chem vse ostal'nye', in Iu. V. Aksiutin (ed.), *N. S. Khrushchev: materialy k biografii* (Moscow, 1989) pp. 27–30.

15. 'Problemy istorii i sovremennosti', *Voprosy istorii KPSS* 2 (February 1989) p. 53; the references are to Voroshilov, Kaganovich and Molotov respectively.
16. L. A. Openkin, *Ottepel': kak eto bylo* (Moscow, 1991) p. 35.
17. *Trud*, 14 March 1991; 'Khrushchevskie vremena', in V. A. Kozlov (ed.), *Neizvestnaia Rossiia: XX vek* (Moscow, 1992) p. 274.
18. *Pravda*, 21 March 1953.
19. Aksiutin and Volobuev, p. 47.
20. Andrei Malenkov takes this view of his father; A. G. Malenkov, *O moem ottse Georgii Malenkove* (Moscow, 1992) especially pp. 57, 61, 70–8.
21. Malenkov, p. 34; L. A. Openkin, 'Na istoricheskom pereput'e', *Voprosy istorii KPSS* 1 (January 1990) p. 107.
22. Openkin, *Ottepel'*, p. 47.
23. For evidence of an early rupture between Malenkov and Beria, see Tompson, pp. 38–40.
24. *Pravda*, 17 December 1953; *Sovetskaia Belorussiia*, 18 April 1953; *Pravda Ukrainy*, 11 April 1953; *Kommunist* (Erevan) 18 April 1953; *Sovetskaia Moldaviia*, 19 April 1953; *Sovetskaia Estoniia*, 28 April 1953; *Sovetskaia Latviia*, 14 April 1953; *Sovetskaia Litva*, 26 April 1953.
25. *Zaria vostoka*, 15 and 16 April 1953.
26. Khrushchev, *Khrushchev Remembers*, p. 332.
27. *Vedomosti Verkhovnogo Soveta SSSR* no. 4 (776) 28 March 1953, p. 1; *Pravda*, 28 March 1953; Khrushchev, *Khrushchev Remembers*, pp. 325–6.
28. *Pravda*, 6 April 1953.
29. *Pravda*, 17 April and 1 May 1953; *Trud*, 17 April 1953; *Izvestiia*, 26 and 28 April 1953; *Zaria vostoka*, 23 April 1953.
30. *Pravda*, 9 October 1952; for an analysis of the speech, see C. H. Fairbanks, Jr, 'National Cadres as a Force in the Soviet System: The Evidence of Beria's Career, 1949–1953', in J. Azrael (ed.), *Soviet Nationality Policies and Practices* (New York, 1978).
31. *Pravda*, 10 March 1953.
32. Khrushchev, *Khrushchev Remembers*, p. 330.
33. For the text of one such decree, see Radio Liberty, *Sobranie dokumentov samizdata* (New York, 1972) 21, no. 1042:3.
34. *Pravda*, 13 June 1952; *Izvestiia*, 19 June 1953.
35. *Pravda Ukrainy*, 12, 18, 19, 21 and 26 June 1953.
36. *Sovetskaia Latviia*, 28 June 1953; *Sovetskaia Litva*, 18 June 1953.
37. *Sovetskaia Rossiia*, 19 February 1989.
38. Wolfgang Leonhard, *The Kremlin since Stalin* (Oxford, 1962) pp. 70–1.
39. 'Plenum TsK KPSS', pp. 143–4, 157–8, 161–3; Molotov's account is closer to the Germans' view; see F. Chuev, *Sto sorok besed s Molotovym* (Moscow, 1991) pp. 332–3.
40. 'Plenum TsK KPSS', pp. 143, 164.
41. A. I. Adzhubei, *Krushenie illiuzii: vremia v sobytiiakh i litsakh*

(Moscow, 1991) p. 39; 'Plenum TsK KPSS', p. 158; Khrushchev, *Khrushchev Remembers*, pp. 326–8.

42. Partarkhiv TsK KPU (Ukrainian Party Archive) f. 1, op. 1, d. 1142; published in *Novaia i noveishaia istoriia* 3 (May–June 1989) pp. 169–76.
43. Khrushchev, *Khrushchev Remembers*, pp. 330–1.
44. Khrushchev, *Khrushchev Remembers*, pp. 331–5; Khrushchev almost certainly exaggerates his own role in the plot to remove Beria, but all of the other principals who have left accounts of the episode agree that he was the prime mover behind Beria's demise. See A. Antonov-Ovseenko, *Kar'era palacha* (Omsk, 1991) pp. 429–34. Even Molotov, a man who never concealed his contempt for Khrushchev, gave him the credit for Beria's defeat – Chuev, p. 343–5; *Literaturnaia gazeta*, 18 April 1990.
45. F. Burlatsky, *Khrushchev and the First Russian Spring* (New York, 1991) p. 36; Antonov-Ovseenko, pp. 429–30.
46. The commander was believed to be loyal to Beria and had therefore been sent to Smolensk Province to watch troop manoeuvres.
47. Khrushchev, *Khrushchev Remembers*, pp. 336–7; Chuev, pp. 343–5.
48. Chuev, pp. 344–5.
49. Khrushchev, *Khrushchev Remembers*, p. 337.
50 *Pravda*, 24 December 1953.
51. 'Plenum TsK KPSS', pp. 141–5.
52. 'Plenum TsK KPSS', pp. 155–6, 159, 169.
53. 'Plenum TsK KPSS', p. 159.
54. 'Plenum TsK KPSS', pp. 145, 147, 149, 155, 159, 166.
55. 'Plenum TsK KPSS', p. 155.
56. 'Plenum TsK KPSS', pp. 147, 166.
57. *Pravda*, 10 July 1953.
58. *Piat'desiat let Kommunisticheskoi partii Sovetskogo Soiuza* (Moscow, 1953) p. 28.
59. See, for example, *Pravda*, 16 April and 13 July 1953.
60. J. F. Hough and M. R. Fainsod, *How the Soviet Union is Governed* (Cambridge, Mass., 1979) pp. 192–3; G. Gill, 'Khrushchev and Systemic Development', in M. McCauley (ed.), *Khrushchev and Khrushchevism* (London, 1987) p. 33.
61. *Pravda*, 16 March 1953; *Vedomosti Verkhovnogo Soveta SSSR* no. 2 (274) p. 2, and no. 3 (275) p. 1.
62. H. Schwartz, *The Soviet Economy since Stalin* (London, 1965) p. 56; A. Nove, *The Soviet Economy*, 3rd edn (London, 1968) p. 70; A. Nove, *An Economic History of the USSR* (London, 1982) p. 296.
63. *Direktivy KPSS i Sovetskogo pravitel'stva po khoziaistvennym voprosam, tom 4: 1953–57 gody* (Moscow, 1958) pp. 7–16.
64. *Pravda*, 19 March, 26 April and 20 May 1953.
65. *Izvestiia*, 1 April 1953; Malenkov was credited with the price cuts by *Kommunist, Bakinskii rabochii, Kazakhstanskaia pravda, Pravda vostoka* and *Pravda Ukrainy*, 1 April 1953. See also Nove, *Economic History*, p. 326.

66. T. H. Rigby, 'Khrushchev and the Resuscitation of the Central Committee', *Australian Outlook* 13, no. 3 (September 1959) p. 68.
67. *Pravda*, 16 April 1953.
68. *Vechnerniaia Moskva*, 19 September 1952.
69. *Pravda*, 8 May 1953.
70. *Pravda*, 14, 28 and 29 May, and 10 June 1953.
71. *Izvestiia*, 18 March 1953; *Voprosy Ekonomiki* 4 (April 1953) pp. 78–95. See S. I. Ploss, *Conflict and Decision-making in Soviet Russia: A Case Study of Soviet Agriculture, 1953–63* (Princeton, 1965) p. 62.
72. *Izvestiia*, 9 August 1953.
73. For statements on this issue in the autumn of 1953, see *Pravda*, 9 August 1953 (Malenkov) and 25 October 1953 (Trade Minister A. I. Mikoian); *Izvestiia*, 1 November 1953 (Minister for the Consumer Goods Industry A. I. Kosygin).
74. *Pravda*, 6 October 1952 and 9 August 1953.
75. *Pravda*, 15 September 1953.
76. *Pravda*, 15 September 1953.
77. *Pravda*, 15 September 1953.
78. M. Efremov, 'O rabote sel'skogo raikoma partii', *Kommunist* 7 (May 1954) pp. 76–85.
79. *Pravda*, 20 November 1953, 1, 10 and 12 February 1954; *Kommunist* (Erevan) 4 December 1953; *Bakinskii rabochii*,16 July 1953.
80. Ernst Kux, 'Technicians of Management versus Managers of Technique', in S. I. Ploss (ed.), *The Soviet Political Process* (London, 1971) p. 176.
81. *Vedomosti Verkhovnogo Soveta* no. 22 (794) (29 December 1953) p. 1.
82. R. Medvedev, *Khrushchev: politicheskaia biografiia* (Moscow, 1991) pp. 74–5; Adzhubei, p. 40.
83. Aksiutin and Volobuev, pp. 9–11.
84. A. Dugin, 'GULAG glazami istorika', *Soiuz* 9 (September 1990) p. 16.
85. *Pravda*, 10 March 1953.
86. *Pravda*, 25 April, 1 and 24 May 1953.
87. M. Beschloss, *MAYDAY: Eisenhower, Khrushchev and the U-2 Affair* (London, 1986) p. 73.
88. *Pravda*, 9 August 1953.
89. *Literaturnaia gazeta*, 23 April and 1 May 1953.
90. *Literaturnaia gazeta*, 16 April 1953 (Berggolts); I. Ehrenburg, 'O rabote pisatelia', *Znamia* 10 (October 1953); K. Paustovskii, 'Poeziia pravdy', *Znamia* 9 (September 1953).
91. V. Pomerantsev, 'Ob iskrennosti v literature', *Novyi Mir* 12 (December 1953); L. Kopelev and R. Orlova, *My zhili v Moskve, 1956–1980* (Moscow, 1990) p. 12.
92. A. Khachaturian, 'O tvorcheskoi smelosti i vdokhnovenii', *Sovetskaia muzyka* 11 (November 1953).
93. Kopelev and Orlova, p. 9.
94. Khrushchev did not like it; Khrushchev, *Last Testament*, p. 78.
95. *Pravda*, 10 March 1963.
96. *Pravda* 6 October 1952. The authorities had decided before the war

that satire had outlived its usefulness: in a socialist society where no class antagonisms remain, there are no objects of satirical comment (M. R. Zezina, 'Iz istorii obshchestvennogo soznaniia perioda "ottepeli": problemy svoboda tvorchestva', *Vestnik Moskovskogo universiteta: seriia 8: istoriia* 6 [November–December 1992] p. 19).

97. *Literaturnaia gazeta,* 30 January and 29 March 1954; *Pravda,* 25 March and 3 June 1954; L. Skorino, 'Razgovor nachistotu', *Znamia* 2 (February 1954).

98. *Literaturnaia gazeta,* 28 March, 15, 19 and 24 June, 1, 8 and 17 July 1954.

99. *Literaturnaia gazeta,* 17 August 1954.

100. *Vtoroi s"ezd sovetskikh pisatelei* (Moscow, 1955) p. 32.

101. *Vtoroi s"ezd,* p. 8.

102. N. S. Khrushchev, *Stroitel'stvo kommunizma v SSSR i razvitie sel'skogo khoziaistva,* vol. 1 (Moscow, 1962) pp. 89, 133, 153, 197, 222.

103. 'Plenum TsK KPSS', p. 153.

104. The other Presidium members' speeches before the 1954 Supreme Soviet elections reveal their lack of interest in Virgin Lands. See *Pravda,* 6–13 March 1954.

105. *Pravda,* 7 March and 27 April 1954 (Khrushchev) and 13 March and 27 April 1954 (Malenkov).

106. *Pravda,* 27 April 1954.

107. *Pravda,* 17 August 1954.

108. *Pravda,* 21 and 28 September, 9, 14 and 20 October, 2, 10, 16, 23 and 25 November and 25 December 1954.

109. K. I. Koval', 'Peregovory I. V. Stalina s Chzhou Enlaem v 1953 g. v Moskve i N. S. Khrushcheva s Mao Tszedunom v 1954 g. v Pekine', *Novaia i noveishaia istoriia* 5 (September–October 1989) pp. 108–11; Koval' was the foreign ministry official heading the Soviet side in the negotiations.

110. Koval', pp. 112–13.

111. Koval', p. 115.

112. Khrushchev, *Last Testament,* pp. 246–50.

113. Khrushchev, *Last Testament,* p. 245.

114. Khrushchev, *Last Testament,* pp. 245–6.

115. Openkin, *Ottepel',* pp. 54–5.

116. *Pravda,* 17 November 1989.

117. Koval', pp. 113–14, 118–19; Openkin, *Ottepel',* p. 55.

118. V. Alekseev, 'Pered "Ottepeliu"', *Glasnost',* 26 December 1991, p. 7.

119. *Pravda,* 11 November 1954.

120. H. Schwartz, *The Soviet Economy since Stalin* (London, 1965) pp. 70–1.

121. *Pravda,* 6 November 1954.

122. See *Voprosy ekonomiki* 11 (November 1954) and 12 (December 1954).

123. *Pravda* and *Izvestiia,* 21 December 1954.

124. *Pravda* and *Izvestiia,* 22–31 December 1954, 1 and 5 January 1955.

125. *Pravda,* 24 January 1955; *Pravda Ukrainy, Sovetskaia Moldaviia, Sovet-*

skaia Belorussiia, 25 January 1955; and *Pravda vostoka*, 27 January 1955.

126. *Pravda*, 3 February 1955.

127. Aksiutin and Volobuev, pp. 59–60.

6 DETHRONING STALIN

1. R. Conquest, *The Great Terror* (Harmondsworth, 1971) p. 59.

2. Khrushchev, *Khrushchev Remembers: The Glasnost' Tapes* (Boston, 1990) pp. 74–5.

3. Khrushchev, *The Glasnost' Tapes*, p. 80.

4. A. Horne, *Harold Macmillan, Vol. II: 1957–1986* (New York, 1989) p. 120.

5. N. S. Khrushchev, *Khrushchev Remembers: The Last Testament* (Boston, 1974) p. 358.

6. A. I. Adzhubei, *Krushenie illiuzii: vremia v sobytiiakh i litsakh* (Moscow, 1991) p. 153.

7. *Soviet News*, 27 May 1955.

8. N. S. Khrushchev, *Khrushchev Remembers* (London, 1971) p. 379; H. Hanak, *Soviet Foreign Policy since the Death of Stalin* (London, 1972) p. 145; E. Crankshaw, *Khrushchev: A Biography* (London, 1966) p. 22.

9. Khrushchev, *Khrushchev Remembers*, pp. 343–4.

10. F. Chuev, *Sto sorok besed s Molotovym* (Moscow, 1991) pp. 349, 351.

11. *Pravda*, 17 November 1989.

12. Chuev, pp. 347–9; *Pravda*, 9 February 1955; *Kommunist* 14 (October 1955).

13. Radio Tbilisi, 22 November 1955; cited in R. Conquest, *Power and Policy in the USSR: The Study of Soviet Dynastics* (London, 1961) pp. 449–51.

14. N. S. Khrushchev, 'O kul'te lichnosti i ego posledstviiakh', *Izvestiia TsK KPSS* 3 (March 1989) p. 157; *Bakinskii rabochii*, 27 May 1956.

15. *Pravda*, 13 July 1955; Khrushchev, *Khrushchev Remembers*, p. 377.

16. Khrushchev, *Khrushchev Remembers*, p. 393.

17. Khrushchev, *Khrushchev Remembers*, p. 395.

18. M. R. Beschloss, *MAYDAY: Eisenhower, Khrushchev and the U-2 Affair* (London, 1986) pp. 162–3.

19. Khrushchev, *Khrushchev Remembers*, pp. 397, 399; Khrushchev, *Last Testament*, p. 363.

20. H. Macmillan, *Tides of Fortune* (New York, 1969) p. 622.

21. Khrushchev, *Khrushchev Remembers*, p.400.

22. *Pravda*, 4 February 1955, 7 March 1955, 29 March 1955; *Izvestiia*, 27 April 1955; *Kommunist* 7 (May 1955) pp. 7–8, 11; 9 (June 1955) p. 45; 10 (July 1955) pp. 6–7.

23. Coverage of the conference can be found in *Pravda* and *Izvestiia*, 17 and 19 May 1955, and in 'Ocherki nashikh dnei – tri dnia v Kremle', *Novyi Mir* 7 (July 1955).

308 *Notes*

24. *Direktivy KPSS i Sovetskogo pravitel'stva po khoziaistvennym voprosam, tom 4: 1953–1957* (Moscow, 1958) pp. 398–9.
25. *Pravda*, 3 and 9 April,10 May and 17 July 1955.
26. *XX S"ezd Kommunisticheskoi Partii Sovetskogo Soiuza: stenograficheskii otchet* (Moscow, 1956) vol. 1, pp. 106–7.
27. Roy D. Laird, 'Decontrols or New Controls? The "Reform" of Soviet Agricultural Administration', *Problems of Communism* VI, no. 4 (July–August 1957) p. 27.
28. *Direktivy*, pp. 365–71.
29. G. A. E. Smith, 'Agriculture', in M. McCauley (ed.) *Khrushchev and Khrushchevism* (London, 1987) p. 100.
30. See, for example, *Pravda*, 15 September 1953, 21 March 1954 and 3 February 1955; for an excellent discussion of Khrushchev's attitudes toward administration, see G. Breslauer, *Khrushchev and Brezhnev as Leaders: Building Authority in Soviet Politics* (London, 1982) pp. 42–6.
31. F. Burlatsky, *Khrushchev and the First Russian Spring* (New York, 1991) p. 14.
32. *Pravda*, 3 March 1955.
33. Conquest, p. 285.
34. These were N. P. Dudorov (MVD) I. A. Serov (KGB) and R. A. Rudenko (Procurator General).
35. *XX S"ezd*, vol. 1, p. 3.
36. *XX S"ezd*, vol. 1, p. 102.
37. Khrushchev, *Khrushchev Remembers*, p. 351.
38. Khrushchev, *Khrushchev Remembers*, p. 348.
39. 'Ulitsa Mandel'shtama', *Ogonek* 1 (January 1991) p. 21.
40. Chuev, pp. 350–1.
41. N. A. Mukhitdinov, '12 let s Khrushchevym', *Argumenty i fakty* 44 (October 1989) p. 5; Khrushchev, *Khrushchev Remembers*, pp. 347–9.
42. Khrushchev, *Khrushchev Remembers: The Glasnost' Tapes* (Boston, 1990) p. 43.
43. *XX S"ezd*, vol. 1, pp. 302, 323, 325–6.
44. Khrushchev, 'O kul'te lichnosti', p. 128.
45. Quoted in M. Frankland, *Khrushchev* (Harmondsworth, 1966) p. 124.
46. Khrushchev, *Khrushchev Remembers*, p. 353, and *Glasnost' Tapes*, p. 44.
47. Khrushchev, 'O kul'te lichnosti', p. 165.
48. *Sovety narodnykh deputatov* 5 (February 1989) p. 110.
49. Aksiutin and Volobuev, pp. 102, 205; S. Vukmanovich-Tempo, 'Revoliutsiia na marshe', *Kommunist vooruzhennykh sil* 10 (October 1989) pp. 86–7.
50. *Sovety narodnykh deputatov* 5 (February 1989) p. 111.
51. *Pravda*, 15 February 1956.
52. *Pravda*, 15 February 1956.
53. *Pravda*, 15 February 1956.
54. *XX S"ezd*, pp. 88–90.
55. Khrushchev, 'O kul'te lichnosti', pp. 151–2.

56. These were: Furtseva (Moscow) Brezhnev (Kazakhstan) Mukhit-dinov (Uzbekistan) and Shepilov (editor of *Pravda*).
57. For a more detailed discussion of the personnel changes at the XX Congress, see W. J. Tompson, *Nikita Khrushchev and the Territorial Apparatus, 1953–1964* (D.Phil. thesis, University of Oxford, 1991) pp. 133–5.
58. L. Vasil'eva, *Kremlevskie zheny* (Moscow, 1993) pp. 445–6.
59. E. Fuller, 'Georgia, Stalin and the Demonstrations of 1956', *Radio Liberty* 190/88 (3 May 1988).
60. 'Khrushchevskie vremena', in V. A. Kozlov (ed.) *Neizvestnaia Rossiia: XX vek* (Moscow, 1992) pp. 297–8.
61. *Pravda*, 28 March and 5 April 1956.
62. W. Leonhard, *The Kremlin since Stalin* (London, 1962) pp. 202, 205.
63. R. Medvedev, *Khrushchev: politicheskaia biografiia* (Moscow, 1990) pp. 108–9.
64. *Pravda*, 20 April 1956.
65. Khrushchev, *Khrushchev Remembers*, p. 413; A. Dallin, *Soviet Foreign Policy after Stalin* (Philadelphia, 1961) p. 238.
66. Khrushchev, *Khrushchev Remembers*, pp. 406–7.
67. *Pravda*, 2 July 1956.
68. *Pravda*, 6 and 24 July 1956.
69. RTsKhIDNI (former Central Party Archive) f. 556, op. 1, d. 608, ll. 157, 242; f. 556, op. 1, d. 603, l. 220; f. 556, op. 2, d. 760, ll. 31–3; M. R. Zezina, 'Iz istorii obshchestvennogo soznaniia perioda 'ottepeli': problemy svobody tvorchestva', *Vestnik Moskovskogo universiteta, seriia 8: istoriia* 6 (November–December 1992) p. 23; B. Nazarova and O. Gridnevoi, 'K voprosu ob otstavanii dramaturgii i teatra', *Voprosy filosofii* 5 (May 1956).
70. Khrushchev, *Last Testament*, pp. 72–3, 79.
71. *XX S"ezd*, vol. 1, p. 117.
72. See the Soviet press reaction to Poznan in *Pravda*, 1 July 1956.
73. AVP RF (Foreign Policy Archive of the Russian Federation) f. 059, op. 36, p. 8, d. 43, ll. 22–9, 37–8; in V. L. Musatov, 'SSSR i vengerskie sobytiia 1956g: novye arkhivnye materialy', *Novaia i noveishaia istoriia* 1 (January–February 1993) p. 7.
74. Musatov, pp. 8–9.
75. Khrushchev, *Last Testament*, pp. 198–9.
76. Khrushchev, *Last Testament*, p. 200, 203–4; *Glasnost' Tapes*, p. 115; Musatov, p. 9.
77. The account of the meeting is based on the stenographic record of an aide to the Czechoslovak leader Novotny; Musatov, p. 10.
78. Musatov, pp. 14–15; Khrushchev, *Glasnost' Tapes*, pp. 122–3.
79. V. Micunovic, *Moskauer Tagebücher, 1956–58* (Stuttgart, 1982) pp. 173–97; Khrushchev, *Khrushchev Remembers*, p. 421.
80. AVP RF, f. 059, op. 36, p. 8, d. 45, ll. 134–8; Musatov, p. 18.
81. Musatov, pp. 18–19.
82. *Pravda*, 6 November 1956.
83. Khrushchev, *Khrushchev Remembers*, p. 436.
84. *The Times*, 19 November 1956.

85. See, for example, the *New York Times*, 17 September 1959.
86. TsGAODgM (former Moscow Party Archive) f. 8132, op. 1, d. 17, l. 112.
87. TsGAODgM, f. 8132, op. 1, d. 13, l. 22.
88. H. Schwartz, *The Soviet Economy since Stalin* (London, 1965) pp. 86–7.
89. *Pravda*, 25 and 26 December 1956.
90. 'Problemy istorii i sovremennosti', *Voprosy istorii KPSS* 2 (February 1989) p. 53.
91. *Pravda*, 19 January 1957.

7 KHRUSHCHEV TRIUMPHANT

1. N. Barsukov, 'Kak byl "nizlozhen" N. S. Khrushchev', *Obshchestvennye nauki* 6 (November 1989) p. 134.
2. *Zasedaniia Verkhovnogo Soveta SSSR: stenograficheskii otchet* 4(6) (Moscow,1957) pp. 15–51, 731.
3. M. McCauley, *Khrushchev and the Development of Soviet Agriculture: The Virgin Lands Programme, 1953–1964* (London, 1976) p. 91.
4. *Pravda*, 16 February 1957.
5. *New York Herald Tribune*, 21 February 1957 (Khrushchev interview with Joseph Alsop).
6. *Pravda* and *Izvestiia*, 30 and 31 March 1957.
7. *Pravda*, 8 May 1957.
8. For a detailed examination of the press discussion of the theses in both central and local papers, see W. J. Tompson, *Nikita Khrushchev and the Territorial Apparatus* (D.Phil. thesis, University of Oxford, 1991) pp. 153–72.
9. See, for example, *Izvestiia*, 5, 12, 16, 20 and 27 April 1957; *Pravda*, 4, 8, 10 and 14 April 1957.
10. V. N. Novikov, 'V gody rukovodstva N. S. Khrushcheva', *Voprosy istorii* 1 (January 1989) p. 108; *Pravda*, 3, 14 ,19 and 25 April, 3 and 7 May 1957; *Izvestiia*, 14 April 1957.
11. For the details of these changes, see Tompson, pp. 157–68.
12. *Pravda*, 8 May 1957.
13. 'Sovershenstvovat' rabotu partiinykh shkol', *Partiinaia zhizn'* 10 (May 1957) pp.29–31.
14. *Pravda*, 24 May 1957.
15. *Plenum Tsentral'nogo Komiteta Kommunisticheskoi Partii Sovetskogo Soiuza, 15–19 dekabria 1958 goda: stenograficheskii otchet* (Moscow, 1958) pp. 421–3.
16. N. A. Barsukov, 'Proval antipartiinoi gruppy', *Kommunist* 8 (May 1990) p. 99. Barsukov's article is based on the stenographic record of the June 1957 Central Committee plenum. Unless indicated otherwise, the account which follows is based on Barsukov's reconstruction of events.
17. Khrushchev later tried to re-write history and cast Malenkov as a conservative all along: the Party press linked him closely with

Molotov and denied his association with post-Stalin reform measures. The 1953 decrees concerning output of consumer goods and processed foods were expunged from the record; they did not appear in the authoritative compendium of economic decrees published the following year; *Direktivy KPSS i Sovetskogo pravitel'stva po khoziaistvennym voprosam*, vol. 4 (Moscow, 1958).

18. *Ustav Kommunisticheskoi Partii Sovetskogo Soiuza* (Moscow, 1952) pp. 3-7.
19. G. I. Voronov, 'Nemnogo vospominanii', *Druzhba narodov* 1 (January 1989) p. 194; P. A. Rodionov, 'Kak nachinalsia zastoi', *Znamia* 8 (August 1989) p. 187.
20. N. A. Mukhitdinov, '12 let s Khrushchevym', *Argumenty i fakty* 44 (November 1989) p. 6; N. G. Egorychev, 'Napravlen poslom', *Ogonek* 6 (February 1989) p. 12.
21. *Pravda*, 4 July 1957.
22. Mzhavanadze, Mazurov, Mukhitdinov, Kalnberzins and Kirilenko respectively.
23. N. S. Khrushchev, 'O kul'te lichnosti i ego posledstviiakh', *Izvestiia TsK KPSS* 3 (March 1989) pp. 145-51.
24. *XXII S"ezd Kommunisticheskoi Partii Sovetskogo Soiuza: stenograficheskii otchet*, vol. 2 (Moscow, 1961) p. 588.
25. N. S. Khrushchev, 'Za tesnuiu sviaz' literatury i iskusstva s zhizn'iu naroda', *Kommunist* 12 (August 1957) pp. 11-29; *Pravda*, 7 November 1957.
26. M. R. Zezina, 'Iz istorii obshchestvennogo soznaniia perioda "ottepeli": problemy svobody tvorchestva', *Vestnik Moskovskogo universiteta, seriia 8: istoriia* 6 (November–December 1992) p. 24.
27. S. I. Chuprinin (ed.) *Ottepel', 1957-1959: stranitsy russkoi sovetskoi literatury* (Moscow, 1990) p. 375.
28. Unless indicated otherwise, the account of Zhukov's removal which follows is based on published excerpts from the October 1957 Central Committee Plenum. See 'Khrushchev protiv Zhukova', *Glasnost'* 3, 10 and 17 October 1991.
29. *Pravda*, 16 July 1957.
30. *Krasnaia zvezda*, 5 July 1957.
31. Novikov, p. 108.
32. *Pravda*, 8 May 1957; *Zasedaniia Verkhovnogo Soveta SSSR: stenograficheskii otchet* 5(2) (Moscow, 1957) pp. 693-4.
33. Novikov, p. 108.
34. A. I. Adzhubei, *Krushenie illiuzii: vremia v sobytiiakh i litsakh* (Moscow, 1991) p. 196.
35. *Pravda*, 3 November 1957.
36. A. Horelick and M. Rush, *Strategic Power and Soviet Foreign Policy* (Chicago, 1966) p. 43.
37. *Pravda*, 22 December 1957.
38. N. S. Khrushchev, *Khrushchev Remembers: The Last Testament* (Boston, 1974) p. 126; *Plenum Tsentral'nogo Komiteta KPSS, 15-19 dekabria 1958 goda: stenograficheskii otchet* (Moscow, 1959) p. 422.
39. *Pravda*, 1 and 14 March 1958.

40. *Pravda*, 26 January 1958; N. S. Khrushchev, *Stroitel'stvo kommunizma v SSSR i razvitie sel'skogo khoziaistva*, vol. 3 (Moscow, 1962) pp. 131–2.
41. *Pravda*, 8 May 1957.
42. *Pravda*, 31 January 1958.
43. M. Tatu, *Power in the Kremlin: From Khrushchev's Decline to Collective Leadership* (London, 1969) p. 117.
44. *Vedomosti Verkhovnogo Soveta SSSR* 9 (May 1958) p. 499.
45. The memorandum was subsequently published in *Pravda*, 21 September 1958 and as a pamphlet: N. S. Khrushchev, *Ob ukreplenii sviazi shkoly s zhizn'iu* (Moscow, 1958).
46. *Pravda*, 16 November 1958.
47. Khrushchev, *Khrushchev Remembers*, p. 472; *Last Testament*, pp. 259–60; *Glasnost Tapes*, pp. 148–51.
48. N. T. Fedorenko, 'Vizit N. Khrushcheva v Pekin', in N. V. Popov (ed.) *Arkhivy raskryvaiut svoi tainy* (Moscow, 1991) pp. 184–5.
49. *Pravda*, 11 November 1958.
50. M. Beschloss, *MAYDAY: Eisenhower, Khrushchev and the U-2 Affair* (London, 1986) p. 152.
51. *Pravda*, 26 January 1958.
52. R. Barnet, *The Alliance: America, Europe, Japan: Makers of the Postwar World* (New York, 1983) p. 181.
53. Chuprinin, p. 406.
54. Chuprinin, p. 408.
55. *Ogonek* 24 (June 1989) p. 24.
56. *Literaturnaia gazeta*, 4 and 6 November 1958.
57. See, for example, *Pravda*, 26 October and 6 November 1958; *Literaturnaia gazeta*, 25 October and 1 November 1958.
58. Adzhubei, p. 260.
59. Khrushchev, *Glasnost Tapes*, pp. 195–6.
60. S. I. Chuprinin, pp. 418–20.
61. V. E. Semichastnyi, 'Ia by spravilsia s liuboi raboty', *Ogonek* 24 (June) 1989, p. 24.
62. Tatu, p. 55.
63. McCauley, pp. 91–2.
64. *Pravda*, 14 November 1958.
65. *Plenum Tsentral'nogo Komiteta Kommunisticheskoi Partii Sovetskogo Soiuza, 15–19 dekabria 1958 goda: stenograficheskii otchet* (Moscow, 1959).
66. Barsukov, p. 125.
67. Barsukov, p. 125.
68. Barsukov, p. 125; A. Adzhubei, 'Po sledam odnogo iubileia', *Ogonek* 41 (October 1989) p. 8.

8 FRUSTRATION

1. *Pravda*, 28 January 1959.
2. *Pravda*, 28 January 1959.

3. *Pravda*, 29 January 1959.
4. *Pravda*, 28 January 1959.
5. *Pravda*, 26 November and 16 December 1958.
6. *Pravda*, 5 February 1959.
7. *Pravda*, 28 January 1959.
8. M. R. Beschloss, *MAYDAY: Eisenhower, Khrushchev and the U-2 Affair* (London, 1986) pp. 173-6.
9. A. Horne, *Harold Macmillan, Vol: II, 1957-1986* (New York, 1989) p. 128.
10. S. I. Chuprinin, *Ottepel', 1957-1959: stranitsy russkoi sovetskoi literatury* (Moscow, 1990) pp. 418-20.
11. Chuprinin, pp. 423, 425.
12. *Pravda*, 25 June through 3 July 1959.
13. *Spravochnik partiinogo rabotnika* (Moscow, 1961) pp. 555-61.
14. Khrushchev, *Last Testament*, pp. 364-5.
15. Khrushchev, *Last Testament*, p. 369.
16. Beschloss, pp. 177-8.
17. Khrushchev, *Last Testament*, pp. 369-72.
18. Beschloss, p. 190.
19. Khrushchev, *Last Testament*, p. 376.
20. Beschloss, p. 193.
21. Khrushchev, *Last Testament*, p. 381.
22. Khrushchev, *Khrushchev Remembers*, p. 371.
23. Beschloss, pp. 204-7, 211-13.
24. Khrushchev, *Last Testament*, pp. 410-12, 415.
25. A. I. Adzhubei (ed.) *Litsom k litsu s Amerikoi* (Moscow, 1959).
26. J. Nogee and R. Donaldson, *Soviet Foreign Policy since World War II* (New York, 1984) p. 227.
27. Khrushchev, *Last Testament*, pp. 263, 308.
28. Nogee and Donaldson, p. 227.
29. *Pravda*, 29 January 1959.
30. *Pravda*, 25 December 1959.
31. *Pravda*, 13 January 1960.
32. *Pravda*, 7 January 1959.
33. *Pravda*, 28 January 1959.
34. *Pravda*, 16 December 1959.
35. 'Khrushchevskie vremena', in V. A. Kozlov (ed.) *Neizvestnaia Rossiia: XX vek* (Moscow, 1992) pp. 275-6.
36. *Pravda*, 15 January 1960.
37. *Pravda*, 15 January 1960.
38. *Pravda*, 16 and 18 October 1959.
39. Khrushchev, *Last Testament*, p. 305.
40. *Pravda*, 27 February 1960.
41. Khrushchev, *Last Testament*, pp. 437-8, 440-2.
42. See, for example, *Pravda*, 26 and 27 April 1960; *New York Times*, 26 April 1960.
43. Beschloss, p. 9.
44. *Pravda*, 5 May 1960.
45. C. Linden, *Khrushchev and the Soviet Leadership with an Epilogue on*

Gorbachev (Baltimore, 1990) pp. 91–106; M. Tatu, *Power in the Kremlin: From Khrushchev's Decline to Collective Leadership* (trans. H. Katel) (London, 1969) pp. 69–100.
46. *Pravda*, 26 April 1960; *New York Times*, 26 April 1960.
47. A. Karaulov, *Vokrug kremlia: kniga politicheskikh dialogov* (Moscow, 1990) p. 35; N. Mukhitdinov, '12 let s Khrushchevym', *Argumenty i fakty* 44 (October 1989) p. 6; S. Khrushchev, *Khrushchev on Khrushchev: An Inside Account of the Man and His Era* (Boston, 1990) pp. 91, 115; Interview with P. Shelest (former Ukrainian party chief) Moscow, 26 December 1990.
48. Mukhitdinov, p. 6; S. Khrushchev, p. 29.
49. *Pravda*, 6 May 1960.
50. *Pravda*, 2 April 1960.
51. *Pravda*, 6 May 1960.
52. Khrushchev, *Last Testament*, pp. 443–4.
53. *Pravda*, 8 May 1960.
54. Khrushchev, *Last Testament*, p. 447; *Pravda*, 13 May 1960.
55. Khrushchev, *Last Testament*, pp. 447–8.
56. Beschloss, p. 257.
57. Khrushchev, *Last Testament*, pp. 451–2.
58. Khrushchev, *Khrushchev Remembers*, pp. 450–2.
59. *Pravda*, 16 May 1960.
60. C. de Gaulle, *Memoirs of Hope: Renewal, 1958–1962* (trans. T. Kilmartin) (London, 1971) pp. 247–9; H. Macmillan, *Pointing the Way, 1959–1961* (New York, 1972) p. 202.
61. Beschloss, p. 279.
62. Khrushchev, *Last Testament*, p. 454.
63. Beschloss, pp. 284–8.
64. Beschloss, pp. 299–300.
65. *Pravda*, 18 May 1960; *Pravda Ukrainy*, 31 May 1960.

9 FROM CRISIS TO CRISIS

1. *Pravda*, 22 September 1964.
2. *Pravda*, 12 and 20 June 1960.
3. *The Observer*, 12 and 19 February 1961.
4. N. S. Khrushchev, *Khrushchev Remembers: The Glasnost Tapes* (Boston, 1990) pp. 153–4.
5. N. S. Khrushchev, *Khrushchev Remembers: The Last Testament* (Boston, 1974) p. 268; *The Observer*, 19 February 1961.
6. Beschloss, *MAYDAY: Eisenhower, Khrushchev and the U-2 Affair* (London, 1986) p. 338.
7. Beschloss, pp. 338–9.
8. A. Horne, *Harold Macmillan: Volume II, 1957–1986* (New York, 1989) p. 279.
9. M. McCauley, *Khrushchev and the Development of Soviet Agriculture* (London, 1976) p. 93.
10. *Pravda*, 29 December 1959.

11. *Pravda*, 21 and 22 January 1961.
12. For further attacks on 'hoodwinking' see *Pravda*, 27 and 31 January 1961.
13. *Pravda*, 1, 5 and 12 February 1961.
14. *XXII S"ezd Kommunisticheskoi Partii Sovetskogo Soiuza: stenograficheskii otchet*, vol. 1 (Moscow, 1962) p. 374.
15. *Sovetskaia Rossiia*, 19 February 1989.
16. N. S. Khrushchev, *Stroitel'stvo kommunizma v SSSR i razvitie sel'skogo khoziaistva*, vol. 4 (Moscow, 1962) p. 109.
17. Khrushchev, *Stroitel'stvo kommunizma*, vol. 4, p. 162.
18. *Spravochnik partiinogo rabotnika* (Moscow, 1961) p. 325.
19. *Pravda*, 21 and 22 January 1961; Khrushchev, *Stroitel'stvo kommunizma*, vol. 5, p. 319.
20. M. Beschloss, *The Crisis Years: Kennedy and Khrushchev* (New York, 1991) p. 233.
21. *New York Times*, 2 January 1961.
22. Beschloss, *Crisis Years*, p. 180.
23. Accounts of Khrushchev's conversations with Kennedy in Vienna are to be found in G. M. Kornienko, 'Upushchennaia vozmozhnost': vstrecha N. S. Khrushcheva i Dzh. Kennedi v Vene v 1961 g.', *Novaia i noveishaia istoriia* 2 (March–April 1992) pp. 98–101 (based on the Soviet side's notes on the meetings) and in Beschloss, *Crisis Years*, pp. 194–231 (based on memoranda drawn up by Kennedy's interpreter).
24. Khrushchev, *Last Testament*, pp. 495–7.
25. Beschloss, *Crisis Years*, p. 234.
26. Horne, p. 303.
27. Associated Press, *The Torch is Passed* (Washington, 1964) p. 40.
28. Khrushchev, *Last Testament*, pp. 497–8, 500; S. Khrushchev, *Khrushchev on Khrushchev: An Inside Account of the Man and His Era* (Boston, 1990) pp. 50–1.
29. G. Kornienko, 'Novoe o karibskom krizise', *Novaia i noveishaia istoriia* 3 (May–June 1991) p. 82.
30. F. Burlatsky, *Khrushchev and the First Russian Spring* (New York, 1991) pp. 162–3.
31. Khrushchev, *Last Testament*, p. 488.
32. Kornienko, 'Upushchennaia vozmozhnost'', pp. 104–5.
33. N. Khrushchev, *Khrushchev Remembers* (London, 1971) p. 456.
34. Khrushchev, *Last Testament*, p. 506.
35. A. Sakharov, *O strane i mire* (New York, 1976) pp. vii–viii.
36. Beschloss, *Crisis Years*, p. 321.
37. *Pravda*, 18 October 1961.
38. RTsKhIDNI (former Central Party Archive) f. 586. op. 1, d. 201, ll. 1–46.
39. 'Dva pis'ma O. V. Kuusinena N. S. Khrushchevu', *Voprosy istorii KPSS* 5 (May 1991) p. 5.
40. RTsKhIDNI, f. 586, op. 1, d. 213, ll. 1–7.
41. *Pravda*, 18 October and 2 November 1961.
42. *Pravda*, 22 September 1964.

316 *Notes*

Notes

43. RTsKhIDNI, f. 586, op. 1, d. 201, ll. 7–8.
44. RTsKhIDNI, f. 586, op. 1, d. 201, l. 7.
45. RTsKhIDNI, f. 586, op. 1, d. 201, l. 11.
46. RTsKhIDNI, f. 586, op. 1, d. 201, ll. 10, 19.
47. RTsKhIDNI, f. 586, op. 1, d. 201, ll. 3–4, 21–26.
48. RTsKhIDNI, f. 586, op. 1, d. 201, ll. 13–14. Khrushchev also hinted publicly that his thinking was moving in this direction; *New York Times*, 21 May 1961.
49. *Pravda*, 30 July 1963.
50. *Pravda*, 18 October 1961.
51. RTsKhIDNI, f. 586, op. 1, d. 212, ll. 1–4; d. 201, l. 1.
52. RTsKhIDNI, f. 586, op. 1, d. 202.
53. *Pravda*, 2 November 1961.
54. *Pravda*, 28 October 1961.
55. *XXII S"ezd*, vol. 3, p. 121.
56. *Argumenty i fakty* 50 (December 1988) p. 3.
57. *XXII S"ezd*, vol.3, p. 344.
58. *XXII S"ezd*, vol. 1, pp. 252–4; F. Burlatsky, p. 130.
59. Burlatsky, pp. 129–30.
60. *Trud*, 26 November 1989; A. Adzhubei, 'Te desiat' let', *Znamia* 7 (July 1988) p. 129; *Pravda*, 13 March 1987, p. 2.
61. 'Khrushchevskie vremena' in V. A. Kozlov (ed.) *Neizvestnaia Rossiia: XX vek* (Moscow, 1992) p. 298; N. Barsukov, 'Kak byl "nizlozhen" N. S. Khrushchev', *Obshchestvennye nauki* 6 (November 1989) p. 124; N. Mukhitdinov, '12 let s Khrushchevym', *Argumenty i fakty* 44 (October 1989) p. 6.
62. A. I. Adzhubei, *Krushenie illiuzii: vremia v sobytiiakh i litsakh* (Moscow, 1991) pp. 248–9.
63. S. Khrushchev, pp. 91, 115; Mukhitdinov, p. 6.
64. *Pravda*, 6 March 1962.
65. *Pravda*, 6 March 1962.
66. *Pravda*, 11 March 1962.
67. See, for example, *Pravda*, 9 and 24 May 1962.
68. *Komsomol'skaia pravda*, 2 June 1989 and 3 June 1990.
69. N. S. Khrushchev, *Khrushchev Remembers: The Glasnost Tapes* (Boston, 1990) pp. 196–7.
70. N. S. Khrushchev, *Stroitel'stvo kommunizma v SSSR i razvitie sel'skogo khoziaistva*, vol. 7 (Moscow, 1963) p. 163; S. Khrushchev, p. 20; G. Voronov, 'Nemnogo vospominanii', *Druzhba narodov* 1 (January 1989) p. 199.
71. *Plenum Tsentral'nogo Komiteta KPSS, 19–23 noiabria 1962 goda: stenograficheskii otchet* (Moscow, 1963) p. 16.
72. G. Hodnett, 'The Obkom First Secretaries', *Slavic Review* 24, no. 4 (December 1965) p. 642.
73. This account of the genesis of Khrushchev's idea is based on a letter from Khrushchev to Castro; F. Burlatsky, 'The Lessons of Personal Diplomacy', *Problems of Communism* XLI (Special Issue, Spring 1992) p. 8.
74. Bruce J. Allyn *et al.*, 'Essence of Revision: Moscow, Havana and the

Cuban Missile Crisis', *International Security* 14 no. 3 (Winter 1989–90) p. 142.
75. See Kornienko, 'Novoe o karibskom krizise', p. 80, on Moscow's assessment of US intentions towards Cuba.
76. N. S. Khrushchev, *Khrushchev Remembers* (London, 1971) pp. 393–5.
77. All of the Soviet participants in the crisis agree that the Presidium backed Khrushchev's initiative from the beginning. See Allyn *et al.*,, p. 147; Vladislav M. Zubok, 'The Missile Crisis and the Problem of Soviet Learning', *Problems of Communism* vol. XLI (Special Issue, Spring 1992) pp. 21–2.
78. Khrushchev, *Last Testament*, p. 511; *Glasnost Tapes*, p. 171; Allyn *et al.*, pp. 141, 148.
79. A. Schlesinger, Jr, 'Onward and Upward from the Cuban Missile Crisis', *Problems of Communism* vol. XLI (Special Issue, Spring 1992) p. 6
80. Allyn, *et al.*, pp. 150–1.
81. Beschloss, *Crisis Years*, p. 393.
82. Allyn *et al.*,, p. 153.
83. The texts of the 25 letters exchanged by Kennedy and Khrushchev between 22 October and 14 December 1962 have been published in *Problems of Communism* vol. XLI (Special Issue, Spring 1992) pp. 28–120. All further references to their correspondence are based on these texts.
84. Beschloss, *Crisis Years*, pp. 317–20, 325–6.
85. Reuters, 21 January 1992.
86. Beschloss, *Crisis Years*, pp. 546–7.
87. Castro did not, however, urge a pre-emptive strike against the United States, as is claimed in Khrushchev, *Glasnost Tapes*, p. 177. This claim reflects Khrushchev's misunderstanding of the text of Castro's letter (now published in L. Chang and P. Kornbluh, *The Cuban Missile Crisis, 1962: A National Security Archive Documents Reader* (New York, 1992) p. 189) and an erroneous translation of the *Glasnost Tapes* material.
88. Schlesinger, p. 7.
89. P. Brenner, 'Kennedy and Khrushchev on Cuba: Two Stages, Three Parties', *Problems of Communism* XLI (Special Issue, Spring 1992) p. 25.
90. S. Khrushchev, p. 20; the stenographic account of the November plenum confirms Sergei Khrushchev's testimony, as does Voronov, 'Nemnogo vospominaniia', p. 199.
91. *Pravda*, 26 December 1962; *Izvestiia*, 19 December 1962 and 8 February 1963; *Ekonomicheskaia gazeta*, 26 January 1963.
92. *Pravda*, 28 September 1962.
93. *Pravda*, 5, 7 and 8 December 1962.
94. *Plenum Tsentral'nogo Komiteta KPSS, 24–26 marta 1965 goda: stenograficheskii otchet* (Moscow, 1965) p. 89; RTsKhIDNI f. 17, op. 94, d. 969, ll. 18–19; *Sovetskaia Rossiia*, 19 February 1989.
95. Voronov, p. 199.
96. A. Baranov and F. Liberman, 'Polozheniia proizvodstvennykh

postavlenii', *Planovoe khoziaistvo* 9 (September 1959) pp. 39–40; *Spravochnik partiinogo rabotnika* (Moscow, 1961) pp. 374ff; *Sobranie postanovlenii pravitel'stva SSSR* (Moscow, 1960) pp. 386–405; W. Tompson, *Nikita Khrushchev and the Territorial Apparatus, 1957–1964* (D.Phil. thesis, University of Oxford, 1991) pp. 241–4; *Vedomosti Verkhovnogo Soveta SSSR* no. 27 (1011) (11 July 1960) p. 447; V. G. Vishniakov and A. I. Zavgorodenko, 'Nekotorye voprosy dal'neishego sovershenstvovaniia upravleniia promyshlennost'iu', *Sovetskoe gosudarstvo i pravo* 12 (December 1960) pp. 3–11.

97. L. A. Openkin, 'Byli li povoroty v sovetskom obshchestve v 50-kh i 60-kh godax?' *Voprosy istorii KPSS* 18 (August 1988) p. 463; S. Khrushchev, pp. 18–20; A. Strelianyi, 'Sub'ektivnye zametki ob N. S. Khrushcheve', in Iu. V. Aksiutin (ed.) *Nikita Sergeevich Khrushchev: materialy k biografii* (Moscow, 1989) p. 190.

10 THE FALL

1. P. Johnson, *Khrushchev and the Arts: The Politics of Soviet Culture, 1962–1964* (Cambridge, Mass., 1965) pp. 103–4.
2. *Pravda*, 2 December 1962.
3. *Izvestiia*, 4 December 1962.
4. N. S. Khrushchev, *Khrushchev Remembers: The Last Testament* (Boston, 1974) p. 82; S. N. Khrushchev, 'That Was How the Time Judged...' in A. Serov (ed.) *Nikita Khrushchev: Life and Destiny* (Moscow, 1989) p. 46.
5. This is also the view of former Presidium member Gennadii Voronov and former Moscow party chief N. G. Egorychev. G. I. Voronov, 'Nemnogo vospominanii', *Druzhba narodov* 1 (January 1989) p. 197; N. G. Egorychev, 'Posle XX S"ezda', *Voprosy istorii KPSS* 5 (May 1991) p. 102.
6. R. Medvedev, *N. S. Khrushchev: politicheskaia biografiia* (Moscow, 1990) p. 253.
7. *Pravda*, 20 June 1962.
8. *Pravda*, 26 April and 19 May 1963.
9. *Pravda*, 22 December 1963.
10. *New York Times*, 29 November 1962.
11. *Literatura i zhizn'*, 24 November 1962.
12. V. Aksenov, 'Kak Nikita possorilsia s pisateliami', *Argumenty i fakty* 45 (November 1991) p. 6.
13. *Pravda*, 29 June 1963.
14. *One Day in the Life* appeared in book form in early 1963, as did other anti-Stalinist works, including Kozevnikov's *The Fleeting Day* and Stadniuk's *Men are not Angels* (Johnson, p. 25).
15. *Pravda*, 10 March 1963.
16. *Pravda*, 10 March 1963.
17. M. Tatu, *Power in the Kremlin: From Khrushchev's Decline to Collective Leadership* (London, 1969) p. 309.

18. See *Pravda*, 10 and 13 December 1962, 7 January, 10 and 14 February 1963.
19. *Pravda*, 14 March and 3 April 1963.
20. *Pravda*, 28 February 1963.
21. *Pravda*, 3 April 1963.
22. *Pravda*, 25 April 1963.
23. *Pravda*, 29 June 1963.
24. *Izvestiia*, 20 June 1963; see *Pravda*, 17 March 1937.
25. *Moscow Radio Home Service*, 19 July 1963, cited in C. Linden, *Khrushchev and the Soviet Leadership: With an Epilogue on Gorbachev* (Baltimore, 1990) pp. 180-1. The published version of the speech is in *Pravda*, 20 July 1963.
26. *Pravda*, 10 May 1958.
27. *Pravda*, 29 June 1963.
28. N. S. Khrushchev, *Stroitel'stvo kommunizma v SSSR i razvitie sel'skogo khoziaistva*, vol. 8 (Moscow, 1964) pp. 23-43.
29. *Pravda*, 11 August 1963.
30. *Literaturnaia gazeta*, 27 June 1963; *Pravda*, 29 June 1963.
31. *Pravda*, 6 September 1963 (Ehrenburg); *Iunost'* 9 (September 1963) (Evtushenko); *Pravda*, 13 October 1963.
32. M. McCauley, *Khrushchev and the Development of Soviet Agriculture: The Virgin Lands Programme, 1953-1964* (London, 1976) p. 95.
33. *Trud*, 29 October 1963; *Pravda*, 27 October and 10 December 1963.
34. *Pravda*, 10 December 1963.
35. *Pravda*, 10 December 1963 and 15 February 1964.
36. *Pravda*, 15 February 1963.
37. *Izvestiia*, 22 December 1963; *Pravda*, 7 and 10 January 1964; such articles appeared frequently in the military newspaper, *Krasnaia zvezda*, as well.
38. *New York Times*, 21 May 1961; Khrushchev, *Last Testament*, p. 146.
39. M. R. Beschloss, *The Crisis Years: Kennedy and Khrushchev, 1960-1963* (New York, 1991) p. 663.
40. *Pravda*, 8 November 1963.
41. N. Barsukov, 'Kak byl "nizlozhen" N. S. Khrushchev', *Obshchestvennye nauki* 6 (November 1989) pp. 124-5.
42. Voronov, pp. 194, 197; *Sovetskaia Rossiia*, 19 February 1989; *Trud*, 14 March 1991; 'Khrushchevskie vremena' in V. A. Kozlov (ed.) *Neizvestnaia Rossiia: XX vek* (Moscow, 1992) pp. 298-9; Interview with P. E. Shelest, Moscow, 26 December 1990.
43. P. Shelest, 'O Khrushcheve, Brezhneve i drugikh', *Argumenty i fakty* 2 (January 1989) pp. 5-6; V. E. Semichastnyi, 'Kak smeshchali N. S. Khrushcheva', *Argumenty i fakty* 20 (May 1989) p. 5; *Trud*, 26 November 1989; S. Khrushchev, *Khrushchev on Khrushchev*, pp. 46-7, 93-6.
44. P. Rodionov, 'Kak nachinalsia zastoi', *Znamia* 8 (August 1989) pp. 185-6, 189-90; N. G. Egorychev, 'Napravlen poslom', *Ogonek* 6 (February 1989) p. 7; *Trud*, 26 November 1989; S. Khrushchev, *Khrushchev on Khrushchev*, pp. 93-6.

45. S. Khrushchev, *Khrushchev on Khrushchev*, pp. 49–50; *Sovetskaia Rossiia*, 19 February 1989.
46. S. Khrushchev, *Khrushchev on Khrushchev*, p. 89, 138, 160; M. Sturua, 'Dve fotografii k odnomu portretu', *Nedelia* 43 (October 1988) p. 17; Semichastnyi, p. 5.
47. S. Khrushchev, *Khrushchev on Khrushchev*, pp. 88–9.
48. S. Khrushchev, *Khrushchev on Khrushchev*, pp. 107–9, 160; Rodionov, p. 189; Sturua, p. 17; A. I. Adzhubei, 'Te desiat' let', *Znamia* 7 (July 1988) p. 129; A. Strelianyi, 'Poslednii romantik', *Druzhba narodov* 11 (November 1988) p. 226.
49. S. Khrushchev, *Khrushchev on Khrushchev*, pp. 18–19, 47, 70, 72, 75–6; A. I. Adzhubei, 'Po sledam odnogo iubileia', *Ogonek* 41 (October 1989) p. 9; Egorychev, 'Posle XX S"ezda', pp. 98–9.
50. *Pravda*, 21 April 1964.
51. *Trud*, 14 March 1991.
52. Rodionov, p. 191; Strelianyi, p. 225; *Trud*, 26 November 1989 and 14 March 1991; N. Barsukov, 'Kak byl "nizlozhen" N. S. Khrushchev', *Obshchestvennye nauki* 6 (November 1989) pp. 130–1; S. Khrushchev, *Khrushchev on Khrushchev*, p. 95.
53. Egorychev, 'Posle XX S"ezda', p. 99; Egorychev, 'Napravlen poslom', p. 7; Barsukov, p. 130.
54. S. Khrushchev, *Khrushchev on Khrushchev*, pp. 18–19.
55. See, for example, *Pravda*, 24–25 February 1964; *Ekonomicheskaia gazeta* 16 April 1964.
56. *Pravda*, 15 December 1963 and 14 July 1964.
57. *Pravda*, 25 July, 22 September and 2 October 1964.
58. Semichastnyi, p. 5; S. Khrushchev, *Khrushchev on Khrushchev*, p. 136; *Trud*, 26 November 1989.
59. Interview with Petr Shelest, Moscow, 26 December 1990.
60. S. Khrushchev, *Khrushchev on Khrushchev*, pp. 136–7, 139, 160; Sturua, p. 17; Semichastnyi, pp. 5–6.
61. Rodionov, p. 186; S. Khrushchev, *Khrushchev on Khrushchev*, p. 135.
62. S. Khrushchev, *Khrushchev on Khrushchev*, pp. 133–6, 139–140n; *Trud*, 26 November 1989; Adzhubei, 'Te desiat' let', p. 129; Semichastnyi, p. 5; A. Karaulov, *Vokrug kremlia: kniga politicheskikh dialogov* (Moscow, 1990) p. 146.
63. Semichastnyi, p. 5.
64. Semichastnyi, p. 5
65. *Trud*, 26 November 1989; S. Khrushchev, *Khrushchev on Khrushchev*, pp. 68–70; Semichastnyi, p. 5.
66. S. Khrushchev, *Khrushchev on Khrushchev*, p. 148; Semichastnyi, p. 5.
67. Semichastnyi, p. 5; Barsukov, p. 133; Egorychev, 'Napravlen', p. 7.
68. S. Khrushchev, *Khrushchev on Khrushchev*, pp. 151–4.
69. Adzhubei, 'Te desiat' let', p. 130.
70. Shelest, p. 5; S. Khrushchev, *Khrushchev on Khrushchev*, pp. 156–7.
71. Shelest, p. 5.
72. Adzhubei, 'Po sledam', p. 8.
73. Tatu, p. 389.

74. S. Khrushchev, *Khrushchev on Khrushchev*, pp. 132–3; F. Burlatsky, 'Mirnyi zagovor protiv N. S. Khrushcheva', in Iu. V. Aksiutin (ed.) *Nikita Sergeevich Khrushchev: materialy k biografii* (Moscow, 1988) p. 211.
75. Barsukov, pp. 124–33; Voronov, pp. 199–201; *Izvestiia*, 18 November 1988; Adzhubei, 'Te desiat' let', p. 129; Adzhubei, 'Po sledam', p. 8; Rodionov, pp. 188, 191; Egorychev, 'Napravlen', p. 7.
76. *Moskovskaia pravda*, 18 August 1989; E. Zubkova, 'Oktiabr' 1964 goda: povorot ili perevorot?', *Kommunist* 13 (September 1989) pp. 93–4; S. Khrushchev, *Khrushchev on Khrushchev*, pp. 70–2, 75–6; Adzhubei, 'Te desiat' let', p. 130.
77. S. Khrushchev, *Khrushchev on Khrushchev*, pp. 149, 153–4; *Trud*, 26 November 1989; *Izvestiia*, 18 November 1988; Rodionov, p. 190; Shelest, p. 5.
78. S. Khrushchev, *Khrushchev on Khrushchev*, pp. 149–50; *Trud*, 26 November 1989.
79. S. Khrushchev, *Khrushchev on Khrushchev*, p. 150.
80. Barsukov, pp. 133–4.
81. Barsukov, pp. 133–4.
82. Shelest, p. 5.
83. S. Khrushchev, *Khrushchev on Khrushchev*, pp. 28, 125; Rodionov, p. 192; Strelianyi, p. 226.
84. Adzhubei, 'Po sledam', p. 9; Voronov, p. 201.
85. Semichastnyi, pp. 5–6; S. Khrushchev, *Khrushchev on Khrushchev*, pp. 158–9.
86. S. Khrushchev, *Khrushchev on Khrushchev*, p. 155.
87. Semichastnyi, p. 6; Barsukov, p. 133; *Izvestiia*, 18 November 1988; Egorychev, 'Napravlen', p. 7; S. Khrushchev, *Khrushchev on Khrushchev*, p. 160.
88. Medvedev, p. 245.
89. S. Khrushchev, *Khrushchev on Khrushchev*, pp. 161–2.
90. Rodionov, 'Kak nachinalsia', p. 191.
91. *Pravda*, 16 October 1964.
92. *Pravda*, 17 October 1964.
93. Khrushchev, *Last Testament*, p. 3.
94. S. Khrushchev, *Khrushchev on Khrushchev*, p. 166.
95. A. I. Adzhubei, *Krushenie illiuzii: vremia v sobytiiakh i litsakh* (Moscow, 1991) p. 13.
96. S. Khrushchev, *Khrushchev on Khrushchev*, pp. 172–3.
97. Adzhubei, *Illiuzii*, pp. 12–13.
98. S. Khrushchev, *Khrushchev on Khrushchev*, pp. 234–8.
99. S. Khrushchev, *Khrushchev on Khrushchev*, pp. 187–8, 227–8.
100. Adzhubei, *Illiuzii*, pp. 122–3.
101. Khrushchev, *Khrushchev on Khrushchev*, pp. 224–5, 325.
102. The Presidium was renamed the Politburo at the time of the XXIII Congress in 1966.
103. Khrushchev, *Khrushchev on Khrushchev*, pp. 246–7.
104. Khrushchev, *Khrushchev on Khrushchev*, pp. 248–52.
105. Khrushchev, *Khrushchev on Khrushchev*, pp. 280–91, 300.

106. Adzhubei, *Illiuzii*, pp. 19–20.
107. Khrushchev, *Last Testament*, p. xv.
108. S. Khrushchev, *Khrushchev on Khrushchev*, pp. 303–4.
109. Khrushchev, *Khrushchev on Khrushchev*, pp. 324, 329.
110. Adzhubei *Illiuzii*, p. 18.
111. A. Zlobin, 'Sanitarnyi den'', *Novoe Vremia* 12 (March 1993) pp. 48, 51.
112. *Pravda*, 13 September 1971.

Bibliography

ARCHIVES

Rossiiskii Tsentr Khraneniia i Izucheniia Dokumentov Noveishei Istorii (All-Russian Centre for the Preservation and Study of Documents of Recent History), funds 17, 556, 586 and 629.
Tsentral'nyi Gosudarstvennyi Arkhiv Obshchestvennykh Dvizhenii g. Moskvy (Central State Archive of Social Movements of the City of Moscow), funds 3, 4, 63, 69 and 160.

DAILY AND WEEKLY NEWSPAPERS

Argumenty i fakty
Bakinskii rabochii
Ekonomicheskaia gazeta
Glasnost'
Izvestiia
Kazakhstanskaia pravda
Kolomenskaia pravda
Kommunist (Erevan)
Komsomol'skaia pravda
Krasnaia zvezda
Literatura i zhizn'
Literaturnaia gazeta
Moskovskaia pravda
New York Herald-Tribune
New York Times
The Observer
Pravda
Pravda Ukrainy
Pravda vostoka
Rabochaia Moskva
Sovetskaia Belorussiia
Sovetskaia Estoniia
Sovetskaia Latviia
Sovetskaia Litva
Sovetskaia Moldaviia
Sovetskaia Rossiia
Sovety narodnykh deputatov
Soviet News
The Times (London)
Trud
Vecherniaia Moskva

324 *Bibliography*

Vedomosti Verkhovnogo Soveta SSSR
Visti VTsVK
Zaria vostoka

SOURCES IN RUSSIAN AND UKRAINIAN

Adzhubei, A. I. *Krushenie Illiuzii: vremia v sobytiiakh i litsakh.* Moscow, 1991.
Adzhubei, A. I. *Litsom k litsu s Amerikoi.* Moscow, 1959.
Adzhubei, A. I. 'Po sledam odnogo iubileia'. *Ogonek* 41 (October 1989).
Adzhubei, A. I. 'Te desiat' let'. *Znamia* 7 (July 1988).
Adzhubei, A. I. *Te desiat' let.* Moscow, 1989.
Aksenov, V. 'Kak Nikita possorilsia s pisateliami'. *Argumenty i fakty* 45 (November 1991).
Aksiutin, Iu. V. (ed.) *Nikita Sergeevich Khrushchev: materialy k biografii.* Moscow, 1989.
Aksiutin, Iu. V. and Volobuev, O. V. *XX S"ezd KPSS: novatsii i dogmy.* Moscow, 1991.
Alekseev, V. 'Pered ottepeliu'. *Glasnost'*, 26 December 1991.
Antonov-Ovseenko, A. *Kar'era palacha.* Omsk, 1991.
Bagramian, I. Kh. *Tak nachalas' voina.* Moscow, 1977.
Baranov, A. and Liberman, F. 'Polozheniia proizvodstvennykh postavlenii'. *Planovoe khoziaistvo* 9 (September 1959).
Barsukov, N. 'Kak byl "nizlozhen" N. S. Khrushchev'. *Obshchestvennye nauki* 6 (November 1989).
Barsukov, N. 'Proval antipartiinoi gruppy'. *Kommunist* 8 (May 1990).
Bogdanov, P. *Rasskaz o pochetnom shakhtere: N. S. Khrushchev v Donbasse.* Stalino, 1961.
Brokgauz, F. A. and Efron, I. A. *Entsiklopedicheskii slovar'.* St Petersburg, 1903.
Chuev, F. *Sto sorok besed s Molotovym.* Moscow, 1991.
Chuprinin, S. I. *Ottepel' 1957-1959: Stranitsy russkoi sovetskoi literatury.* Moscow, 1990.
Desiatii z'izd Komunistichnoi Partii (Bil'shovikiv) Ukraini: stenografichnii zvit. Khar'kov, 1928.
Direktivy KPSS i Sovetskogo pravitel'stva po khoziaistvennym voprosam, tom 4: 1953-57. Moscow, 1958.
Dugin, A. 'GULAG glazami istorika'. *Soiuz* 9 (September 1990).
Efremov, M. 'O rabote sel'skogo raikoma partii'. *Kommunist* 7 (May 1954).
Egorychev, N. G. 'Napravlen poslom'. *Ogonek* 6 (February 1989).
Egorychev, N. G. 'Posle XX S"ezda'. *Voprosy istorii KPSS* 5 (May 1991).
Ehrenburg, I. 'O rabote pisatelia'. *Znamia* 10 (October 1953).
Fedorenko, N. T. 'Vizit N. Khrushcheva v Pekin'. In Popov, N. V. (ed.) *Arkhivy raskryvaiut svoi tainy.* Moscow, 1991.
Ivanova, G. V. (ed.) *Ot ottepelia do zastoia.* Moscow, 1990.
Kak my stroili metro. Moscow, 1935.
Karaulov, A. *Vokrug Kremlia: kniga politicheskikh dialogov.* Moscow, 1990.

Khachaturian, A. 'O tvorcheskoi smelosti i vdokhnovenii'. *Sovetskaia muzyka* 11 (November 1953).

Khrushchev, N. S. *Itogi dekabr'skogo plenuma i zadachi moskovskikh bol'shevikov.* Moscow, 1936.

Khrushchev, N. S. *Itogi iiunskogo Plenuma TsK VKP(b) i zadachi moskovskoi partiinoi organizatsii.* Moscow, 1935.

Khrushchev, N. S. *Nashi zadachi v vosstanovlenii i blagoustroistve gorodov i stroitel'stve v selakh i kolkhozakh.* Moscow, 1945.

Khrushchev, N. S. *Ob ukreplenii sviazi shkoly s zhizn'iu.* Moscow, 1958.

Khrushchev, N. S. 'O kul'te lichnosti i ego posledstviiakh'. *Izvestiia TsK KPSS* 3 (March 1989).

Khrushchev, N. S. *Otchetnyi doklad na moskovskoi X oblastnoi partiinoi konferentsii o rabote MK VKP(b).* Moscow, 1952.

Khrushchev, N. S. *Rech' na obshchegorodskom mitinge trudiashchikhsia Kieva; rech' na IV Kievskoi oblastnoi partiinoi konferentsii.* Kiev, 1938.

Khrushchev, N. S. *Rech' tovarishcha N. S. Khrushcheva na pervom Vsesoiuznom soveshchanii rabochikh i rabotnits stakhanovtsev.* Iakutsk, 1935.

Khrushchev, N. S. *Stroit' prochno, bystro, krasivo i deshevo.* Moscow, 1935.

Khrushchev, N. S. *Stroitel'stvo kommunizma v SSSR i razvitie sel'skogo khoziaistva,* vols 1–8. Moscow, 1962–4.

Khrushchev, N. S. 'Za tesnuiu sviaz' literatury i iskusstva s zhizn'iu naroda'. *Kommunist* 12 (August 1957).

'Khrushchev protiv Zhukova'. *Glasnost',* 3, 10 and 17 October 1991.

Koval', K. I. 'Peregovory I. V. Stalina s Chzhou Enlaem v 1953 g. v Moskve i N. S. Khrushcheva s Mao Tszedunom v 1954 g. v Pekine'. *Novaia i noveishaia istoriia* 5 (September–October 1989).

Kozlov, V. A. (ed.). *Neizvestnaia Rossiia: XX vek.* Moscow, 1992.

Kirpotin, V. 'Russkaia kul'tura'. *Bol'shevik* 12 (June 1938).

Kirshner, L. *Svet i teni velikogo desiatiletiia: N. S. Khrushchev i ego vremia.* Leningrad, 1989.

Kolesnik, A. N. 'Letchik L. N. Khrushchev'. *Voenno-istoricheskii zhurnal* 11 (November 1989).

Kommunisticheskaia Partiia Sovetskogo Soiuza v resoliutsiiakh i resheniiakh s"ezdov, konferentsii i plenumov TsK, vol. 1. Moscow, 1971.

Kopelev, L. and Orlova, R. *My zhili v Moskve, 1956–1980.* Moscow, 1990.

Kornienko, G. M. 'Novoe o karibskom krizise'. *Novaia i noveishaia istoriia* 3 (May–June 1991).

Kornienko, G. M. 'Upushchennaia vozmozhnost': vstrecha N. S. Khrushcheva i Dzh. Kennedi v Vene'. *Novaia i noveishaia istoriia* 2 (March–April 1992).

Kozhukalo, I. P. and Shapoval, Iu. I. 'N. S. Khrushchev na Ukraine'. *Voprosy istorii KPSS* 9 (September 1989).

Kozlov, F. R. 'Bditel'nost' – obiazannost' chlena partii'. *Kommunist* 1 (January 1953).

Kuusinen, O. V. 'Dva pis'ma O. V. Kuusinena N. S. Khrushchevu'. *Voprosy istorii KPSS* 5 (May 1991).

Malenkov, A. G. *O moem ottse, Georgii Malenkove.* Moscow, 1992.

Malenkov, G. M. 'V bor'be za tempy'. *Partiinoe stroitel'stvo.* 2(4) (February 1930) pp. 35–40.

Mazurov, K. T. 'Ia govoriu ne tol'ko o sebe'. *Sovetskaia Rossiia,* 19 February 1989.

Medvedev, R. *Khrushchev: politicheskaia biografiia.* Moscow, 1990.

Modestov, V. *Rabochee i professional'noe dvizhenie v Donbasse do Velikoi Oktiabr'skoi Sotsialisticheskoi Revoliutsii.* Moscow, 1957.

Moskovskii Komsomol na metro. Moscow/Leningrad, 1934.

Mukhitdinov, N. A. '12 let s Khrushchevym'. *Argumenty i fakty* 44 (October 1989).

Musatov, V. L. 'SSSR i Vengerskie sobytiia 1956g: novye arkhivnye materialy'. *Novaia i noveishaia istoriia* 1 (January–February 1993).

Narisi istorii Komunistichnoi Partii Ukraini. Kiev, 1964.

Nazarova, B. and Gridnevoi, O. 'K voprosu ob otstavanii dramaturgii i teatra'. *Voprosy filosofii* 5 (May 1956).

'Nekotorye voprosy rukovodstva vooruzhennoi bor'boi letom 1942 goda'. *Voenno-istoricheskii zhurnal* 8 (August 1965).

Novikov, V. N. 'V gody rukovodstva N. S. Khrushcheva'. *Voprosy istorii* 1 (January 1989) and 2 (February 1989).

'Ob obiazatel'nom izuchenii russkogo iazyka v shkolakh natsional'nykh respublik i oblastei'. *Izvestiia TsK KPSS* 3 (March 1989).

'Ob organizatsii oborony Kievskogo ukrepraiona'. *Izvestiia TsK KPSS* 9 (September 1990).

'Ob organizatsii partizanskikh otriadov'. *Izvestiia TsK KPSS* 9 (September 1990).

'Ocherki nashikh dnei: tri dnia v Kremle'. *Novyi Mir* 7 (July 1955).

Openkin, L. A. 'Byli li povoroty v sovetskom obshchestve v 50-kh i 60-kh godakh?' *Voprosy istorii KPSS* 18 (August 1988).

Openkin, L. A. 'Na istoricheskom pereput'e'. *Voprosy istorii KPSS* 1 (January 1990).

Openkin, L. A. *Ottepel': kak eto bylo.* Moscow, 1991.

'O poriadke evakyatsii i unichtozhenii imushchestva'. *Izvestiia TsK KPSS* 7 (July 1990).

'O sozdanii oboronitel'noi linii na levom beregu Dnepra'. *Izvestiia TsK KPSS* 9 (September 1990).

'O tak nazyvaemom natsional-uklonizme'. *Izvestiia TsK KPSS* 9 (September 1990).

'O zashchite pravoberezh'ia Dnepra'. *Izvestiia TsK KPSS* 7 (July 1990).

Parsadanova, V. S. 'Deportatsiia naseleniia iz zapadnoi Ukrainy i zapadnoi Belorussii'. *Novaia i noveishaia istoriia* 2 (March–April 1989).

Paustovskii, K. 'Poeziia pravdy'. *Znamia* 9 (September 1953).

'Plenum TsK KPSS: iiul' 1953 goda: stenograficheskii otchet'. *Izvestiia TsK KPSS* 1 (January 1991) and 2 (February 1991).

Per'sha vseukrain'ska konferentsiia KP(b)U (17–21 zhovtnia 1926 roku): stenografichnii zvit. Khar'kov, 1926.

Pestov, B. E. 'Pogib? Popal bez vesti? Zhiv?' *Voenno-istoricheskii zhurnal* 4 (April 1990).

Piat' let moskovskogo metro. Moscow, 1940.

Piat'desiat' let Kommunisticheskoi Partii Sovetskogo Soiuza. Moscow, 1953.

Plenum Tsentral'nogo Komiteta Kommunisticheskoi Partii Sovetskogo Soiuza, 15–19 dekabria 1958 goda: stenograficheskii otchet. Moscow, 1958.

Plenum Tsentral'nogo Komiteta Kommunisticheskoi Partii Sovetskogo Soiuza, 19–23 noiabria 1962 goda: stenograficheskii otchet. Moscow, 1963.

Plenum Tsentral'nogo Komiteta Kommunisticheskoi Partii Sovetskogo Soiuza, 24–26 marta 1965 goda: stenograficheskii otchet. Moscow, 1965.

Pomerantsev, V. 'Ob iskrennosti v literature'. *Novyi Mir* 12 (December 1953).

Ponomarev, A. N. *N. S. Khrushchev: put' k liderstvu.* Moscow, 1990.

Popov, G. Kh. 'Dva tsveta vremeni, ili uroki Khrushcheva'. *Ogonek* 42 (October 1989).

'Problemy istorii i sovremennosti'. *Voprosy istorii KPSS* 2 (February 1989).

Radio Liberty. *Sobranie dokumentov samizdata.* New York, 1972.

Rasskazy stroitelei metro. Moscow, 1935.

Rezoliutsii XX S"ezda Kommunisticheskoi Partii. Moscow, 1956.

Rodionov, P. A. 'Kak nachinalsia zastoi'. *Znamia* 8 (August 1989).

Sakharov, A. *O strane i mire.* New York, 1976.

Sed'maia sessiia Verkhovnogo Soveta USSR 1-go sozyva: stenograficheskii otchet. Kiev, 1945.

Semichastnyi, V. E. 'Ia by spravilsia s liuboi rabotoi'. *Ogonek* 24 (June 1989).

Semichastnyi, V. E. 'Kak smeshchali N. S. Khrushcheva'. *Argumenty i fakty* 20 (May 1989).

Shapoval, Iu. I. *M. S. Khrushchov na Ukraini.* Kiev, 1990.

Shapoval, Iu. I. 'Stalinskyi poslanets na Ukraini'. *Pid praporom Leninizmu* 20 (October 1989).

Shelepin, A. N. 'Istoriia – uchitel' surovyi'. *Trud,* 14 March 1991.

Shelest, P. E. 'O Khrushcheve, Brezhneve i drugikh'. *Argumenty i fakty* 2 (January 1989).

'Skol'ko delegatov XVII S"ezda golosovali protiv Stalina?' *Izvestiia TsK KPSS* 7 (July 1991).

Skorino, L. 'Razgovor na chistotu'. *Znamia* 2 (February 1954).

Sobranie postanovlenii pravitel'stva SSSR. Moscow, 1960.

'Sovershenstvovat' rabotu partiinykh shkol'. *Partiinaia zhizn'* 10 (May 1957).

Spravochnik partiinogo rabotnika. Moscow, 1961.

Stalin, I. V. *Sochineniia.* Moscow, 1949.

Strelianyi, A. 'Poslednii romantik'. *Druzhba narodov* 11 (November 1989).

Sturua, M. 'Dve fotografii k odnomu portretu'. *Nedelia* 43 (October 1988).

'Sud'ba chlenov i kandidatov v chleny TsK KPSS VKP(b) izbrannogo XVII S"ezdom partii'. *Izvestiia TsK KPSS* 12 (December 1989).

'Telegramma iz Khar'kova. 13 sentiabria 1941 goda'. *Izvestiia TsK KPSS* 10 (October 1990).

'Telegramma komandovaniia Iuzhnogo fronta I. V. Stalinu i S. M. Budennomu'. *Izvestiia TsK KPSS* 9 (September 1990).

Tret'ia Moskovskaia oblastnaia i vtoraia gorodskaia konferentsii VKP(b): Biulleten', no. 4. Moscow, 1932.

Turetskii, V. 'Pravo na obrazovanie v sovetskom gosudarstve'. *Sovetskoe gosudarstvo i pravo* 9 (September 1936).

'Ulitsa Mandel'shtama'. *Ogonek* 1 (January 1991).

Ustav Kommunisticheskoi Partii Sovetskogo Soiuza. Moscow, 1952.

Vasil'eva, L. *Kremlevskie zheny.* Moscow, 1993.

Vasil'evskii, A. M. *Delo vsei zhizni.* Moscow, 1978.

Vishniakov, V. G. and Zavgorodenko, A. I. 'Nekotorye voprosy dal'neishego sovershenstvovaniia upravleniia promyshlennost'iu'. *Sovetskoe gosudarstvo i pravo* 12 (December 1960).

Voronov, G. I. 'Nemnogo vospominanii'. *Druzhba narodov* 1 (January 1989).

Voronov, G. I. 'Ot ottepeli do zastoia'. *Izvestiia*, 18 November 1988.

Vos'maia sessiia Verkhovnogo Soveta USSR 1ogo sozyva. Kiev, 1946.

'Vot gde pravda, Nikita Sergeevich!' *Voenno-istoricheskii zhurnal* 12 (December 1989), 1 (January 1990) and 2 (February 1990).

'Vozglavlial li Khrushchev nelegal'nyi TsK KP(b) Ukrainy?' *Izvestiia TsK KPSS* 2 (February 1990).

Vtoraia sessiia Verkhovnogo Soveta SSSR I sozyva: stenograficheskii otchet. Moscow, 1938.

Vtoroi s"ezd sovetskikh pisatelei. Moscow, 1955.

'Zapis'ka P. N. Pospelova ob ubiistve Kirova'. *Svobodnaia mysl'* 8 (April 1992).

Zasedaniia Verkhovnogo Soveta SSSR, 5-go sozyva, 2-aia sessiia: stenograficheskii otchet. Moscow, 1957.

Zezina, M. R. 'Iz istorii obshchestvennogo soznaniia perioda "ottepeli": problemy svoboda tvorchestva'. *Vestnik Moskovskogo universiteta: seriia 8: istoriia* 6 (November-December 1992).

Zhukov, G. K. *Vospominaniia i razmyshleniia,* 11th edn. Moscow, 1992.

Zima, V. F. 'Golod v Rossii 1946–47 godov'. *Otechestvennaia istoriia* 1 (January 1993).

Zlobin, A. 'Sanitarnyi den''. *Novoe vremia* 12 (March 1993).

Zubkova, E. Ia. 'Khrushchev, Malenkov i "ottepel'"'. *Kommunist* 13 (September 1990).

Zubkova, E. Ia. 'Oktiabr' 1964 goda: povorot ili perevorot?' *Kommunist* 13 (September 1989).

Zubkova, E. Ia. 'Opyt i uroki nezavershennykh povorotov 1956 i 1965 godov'. *Voprosy istorii KPSS* 4 (April 1988).

IV Moskovskaia oblastnaia i III gorodskaia konferentsii VKP(b): stenograficheskii otchet. Moscow, 1934.

XIV S"ezd Vsesoiuznoi Kommunisticheskoi Partii (Bol'shevikov): stenograficheskii otchet. Moscow, 1926.

XIV z'izd Komunistichnoi Partii (Bil'shovikiv) Ukraini: stenografichnii zvit. Kiev, 1938.

XVI z'izd Komunistichnoi Partii (Bil'shovikiv) Ukraini: stenografichnii zvit. Kiev, 1949.

XVII S"ezd Vsesoiuznoi Kommunisticheskoi Partii (b): stenograficheskii otchet. Moscow, 1934.

XVIII S"ezd Vsesoiuznoi Kommunisticheskoi Partii (Bol'shevikov): stenograficheskii otchet. Moscow, 1939.

XX S"ezd Kommunisticheskoi Partii Sovetskogo Soiuza: stenograficheskii otchet. Moscow, 1956.
XXII S"ezd Kommunisticheskoi Partii Sovetskogo Soiuza: stenograficheskii otchet. Moscow, 1961.

SOURCES IN ENGLISH

Alliluyeva, S. I. *Twenty Letters to a Friend.* London, 1967.
Allyn, B. *et al.* 'Essence of Revision: Moscow, Havana and the Cuban Missile Crisis'. *International Security* 14, no. 3 (Winter 1989–90).
Armstrong, J. A. *Soviet Partisans in World War II.* Madison, 1964.
Bailes, K. B. *Technology and Society under Lenin and Stalin: Origins of the Soviet Technical Intelligentsia, 1917–1941.* Princeton, 1978.
Barnet, R. *The Alliance: America, Europe, Japan: Makers of the Postwar World.* New York, 1983.
Beschloss, M. *The Crisis Years: Kennedy and Khrushchev.* New York, 1991.
Beschloss, M. *MAYDAY: Eisenhower, Khrushchev and the U-2 Affair.* London, 1986.
Bialer, S. *Stalin's Successors: Leadership, Stability and Change in the Soviet Union.* Cambridge, 1980.
Bilinsky, Y. *The Second Soviet Republic: The Ukraine after World War II.* New Brunswick, NJ, 1964.
Brenner, P. 'Kennedy and Khrushchev on Cuba: Two Stages, Three Parties'. *Problems of Communism* XLI (Special Issue, Spring, 1992).
Breslauer, G. *Khrushchev and Brezhnev as Leaders: Building Authority in Soviet Politics.* London, 1982.
Burlatsky, F. *Khrushchev and the First Russian Spring,* trans. D. Skillen. New York, 1991.
Burlatsky, F. 'The Lessons of Personal Diplomacy'. *Problems of Communism* XLI (Special Issue, Spring 1992).
Carrére d'Encausse, H. *Stalin: Order Through Terror,* trans. V. Ionescu. London, 1981.
Chang, L. and Kornbluh, P. *The Cuban Missile Crisis, 1962: A National Security Archive Documents Reader.* New York, 1992.
Conquest, R. *Harvest of Sorrow: Soviet Collectivization and the Terror-Famine.* London, 1988.
Conquest, R. *The Great Terror.* Harmondsworth, 1971.
Conquest, R. *The Great Terror: A Reassessment.* New York, 1990.
Conquest, R. *Power and Policy in the USSR: The Study of Soviet Dynastics.* London, 1961.
Conquest, R. *Stalin and the Kirov Murder.* New York, 1989.
Crankshaw, E. *Khrushchev: A Biography.* London, 1966.
Dallin, A. *Soviet Foreign Policy after Stalin.* Philadelphia, 1961.
de Gaulle, C. *Memoirs of Hope: Renewal, 1958–1962,* trans. T. Kilmartin. London, 1971.
Erickson, J. *The Road to Stalingrad: Stalin's War with Germany,* vol. 1. London, 1975.
Fairbanks, C. H. 'National Cadres as a Force in the Soviet System: The

Evidence of Beria's Career'. In Azrael, J. (ed.) *Soviet Nationality Policies and Practices*. New York, 1978.

Filtzer, D. *Soviet Workers and Stalinist Industrialisation*. London, 1986.

Fitzpatrick, S. *The Russian Revolution, 1917–1932*. Oxford, 1982.

Frankland, M. *Khrushchev*. Harmondsworth, 1966.

Friedgut, T. H. *Iuzovka and Revolution*, vol. 1: *Life and Work in Russia's Donbass, 1869–1924*. Princeton, 1989.

Fuller, E. 'Georgia, Stalin and the Demonstrations of 1956'. *Radio Liberty* 190/88 (3 May 1988).

Getty, J. A. *Origins of the Great Purges: The Soviet Communist Party Reconsidered, 1933–1938*. Cambridge, 1985.

Gonzalez, V. and Gorkin, J. *Life and Death in Soviet Russia*. New York, 1952.

Hanak, H. *Soviet Foreign Policy since the Death of Stalin*. London, 1972.

Hodnett, G. 'The Obkom First Secretaries'. *Slavic Review* 24, no. 4 (December 1965).

Horelick, A. and Rush, M. *Strategic Power and Soviet Foreign Policy*. Chicago, 1966.

Horne, A. *Harold Macmillan*, vol. II: *1957–1986*. New York, 1989.

Hough, J. and Fainsod, M. *How the Soviet Union is Governed*. Cambridge, Mass., 1979.

Jasny, N. 'Kolkhozy, the Achilles Heel of the Soviet Regime'. *Soviet Studies* III no. 2 (October 1951).

Johnson, P. *Khrushchev and the Arts: The Politics of Soviet Culture, 1962–1964*. Cambridge, Mass., 1965.

Khrushchev, N. S. *Khrushchev Remembers*. trans. S. Talbott. London, 1971.

Khrushchev, N. S. *Khrushchev Remembers: The Last Testament*, trans. S. Talbott. Boston, 1974.

Khrushchev, N. S. *Khrushchev Remembers: The Glasnost' Tapes*, trans. J. L. Schechter with V. Luchkov. Boston, 1990.

Khrushchev, S. N. *Khrushchev on Khrushchev: An Inside Account of the Man and His Era*, trans. W. Taubman. Boston, 1990.

Kux, E. 'Technicians of Management versus Managers of Technique'. In S. I. Ploss (ed.), *The Soviet Political Process*. London, 1971.

Laird, R. D. 'Decontrols or New Controls? The "Reform" of Soviet Agricultural Administration'. *Problems of Communism* VI, no. 4 (July–August 1957).

Leonhard, W. *The Kremlin since Stalin*, trans. E. Wiskeman and M. Jackson. Oxford, 1962.

Linden, C. *Khrushchev and the Soviet Leadership: With an Epilogue on Gorbachev*. Baltimore, 1990.

Macmillan, H. *Pointing the Way, 1959–1961*. New York, 1972.

Macmillan, H. *Tides of Fortune, 1945–1955*. New York, 1969.

Marples, D. R. *Stalinism in Ukraine in the 1940s*. Basingstoke, 1992.

McCauley, M. *Khrushchev and the Development of Soviet Agriculture: The Virgin Lands Programme, 1953–1964*. London, 1976.

McCauley, M. *Khrushchev and Khrushchevism*. London, 1987.

Medvedev, R. and Medvedev, Zh. *Khrushchev: The Years in Power*. Oxford, 1977.

Merridale, C. *Moscow Politics and the Rise of Stalin*. Basingstoke, 1990.
Nahaylo, B. and Swoboda, V. *Soviet Disunion: A History of the Nationalities Problem in the USSR*. London, 1990.
Nogee, J. and Donaldson, R. *Soviet Foreign Policy Since World War II*. New York, 1984.
Nove, A. *An Economic History of the Soviet Union*. London, 1982.
Nove, A. *The Soviet Economy*, 3rd edn. London, 1968.
Paloczi-Horvath, G. *Khrushchev: The Road to Power*. London, 1960.
Paustovskii, K. *Slow Approach of Thunder*, trans. M. Harari and M. Duncan. London, 1965.
Pethybridge, R. *A Key to Soviet Politics: The Crisis of the 'Anti-Party' Group*. London, 1962.
Pistrak, L. *The Grand Tactician: Khrushchev's Rise to Power*. London, 1961.
Ploss, S. I. *Conflict and Decision-making in Soviet Russia: A Case Study of Soviet Agriculture, 1953-63*. Princeton, 1965.
Problems of Communism XLI (Special Issue, Spring 1992).
Rigby, T. H. 'Khrushchev and the Resuscitation of the Central Committee'. *Australian Outlook* 13, no. 3 (September 1959).
Schlesinger, A., Jr, 'Onward and Upward from the Cuban Missile Crisis'. *Problems of Communism* XLI (Special Issue, Spring, 1992).
Schwartz, H. *The Soviet Economy since Stalin*. London, 1965.
Serov, A. (ed.) *Nikita Khrushchev: Life and Destiny*. Moscow, 1989.
Siegelbaum, L. *Stakhanovism and the Politics of Productivity in the USSR*. Cambridge, 1988.
Sullivant, R. S. *Soviet Politics and the Ukraine, 1917-1957*. New York, 1962.
Tatu, M. *Power in the Kremlin: From Khrushchev's Decline to Collective Leadership*, trans. H. Katel. London, 1969.
Tompson, W. J. *Nikita Khrushchev and the Territorial Party Apparatus*. D.Phil. thesis, University of Oxford, 1991.
Troitskaia, Z. *The L. M. Kaganovich Metropolitan Railway of Moscow: Moscow's Metro*. Moscow, 1955.
Ulam, A. *Stalin: The Man and His Era*. New York, 1973.
Volkogonov, D. *Stalin: Triumph and Tragedy*, trans. H. Shukman. Rocklin, Calif., 1992.
Werth, A. *Russia at War*. London, 1964.
Zubok, V. M. 'The Missile Crisis and the Problem of Soviet Learning'. *Problems of Communism* XLI (Special Issue, Spring 1992).

Index

Abakumov, Egor 13
Abakumov, V. S. 106, 139, 140, 146
Academy of Sciences of the USSR 217, 270
Adenauer, Konrad 144–5, 196
Adzhubei, Aleksei Ivanovich 58, 93, 94, 95, 96, 203, 212, 244, 249–50, 263, 270, 273, 274, 281, 282, 284
Adzhubei, Rada Nikitichna (Khrushchev) 29, 82, 268
Afghanistan 149, 218
agriculture 92–3, 104, 123, 127–8, 151–2, 263
    collectivization of: and First Five-Year Plan 30, 42, 158, 195, 214–17; Khrushchev's involvement in 47, 68, 72, 88–9, 92, 95, 96
    investment in 96, 215–16, 231–2
    Khrushchev's policies towards: administrative reorganisations 129, 151–2, 231, 244, 269–70; agrotown scheme 96–7, 101–3; kolkhoz amalgamation 48, 100–1, 103; link system replaced 100; maize campaign 128–9, 151, 216; material incentives 126, 128, 179; MTS sell-off 179, 190–1, 214; post-war Ukraine 86–9, 91, 92, 95, 96–7, 128; private plots restricted 269; procurement prices 127, 128, 214, 244–5; technical issues 68–9, 103, 216; TPAs 244; Virgin Lands Programme

128, 134–5, 137, 174, 198, 201, 214, 230, 264
    performance: under Stalin 91–2, 95, 128; under Khrushchev 174, 198, 214, 215, 230, 254–5, 264, 267;
    see also Lysenko, Trofim Denisovich
Aksenov, Vasilii Pavlovich 259–60
Albania 187, 213, 230
Aleksandr I, Tsar 282
Alliluyeva, Nadezhda Sergeevna 33–4
Alliluyeva, Svetlana Iosifovna 159
America
    economic competition with 171–2, 178, 179, 200, 214, 266
    Khrushchev visits 206-12
    Soviet relations with 132, 148–9, 170–1, 193, 206–12, 219–20, 222–8, 232–7, 247–53, 261–3, 266;
    see also Berlin, Cuban missile crisis, détente, Geneva summit, 'missile gap' deception, Paris summit, Suez crisis, U-2 incident
Andreev, A. A. 92, 99–100
Andropov, Yurii Vladimirovich 169
anti-party group 94, 179–83, 184, 191, 198, 202–3, 241, 242, 267
Aristov, Averkii Borisovich 183
Austrian State Treaty 143–4

Bagramian, Ivan Khristoforovich 79–81
Bauman district 33–6
Bauman, Karl Ianovich 31, 48